William Wordsworth: A Poetic Life

William Wordsworth

A POETIC LIFE

John L. Mahoney

Fordham University Press
New York
1997

Copyright © 1997 Fordham University Press
All rights reserved.
LC 96-39355

ISBN 0-8232-1715-9 (*hardcover*)
ISBN 0-8232-1716-7 (*paperback*)

Library of Congress Cataloging-in-Publication Data

Mahoney, John L.
  William Wordsworth, A poetic life / by John J. Mahoney
     p.   cm.
  ISBN 0-8232-1715-9. — 1716-7 (pbk.)
     1. Wordsworth, William, 1770–1851—Biography.   2. Poets, English—19th
century—Biography.   I. Title.
  PR5881.M33   1997
  821'.7—dc21
  [B]   96-39355
                                                                        CIP

Printed in the United States of America

For Ann, as always

CONTENTS

ACKNOWLEDGMENTS

This book has been a good while in the making. Having published a study of William Hazlitt as Romantic critic and a book on the evolution of a Romantic *mimesis*, and having co-edited and contributed to a collection of essays on Coleridge, Keats, and the imagination, I wanted to do something biographical. As always, I discussed the idea with my former teacher and continuing mentor, Walter Jackson Bate. He responded most helpfully to my plan for what I have called a literary life, and has continued to be a good and generous adviser as the work has gone forward. James Engell continues to be most supportive of all my efforts in the general area of our mutual interest, the period from 1660 to 1830 in British literature and criticism. J. Robert Barth, s.j., Dean of the College of Arts and Sciences at Boston College and my colleague in the English Department, has afforded me many opportunities to tap his rich knowledge of Wordsworth and Coleridge, and has read and offered candid and constructive criticism of sections of my work. Mark Reed made vital suggestions at the beginning and end of the project, and has remained a willing and helpful adviser.

Yet nothing has been more instructive, indeed inspirational, to me than the classes I have taught in recent years and the conversations I have had with colleagues in colloquia and in informal settings. The continuing "Romanticism" seminars of the Harvard University Center for Literary and Cultural Studies, especially the contributions of David Perkins and Charles Rzepka, are notable examples. In these settings I have learned in a special way how to nourish my knowledge and admiration of Wordsworth's poetry and have lost some of the critical innocence that has limited my ability to view that poetry from some of the vantage points provided by the extraordinary theoretical developments of the last twenty-five years.

The names I mention in what I hope is not simply a *de rigueur* list of present and former Boston College colleagues may surprise some of them, may even make them struggle to recall a specific occasion, but they should be assured that not only advice but example have helped me to shape my reading of and approaches to the poetry and criticism over the years. John Anderson, Joseph Appleyard, S.J., M. J. Connolly, Alan Crowley, Paul Doherty, Anne Ferry, Dayton Haskin, Robert Kern, Thomas Lloyd, John McCarthy, Alan Richardson, Richard Schrader, Dennis Taylor, Andrew Von Hendy, William Youngren, Christopher Wilson, and Judith Wilt are stimulating, supportive, and properly critical teacher-scholars who make the community in which I ply my wares such a splendid place to be. Professors Anderson, Richardson, Schrader, and Taylor were especially generous in reading and commenting on various sections of the developing manuscript. Professor Schrader was my never-failing consultant on matters bibliographical and editorial.

Two of the colleagues above have been Department Chairs during the progress of my work—Professors Doherty and Wilt—and their support in providing teaching assignments, secretarial assistance, and computer facilities has been considerable. Professor Wilt embodies those qualities of friendship and colleagueship that are rare gifts in the profession. And speaking of secretarial assistance, I offer special thanks to Claudette Picklesimer, Judith Plank, and Patrice Scott for never-failing help.

Elaine Tarutis continues to be my editorial assistant, and without her superb skills and sharp and critical eye, this book would have been a poor and paltry thing. William B. Neenan, S.J., Academic Vice President and Dean of Faculties, and Donald J. White, former Associate Dean of Faculties and Dean of the Graduate School of Arts and Sciences, of Boston College are superior examples of academic administrators who are keenly concerned with the work and special needs of their faculty.

My thanks to the Boston College Faculty Fellowship program, to the American Philosophical Society, and to the Thomas F. Rattigan Chair Research Fund for generous grants that provided the time and financial support for a project of this kind. The resources of the Wordsworth Library in Grasmere, England, and the unstinting courteous and efficient help of its Secretary, Jeff Cowton; of the New York Public Library; of the Andover-Newton Theological School Library; of the Harvard College Library; of the O'Neill Library of Boston College have been invaluable.

My wife, Ann Dowd Mahoney, continues to be not only the best research companion, but also the wisest friend and adviser a scholar could have. From Boston to New York to London; from Grasmere to Bristol, she has been there keeping meticulous journals—and taking photographs (see following page 284). She has also continued to reveal her uncanny sense of how to separate what is important from what is diversionary in one's work, and especially of how to see one's work in the context of a larger life.

I am, as always, thankful for the love and support of my family— John, Pat, Bill, Lenor, Jim, Elvie, and the littlest members, Alison, Emma, and Emily. And, again as always, I'm grateful for the friendship and artistry of Harry Locke and Jackie and Roy Kral who make all seasons sweet.

Boston College   JOHN L. MAHONEY

Permission to use the Benjamin Haydon portrait of Wordsworth and to quote from the letters of Wordsworth has been granted by The Wordsworth Trust, Grasmere, England.

Quotations from the following editions of the Cornell Wordsworth, under the general editorship of Stephen M. Parrish, are used with the permission of the publisher, Cornell University Press:

The Borderers, ed. Robert Osborn (Ithaca, N.Y.: Cornell University Press, 1982)

Descriptive Sketches, ed. Eric Birdsall (Ithaca, N.Y.: Cornell University Press, 1984)

An Evening Walk, ed. James Averill (Ithaca, N.Y.: Cornell University Press, 1984)

Lyrical Ballads and Other Poems, ed. James Butler and Karen Green (Ithaca, N.Y.: Cornell University Press, 1992)

Poems in Two Volumes, and Other Poems, 1800–1807, ed. Jared Curtis (Ithaca, N.Y.: Cornell University Press, 1983)

Wordsworth's Shorter Poems, 1807–1820, ed. Carl Ketchan (Ithaca, N.Y.: Cornell University Press, 1989).

The author wishes to thank Judith Steinberg for permission to quote her poem "Now that we're middle-aged, we're reciting Wordsworth" from *Past Time.*

INTRODUCTION

STUDYING THE LIFE OF William Wordsworth, 1770–1850, for many readers the high priest and master spirit of what has come to be called the Romantic Movement in England, the promulgator of many of its central tenets, a poet who wrote steadily from his earliest school days at Hawkshead to his final years as the Squire of Rydal Mount—a career of some sixty, even seventy years! The idea boggles the mind, quite properly, not just because of the enormity of the task, but also because two major biographers have, relatively recently, achieved a degree of success in the ways they handled that task.

How to deal with a writer whose career moves from the age of Johnson to the age of Victoria; who writes from adolescence to old age, from a period of youthful radicalism to middle-aged moderatism to later-life conservatism; whose emotional range—at least on the surface—develops from early optimism about the possibilities of human nature, when a young and free and healthy imagination can explore and find meaning in the beauties of nature, to later periods of deep anxiety and even profound doubt about the power of mind as it confronts the claims of the great world beyond? How, without the burden of preconception or a fixed mode of critical discourse, to find, or perhaps not to find, the sense of a life, of certain persisting concerns, dominant themes and images in descriptive and narrative poems like *An Evening Walk, Descriptive Sketches*, and *Guilt and Sorrow: Incidents Upon Salisbury Plain*; rustic ballads like "Goody Blake and Harry Gill," "Simon Lee," "We Are Seven," and others; poems of the interior life extending from *Tintern Abbey* and the epic-autobiographical *Prelude*; the wonderfully varied poems of his two 1807 volumes, *Ode: Intimations of Immortality* and *Ode to Duty*; sonnets ranging from the more personal "Composed Upon Westminster Bridge" to the more public "The world is too much with us," still other forms like those of "The Solitary Reaper," "Elegiac Stanzas," and the "Celandine" poems; later work as different as the narrative-dramatic

Excursion and the massive poetico-historical *Ecclesiastical Sonnets*; and still later work like *Yarrow Revisited, and Other Poems*; and even later efforts extending to the year of his death.

One can, of course, keep adding to the problems arising from the attempt to write any kind of literary-biographical study of a poet so dominant for so long that, at least through the nineteenth century, he was consistently placed just below Shakespeare, Milton, and Chaucer in rankings of the great English poets, and so innovative in subject matter and technique, in poetic theory and practice, that he has in this century been regularly regarded as one of the first modern poets. Consequently, one can perhaps depend on a consensus among readers of Wordsworth as to the dimensions of the task and the complexity of the problem, and proceed to think about ways of dealing with them.

As already suggested, Wordsworth has been a subject for many biographers, men and women who have taken on the formidable task of dealing with the whole life—eighty years—or with particular parts of it—early or late, for example—and who have provided for those who come to the task later the kinds of material without which anything like what the present writer proposes would be impossible. Foremost among these are Mary Moorman and Stephen Gill, whose work to this date must stand as definitive.[1] Prodigious in their amassing of what seems to be every detail of private and public life, family, friends, literary relationships; informed, sensitive, and properly distinctive in their painstaking accounts of the poetry and its contexts; admirably objective in their treatment of the many nuances of such a long life, they are models of a certain kind of biography.

As early as 1851, of course, Wordsworth's nephew Christopher, with the propriety of an admiring relative, undertook a two-volume "biographical commentary on the poet's works."[2] In the first volume he writes of visiting Rydal Mount in 1847 and discussing with his

[1] Mary Moorman, *William Wordsworth: A Biography*. I. *The Early Years, 1770–1803* (Oxford: Clarendon, 1957); II. *The Later Years, 1803–1850* (Oxford: Clarendon, 1965). Stephen Gill, *Wordsworth: A Life* (Oxford: Oxford University Press, 1989).

[2] Christopher Wordsworth, *Memoirs of William Wordsworth*, 2 vols. (London, 1851), 1:3.

uncle the general subject of the lives of departed poets. "On that occasion," he writes, "as on many others, he expressed an opinion, that a poet's *Life* is written in his WORKS; and this is undoubtedly true, in a remarkable manner, in his own particular case."[3] Christopher Wordsworth seems firm in his conviction that "His Works, therefore, are his Life," and sounds both possessive and protective in his almost biblical exclamation, "Let them retain their supremacy in this respect; and let no other Life of Wordsworth be composed beside what has thus been written with his own hand."[4] Yet, despite this scenario, he calls the poems "no visionary dreams but practical realities," arguing that Wordsworth "wrote as he lived, and he lived as he wrote," and that as a result many of the poems "will be very obscure to those persons who are not acquainted with the circumstances of his life." He even proposes a chronological strategy for his study as an opportunity to read "profitably" and to develop a greater awareness of the poet's artistic development.[5]

Wordsworth, we are told, provided his nephew "with a brief sketch of the most prominent circumstances in his life" and actually dictated autobiographical memoranda. What emerges is essentially familial biography with little attention to the poems as poems, useful if kept in perspective but lacking the kind of objectivity and critical insight that might have strengthened the relationship between biographer and subject. Not, for example, that an account of the love affair between the poet and his French mistress, Annette Vallon, and of the birth of a child to them would have dramatically altered the configuration of the biography, but certainly the absence of any mention of the episode—granted the writer's somewhat prissy observations on the young lonely poet in France in the early 1790s, on his being subjected to "strong temptations," on "the dangers which surround those who in an ardent emotion of enthusiasm put themselves in a position of peril without due consideration of the circumstances which ought to regulate their practice" and the somewhat facile resolve "to chronicle the events of his life except so far as they illustrate his writings")—leaves the critic without a ray

---

[3] Ibid., 1:1.
[4] Ibid., 1:2.
[5] Ibid., 1:4.

of human emotion that might illuminate the moral and aesthetic development of a young artist and his work.[6]

Fortunately, the biographical work of Émile Legouis brought this crucial episode to light, as, in his chronology of events surrounding Wordsworth's days in France, he recounts hearing from Thomas Hutchinson "a well-established tradition in the Coleridge family that William Wordsworth, during his stay in France, had by a young French lady a son, who afterwards visited him at Rydal Mount,"[7] a matter not included in Legouis's *Early Life of Wordsworth*,[8] but later told to George Harper, an early and important Wordsworth biographer. Harper subsequently discovered in the British Museum a series of letters from Dorothy Wordsworth to Catharine Clarkson in which there is a specific mention of a Madame Vallon and a daughter, Caroline. whom Dorothy describes as her niece. The first sketch of the finding is in Harper's *William Wordsworth: His Life, Work, and Influence*,[9] but more important is Harper's discovery during his service in World War I that Annette was the sister-in-law of a Madame Vallon whose memoirs of the French Revolution appeared in 1913. Returning to America after the War, he urged Legouis to tell the whole story, which Legouis did in a new edition of his *Early Life of Wordsworth*. Legouis's biography, his *Wordsworth and Annette Vallon*,[10] and *Wordsworth in a New Light*, combined to locate this crucial episode in the larger context of the poet's life.

There are also useful specialized biographies and biographical studies of the poet—Ernest De Selincourt's *The Early Wordsworth*; Willard Sperry's *Wordsworth's Anti-Climax*; Russell Noyes's *William Wordsworth*, recently updated by John Hayden; W. W. Douglas's *Wordsworth: The Construction of a Personality*; Natalie Bober's *William Wordsworth: The Wandering Poet*; Hunter Davies's *William Wordsworth: A Biography*; Robert Gittings and Jo Manton's *Dorothy Wordsworth*; William Heath's *Wordsworth and Coleridge: A Study of Their Literary Relations in 1801–1802*; and others. And beyond biographical studies

---

[6] Ibid., 1:75.

[7] *Wordsworth in a New Light* (Cambridge, Mass.: Harvard University Press, 1923), p. 7.

[8] Trans. J. W. Matthews (London: J. W. Dent, 1921).

[9] 2 vols. (New York: Charles Scribner's Sons, 1916).

[10] (New York: E. P. Dutton, 1922).

there is a massive body of scholarship representing almost every critical point of view—from the pioneering approaches of M. H. Abrams, Harold Bloom, David Ferry, Geoffrey Hartman, and David Perkins to the deconstructive readings of Paul de Man and J. Hillis Miller; the feminist critiques of Susan Levin, Anne Mellor, and Camille Paglia; and the currently forceful New Historicist views of James Chandler, Marjorie Levinson, Alan Liu, and Jerome McGann. To cite even these major forces is to invite suggestions of other important biographical-critical studies.

Then there are, of course, certain continuing central questions that seem obvious and perhaps old-fashioned and yet, in our preoccupation with the complex and the novel, we push aside a little too easily. Is there a discernible shape to this poet's life and work, a consistency that ties together the early, later, and late? Are there really two Wordsworths: the passionate, radical poet of nature and imagination of the first forty years, and the patriarchal, didactic Tory humanist of the last forty? Is Wordsworth a continuation of the English poetic tradition with perhaps a more fully developed sense of landscape, a sharper image of the poet as a private figure of strong feeling, and a greater need to find a subject matter and language more faithful to the comings and goings of real men and women? Or does he represent a major break with tradition, a poet with a new sensibility, private and eager to explore the ebb and flow of the inner life unencumbered by the forces, prejudices, and intimidations of society and committed to the individual's discovery of value in a milieu that has lost faith in the medieval-Renaissance religious outlook and the smug scientific rationalism of the Enlightenment? Or, perhaps, is he very much the creature of a particular historical moment, a prisoner of an ideology—male, privileged, conservative— whose work represents a kind of evasion by sublimation?

Then there is another question, today perhaps unfashionable, the kind of question posed to the literary biographer a good many years ago. In remarks made at centenary celebrations of Wordsworth's death in 1950, Douglas Bush offered, in the midst of otherwise fulsome eulogies, what he called "A Minority Report." Recalling Matthew Arnold's provocative observation that Wordsworth turned away from half of human experience, and suspicious himself of "writers who draw a main part of their spiritual sustenance from nature," he posed his problem in disarmingly blunt fashion. Addressing "the general body of readers—never in any age a large body—who take poetry seriously, who read it with their whole being and not merely with detached historical or aesthetic intelligence, who think of it as the record of man's moments of vision, as the distillation of his highest and deepest experience," he challenged them with this question: "What does Wordsworth now actually mean to me? Do I find myself going back to him continually because he gives the kind of profound stimulus and satisfaction that I want?"[11]

There are echoes of Bush, although the context is decidedly different, in a remarkable recent essay by Gene Ruoff. Bemoaning the growing gap between "Romantics and Us" generated by current theoretical controversies, he sees critics and teachers "unable to face the specter of doctrine in poetry: our eyes go funny and we cease reading," and he worries about the "consequences for our criticism, our teaching, and our loss of a public audience of poetry,"[12] and about the "distance between us, as academic readers, and the rest of us—them, as we are wont to think of that substantial portion of the world's population for which belief, creed, and doctrine remain central determinants for action."[13] And Don Bialostosky, still another important contemporary critic of Wordsworth, is concerned about current characterizations of poetry as "anti-historical aestheti-zation" or "sheer language" and about how they "leave unresolved the problem of how to describe and value the poet's voice and the voices of others he reports."[14] His plea is for a dialogic—to some extent Bakhtinian—approach that does not exclude or silence but includes competing voices to deal with the complexity and tentativeness of literature and of life.[15] He finds in Wordsworth a continu-

---

[11] "Wordsworth: A Minority Report," in *The English Romantics: Major Poetry and Critical Theory*, ed. John L. Mahoney (Lexington, Mass.: D. C. Heath, 1978), pp. 691–692.

[12] "Romantic Lyric and the Problem of Belief," in *Romantic Poetry: Recent Revisionary Criticism*, ed. Karl Kroeber and Gene W. Ruoff (New Brunswick, N.J.: Rutgers University Press, 1993), p. 242.

[13] Ibid., p. 249.

[14] *Wordsworth, Dialogics, and the Practice of Criticism* (New York and Cambridge: Cambridge University Press, 1992), p. xviii.

[15] See my review of Bialostosky's book in *Nineteenth-Century Contexts*, 17, No. 2 (1993), 271–272.

ity between "ordinary" and "aesthetic" experience, an ambivalence toward, rather than a Coleridgean "contempt" for, popular culture.[16]

These are but a few of the questions and issues, and they are not easily dealt with in straight scholarly biography or in unadorned textual analysis. Wordsworth is no easy man to understand. He is simple and complex, affirmative and negative, radical and conservative, and his works are the same. Yet I see few sudden and sharp breaks, and find a good many motifs and responses that persist throughout his poetry. He seems a man and artist who could affirm the presence of divinity in nature and yet be torn by episodes of profound doubt. He is a writer who could find in the images of the creative mind occasions of value, moments to live by, yet who must reckon with the demands of the world beyond, with periods of pain and loss. He is a poet struck by the ministering power of sea, sky, mountain, and flower, yet possessed of an extraordinary sense of time and place, keen to experience the power of cities, of institutions, of human beings.

Methodology is a challenge. A good many years ago Herbert Read spoke confidently of our knowing "enough about the personal life of Wordsworth to be able to say when and where this life with its emotional tangles affects the course of his work." At the same time he saw "no simple choice between the biographical and the critical approach to Wordsworth. Both are essential to our understanding of his poetry."[17] One must, it seems, in the kind of study I propose, confront the poetry, yet not just in the context of the inner life of the artist or of what has come to be called Romantic discourse, but also in the larger contexts of people and places and events that engage and influence the life. I need to steer a course that will allow me to advance a relatively full and fresh view of a major literary life, or, lest the charge of vanity be leveled, at least of key episodes; to read representative works not merely as occasions, but also as ways of telling the story more fully than even the richest account of names, dates, and facts.

If I have any model for the task, it is William Pritchard, who, eager to tell the story of Robert Frost's life and work, realized how

---

[16] *Wordsworth, Dialogics, and the Practice of Criticism*, p. 28.

[17] *Wordsworth* (London: Faber & Faber, 1930; repr. 1948), pp. 28–29.

powerfully Lawrence Thompson had been there before him. Feeling more than mildly intimidated by Thompson's three-volume life, and recognizing its indispensability for anyone proposing to deal with Frost's life and work, he is nevertheless unhappy with the biographer's approach and convinced that Thompson's "biographical style made Frost into a particularly unattractive presence, so much at variance with what many who knew him (including myself, briefly) remembered of him, that something perhaps had gone amiss."[18] Thompson's interest in the poetry, while genuine and generally favorable, was largely a process of "relating a particular poem to some incident in the life from which it may have sprung." Hence, Pritchard, in his quest for a "literary life," wants "to identify and describe Frost's play of mind as it reveals itself in an art which is notable for the amount of felt life that it contains, and is a life which is notably artful, constantly shaped by the extravagant designs of his imagination." His biographical strategy is "to move back and forth between life and art, often blurring the distinctions in the interest of telling a story of a literary life." Underlying the strategy is a conviction that "whatever he [Frost] did, for better or for worse, was done poetically, was performed in a style which must not be pushed out of the way in order to get at the 'real' or 'deeper' motives that supposedly underlay it."[19]

I find myself at this beginning point in a situation like Pritchard's as I, on the one hand, look back admiringly, even anxiously, at the splendid biographies by Moorman and Gill, yet, on the other, feel that their ultimate purpose was not primarily literary, but, perhaps quite properly, more strictly biographical: to set down as fully as possible a record of the longest life of the English Romantics, setting the poems in the context of that life. They are definitive biographies, to be sure, and one leaves them with a feeling of scholarly gratitude, but also with a felt need for something more, a need caught in a review of Moorman's book that contends "her work is not distinguished as literary criticism, though it uses the poems very well as biographical documents,"[20] or in Gill's remarkably candid re-

---

[18] *Robert Frost: A Literary Life Reconsidered* (New York: Oxford University Press, 1984), p. xiii.

[19] Ibid., pp. xvi–xviii.

[20] In Frank Jordan, ed., *The English Romantic Poets: A Review of Research and Criticism* (New York: Modern Language Association, 1972), p. 80.

mark in his preface that his "main purpose" is "to offer the general reader a life of Wordsworth that takes account of th[e] new information" that followed hard upon the publication of Moorman's first volume and heralded "a golden age of Wordsworth and Coleridge studies." Gill promises "a biography, not an 'intellectual history' exegesis of specific works and phases of thought."[21] And he has fulfilled that promise, taking advantage of new editions of the works, of Mark Reed's splendid chronology, of notable studies of the earlier life, of the Cornell edition of Wordsworth with its dramatization of the poet's mode of composition, of new materials like the crucial family papers acquired by the Wordsworth Library in Grasmere in 1977.

And so, interested in both life and work and at the same time recognizing the length of that life and the enormous volume of poetry, I look for an approach, one that eschews mere chronology, easy categories, and facile generalizations as it tries to connect life and work more closely, to develop a way of thinking about the life as it nourishes the work and the work as it illuminates the life. It is the latter emphasis that seems most intriguing and most helpful for understanding Wordsworth—how the poetry of the now often arbitrarily defined periods can, with careful and, I hope, insightful attention to textual nuances and context, offer a fuller and richer portrait of a poet and a life, or of a truly poetic life.

I propose—and the charge of foolhardiness can still be raised—nothing so comprehensive as a year-by-year following of Wordsworth's life and work. Moorman, Gill, and others have done it so well that there are few new discoveries to add to the biographical and the bibliographical treasury. What can, I think, be profitably done—and again Pritchard on Frost comes to mind—is to focus on what I am calling "episodes in a poetic life" and to study important poems at certain key points of intersection between private and public. Such an approach may open up new ways of thinking about Wordsworth and the special and continuing significance of his work.

Choices can, of course, be arbitrary, even biased, no matter how great the desire for a certain critical objectivity may be, but this book will be attentive to certain central and unavoidable facets of the

---

[21] *Wordsworth: A Life*, p. vii.

poet's life and career—the circumstances of his birth, family, education, personal and political crises; the magical meeting with Coleridge in the southwest of England in 1795; the experimental
theorizing and new poetry of the *Lyrical Ballads*; the humble and
rustic emphases, on the one hand, and the intensely private and
lyrical thrust of poems like *Tintern Abbey*, on the other; the continuing struggle with the writing of a long autobiographical poem that
results in *The Prelude*; the many-splendored variety of the two 1807
volumes; and, surely, the events and work of the post-1810 career,
all too often regarded as the period of anti-climax, of turncoat conservatism and poetic decline.

If this book has a thesis to be tested, it is one that is suspicious
of sharp patterns of development and decline, one that argues—not
simply for professional Wordsworthians but also for Gene Ruoff's
"public audience for poetry," for Douglas Bush's "general body of
readers . . . who take poetry seriously" and who look to poetry to
find some meaning for their lives—that Wordsworth found powerful
questions about meaning in a solitary confrontation with nature, a
faith in the power of the individual mind to connect certain points
in an individual existence, a belief that poetry, far from being a mere
helpmate in the service of hard knowledge, was itself a kind of
knowledge, a hope for the good society. It sees these tenets embodied exuberantly in the poet's years of great creativity, modified and
tempered by the realities of time, age, and death, and sharply qualified by radical upheavals in the social, political, and religious worlds.

If I can lay any claim to distinctiveness, it is my continuing argument that Wordsworth's confidence in nature, mind, and poetry was
almost always shaded, that even in seemingly confident poems that
celebrate a "faith that looks through death," Wordsworth, however
subtly or guardedly, imagines the dark side of things, the "limits of
mortality." And it is this hesitation about limits, all too fully human,
that makes him not a Utopian, not, as Arnold and Bush and others
would have it, one who turns away from evil and suffering, but actually one of us. He is the poet who in the midst of things can hold
out a vision of unity, of joy in communion with nature, of delights in
the pleasures of imagination, while growing and maturing as a human
being and an artist in a realization of the worldly freight that clouds
that vision and challenges one to articulate it more passionately or

to show its autumnal colors as youth gives way to age, confidence to need.

Nowadays who can remain coy about the theoretical underpinnings of a study like this one? Few bodies of literature have evoked the rich response of critics and theorists as what has come to be known as Romanticism. Following the dominance of what we today call the "old literary history," the earliest manifestations of British and American New Criticism tested the rigors and delights of close reading. With I. A. Richards as moving force, Cleanth Brooks was clearly a pioneer, and Earl Wasserman a faithful practitioner, in probing the irony, paradox, and linguistic nuance in the major poems of Wordsworth, Coleridge, and Keats. M. H. Abrams and Geoffrey Hartman were certainly leaders in bringing the history-of-ideas approach to bear on poetry and critical theory, and Northrop Frye almost singlehandedly summoned Blake from the dead, with mythological readings of his poetry and the poetry of other Romantic writers.

Yet, as I write, there are other and more powerful forces at work. In the work of Jacques Derrida, the late Paul de Man, J. Hillis Miller, and others, the deconstructive impulse has been strong and influential, with its savoring of the ambivalence—indeed, instability—of a range of poems and its detailed and playful explorations of language and imagery. At its best this impulse has brought a healthy concern for the ahistorical quality of many of the poems and for the opportunities afforded readers to encounter texts more actively. The poetry of Wordsworth and other Romantics has, in the hands of such critics, found itself isolated from biographical speculation about authorial intention; and the result, displeasing to many traditional readers and even viewed as anti-humanistic by readers with special moral or religious concerns, has often been to give the poems a richer life, an uncertainty not so much crudely negative as constructively unsettling when it comes to establishing definitive interpretations, sharp contours of form. While my own temperament cannot be described as deconstructive, I have learned valuable lessons about the heuristic and pleasurable possibilities of seeing varied and often conflicting meanings in a text as in the larger text of human experience, and such learning will, I trust, be apparent from time to time as I follow episodes in Wordsworth's poetic career.

I have profited greatly from some aspects of what has come to be called the New Historicism, although the rigidly ideological frameworks frequently employed by many of its practitioners often leave me with a sense of frustration as the artist appears as almost a prisoner of a particular power base—class, race, gender, religion, politics—and the poem as irrevocably conditioned by this imprisonment. I find myself in sympathy with some aspects of the enormously influential and impressive work of Jerome McGann, especially the central argument of his masterwork *The Romantic Ideology*: that "Western cultural history since 1789 is richer and more diverse than its various Romantic characterizations and that these characterizations—both artistic and critical—can be usefully studied by placing them in a critical context which attempts to understand them in terms other than their own self-definitions."[22] "Romantic," like so many literary–historical labels, while useful to a degree, is too sweeping, too popular a term to describe so rich and complex a poet as Wordsworth, to say nothing of a body of poetry that includes his along with that of other long-canonized writers such as Blake, Coleridge, Byron, Shelley, and Keats, as well as the work of a number of only recently recognized non-canonical writers.

Marjorie Levinson, certainly in the McGann tradition, bemoans the stalemate between close readers and historians, and her essays on *Tintern Abbey*, the *Ode: Intimations of Immortality*, *Michael*, and "Peele Castle," while tied to a rigorous—indeed, rigid—historical orientation, are consistently provocative. She sees in *Tintern Abbey*, for example, "a conversion of public to private poetry, history to poetry." For her, "*Michael's* sheepfold is explicitly offered to the reader as a historical landmark testifying to an earlier, more satisfying way of life; at the same time, the narrator persuades us that the passage of that historical moment has brought about a finer tone in social bonding."[23] And "'Peele Castle,' or rather the two elegiac representations of it (before and after the poet's revelation of a 'Nature, red in tooth and claw'), reflect an absent object, the French Revolution."[24]

---

[22] *The Romantic Ideology: A Critical Investigation* (Chicago and London: The University of Chicago Press, 1983), p. ix.

[23] *Wordsworth's Great Period Poems: Four Essays* (Cambridge: Cambridge University Press, 1986), p. 37.

[24] Ibid., p. 120.

James Chandler, another critic in the general New Historicist mold, complains that Abrams, Bloom, and Hartman "all miss or misplot Wordsworth's position on the crucial intellectual axes represented by Burke and Rousseau,"[25] and contends that as early as *The Prelude*, the poet's ideological perspective is "thoroughly Burkean."[26] For Chandler, "the redemptive spots of time are, like Burke's moral sentiments, strongly allied with early prejudice, insensibly formed in particular circumstances, and profoundly indebted to the English past."[27]

Alan Liu, whose massive *Wordsworth: The Sense of History* represents the most thoroughgoing use of New Historicism in studying the poet, moves beyond Chandler to suggest that "the influence behind such ideology was not only Burke's philosophy of prejudice applied against a specific French philosophy but also a pre-philosophical exercise of denial—an effort by the Imagination to contain the phenomenal event that most seized imagination at the time of composition."[28] While Liu can admire the possibilities of deconstructive reading in "the sense that literature's world is the trust of value," it is somewhat like the New Criticism with this trust and yet "tremendously resistant to the declaration of any normative frame of reference upon which to secure the determination of values."[29]

France and the Revolution, with all the implications of that momentous event, form the matrix against which Wordsworth's poetry must be read, but, in Liu's copiously and curiously developed argument, the poet—and for that matter the Romantics generally—is involved in not just an avoidance but also a "denial of history,"[30] "an émigré flight from narrative."[31] Such escapism, he contends, can account for the "rustic transcendency of history that Wordsworth embraced in his Great Decade of poetry after the 1790s." "Here was room for the Mind to expand into its empire."[32]

---

[25] *Wordsworth's Second Nature: A Study of the Poetry and Politics* (Chicago and London: The University of Chicago Press, 1984), p. xxi.

[26] Ibid., p. 32.

[27] Ibid., p. 61.

[28] (Stanford: Stanford University Press, 1989) p. 395.

[29] Ibid., p. 393.

[30] Ibid., p. 35.

[31] Ibid., p. 51.

[32] Ibid., p. 214.

The New Historicist reading of the Romantics and of Wordsworth in particular, especially the staggering amassing of historical
evidence in Liu's work, is compelling, to be sure, but, as I suggested
earlier, the lines of such a critical approach seem too confining to
me, too unforgiving of those alternative readings that see the poem
in history but not utterly determined by history, too ready to see the
artist as a creature of the power centers of a time and place and
inevitably faced with the choice of recognizing this historical posi-
tioning or of engaging in some process of projection or outright denial. Peter Manning's tribute to New Historicism's invigoration of
the study of Romantic poetry—"renewing our sense of the depth,
particularity, and strength of the poets' engagement with their
world"—yet his caution about "restricting the meaning of the poetic
text to the generalized ideological matrix to which it is declared to
belong," catches this writer's attitude and approach nicely.[33]

In calling attention to certain attractive features of the deconstructive and New Historicist impulses, and then taking back some
of the compliment, I may appear indecisive. But what I propose in
this book is a literary life of a major nineteenth-century poet for
contemporary readers. Or should I say that this book attempts to
show the essential literariness of Wordsworth's life, recalling his first
biographer's contention that the poet "wrote as he lived, and he
lived as he wrote,"[34] or Pritchard's desire, in writing about Frost, to
demonstrate his poet's "play of mind as it reveals itself in an art
which is notable for the amount of felt life that it contains"?[35] Or
perhaps that there is no convincing way of separating life and work,
that the poetry is the best way of telling the story of the life?

---

[33] "Wordsworth at St. Bees: Scandals, Sisterhoods, and Wordsworth's Later
Poetry," *Reading Romantics: Texts and Contexts* (New York and Oxford: Oxford University Press, 1990), p. 300. See also Leopold Damrosch's interesting and instructive
view of New Historicist developments in eighteenth-century studies in his *The
Imaginative World of Alexander Pope* (Berkeley and Los Angeles: University of California Press, 1987), p. 9. Praising those developments when they teach "a scholarly
skepticism and humility, recognizing that the life of the past is densely complicated
by factors which are almost impossible to recover today, and that what went unsaid
was often as significant as what was said," he nevertheless finds it "a rare scholar (I
am not one) who can master social history deeply enough to prove that literary texts
are direct expressions of institutional structures."

[34] Christopher Wordsworth, *Memoirs of William Wordsworth*, 1:4.

[35] *Robert Frost*, pp. xvii–xviii.

As I have already said, a full-scale biography or a running commentary on the complete works is beyond the scope of this study. I suppose what I most fancy is a magical middle ground. Wordsworth's poetry, at least what I consider to be certain crucial poems as they catch the shaping of a life, will be the center of attention, and I will treat these poems not simply as biographical documents, but also as richly complex texts commanding critical rigor. What else but the poems can be this center for those whose basic concern is literature and literary study? Wordsworth himself saw the poet as a teacher and poetry as a way of giving shape to the workings of the mind.[36]

This study will also, beyond the pleasures of encountering the poetry, attempt to ensure its biographical contexts. But biography and history will, I hope, be servants, not masters. Nor will poems simply become verbal constructs masking larger personal and historical dimensions and in the process losing the special independence that empowers them as the poet's mode of communication. I see the work of art as a human document, like experience itself richly nuanced and occasionally undecidable, yet at times lending itself to sensitive readings, but also as the creature of a particular writer, a particular time and place. While it may not be possible to achieve the magical middle ground, this literary life of Wordsworth will always be seeking it out—the poet and his work in their historical contexts, consistently asserting independence while consistently calling attention to those forces that give them focus and remove them from some general fund of human experience and linguistic expression.

I have always been greatly impressed and influenced by the central argument of Lawrence Lipking's *The Life of the Poet: Beginning and Ending Poetic Careers.* Starting from the premise that for "much of this century intellectual critics have made a point of not reading the lives of the poets," and arguing that the poem itself "must acquire

---

[36] In a March 16, 1988 letter to me, Mark Reed offers this remarkable comment: "STC said—and W. W. said!—that from a v. early age W. W. had one pursuit to which he devoted himself—poetry. Few people who write about WW seem to ponder (much less pursue the consequences of) the implication that he primarily meant his best expressions to be poems (as distinguished from his meaning that his poems be his best expressions of something else—biography, philosophy, religion, politics, etc.)."

a life of its own,"[37] he proposes his strategy of "listening carefully both to what poets say about their works and to what works say about themselves." For Lipking, "the poems themselves, above all, declare the life of the poet"; he will write "not the biographies of poets, but the biography that gets into poems; the life that has passed through a refining poetic fire."[38] And, interesting for my purposes, he singles out Blake and Wordsworth as his key examples of poets who "tell their own stories" and set the pace for "most subsequent poets." "The 'modern epic,' " he says, "is dominated by one story and one story only: the life of the poet."[39] It is time to begin our story.

---

[37] (Chicago and London: The University of Chicago Press, 1981), p. vii.

[38] Ibid., pp. ix–x.

[39] Ibid., p. 70.

1

Becoming a Poet: Education and Early Poems

"Now it is manifest that no human being can be so besot-
ted and debased by oppression, penury, or any other evil
which unhuma[nizes] man, as to be utterly insensible to
the colours, forms, or smell of flowers, the [voices?] and
motions of birds and beasts, the appearances of the sky
and heavenly bodies, the [genial?] warmth of a fine day,
the terror and general uncomfortableness of a storm, etc.,
etc. How dead soever many full-grown men may out-
wardly seem to these th[ings,] they all are more or less
affected by them; and in childhood, in the first practice
and exercise of their senses, they must have been not the
nourish[ers] merely, but often the fathers of their passions."

W. W. to John Wilson
June 7, 1803

"But let this
Be not forgotten, that I still retained
My first creative sensibility;
That by the regular action of the world
My soul was unsubdued. A plastic power
Abode with me; a forming hand, at times
Rebellious, acting in a devious mood;
A local spirit of his own, at war
With general tendency, but for the most,
Subservient strictly to external things
With which it communed."

1850 *Prelude*

> "William has a great attachment to poetry . . . which is
> not the most likely thing to produce his advancement in
> the world; his pleasures are chiefly of the imagination, he
> is never so happy as when in a beautiful country. Do not
> think from what I have said that he reads not [at] all, for
> he does read a great deal and not only poetry and those
> languages he is acquainted with but history &c. &c."
>
> D. W. to Jane Pollard
> June 26 [1791]

IT IS KEATS who seems to have the best lines to capture the drama
of a poetic life like Wordsworth's, if indeed he ever had any other
kind of life. We remember Keats, in an April 18, 1817 letter to John
Hamilton Reynolds, saying, "I find that I cannot exist without
poetry—without eternal poetry—half the day will not do—the
whole of it—I began with a little, but habit has made me a Levia-
than."[1] And there is, of course, the celebrated—and, in the context
of this book, ironic—outburst in the October 27, 1818 letter to Richard Woodhouse when, speaking of the "poetical Character itself, (I
mean that sort of which, if I am anything, I am a Member; that sort
distinguished from the Wordsworthian or egotistical sublime; which
is a thing per se and stands alone"), he proceeds to develop with
great intensity the strength of his commitment and the virtual in-
separability of poetry from the activities of his life.[2]

Wordsworth, perhaps characteristically, speaks of the poetic vocation on occasion, but with what many would regard as considerably
less gusto. His nephew and first biographer, Christopher Wordsworth. records, as I have already noted, the poet's rather straightforward "opinion, that a poet's *Life* is written in his WORKS."[3] To Anne
Taylor, who had written to Wordsworth to express her pleasure in
his poetry and to ask for an account "of such events in my life as
may have had an influence in forming my present opinions," he replies that he "should have complied with great pleasure, had the

---

[1] *The Letters of John Keats, 1814–1821*, ed. Hyder Edward Rollins, 2 vols. (Cambridge, Mass.: Harvard University Press, 1958), 1:133.

[2] Ibid., 1:386–387.

[3] See above, p. xv.

task been more difficult, but the history of my life is very short." After the barest of summaries of his life to that date, he speaks of having "taken a house in the Vale of *Grasmere*, (a very beautiful spot of which almost every body has heard,) and I live with my Sister, meaning, if my health will permit me, to devote my life to literature." He has little to "throw any light on my writings" or to reveal how "I came to adopt the opinions" in the "Preface" to the 1800 *Lyrical Ballads*, "but in truth my life has been unusually barren of events, and my opinions have grown slowly, and, I may say, insensibly."[4] To Lady Beaumont, wife of his friend and patron Sir George Beaumont, he writes concerning his 1807 poems, which had met with severe critical reception, that he has "calm confidence that these Poems will live," that "every great and original writer . . . must himself create the taste by which he is to be relished." He hopes that Lady Beaumont "will share with me an invincible confidence that my writings . . . will co–operate with the benign tendencies in human nature and society, wherever found."[5] And, considerably later, in a February 6, 1812, letter to the Earl of Lonsdale, he seeks a civil service post to provide the financial security to follow a literary career. "Literature," he writes, "has been the pursuit of my Life; a Life-pursuit justified (as I believe are those of most men distinguished by any particular features of character) partly through passionate liking and partly through calculations of judgement."[6]

But if Keats has the exciting lines, Wordsworth has the long life to figure them, to give shape to a vocation to which he committed himself from his earliest days, even when that commitment, at times not fully understood and certainly not sharply articulated, seemed clouded by financial problems or by expectations, familial and social,

---

[4] April 9, 1801. *EY* 1:327. Unless otherwise noted, all references to the letters are to *The Letters of William and Dorothy Wordsworth*, ed. Ernest De Selincourt, 7 vols.: *The Early Years, 1787–1805*, rev. Chester L. Shaver (Oxford: Clarendon, 1967) [EY]; *The Middle Years, Part I. 1806–1811*, rev. Mary Moorman (Oxford: Clarendon, 1969); *The Middle Years. Part II. 1812–1820*, rev. Mary Moorman and Alan G. Hill (Oxford: Clarendon, 1970) [*MY*]; *The Later Years, 1821–1853*, rev. Alan G. Hill, 4 vols. (Oxford: Clarendon, 1978–1988) [*LY*]. In the references to *MY* and *LY*, the first number refers to the volume number in the series as a whole; the second, to the volume within the subseries of *MY* and *LY*.

[5] May 21, 1807. *MY* 2.1:150.

[6] February 6, 1812. *MY* 2.2:2.

of a career in the church or the law. He was born in the small town of Cockermouth on the northern border of the English Lake District, still a rather quiet place. His house had—and still has—the look of a mansion, a two-story building, multi-windowed, and surrounded by a stone wall, and with a rather formal entrance approached from a wooden gate. The imposing quality of the house stands in marked contrast to what surrounds it and especially to the Derwent River, which flows by the lawn and garden at the rear. It is as if formal and natural are competing forces in a drama. The sounds of the river are noted with pleasure and pensiveness early in *The Prelude*, the poet's spiritual autobiography, which will discussed at length later. Pleasure and pensiveness indeed, for, as the mature Wordsworth has it, "the fairest of all rivers, loved to blend his murmurs with my nurse's song," and "sent a voice / That flowed along my dreams." The young boy's earliest education in nature is poetic, preceding the wondrous later episodes of the Lakes, for the Derwent, even as he was "a babe in arms," made "ceaseless music that composed my thoughts / To more than infant softnĕss, giving me / Amid the fretful dwellings of mankind / A foretaste, a dim earnest, of the calm / That Nature breathes among the hills and groves" (1.270–281).[7]

The workings of the mind in the midst of the great world beyond becomes a motif established early by the poet. As he and his beloved sister, Dorothy, roamed the surrounding area, he, "a five years' child, / In a small mill-race severed from his stream, / Made one long bathing of a summer's day; / Basked in the sun, and plunged and basked again / Alternate, all a summer's day" (1.288–292). A memory of light unblemished by shade, of sun undisturbed by the intrusion of cloud, of youth still unaware of the oncoming of age—the beginning of still another motif that will persist, with variations, throughout the poetry.

Wordsworth was the second child of John Wordsworth and Ann Crackanthorpe, born on April 7, 1770. An elder brother, Richard, was born in 1768, then John in 1772, and Christopher in 1774. His only

---

[7] Unless otherwise noted, all references are to *The Prelude* of 1850 in *The Prelude 1799, 1805, 1850*, ed. Jonathan Wordsworth, M. H. Abrams, and Stephen Gill (New York and London: W. W. Norton, 1979).

sister, Dorothy, born in 1771, plays a major role in the poet's life as close friend, supporter of his vocation as writer, editor, secretary, almost his "all in all." Her special place in the poet's life—often exaggerated, often underestimated—is a topic we shall return to often in the course of these pages.

Wordsworth's parents—essentially middle class—represent an interesting contrast, a contrast often apparent, it seems, in the personality and thought of their son. His mother, a gentle woman who loved her children, gave them room to grow and trusted the rhythms of their inner lives and their hopes for happiness even when her own parents felt that she was not enough of a disciplinarian. Her teaching was not so much a formal thing, a regimen of books and study, as the holding up of an ideal of morality and learning and the embodiment of those "little acts of kindness and of love" so powerful in the development of a child. Women are to play major roles in Wordsworth's life—Dorothy; Mary Hutchinson, his wife, and Sara, her sister; his daughter, Dora; and many others who will enter this story—but the power of the maternal imagery in *The Prelude* points up, as no mere biographer can, the impact of his mother. As he traces "Our Being's earthly progress," he calls the baby "blest," "Nursed in his Mother's arms, who sinks to sleep / Rocked on his Mother's breast; who with his soul / Drinks in the feelings of his Mother's eye!" She is for him "one dear Presence" with "A virtue which irradiates and exalts / Objects through widest intercourse of sense" (2.232–240).

John Wordsworth, the poet's father, was a formidable figure, a Cockermouth lawyer and—most important for an understanding of the family's continuing financial worries—a kind of business manager for Sir James Lowther, later to be Lord Lonsdale, perhaps one of the most successful and influential men in Cumberland. He was a man who worked hard to support a large family, but who needed to be away from home for long periods, entrusting the day-to-day care of his children to his wife. Yet he loved his children and, despite his absences, was concerned about their moral, emotional, and intellectual well-being. Wordsworth was unquestionably fortunate in having such parents.

The contrast between mother and father is nowhere more evident than in the kind of reading encouraged by each. Books for the young Wordsworth were not "a dull and endless strife." His earliest reading—under his mother's loving eye—was, predictably enough, in children's stories, but in good ones—in "Jack the Giant Killer," "St. George and the Dragon," "Robin Hood," and the like—stories that would have stirred the imagination of a lively child (5.341–346). He recalls in *The Prelude* savoring the delights of *The Arabian Nights* (5.460–477). His father had a better-than-ordinary library for the time, and, thanks to his encouragement and example, the boy read and memorized a good deal of Spenser, Shakespeare, and Milton, formidable writers indeed. As he roamed at will in his father's library, he read, before he was thirteen, *Gulliver's Travels, Tale of a Tub*, all of Fielding, *Don Quixote*, and *Gil Blas*.[8] Even though sea, sky, mountain, and stream nourished his youthful spirit, Wordsworth was hardly an untutored child of nature. Is it any wonder that the young poet of *The Prelude* should so often tell the story of his life by rendering actual situations in the fashion of a poetic storyteller?

Wordsworth, of course, devotes Book 5 of *The Prelude* to the presence and power of books in his early life, to an explanation of how education in nature is complemented by the richness of story. "Twice five years / Or less I might have seen, when first my mind / With conscious pleasure opened to the charm / Of words in tuneful order, found them sweet / For their own *sakes*, a passion, and a power" (5.552–556). Most striking is his tribute to the power of language not just to please, but to widen awareness, to nourish the mind, to inform the spirit, aspects of the literary experience that will become central to Wordsworth's thinking about art and his new *apologia* for literature.[9] Indeed, there is the ring of modernity, even of contemporary theoretical discussion of language, in his praise of "the great Nature that exists in works / Of mighty Poets," something as great as the "living Nature" he loved from his earlier days.

> Visionary power
> Attends the motions of the viewless winds,
> Embodied in the mystery of words:

---

[8] *The Prose Works of William Wordsworth*, ed. W. J. B. Owen and Jane Worthington Smyser, 3 vols. (Oxford: Oxford University Press, 1974), 3:372. Unless otherwise noted, all references to Wordsworth's prose are to this edition.

[9] See John L. Mahoney, *The Whole Internal Universe: Imitation and the New Defense of Poetry in British Criticism, 1660–1830* (New York: Fordham University Press, 1985), pp. 99–111.

There, darkness makes abode, and all the host
Of shadowy things work endless changes there,
As in a mansion like their proper home.
Even forms and substance are circumfused
By that transparent veil with light divine,
And, through the turnings intricate of verse,
Present themselves as objects recognised,
In flashes, and with glory not their own [5.594–605].

Wordsworth's own words, dictated to his nephew Christopher at Rydal Mount in November 1847, are especially revealing on the subject: "Of my earliest days at school I have little to say, but that they were very happy and chiefly because I was left at liberty, then and in the vacations, to read whatever works I liked."[10]

The next phase of Wordsworth's education was somewhat different. Like Keats, the poet was to lose both parents when he was still very young, and the spectacle of five orphaned children was not an episode in a fairy tale, but a harsh reality. His mother died on March 9, 1778, and with her death the poet felt the loss of tenderness and familial nourishment that was central to his life. "Early died / My honoured Mother, she who was the heart / And hinge of all our learnings and our loves: / She left us destitute, and, as we might, / Trooping together" (5.256–260). This is not to say that John Wordsworth was not a good parent; he was in every way concerned about his sons and daughter, about their moral training, their education, and their relationships to each other, to relatives, to home. The fact remained, however, that he was not a wealthy man, and, as already noted, his work regularly took him away from home. What he did was what most widowers in his situation would do: find the kind of setting in which his children would know love, concern, and care, and continue to support them with the salary he drew from the demanding work in which he was engaged.

But paternal anxiety meant family disruption as Dorothy was sent to live with her mother's cousin Elizabeth Threlkeld in Halifax and the boys with their maternal grandparents in Penrith. William and Ann Cookson were concerned but grim, and Wordsworth rebelled, giving vent to what many Wordsworth biographers have

---

[10] *Memoirs of William Wordsworth*, 1:10.

noted as a streak of stubbornness and boisterousness in his personality. Natalie Bober tells the familiar stories of the boy's destroying a family portrait, threatening suicide, all of which "seemed to be fulfilling the undesirable aspect of his mother's earlier prophecy that he would be remarkable either for good or for evil."[11]

Wordsworth and his brothers found life with his stern Cookson grandparents increasingly difficult and eventually unbearable, and after two years they went to live in the small village of Colthouse under the care of Ann Tyson, the "Dame" who was to mean so much in their motherless upbringing, and her husband, Hugh. "While my heart / Can beat never will I forget thy name," he writes of her in *The Prelude* (4.31–32). His years with the Tysons—some eight while at Hawkshead School and the two long summer vacations while at Cambridge—were happy ones, although his letters reveal how much he missed Dorothy and what little prospect there was of a family reunion. Colthouse offered a setting of extraordinary beauty, set in the valley of Esthwaite with the hills of High Furness as a backdrop. The young boy lived in a poetic world, delighting in the greenness of the landscape, in rainbows after storms; savoring adventurous nutting expeditions; and awe-struck by the fearsome presences that surrounded him. *The Prelude* tells the story better than any biographer as he recalls, "Fair seed-time had my soul, and I grew up / Fostered alike by beauty and by fear" (1.301–302).

Hawkshead was the site of a famous grammar school; Ben Ross Schneider has described it as "from a purely academic standpoint . . . one of the best schools in England"—what nowadays we would call a classical or Latin school—and John sent William and his brother Richard there in 1779.[12] His earliest teachers had been Rev.

---

[11] *William Wordsworth: The Wandering Poet* (Nashville and New York: Thomas Nelson, 1975), p. 21. See Mark Reed's study of Charles Wordsworth's *Annals of My Early Life, 1806–1846*, especially the following remembrance: "My Grandmother was 29 when she died—and my grandfather who died 4 or 5 years after was 40. An old Lady now living is near 100 yrs remembers very well my Grandmother saying that she had no fears about any of her children—but only for William—whose disposition was so remarkeable that she was sure he wd turn out something great *either for good or evil.*" "Wordsworth on Wordsworth and Much Else: New Conversational Memoranda," *Papers of the Bibliographical Society of America*, 81 (1987), 451–458.

[12] *Wordsworth's Cambridge Education* (Cambridge: Cambridge University Press, 1957). I am also greatly indebted to T. W. Thompson, *Wordsworth's Hawkshead*, ed. Robert Woof (London: Oxford University Press, 1970).

Mr. Gillbanks at Cockermouth and Mrs. Anne Birkett at Penrith.[13] Founded in 1585 by Edwin Sandys, then Archbishop of York, Hawkshead was free of charge to children of the district. The best accounts of Hawkshead describe its atmosphere of learning, its fairly strict curriculum, yet its joyous and free spirit. The headmasters, graduates of Cambridge, were all Anglican clergymen, many of them with their eye on the prize of ecclesiastical advancement. A student like the young Wordsworth would have been exposed to a curriculum that included Latin; Greek; the mathematics of Euclid; classical writers like Homer, Demosthenes, Sophocles, Virgil, Horace, and Cicero; and a healthy dose of English poetry. Most recently, following the tradition of Schneider and of T. W. Thompson, Richard Clancey has written exhaustively about the classical bent of Wordsworth's education at Hawkshead and later at Cambridge, a bent that will reveal itself as an "undersong" in *The Prelude*. At Hawkshead, says Clancey, both "mountains" and "classical texts" engaged the young Wordsworth. "He was challenged to compete with Virgil, Milton, and others; he was educated to inspire us to do the same."[14] One William Taylor presided over the school from 1782 to 1786, and, like special teachers and headmasters in any age, won the affection of students and widened their intellectual horizons not only in literature, but also in Bacon, Newton, and the growing scientific approach to knowledge. The young Wordsworth, quite typically, also moved beyond formal curricular requirements to satisfy a zest for all kinds of literary works—fairy tales, biography, and travel books in particular.

Yet he enjoyed not only books, but also the beauty of the setting at Hawkshead where he roamed at will in a spirit of independence, finding in nutting expeditions, ice-skating, boating on the lake, and other youthful escapades the pleasure of physical sensation and, strikingly, the dawning of a richer awareness of spiritual presence. And there were holiday visits to relatives at Cockermouth and to the spectacular setting of the port city of Whitehaven, where his Uncle Richard was a Controller of Customs. Yet one of these vacations

---

[13] Moorman, *William Wordsworth*, 1:15.

[14] "Wordsworth's Classical Undersong: Rhetorical Learning and the 'Blended Might' of a New Creation," unpubl, 1993.

brought another youthful traumatic experience. The scenario has all
the elements of a drama. The time is Christmas of 1783; Wordsworth is thirteen and he impatiently waits for the horses that will
take him and his brothers home from Hawkshead for the holiday. As
it happened, John Wordsworth, ever the devoted but busy parent,
hurrying home on horseback from his work, had become lost, and
was forced to spend a night without lodging in the mountains of
Cold Fell. The father, who never fully assuaged the grief that followed his wife's death, literally caught his death of cold. It is a Keatsian scene as Wordsworth and his brothers Richard and John—now
truly orphans—stood at graveside in the Cockermouth cemetery as
their father, the familial anchor, was buried. Although Wordsworth
and his father were never really close, loss and especially a sense of
guilt about his anxiety for the return home combined to sharpen a
sense of isolation and a need for new sources of stability. W. Jackson
Bate in his memorable life of Samuel Johnson captures poignantly
the guilt Johnson felt many years after refusing his ailing father's
request to take charge of his book stall. "Now, on a rainy day exactly
fifty years later, he forced himself, in a way that could seem almost
like an act of religious penance, to do what he had once denied the
helpless Michael." "He went" to Uttoexeter, and "going into the
market at the time of high business, uncovered my head, and stood
with it bare an hour before the stall which my father had formerly
used, exposed to the sneers of the standers–by and the inclemency
of the weather."[15]

Circumstances are different, to be sure, but there is something
of the same human feeling of loss and guilt and reparation in Wordsworth's recalling and dramatizing this episode with great power in
Book 12 of *The Prelude*:

> The event,
> With all the sorrow that it brought, appeared
> A chastisement; and when I called to mind
> That day so lately past, when from the crag
> I looked in such anxiety of hope;
> With trite reflections of morality,

---

[15] *Samuel Johnson* (New York and London: Harcourt Brace Jovanovich, 1975; repr.
1977), p. 129.

Yet in the deepest passion, I bowed low
To God, Who thus corrected my desires [12.309–316].

Now truly orphans, the brothers Wordsworth were cared for by legal guardians, their uncles Richard Wordsworth and Christopher Cookson. The first task was to collect the money owed to their father, especially the £4,500 owed by his employer, Sir James Lowther, now a prestigious Earl of Lonsdale, for loyal service. It was a long and frustrating process of legal wrangling that was not to be fully settled until 1802. Meanwhile, the boys continued their Hawkshead education, and the setting of the school continued to be a source of even richer learning for the young William. Lacking a father, Wordsworth seems to have found a surrogate in his beloved teacher William Taylor. Here he probably formed his first images of the poet and his mission as he and his friend John Fleming read aloud James Beattie's *The Minstrel*, lent him by Taylor. Here also he saw in the poems of the "marvelous boy" Thomas Chatterton, someone not much older than he was, the possibilities of poetry as he read in Chatterton's *Miscellanies in Prose and Verse*, another gift from Taylor. Ben Ross Schneider contends that he learned the meaning of literary melancholy from Taylor, who loved Chatterton and that remarkable cluster of eighteenth-century writers who came to be known as Poets of Sensibility.

Taylor was always more than a lender of good books. He was one of those teachers able to see something of promise, however primitive, in a student and to support and encourage it with honesty and concern. The lovely inscription in the flyleaf of Wordsworth's copy of Chatterton's *Miscellanies*, a book discovered by T. W. Thompson, exemplifies a student's admiration: "To the Revd. William Taylor, Master of the Free Grammar School at Hawkshead, to mark my appreciation of his luminous and pertinent reflections on the poets of our time, and especially the unhappy boy whose genius is evident in many of the pieces contained in this slender volume."[16] Wordsworth's Hawkshead poems do not offer us any artist as *enfant terrible* image; they are first attempts, lacking in artistry, but not in a sense of commitment. Among them are the "Lines Written as a School

---

[16] *Wordsworth's Hawkshead*, p. 77.

Exercise at Hawkshead, Anno Aetatis 14," with its abstractions of Truth, Industry, and Passion, its preachy couplets, its praise of the school and its history, yet still a notable Popean imitation for a young teenager. And there are the assigned imitations of Anacreon, with the interesting address to Sir Joshua Reynolds, and the embarrassing "idyllium" on the death of his dog, with its unabashedly Miltonic, "Where were ye nymphs, when the remorseless deep / Closed o'er your little favourite's helpless head?" There is also the notable descriptive poem *The Vale of Esthwaite*, surviving now only in fragments but certainly revealing signs of the loco-descriptive qualities to be found in his *An Evening Walk* and *Descriptive Sketches*. It was also at Hawkshead—at the very end of his studies there—that he composed the mawkishly precious "Sonnet, On Seeing Miss Helen Maria Williams Weep at a Tale of Distress," his first published poem and an early example of a continuing, indeed lifelong, interest in women writers.

As he begins to write, he continues to nourish his love of natural beauty. He boated and skated on Esthwaite Water, often walked along around the five-mile perimeter of Lake Windemere, and sometimes even visited families in the area. He would on occasion take the ferry (nowadays there is a convenient pedestrian and automobile ferry) to Bowness on the other side of the lake. Perhaps the best-known story in this connection recounts a trip across the lake, a visit to the White Lion Inn (today the Royal) in Bowness near the shore for a treat of bowling and of strawberries and cream. He would also rent a boat and sail to many of the islands of Windemere—to Belle Isle, his favorite, or St. Mary's, or perhaps others. He also loved to ride horseback to Furness Abbey some twenty miles away, with its ruins so evocative of the medieval and the Gothic.

It was a magical time as the lively, exuberant boy—at one with nature, his imagination stirred by books and monuments, his social sense nourished by friends and neighbors—moved through what he thought of as an earthly paradise. Recalling the time poetically, he again uses the sun to catch his feeling, but, as he suggests, a particular image of the sun:

> already I began
> To love the sun; a boy I loved the sun,

Not as I since have loved him, as a pledge
And surety of our earthly life, a light
Which we behold and feel we are alive;
Nor for his bounty to so many worlds—
But for this cause, that I had seen him lay
His beauty on the morning hills, had seen
The western mountains touch his setting orb,
In many a thoughtless hour, when, from excess
Of happiness, my blood appeared to flow
For its own pleasure, and I breathed with joy [2.177–188].

Having found both security and inspiration under the guidance of Taylor, he was to see them slip away again as he and several of his senior classmates at Hawkshead were called to their teacher's bedside as he lay dying. Taylor died a few days after this visit of June 12, 1786, at the age of thirty-two, and was succeeded as Headmaster by one Thomas Bowman, a worthy educator who, though he never had the impact of Taylor, encouraged Wordsworth's literary leanings. He lent the young poet copies of Cowper's *The Task* and the poetry of Burns, the latter remaining a strong influence for many years with its vivid portraits of peasant–rustic folk who lived and worked close to the soil and spoke a natural, unspoiled, musical language.

But Taylor's personal and literary influence lingered long for the adolescent and the older Wordsworth. He recalls in *The Prelude* how, returning from a visit to his cousins at Rampside in August and September 1794—a visit made memorable by his later poem "Elegiac Stanzas Suggested by a Picture of Peele Castle"—he came upon Cartmel Priory near Ulverston where Taylor was buried. The Priory evoked a memory—Taylor's gravestone, with lines from Gray's *Elegy*, can still be seen in the churchyard—and he "turned aside / To seek the ground where, 'mid a throng of graves, / An honoured teacher of my youth was laid, / And on the stone were graven by his desire / Lines from the churchyard elegy of Gray." Wordsworth's method is to create a poetic drama in two acts. In the first act there is the recreation of the Hawkshead student and his teacher: Taylor "speaking from his death–bed, / Added no farewell to his parting counsel, / But said to me, 'My head will soon lie low'; / And when I saw the turf that covered him, / After the lapse of full eight years, those words, / With sound of voice and countenance of the Man, / Came back upon me, so that some few tears / Fell from me in my own despite." In the second act he imagines, "whispering to myself: / He loved the Poets, and, if now alive, / Would have loved me, as one not destitute / Of promise, nor belying the kind hope / That he had formed, when I, at his command, / Began to spin, with toil, my earliest songs" (10.532–552).

Wordsworth left Hawkshead School in the spring of 1787 and was admitted as a sizar (a scholarship student) to St. John's College, Cambridge. His memories on leaving the school are generally happy ones, whether he speaks of the people, the locale, or, most important, the quality of the educational experience. Robert Woof reminds us of the fascinating letter Wordsworth wrote to H. S. Tremenheere, as Inspector of Schools, on December 16, 1845, as the elderly poet looks back over his school days at all levels and unfolds what amounts to a philosophy of education. Hawkshead must certainly be seen as a key contributor to that philosophy, perhaps a crucial part given his infant-school experiences and his somewhat unhappy days at Cambridge.[17] "Is not," he writes, "the Knowledge inculcated by the Teacher, or derived under his managem[en]t, from books, too exclusively dwelt upon, so as almost to put out of sight that which comes, without being sought for, from intercourse with nature and from experience in the actual employments and duties which a child's situation in the Country, however unfavorable, will lead him to or impose upon him?"

He respectfully disagrees with the opinion of a supporter of "in the classroom" education as one way of saving the expense of clothing and shoe-leather, while characterizing himself blithely as "one who spent half of his boyhood in running wild among the Mountains." And he closes this remarkable letter—he is now seventy-five—with an expression of regret that "too little attention is paid to books of imagination which are eminently useful in calling forth intellectual power." He is convinced that students must have not only "Knowledge but the means of wielding it, and that is done infinitely more thro' the imaginative faculty assisting both in the collection and application of facts."[18]

---

[17] In ibid., pp, 116–117.
[18] December 16, 1845. *LY* 7.4:733.

The summer following graduation from Hawkshead was an unusually full one. Dorothy, after a nine-year absence while living with her late mother's cousin Elizabeth Threlkeld in Halifax, returns to live with her grandparents at Penrith, a situation, as she confides to her friend Jane Pollard, that proves a source of great unhappiness to her. Overriding all of this disappointment, however, is the joy of reunion, for her, but even more so for her brother who found in her the firm ground, the source of stability, that was always so crucial for his inner peace. To Coleridge, the most prominent listener in *The Prelude*, Wordsworth speaks of being "blest with the presence, Friend! / Of that sole Sister, she who hath been long / Dear to thee also, thy true friend and mine, / Now, after separation desolate, / Restored to me—such absence that she seemed / A gift then first bestowed" (6.197–203). And in what is perhaps his most celebrated poetic tribute—in his "The Sparrow's Nest"—he again uses the religious image to express the sense of the real that Dorothy brought to his life early and late. She, "The Blessing of my later years / Was with me when a Boy," and to one given to the ways of imagination, "She gave me eyes, she gave me ears; / And humble cares, and delicate fears; / A heart, the fountain of sweet tears; / And love, and thought, and joy" (15–20).[19]

The Prelude records happy episodes, both of this summer and those ahead, as they celebrate reunion, renew their friendship with Mary Hutchinson—later to be Wordsworth's wife—roaming the countryside, talking about happy childhood days at Cockermouth, reading to each other at Brougham Castle near Penrith, climbing the Penrith Beacon where the poet had experienced one of his epiphanic moments years before. Brother and sister rediscover themselves; they seem always to be together, walking enormous distances, talking, planning. There will be occasion later on to talk about a brother–sister relationship that over the years has evoked among some critics a curiosity about incest, or at least abnormal familial closeness. Recent criticism has pretty much dispelled such speculation, focusing on the intensity of devotion felt by each, the depth of commitment brought by Dorothy to furthering her brother's poetic ambition,

---

[19] All references are to "The Sparrow's Nest," in *Poems in Two Volumes, and Other Poems, 1800–1807*, ed. Jared Curtis (Ithaca, N.Y.: Cornell University Press, 1993).

Wordsworth's male dominance, and Dorothy's submergence of her own needs to what she considered to be the greater good of her brother. Mary Moorman sees no need for "morbid implications." "Theirs," she says, "was a love that found its daily food in a thousand tiny incidents, . . . and it was firmly based on the strongest ground of all, a common inheritance from earliest childhood of memories and associations that were entirely happy." "Dorothy believed that her brother was a poet, and set about recreating that belief in him."[20] Most recently, and especially in such critics as Susan Levin and Anne Mellor, the emphasis has shifted to the peculiarly female qualities that characterize her poetry and particularly her journals, her "different voice," and these critics view her as a key part of the Grasmere literary community.[21] Critical disputes aside, it was a time of happiness and excitement for both brother and sister. Wordsworth catches the time and presents Dorothy and himself as characters in an adventure story, its setting Brougham Castle on the River Eamont:

> —that river and those mouldering towers
> Have seen us side by side, when, having clomb
> The darksome windings of a broken stair,
> And crept along a ridge of fractured wall,
> Not without trembling, we in safety looked
> Forth, through some Gothic window's open space,
> And gathered with one mind a rich reward
> From the far-stretching landscape, by the light
> Of morning beautified, or purple eve [6.211–219].

It was also a time of great excitement in the larger world, with political upheaval in America, India, and France stirring the interest and concern of young men like Wordsworth who had developed from their earliest days a faith in the goodness of human beings, the beauty of external nature, the force of democracy. Further, the large phenomenon of the Industrial Revolution could now be seen in microcosm by Wordsworth as he watched the idyllic cottage textile

---

[20] *William Wordsworth: A Biography*, 1:281–282.

[21] Susan Levin, *Dorothy Wordsworth and Romanticism* (New Brunswick, N.J.: Rutgers University Press, 1987); Anne Mellor, *Romanticism and Gender* (New York and London: Routledge, 1993), pp. 144–169.

industries of Hawkshead and Penrith give way to factories, with all the implications for the blemishing of nature and the dehumanization of workers. As Wordsworth grew older, he became an increasingly strong advocate for the purity of the environment and an equally strong foe of the incursions of buildings, factories, and railways into his beloved Lake District. The modern visitor marvels at the beauty of Rydal, Grasmere, and other sections of this area—the beauty of lakes and mountains, the cleanness of the air, the quiet (July and August notwithstanding) of the setting. Those pleasures are due in no small part to the National Trust and to contemporary activists, but the early pioneers like Wordsworth created this Lake spirit of pride and concern for preservation not just of historical sites but also of the monuments of nature. His 1835 *Guide to the Lakes* continues to be both his personal memoir and also an invaluable resource for modern travelers.

Add together the high spirits triggered by his reunion with Dorothy, his concern with the events of the larger world, his first steps in the profession of poetry, and the expectation of a university education at Cambridge, and you have an ebullient Wordsworth in the summer of 1787. In October 1787 the grand journey to the university was launched, and with his kind and caring uncle William Cookson and his cousin John Myers, a fellow prospective Cantabrigian, he arrived at Cambridge on October 30.

Ben Ross Schneider, who has written extensively on Cambridge in the eighteenth century, speculates that William Cookson "entered Wordsworth at St. John's because he knew that a fellowship would be waiting for him upon graduation." As a fellow of the college and a clergyman himself, he saw ecclesiastical and legal opportunities for his nephew in the future. And, given the remarkably scientific orientation of Cambridge at the time, Wordsworth would seem to have been, at least academically, well prepared. He had already, thanks to Taylor, been introduced to Bacon, Newton, and the scientific method. He had studied the mathematics of Euclid. Following the revolution triggered by Newton's great discoveries, "Cambridge gave an increasingly large place in its course of studies to mathematics and natural philosophy at the expense of classics and moral philosophy. By Wordsworth's time, only proficiency in Newtonian science could secure high honors for a B.A. degree candidate." A kind of mechanical materialism and utilitarianism dominated the thinking of the university, and, as Schneider notes, "many Cambridge men were deists, often accused of being atheists."[22]

Yet Wordsworth's hopes were high as he arrived at school, like the hopes of generations of first-year college and university students arriving for orientation days, with expectations idealistic, indeed unrealistic feelings of hope that no human institution can fulfill—a full round of exciting courses taught by brilliant and enthusiastic lecturers, a curriculum that would bring present pleasure and later success in the great world beyond, and a full round of social life with charming friends both tried and true.

He certainly did not lack friends. His cousin John Myers just beginning; his good friend from Hawkshead, John Fleming, starting his third year; William Penny, Edward Burkett, Fletcher Raincott, Robert Greenwood, Thomas Gawthorp, and others—all of these provided protection against the loneliness and homesickness that many beginning students experience. Dorothy had prepared his wardrobe, and he seemed ready, as he himself records, again in the form of a poetic mini-drama touched by gentle self-mockery, the grand arrival. There is the first scene, a suspenseful approach, a first view: "It was a dreary morning when the wheels / Rolled over a wide plain o'erhung with clouds, / And nothing cheered our way till first we saw / The long-roofed chapel of King's College lift / Turrets and pinnacles in answering files / Extending high above a dusky grove." And then there is the campus itself, as, with a light satiric touch, the hero of the play spies along the street "A student clothed in gown and tasselled cap, / Striding along as if o'ertasked by Time, / Or covetous of exercise and air." Little by little the dream of expectation meets the reality; "As near and nearer to the spot we drew, / It seemed to suck us in with an eddy's force."

The young Wordsworth's "spirit was up, my thoughts were full of hope." There were friends to offer "Questions, directions, warnings and advice." There was the first sense of self-confidence, even delight, as "to myself I seemed / A man of business and expense, and went / From shop to shop about my own affairs, / To Tutor or to Tailor, as befel, / From street to street with loose and careless mind."

---

[22] *Wordsworth's Cambridge Education*, pp. 4–10.

Yet, he feels, "I was the Dreamer, they the Dream; I roamed / Delighted through the motley spectacle," certainly "Migration strange for a stripling of the hills, / A northern villager" (3.1–35).

Dream, to be sure, for he was quickly awakened to a rather different reality, a phenomenon not unfamiliar to many young men and women today who create a sort of Platonic ideal that simply cannot be fulfilled. But the problem was compounded at Cambridge where the curriculum seemed in a state of decline and disarray, the student body anti-humanistic and hyper-competitive, many of the administration and faculty concerned with their own careers and aspirations.

Schneider's detailed study of Wordsworth's Cambridge education argues that the university at that time was theoretically governed by statutes passed down from Elizabethan times. The Thirty-Nine Articles, he contends, were certainly anti-freethinking and clearly not in tune with scientific and social advances. The statutes "were therefore disregarded or 'reinterpreted' so often as to encourage disrespect for law and order. In a time of moral laxity, this state of affairs was bad for Cambridge." Though some reform was under way, the university "still seethed with intrigue, favouritism and injustice, a fact he must soon have sensed. In the midst of this spectacle the manner and attire of the North Country boy seemed gauche to the witty and stylish."[23] His room, we know, was one of the shabbiest in the university. Whatever prestige he had as a bright young man and would-be poet at Hawkshead gave way to a state of near oblivion at Cambridge. He was now the proverbial small fish in a big pond.

It is a mistake to paint too idealistic a picture of Wordsworth at this time, of an unwavering, devout, studious young man interested only in study and learned discussions of books and ideas. He did enjoy the friendship of old Hawkshead classmates and of new Cambridge friends. And he took delight in good parties, boating on the Cam, and other pleasures. Yet he must have shuddered when he realized that an honors degree required Newtonian science.[24] No other field counted. He clearly rejected the regular course of study, despised ambitious deans and clergy, and might be described as de-

---

[23] Ibid., p. 11.
[24] Ibid., pp. 4–5.

cidedly anti-clerical. We have no hard evidence that he had any genuine interest in organized religion. In a dramatic and oft-quoted section of *The Prelude*, he captures the routinization and boredom of university life, and also offers a vivid graph of his own psychic state in the midst of it all.

> Of College labours, of the Lecturer's room
> All studded round, as thick as chairs could stand,
> With loyal students faithful to their books
> Half-and-half idlers, hardy recusants,
> And honest dunces—of important days,
> Examinations, when the man was weighed
> As in a balance! of excessive hopes,
> Tremblings withal and commendable fears,
> Small jealousies, and triumphs good or bad,
> Let others that know more speak as they know.
> Such glory was but little sought by me,
> And little won [3.64–75].

While he is eager "to hope" and anxious about his "future worldly maintenance," it is his sense of isolation that strikes us most, an inner stirring unformed, unfigured, "a strangeness in the mind, / A feeling that I was not for that hour" (3.77–81).

This combination of disillusionment, anxiety, and hope developed quickly, and, after such an academic year, he was delighted to return to Ann Tyson's cottage in Hawkshead for holidays. Here was his natural habitat, his Eden with the sights and sounds of nature unadulterated, the faces and speech of men and women of honesty and directness, the simple pleasures of walking, boating, even attending parties and a country dance. All these seemed more nurturing to the young man than the learning and acclamation of the university—he had been one of twenty-one in a class of forty-five who received first-class honors—the popularity with friends, the promise of a secure position after graduation. During his first year at Cambridge he had found much to disenchant him; he had perhaps even taken a trip to London and tasted its noise and turbulence. Yet during this summer, especially in the accounts in *The Prelude*, he develops a sense of what he does not want to do with his life, a feeling of what a life devoted to poetry might involve and of what kind of poet he might become.

He speaks of having "inward hopes / And swellings of the spirit," and "glimmering views / How life pervades the undecaying mind; / How the immortal soul with God–like power / Informs, creates, and thaws the deepest sleep / That time can lay upon her" (4.162–168). He further records, "A freshness also found I at this time / In human Life, the daily life of those / Whose occupations really I loved," and how this love for the humble and rustic is matched by a deep concern with the pleasures of the inner life (4.191–193). These ruminations of the young first-year college student offer fertile anticipation of a lifelong poetic and personal tension between the claims of the individual mind and those of the larger external reality. It is a tension fundamental to an understanding and appreciation of Wordsworth's literary—and personal—life, of the continuities and discontinuities of his poetry and his life.

Cambridge ceases to engage the maturing young poet, and the St. John's examination reports for June 1788 reveal a second-class ranking. College is now, at best, something to be gotten through, perhaps to please his family or to secure credentials of a sort for the eyes of society. Schneider may attribute too much to an eighteen-year-old in his claim that "Wordsworth's revolt in 1788 against Cambridge foreshadows, parallels, and helps to explain his revolt in 1798 against eighteenth-century culture";[25] yet it is an interesting theory of the case, a case that sees Wordsworth, no mere recluse, annoyed by the academic corruption he saw everywhere, finding a richer life in the imaginative surroundings of Cambridge, thinking about the vocation not of church or law, but of poetry. One thinks especially of this new concern, and even commitment, in the lines of *The Prelude*, "I made no vows, but vows / Were then made for me; bond unknown to me / Was given, that I should be, else sinning greatly, / A dedicated Spirit" (4.334–337). Mary Moorman speculates that the vocation of poetry becomes more fixed in Wordsworth's mind this summer and that "it was during this vacation that he began to write *An Evening Walk*, a poem both in form and content far more mature than *The Vale of Esthwaite* and more likely to achieve publication."[26] We will return to *An Evening Walk* below as an important early work in the evolution of the poet's literary life.

---

[25] Ibid., p. 17.
[26] *William Wordsworth: A Biography*, 1:110.

We know relatively little of Wordsworth's 1788–1789, 1789–1790 Cambridge years. His disillusionment was certainly reinforced, especially after happy vacation times at Hawkshead. He is clearly reading at will now, showing little enthusiasm for science and mathematics, and widening his circle of friends—Robert Jones, who will accompany him on his later trip to France and Switzerland and who will remain a favorite traveling companion; William Mathews, a regular correspondent, who was to die in his early thirties of yellow fever in the West Indies; his cousin John Myers, already mentioned; and fellow St. John's students William Terrot, John Fisher, and John Gisborne (he was a nature poet and a convert to Methodism). Schneider speculates that since Wordsworth knew Francis Wrangham, a scholar and a clergyman, and John Tweddell after leaving St. John's, "there is some probability that he knew them while still there. They were both members of a brilliant group of young men who graduated in 1790." Such a group would have been intellectually and artistically stimulating to a young man feeling his first poetic stirrings. Also worthy of special note is Schneider's suggestion that he may have met one Willis John Webb, a student of the Utopian political philosopher William Godwin, whose work will later exert its influence on Wordsworth.[27]

Wordsworth was, of course, admirably prepared for a program of wide-ranging reading. The dimensions of his own library can be seen in his daughter Dora's hand in the Manuscript Catalogue at the Houghton Library of Harvard University. While Hawkshead may have placed a great emphasis on algebra and geometry for its students, this emphasis hardly inhibited the young poet's literary instincts. He had been well prepared in Latin, as had all his classmates headed for the philosophical studies of Cambridge. At Cambridge he certainly encountered John Locke's central statement of British empirical psychology, *An Essay Concerning Human Understanding*, a treatise that, according to Schneider, ranked second only to Newton's *Principia* in order of academic importance.[28] Locke was, of course, not only the high priest of British empiricism, but also a strong influence on David Hartley's psychological work, the *Observa-*

---

[27] *Wordworth's Cambridge Education*, p. 66.
[28] Ibid., p. 106.

tions on Man, an important book for the young Wordsworth and Coleridge. In Locke and Hartley they would have found a strong physiological–mechanistic epistemology, an emphasis on the power of sensation, especially sight, as a basis for knowledge. More important, they would have, in Locke's presentation of the primary and secondary qualities of matter, later popularized in Addison's *Spectator* papers on "The Pleasures of Imagination," became aware of the power of mind to shape experience, to bring those lights and shades and feelings to the object found not in the object itself, but in the psyche of the viewer. How vividly lines from *Tintern Abbey* describe the early psychology of Wordsworth, his faith in a collaboration of mind and nature to make meaning and value. Looking back over the phases of his own psychological development from childhood to adolescence to maturity, he offers a summation of a continuing faith, a statement of his state of mind in the late 1790s:

> Therefore am I still
> A lover of the meadows and the woods,
> And mountains; and of all that we behold
> From this green earth; of all the mighty world
> Of eye, and ear, both what they half-create,
> And what perceive; well pleased to recognize
> In nature and the language of the sense,
> The anchor of my purest thoughts, the nurse,
> The guide, the guardian of my heart, and soul
> Of all my moral being [103–112].[29]

And how movingly this faith in the power of the object and the creativity of mind is caught in the memorable lines of *The Prelude*. He speaks of the "plastic power" within, of how

> An auxiliar light
> Came from my mind, which on the setting sun
> Bestowed new splendour; the melodious birds,
> The fluttering breezes, fountains that ran on
> Murmuring so sweetly in themselves, obeyed
> A like dominion, and the midnight storm
> Grew darker in the presence of my eye:

---

[29] All references to *Tintern Abbey* are to *Lyrical Ballads and Other Poems, 1797–1800*, ed. James Butler and Karen Green (Ithaca, N.Y.: Cornell University Press, 1992).

Hence my obeisance, my devotion hence,
And hence my transport [2.368–376].

One should also be aware of the revolutionary spirit in the Cambridge air at the time, a spirit that Wordsworth imbibed. It is, I think, a mistake to regard the famous meeting with Michael Beaupuy, important though it was, as a sudden beginning of Wordsworth's ardor for the French Revolution. Schneider is especially helpful in sketching the dimensions of radicalism on the campus at the time, especially at Trinity, at Jesus (Coleridge's college), and at St. John's (Wordsworth's). The Cambridge Dissentients, strong supporters of the American Revolution and the early days of the French Revolution, arguers for reform, political, educational, other, must certainly have caught his attention and held it. "Three of the elder *philosophes* represented Cambridge at the historic meeting of the Revolution in London on November 5, 1789 when Richard Price delivered the sermon that inspired Edmund Burke's *Reflections on the Revolution in France*. . . . Godwin was also there."[30] Both Godwin and Burke were to be important figures in the young Wordsworth's intellectual history and political development. He met Godwin in 1795 and for a time came under his spell, taken by his ideas of reform not by violent upheaval but by the gradualism of sweet reasonableness. And, according to James Chandler, Wordsworth's early lessons in the power of nature and "in the simple primary affections and duties" learned from Rousseau were tempered and modified by Burke's "second nature," "the moral wardrobe of the naked shivering nature." Indeed, for Chandler, Wordsworth was to become "a more thoroughgoing traditionalist than Burke himself."[31]

Such were the events and activities that surrounded a somewhat bored Wordsworth during his last two years at Cambridge. Dorothy left Penrith in November 1788 to live with her uncle William Cookson and his new wife, Dorothy Cowper, at Forncett Rectory near Norwich, about fifty miles from Cambridge. Here she ran a small Sunday school for children, and Wordsworth visited her the following June at the end of his final year at Cambridge. He had decided at the time on a walking tour of France and Switzerland with his good

---

[30] Ibid., p. 134.
[31] *Wordworth's Second Nature*, pp. xxi–xxii.

friend Robert Jones. It was the kind of trip, it seems, students able to do so took and continue to take during or, more often, at the end of their college years. For several months they were out of touch completely, with no one knowing their whereabouts, lending further support to the image of maturity and independence they were eager to create.

It was a remarkable trip by any standards, nearly three thousand miles, according to Stephen Gill, and a large part of it walking.[32] Wordsworth—indeed, one might say the whole Wordsworth circle— gave new meaning to the activity of walking throughout a lifetime. Reaching Dover on June 13, 1790, they crossed the channel to Calais just as Louis XVI was swearing fidelity to a new constitution, an event of great excitement for the two young radicals who had talked and read about the Revolution at a distance. Wordsworth had heard the news of the Fall of the Bastille the year before, and he could sense the excitement and exuberance of the *fédérés*, those delegates from Marseilles to the Federation Festival who were returning home with hopes for a new politics and a new world.

Covering some twenty miles a day, they reached Chalon-sur-Saône on July 17, and enjoyed the beauty and tranquillity of a boat trip with a group of Frenchmen down the Saône toward Lyons, where the young poet fulfilled a dream of viewing the monastery of La Grande Chartreuse. Then on to view the sublime power of Chamonix and Mont Blanc. "My Spirits," he writes to Dorothy from Keswi, on Lake Constance, "have been kept in a perpetual hurry of delight by the almost uninterrupted succession of sublime and beautiful objects which have passed before my eyes during the course of the last month." And with the language of the religious mystic, he describes how "Among the more awful scenes of the Alps, I had not a thought of man, or a single created being; my whole soul was turned to him who produced the terrible majesty before me." Yet in the midst of the awe-inspiring natural scenery, Wordsworth was always quick to note his delight in coming upon the sights of

---

[32] *Wordsworth, A Life*, p. 44. Here, as in all matters of chronology, my invaluable guide has been Mark Reed's *Wordsworth: The Chronology of the Early Years, 1770–1799* (Cambridge, Mass.: Harvard University Press, 1967) and his *Wordsworth: The Chronology of the Middle Years, 1799–1815* (Cambridge, Mass.: Harvard University Press, 1975).

simple shepherds, cottagers, those who lived close to the earth; or, as at Lake Como, to express a desire to heighten his enjoyment of natural scenery "by conversation and exercise of the social affections."[33]

From France they traveled into Switzerland, the occasion of their passing through the Simplon Pass without realizing, in the midst of clouds and fog, that they had already fulfilled a youthful dream of crossing the Alps. The episode, to be discussed at great length in our examination of *The Prelude*, was to be re-created poetically as one of those visionary experiences that he regarded as shaping his spirit and providing a rich awareness of the power of mind. Filled with "hopes that pointed to the clouds," and "Loth to believe" the guide's words, "*that we had crossed the Alps*," he must at the same time come to terms with the reality of the crossing and yet pay tribute to the power that had made the imagining more powerful than that reality. "Imagination" is an "awful Power," and he now can say " 'I recognise thy glory': in such strength / Of usurpation, when the light of sense / Goes out, but with a flash that has revealed / The invisible world" (6.586–603).

Lake Como, Gravedona, and especially the Falls of the Rhine at Schaffhausen display the power of waterfalls as they begin the journey back. At Basel they rent a boat and sail down the Rhine to Cologne, then move on through Belgium to Calais and back to Cambridge by mid–October. Wordsworth returns with an even deeper reverence for the power of nature and the strong bond he feels with this power, with a conviction that "Our destiny, our being's heart and home, / Is with infinitude, and only there" (6.604–605).

A visit to Dorothy at Forncett made her nineteenth birthday a happy one for all concerned. The return to Cambridge was a matter, as we put it nowadays, of "picking up the degree," especially after a summer that had opened a world so much larger, so much more educative, than the confinement of St. John's and even the larger university. He took his degree in January 1790, without honors, yet, as Schneider reminds us, "with a good grounding in classical literature, a valuable knowledge of modern languages and literatures." He

---

[33] W. W. to D. W., September 6 [and 12, 1790]. *EY* 1:32, 34.

had also found in the moral philosophy he read at the university a basis for translating his "private feelings about the aristocracy into the rationale of the French Revolution," a development that was reinforced by his firsthand observation of the radical activities of the Cambridge Dissentients. That philosophy must also have made him more open to the strong force of Godwin's ideas of political justice.[34] Wordsworth may have left Cambridge with a good deal of cynicism about the experience of formal education, but he brought from his reading, his vacation travel, his associations a vision of a new world and a sense of his need to find a special place within that world.

Again, we must remember that Wordsworth was still young, only in his early twenties, and that his departure from the university, like that of undergraduates dissatisfied with what they regard as the limitations of the academy, was not without anxiety, even sadness. His words in a letter to William Mathews capture vividly his state of mind: "You have learned from Myers that, since I had the pleasure of seeing you, I have been do[ing] nothing and still continue to be doing nothing. What is to become of me I know not: I cannot bow down my mind to take orders, and as for the law I have neither strength of mind purse or constitution, to engage in that pursuit."[35] In a sense it represented an end of youth, of endless days of walking, socializing, reading, and hatching schemes for a better world. These are days when one can bravely play the detached intellectual, the privileged imaginative artist, criticizing and satirizing the larger world, offering solutions for its ills, playing the role of prophet for a bright tomorrow. They are also days when one can procrastinate, put off the burdens of career, responsibilities, financial concerns; and Wordsworth, uncertain about the legal actions to recover his father's estate and about how exactly to fulfill his poetic ambitions, in a curious way hated to leave his campus.

But leave he did and went off to London, uncertain of what he would do there, and clearly unconcerned about his family's pragmatic objections. He had already made a first visit during the Christmas holidays of 1789, at that time to be with his brother John before John sailed for India on his ship, the *Earl of Abergavenny*, in January

---

[34] *Wordsworth's Cambridge Education*, pp. 188–189.
[35] February 17 [1794]. *EY* 1:112.

1790. London seemed to have a complex effect on him. On the one hand, there were the crowds, the ugliness and noise of Bartholomew Fair, the poverty, the neglect of those in need, and all of these shocked him. "Oh, blank confusion! true epitome / Of what the mighty City is herself / To thousands upon thousands of her sons, / Living amid the same perpetual whirl / Of trivial objects, melted and reduced / To one identity, by differences / That have no law, no meaning, and no end" (7.722–728). On the other hand, the sensitive man sees in the vast expanse of the city—walking along the Thames, viewing the Abbey, the Tower, and the other monuments of a culture—something more. "The Spirit of Nature was upon me there," he exclaims (7.766).

Wordsworth discerned another dimension of the great city in its architecture, in the artistic performances at Drury Lane, Covent Garden, and Sadler's Wells. And the spirit of place, the play of mind that characterized the great Charles James Fox–Edmund Burke debate on the French Revolution in May 1791, impressed, as he recalls in his 1820 addition to *The Prelude*, a young man of twenty-one. Although hardly ready at the time to share Burke's politics, with its vivid sense of the ordered society and the rule of reason, he describes himself as one of the "rapt auditors" caught by the older statesman offering another way of looking at the world, another way of balancing the conflicting claims of tradition and individual freedom, theory and practical politics, mind and the reality beyond. He uses a wonderfully poetic image to describe the scene of Burke haranguing the Parliament, advancing the cause of tradition and stability. "I see him,—old, but vigorous in age,— / Stand like an oak whose stag-horn branches start / Out of its leafy brow, the more to awe / The younger brethren of the grove." We see Burke bearing "Keen ridicule" from his audience as he denounces "all systems built on abstract rights," and "the majesty proclaims / Of Institutes and Laws, hallowed by time," and celebrates "the vital power of social ties" (7.512–527). Burke had begun to have an impact on Wordsworth even at this early age.

A stern uncle William, alarmed by what he saw as a lack of vocation in the young Wordsworth, drew him back to Cambridge to study the biblical languages, Hebrew and Arabic, in the hope that he would follow an ecclesiastical career. But the young man's mind is elsewhere as he hastens to invent excuses for a return to France. As a phase of his life closes, he may not have made a formal commitment to a poetic career, but his mind and heart are turned toward a world he regards as larger, freer, more hopeful than Hawkshead, Cambridge, London, toward a way of life more open, more creative than the church or the law. And he is certainly continuing to put pen to page, to capture in poetry now, as he did as early as his Hawkshead days, the sights and sounds that engage him. Two diverse critical viewpoints—those of Geoffrey Hartman and Alan Liu—touch on this critical moment. Hartman sees two forces fighting for his soul, "Nature and Milton," nature and imagination, and, rejecting the merely mimetic route, he argues, "Wordsworth set out with less between himself and his imagination than perhaps any poet before him; he is somehow more vulnerable to apocalyptic starts and self–recognition."[36] Liu sees the tour poems which we now discuss as blunting history, substituting description for narration, the picturesque for the sublime, all the while not so much denying as avoiding the specter of Revolutionary violence.[37]

The choices I make may be called arbitrary, of course, but two poems seem to me to emerge from this first episode in Wordsworth's personal and literary life, each in its own way revealing something significant about the poet. *An Evening Walk Addressed to a Young Lady*, composed, as he tells us in the Isabella Fenwick note to the poem, chiefly in 1788 and 1789 at college and during his first two vacations, has to some extent the ring of a writer trying to sound like a writer, a poet conscious not only of Spenser, Shakespeare, Milton, and Pope, but also, more obviously, of the so-called pre-Romantics or Poets of Sensibility like James Thomson, James Beattie, William Collins, poets given to the somewhat delicate expression of feeling not unchecked but controlled, to a poetry self-conscious, stylized, conventional.[38] Addressed to his sister Dorothy, the poem is written

---

[36] *Wordsworth's Poetry, 1799–1814* (Cambridge, Mass. and London: Harvard University Press, 1987), pp. 100–101. Unless otherwise noted, all references to Hartman are to this work.

[37] *Wordsworth: The Sense of History*, p. 11.

[38] For more on Isabella Fenwick, see below, p. 270. See also Jared Curtis, *The Fenwick Notes of William Wordsworth* (London: Bristol Classical Press, 1993). All references are to *An Evening Walk*, ed. James Averill (Ithaca, N.Y.: Cornell University Press, 1984).

in somewhat predictable couplets, regular in their pauses and rhymes, and has a fairly heavy dose of the sentimentality, melancholy, and allegorical personification on which he grew up.

Geographically the poem moves from Cockermouth and Keswick, "Where Derwent rests, and listens to the roar / That stuns the tremulous cliffs of high Lodore," to Grasmere and Windemere, "Where undisturbed by winds, Winander sleeps / 'Mid clustering isles and holly sprinkled steeps," and finally to Hawkshead, "Where twilight glens endear my Esthwaite's shore, / And memory of departed pleasures, more." He seems already the poet of recollection, ready to contrast the energy and exuberance of youth with the relentless coming of age. And in framing this contrast even this early in his career, he uses an image that seems to persist throughout his poetry. How to describe it without falling into the trap of conventional "light–darkness" contrasts is the challenge. Although the image will become increasingly rich and complex with Wordsworth's growing poetic maturity, it is at root and inevitably one of skewed light, of brightness touched by shadings of darkness. Youth was a time of dichotomized living, of "thoughtless gaiety," of "hope" without "pain," of "The sun at morning and the stars at night." But life is brief, and the sad story of time and change and loss can be "found / Depicted in the dial's moral round." Hope brightens the days of youth, but, ominously, "the sport of some malignant power, / He knows but from its shade the present hour." Already there are evidences of the teenager seeing spurts of darkness in the midst of light (1–32).

Quickly the speaker, in the tradition of the landscape and the walk poem, asks his listener to, "with unreluctant ear, / The history of a poet's evening hear" (35–36). Evening's "mild hour invites my step abroad," and the walk begins (89). The Fenwick note is, as usual, helpful and correct at this point, as Wordsworth at age seventy-three recalls the experiences of the poem. The plan of the poem, he says, "has not been confined to a particular walk or an individual place;—a proof (of which I was unconscious at the time) of my unwillingness to submit the poetic spirit to the chains of fact and real circumstances. The Country is idealized rather than described in any of its local aspects."

While Wordsworth had indeed generalized the geography of the poem, content to sketch broadly "crags," "cascade," "brook," covered "bridge," he has digressed to ruminate, in the manner of Horace, on the pleasures of the brook with "Harmonious thoughts, a soul by truth refined, / Entire affection for all human kind" (62–84). Yet there are points where a genuinely poetic voice is emerging, signs of promise and of things to come. Especially interesting is the kind of pacing that suggests, not the sudden coming of a static evening, but the slow evolution of a natural process. He begins like a landscape poet: "How pleasant, as the sun declines, to view / The spacious landscape change in form and hue!" (98–99). But the detail, Wordsworth's Fenwick disclaimer notwithstanding, seems more real, more vivid as daylight brightness slowly gives way to evening dusk. Here "Even the white stems of birch, the cottage white, / Soften their glare below the mellow light." There, "Raised by yon travelling flock, a dusty cloud / Mounts from the road, and spreads its moving shroud." Strikingly, even the human is touched as "The shepherd, all involved in wreaths of fire, / Now shows a shadowy speck, and now is lost entire" (103–112). Darkness slowly envelops everything.

At just about the poem's midpoint comes still another flash of originality, a departure of sorts from the "Poetry of Sensibility" that dominates. It is a scene that again juxtaposes light and darkness, but in that special way already described, light shaded or tempered, light whose power is nuanced by evidences of decline. The sun here cannot fight the inevitable end of its brilliance. As the shepherd directs the "winding dog" with his waving hat and pointing hand to gather the "intercepted flocks," "the day-star lessens still, / Gives one bright glance, and drops behind the hill" (181–190). And night brings not just darkness, but also a good amount of the Gothic machinery—"Strange apparitions"; "The form appears of one that spurs his steed / Midway along the hill with desperate speed"; "horsemen-shadows moving to and fro"—not unfamiliar to a poet who knew Ossian and the popular superstitions of Collins, Burns, and others (194–200).

And still the walk continues and with increasingly vivid images. Wordsworth himself comments on the authenticity of one such image in an Isabella Fenwick note of how "fronting the bright west, yon oak entwines / Its darkening boughs and leaves in stronger lines"

(214–215), imagery that seems to anticipate that of Coleridge's "This Line-Tree Bower My Prison."[39] "Although the image is feebly and imperfectly expressed," he says modestly, he can "recollect distinctly the very spot where this first struck me. It was in the way between Hawkshead and Ambleside, and gave me extreme pleasure." He marks both place and time as "important in my poetical history; for I date from it my consciousness of the infinite variety of natural appearances which had been unnoticed by the poets of any age or Country, so far as I was acquainted with them; and I made a resolution to supply, in some degree, the deficiency. I could not have been at that time above fourteen years of age." The literariness of Wordsworth's life, the first evidences, the resolve to become not just a poet, but a particular kind of poet—all of these seem evident early.

A lovely image of the swan seems to anticipate a similar, and even more striking, one at the beginning of Keats's "To Charles Cowden Clarke"—fresh, engaging, relatively untarnished by the repetitions of convention.[40] Again, he stresses in a Fenwick note how firsthand the experience, the sensation had been, "taken from the daily opportunities I had of observing their habits, not as confined to the gentleman's park, but in a state of nature." It is an image freshly realized, smacking of the kind that will quickly become a central feature of his poetry:

> 'Tis pleasant near the tranquil lake to stray
> Where, winding on along some secret bay,
> The swan uplifts his chest, and backward flings
> His neck, a varying arch, between his towering wings:
> The eye that marks the gliding creature sees
> How graceful, pride can be, and how majestic, ease [216–221].

---

[39] "And that walnut-tree / Was richly ting'd and a deep radiance lay / Full on the ancient ivy, which usurps / Those fronting elms, and now with blackest mass / Makes their dark branches gleam a lighter hue / Through the late twilight." *Coleridge's Poems and Prose*, selected by Kathleen Raine (London: Penguin, 1957), pp. 35–36.

[40] "Oft have you seen a swan superbly frowning, / And with proud breast his own white shadow crowning, / He slants his neck beneath the waters bright / So silently, it seems a beam of light / Gone from the Galaxy: anon he sports,— / With outspread wings the Naiad Zephyr courts, / Or ruffles all the surface of the lake." *The Poems of John Keats*, ed. Jack Stillinger (Cambridge, Mass.: Harvard University Press, 1978), p. 60.

The poem, still under the spell of the midnight mystery and melancholy of the Poetry of Sensibility, stakes out its own poetic claim as it rounds to a graceful close—sights and sounds giving way to the full grip of night. There are inklings of a peculiar Wordsworthian meditativeness, of awe in the presence of nature; and while it is hardly the sense of "something far more deeply interfused" of *Tintern Abbey*, there is clearly something more than the standard machinery of landscape poetry. "Now with religious awe" begins a line that reintroduces the subtle contention of light and darkness in the outer scene, "the farewell light / Blends with the solemn colouring of night" (286–287). The moon makes her way through the night sky "Gilding that cottage with her fondest ray." The human element appears as moonlight brings hope in the darkness, as a cottage looms large in his thoughts while he walks ("Sole bourn, sole wish, sole object of my way"). This is the place, he says to Dorothy, his listener throughout, "Where we, my Friend, to happy days shall rise, / Till our small share of hardly-paining sighs / (For sighs will ever trouble human breath) / Creep hushed into the tranquil breast of death" (347–354).

As the walk draws to its close, with the speaker beguiled by the "song of mountain-streams," *Tintern Abbey* again comes to mind. With the moon at zenith, its light catching "The deepest cleft the mountain's front displays," there comes a feeling of security to the speaker, a sense of home: "Time softly treads; throughout the landscape breathes / A peace enlivened, not disturbed, by wreaths / Of charcoal-smoke, that o'er the fallen wood, / Steal down the hill, and spread along the flood" (355–364). It is an evening walk, to be sure, a walk that revels in the idealized delights of the area around Esthwaite Water. Yet it is a walk not just of natural pleasure, but also of people, a walk that always anticipates the return home to his sister and to the companionship that wards off loneliness.

Wordsworth's second major poem in this episode of a literary life, *Descriptive Sketches Taken During a Pedestrian Tour Among the Alps*, composed in 1791–1792 after his experience in revolutionary France, still has the ring of a "literary" poem, with echoes from classical literature as well as from Milton, Pope, Gray, and others. Liu sees *Descriptive Sketches* beginning, like *An Evening Walk*, "by refusing to describe either Revolutionary France . . . or the Savoy." Such experience, he contends, is not yet describable in the picturesque form. "Before that agony can be told, description must know the politics of violence."[41] Yet if it is not to most readers a great poem, it seems in several ways an impressive advance after *An Evening Walk*. Wordsworth is still proceeding in a somewhat narrowly narrative manner, but the language and imagery are more concrete, more powerfully visual, and the couplets looser, more freely flowing. As he is to say of his later *Lyrical Ballads*, he has tried to look squarely at his subject. And, as in so many of those ballads, he continues to focus on things primitive, on rugged natural settings, on people who live apart from the corruptions of polite society.

The preface to the poem—a dedication to his good friend and Cambridge classmate Robert Jones—is instructive.[42] At first we may be puzzled at the motivation behind his words. He inscribes the volume to Jones because "I consult my heart," and then proceeds to compare a friendship or relationship between "two companions lolling in a post-chaise" and "two travellers plodding slowly along the road, side by side, each with his little knapsack of necessaries upon his shoulders. How much more of heart between the two latter!" Once again, there is the importance of another human being, someone who can contribute to the shaping of a heart, a way of feeling that goes beyond mere observation to include sympathy, a richer awareness of a link between mind and nature. One has the sense, in examining the comment to Jones that "whatever is feeble in my design, or spiritless in my colouring, will be amply supplied by your own memory," that there is more than a beginning of a theory of imagination, that he is inviting Jones, and by implication the reader, to fill in the gaps, to re-create from memory, to "perceive and half-create." Memory seems to take on more than a merely recollective power here; there is even a hint of Addison's secondary pleasure of imagination, of that energy of mind which brings a life and spirit to objective reality.

Once again, the young Wordsworth reveals a high degree of control in meeting the challenges of the landscape-walk poem, a control

---

[41] *Wordsworth: The Sense of History*, pp. 166–167.

[42] All references are to *Descriptive Sketches*, ed. Eric Birdsall (Ithaca, N.Y.: Cornell University Press, 1984).

that prevents the dangers of such a poem's becoming a mere pastiche of settings with no special connections and certainly with no underlying philosophical premise. The opening exemplifies the point quickly as the speaker compares the relative merits of solitude and travel. Yes, nature has a wealth of resources for the person seeking the calm of religious meditation, "a spot of holy ground / Where from distress a refuge might be found, / And solitude prepare the soul for heaven" (1–3). Sounding very Newtonian with a kind of Enlightenment image of God, he continues:

> Sure, nature's God that spot to man had given
> Where falls the purple morning far and wide
> In flakes of light upon the mountain-side;
> Where with loud voice the power of water shakes
> The leafy wood, or sleeps in quiet lakes [4–8].

Reenter the emerging image of skewed light, "flakes of light," to suggest the blend of brightness and darkness in nature as like the same blend in the lives of men and women. Enter another powerful and fertile image of water, now used in a fairly literal way, but already suggesting the richer possibilities of *The Prelude*. On the one hand, it is personified as having the power to shake the woods with its "loud voice" while, on the other, it "sleeps in quiet lakes" (7–8).

Yet the roamer who quits his home shall not be "unrecompensed." Nature is enlivened for this walker; its vitality is more forcefully evident than in the personifications of many eighteenth-century landscape poems: "sod-seats the cottage-door adorn; / And peeps the far-off spire, his evening bourn" (19–20). Dear to him are the "forest" and the "velvet green-sward." More introspective, more sensitive than, for example, the walker in Thomson's *The Seasons*, he beholds "a cloud o'er mid-day's flaming eye," and "Upward he looks—'and calls it luxury.' " The language is at times amateurishly pretty, yet the closing sentiment suggests a developing human–natural link: "Kind Nature's charities his steps attend; / In every babbling brook he finds a friend" (23–26).

Preliminaries completed, the speaker narrows and sharpens his focus as he retraces the steps of a summer journey to the Continent. Again, the genre is not a new one, but it is interesting to observe the new life Wordsworth brings to it, capturing the beauty of imposing natural settings, yet in language that is increasingly fresh and original and with a deepening awareness of the life of things, of animate forces that underlie the natural beauty of mountain, lake, sky. We are guided to France, encouraged by the prospect, "But lo! the Alps ascending white in air, / Toy with the sun and glitter from afar." We are lectured concerning the violence of the Revolution in a dazzling image, "The voice of blasphemy the fane alarms, / The cloister startles at the gleam of arms," that commemorates the Grande Chartreuse (50–60). At Lake Como we witness an evening scene as the traveler tracks "the yellow light from steep to steep, / As up the opposing hills with tortoise-foot they creep," and views in twilight how "half a village shines, in gold arrayed, / Bright as the moon; half hides itself in shade" (95–98). But France and Switzerland bring more than the beauties of nature. The human is again a Wordsworthian concern as the speaker recounts how "By silent cottage-doors, the peasant's home / Left vacant for the day, I loved to roam." And there is the cabin where an old man played the viol—"Stretched at his feet, with steadfast, upward eye / His children's children listened to the sound; / —A Hermit with his family around" (141–151).

On to the town of Locarno and the River Tusa, whose banks one must descend in crossing the Alps by the Simplon Pass. Rich light-dark imagery pervades an evening scene on the banks of the Tusa. Gleaming waters give way to "The dull-red steeps, and, darkening still, aspire / To where afar rich orange lustres glow / Round undistinguished clouds, and rocks, and snow." The chasms of Via Mala hold an awe-inspiring power to contain "The indignant waters of the infant Rhine," where one can "Hang o'er the abyss [whose] else impervious gloom / His burning eyes with fearful light illume" (157–163). Nevertheless, the humble, rustic emphasis makes its appearance as a "vagrant" woman with her child seeks cover from a storm, or a dark night closes her tired eyes. And in the descent from the valley of Urseren, there is the peasant near his cell praying "By many a votive death-cross," marking where others perished, his attention "Fixed on the anchor left by Him who saves / Alike in whelming snows, and roaring waves" (214–219). The evangelical gloom of Cowper's "The Castaway" and early signs of the Christian orthodoxy of the later Wordsworth are evident in this striking image of a point of stability and comfort in a setting of turbulence and terror.

The poem, marked by evidence of an emerging artist, is still imitative in many sections. Personification, stock diction, the conventions of Sensibility are apparent, yet most striking are those increasing moments when the young poet rejects imitation to offer a flashingly original picture of great sublimity. Morning on the heights of Underwalden, sights and sounds of remarkable vitality, seem to anticipate evening on Mount Snowdon.

> 'Tis morn: with gold the verdant mountain glows;
> More high, the snowy peaks with hues of rose.
> Far-stretched beneath the many-tinted hills,
> A mighty waste of mist the valley fills,
> A solemn sea! whose billows wide around
> Stand motionless, to awful silence bound:
> Pines on the coast, through mist their tops uprear,
> That like to leaning masts of stranded ships appear.
> A single chasm, a gulf of gloomy blue,
> Gapes in the centre of the sea—and through
> That dark mysterious gulf ascending, sound
> Innumerable streams with roar profound [420–431].

Romantic primitivism is evident in the image of prelapsarian man—"entirely free, alone and wild," "Nature's child." Still "The traces of primeval Man appear." Memories of the brave Swiss overcoming their oppressors connect him with the past, with the dead (433–442). It is a special kind of knowledge he gropes to describe, in some ways an anticipation of the "shadowy recollections." Images of "other worlds" strike him:

> Awful the light, and holy is the air.
> Fitfully, and in flashes, through his soul,
> Like sun-lit tempests, troubled transports roll;
> His bosom heaves, his Spirit towers amain,
> Beyond the senses and their little reign [471–475].

Indeed it is not just supra-sensual knowledge, but something approaching the religious, for "when that dread vision hath past by, / He holds with God himself communion high" (476–477). Even the powerful sublime forces of oncoming winter cannot shake the man-peasant's calm spirit.

The poem moves toward a note of hope, indeed strong hope as

the speaker bids the gay lark "thy silent song resume!" the "eastern lights, once more the hills illume!" and, sounding like Herbert or Hopkins, "lost fragrance of the heart, return!" Continuing his use of the image of half-light, he observes how human joy fades like the brightness of a cloud in evening. His answer, not Utopian, but clearly anticipating lines in *The Prelude*, affirms: "We still confide in more than we can know; / Death would be else the favourite friend of woe" (543–554).

To the sublimity of the vale of Chamouny the poet turns at last. All seasons play their part in its continuing life as resounding images, cosmic in scope and power, close the section: "From age to age, throughout his lonely bounds / The crash of ruin fitfully resounds; / Appalling havoc! but serene his brow, / Where daylight lingers on perpetual snow; / Glitter the stars above, and all is black below" (594–598).

The poem's conclusion celebrates political and religious freedom—in his native Cumbria, in Scotland, in Italy, elsewhere. But France, as it will continue to be, is his special concern, a country where "Freedom spreads her power / Beyond the cottage-hearth, the cottage-door," where "All nature smiles, and owns beneath her eyes / Her fields peculiar, and peculiar skies" (637–640). Reactionary foes loom large, but the quest for liberty cannot cease. Invoking God's aid for the just cause, the poet gracefully returns to Jones, his companion, and seeks for both the blessings of rest after their reflective journeying. And as night gives way to day and the journey continues, "On the tall peaks the glistening sunbeams play, / With a light heart our course we may renew, / The first whose footsteps print the morning dew" (685–687).

With the publication of the *Descriptive Sketches* in 1793, an episode in Wordsworth's literary life closes. It is an episode of youthful development, of the young man now only in his early twenties, and especially of the young poet. It is a period of education, of early poetic probes, and *An Evening Walk* and *Descriptive Sketches*, along with the evolving *Salisbury Plain/Guilt and Sorrow*" materials, point to the future with their motifs, themes, characters, techniques—the deep concern with nature as a phenomenon of great beauty and as evidence of spiritual presences; with those men and women whose lives are rooted in the earth; with the poor, the oppressed, the victims of war and social injustice; with the corruption of institutions and the hope for the kind of political change evidenced in France; with the need for a new poetic voice. Wordsworth, albeit very young, is, more and more, finding in himself signs of that poetic voice. It is still unsure of exactly how to speak, of exactly what it will speak about. But the sense of vocation is developing, and in the pages ahead we will observe the challenges to and opportunities for that vocation.

2

The Deepening of a Poetic Vocation: Revolution and Response

"I disapprove of monarchical and aristocratical governments, however modified. Hereditary distinctions and privileged orders of every species I think must necessarily counteract the progress of human improvement: hence it follows that I am not amongst the admirers of the British constitution. . . . I recoil from the bare idea of a revolution; yet, if our conduct with reference both to foreign and domestic policy continues such as it has been for the last two years how is that dreadful event to be averted? Aware of the difficulty of this it seems to me that a writer who has the welfare of mankind at heart should call forth his best exertions to convince the people that they can only be preserved from a convulsion by oeconomy in the administration of the public purse and a gradual and constant reform of those abuses which, if left to themselves, may grow to such a height as to render, even a revolution desirable."

W. W. to William Mathews
June 8, 1794

"You have felt that the most sacred of all property is the property of the Poor. The two poems which I have mentioned ["The Brothers" and "Michael"] were written with a view to shew that men who do not wear fine cloaths can feel deeply."

W. W. to Charles James Fox
January 14, 1801

DESPITE THE STRONGEST URGINGS of his protective uncle William, Wordsworth returned to France on November 17, 1791. Indeed, he was skillful in inventing a number of reasons why such a trip would be advantageous—his need to learn French better than he had demonstrated on the earlier trip with Jones or perhaps the opportunity to tutor some wealthy young Englishman interested in traveling and studying abroad. What seems like the strongest explanation is that Wordsworth was twenty-three, a recent and disillusioned graduate of the university, a lover of the world of natural beauty rather than of books, a young man alone and in search of some concrete embodiment of his idealism, some point of value in a *status quo* he found increasingly repulsive. He later recalls for his nephew Christopher, "In the autumn of 1791 I went to Paris, where I stayed some little time, and then went to Orleans, with a view of being out of the way of my countrymen, that I might learn to speak the language fluently. At Orleans, and Blois, and Paris, on my return, I passed fifteen or sixteen months. It was a stirring time. The king was dethroned when I was at Blois, and the massacres of September took place when I was at Orleans."[1] Wordsworth's account is fine as far as it goes. He was, to be sure, back in France in late 1791, in Dieppe, then in Paris, then in Orleans. Paris was alive with revolutionary excitement; the Bastille, although its occupants were few, was nevertheless stormed, and the *ancien regime* was toppled. The Friends of the Revolution—the Girondins—dominated a city where aristocracy and privilege had virtually disappeared, and Wordsworth ultimately became associated with them.

John Goldworth Alger in his study of Paris between 1789 and 1794 says that "Of the enthusiasts drawn from all parts of the world to Paris by the Revolution, the British visitors, as far as I can judge, exceeded those of any other nationality." Alger describes a British dinner at White's Hotel or Hotel d'Angleterre "to celebrate the victories of French arms,"[2] a dinner, according to James Robertson MacGillivray, possibly attended by Wordsworth.[3] A new friend of

---

[1] *Memoirs of William Wordsworth*, 1:5.

[2] *Paris in 1789–1794: Farewell Letters of Victims of the Guillotine* (New York: AMS Press, 1970), p. 325.

[3] "Wordsworth and His Revolutionary Acquaintances, 1791–1797," Ph.D. diss., Harvard University, 1930, p. 98.

Wordsworth's, the poet Charlotte Smith, had given him several letters of introduction, and he used one of them to meet the extraordinary English Jacobin Helen Maria Williams. Williams, according to
MacGillivray, "poetess, novelist, journalist, pamphleteer, was a blue-
stocking of the deepest dye, who, with the possible exception of her
friend Mary Wollstonecraft, was the most famous or notorious of the
English women who acclaimed the French Revolution."[4] "In no political group," says Mary Moorman, "was the heady influence of
Rousseau so clearly traceable."[5]

Richard Holmes, the impressive biographer of Shelley and, more
recently, of Coleridge, and a theorist who emphasizes the importance of the sense of place, of the biographer's getting close to the
scenes and settings of this story, has imagined himself as Wordsworth in France in 1791. While some might complain about his at
times highly subjective approach to the genre, there is certainly a
broad accuracy and intense excitement about his manner. Wordsworth, he imagines, "quartered the city from one end to the other
in a series of long hiking expeditions, as if he were still in his native
Cumberland." We see the poet going to the ruined Bastille, witnessing the guillotine set up in the Place de la Revolution, hearing about
Bastille keys carried through Europe and even finding their way to
the houses of the governor of Newfoundland and Thomas Jefferson
in Virginia. "Tourists and sympathizers like Wordsworth," he says,
"eagerly picked up pieces of stone from the prison rubble to be-
queath to their children. Wordsworth described emotionally how he
watched the west wind, the zephyr (later to be Shelley's 'destroyer
and preserver') whipping through the debris and 'sporting with the
dust of the ruins.' He sat in the open sun and pocketed a relic in the
guise of an enthusiast."

Holmes is undoubtedly right when he describes Wordsworth's
responses as "complicated." He was indeed looking for "something
I could not find"; he was "looking for a wave of revolutionary joy
which did not quite touch him."[6] He is interested in a more peaceful
kind of change, a revolution chiefly of the spirit, and what he sees

---

[4] Ibid., p. 23.

[5] *William Wordsworth: A Biography*, 1:172.

[6] *Footsteps: Adventures of a Romantic Biographer* (New York: Viking, 1985), pp.
80–81.

and hears, while exhilarating to a point, is not quite what he had in mind. A powerful force in his political development is Michael Beaupuy, a French military officer so committed to the ideals of the Revolution that he sold his aristocratic birthright for a role in what he considered to be the events that would shape a better world. Young, enthusiastic, a committed democrat, he was one of a number of officers of the Bassigny regiment living at a house in Blois and preparing for active duty. Long talks, not so much on political strategy as on the concrete situation of France at the time, kept them awake at the Blois patriotic club. The youthful idealist soon became the English Jacobin, persuaded by Beaupuy that the stirrings at the Bastille, the cries of "Liberty, Equality, Fraternity," were no mere ephemeral hemorrhages but, rather, the beginning of a new order where privilege, kingship, poverty, and oppression of the needy and marginalized would give way to a revolution not just French but much larger, one that would bring the light of freedom to a tyrannized world. The intensity of Wordsworth's enthusiasm and the depth of Beaupuy's influence can be seen in the poet's cameo of his friend in *The Prelude*:

> By birth he ranked
> With the most noble, but unto the poor
> Among mankind he was in service bound,
> As by some tie invisible, oaths professed
> To a religious order. Man he loved
> As man; and, to the mean and the obscure,
> And all the homely in their homely works,
> Transferred a courtesy which had no air
> Of condescension; but did rather seem
> A passion and a gallantry, like that
> Which he, a soldier, in his idler day
> Had paid to woman [9.302–313].

Long walks, dreams of the future often gave, as they do for young radicals in any age, to a single scene or episode, a "spot of time" for the poetic Wordsworth, a power that dramatizes a just and noble cause:

> And when we chanced
> One day to meet a hunger-bitten girl,
> Who crept along fittingly her languid gait

> Unto a heifer's motion, by a cord
> Tied to her arm, and picking thus from the lane
> Its sustenance, while the girl with pallid hands
> Was busy knitting in a heartless mood
> Of solitude, and at the sight my friend
> In agitation said, "'Tis against *that*
> That we are fighting,' I with him believed
> That a benignant spirit was abroad
> Which might not be withstood [9.509–520].

At a moment like this one he sees the possibility of a world without privilege, poverty, oppression, with "the people having a strong hand / In framing their own laws; whence better days / To all mankind" (9.530–532). Beaupuy, the devotee of freedom, left Blois for active service, and Wordsworth never saw him again. He became a general and was killed in the battle of the Elz in November 1796, fighting not his countrymen but the Austrians.

But revolutionary fervor was not the only passion felt on this trip to France. When Wordsworth first arrived in Orleans on December 5, 1791, he lived at the residence of M. Gellet-Duvivier, a staunch Royalist. We know that he had in his earliest years not been unaware of or uninterested in feminine beauty and charm, whether at the dances in his native land or in his ramblings with Jones when he describes the special beauty of Italian women. As Émile Legouis puts it, describing the young Englishman, free of university routine, on his own in a country that offered powerful images of the struggle for democracy: "there were in his disposition all the elements which make for a great passion."[7] Biographers, as we know, were slow to learn of the great passion. There is no mention of it in *The Prelude*, and Wordsworth's first biographer, his protective and defensive nephew, Christopher, managed to dispose of any written material relating to a romantic affair. Thanks to the discoveries of George Harper and to Legouis's persistence in following a recurring story among the reading public of "how William Wordsworth, while he lived in France in 1792, fell in love with a French lady called Annette Vallon and had by her a daughter, to whom he gave his name, though

---

[7] *Wordsworth and Annette Vallon*, p. 7.

he never would or could marry the mother,"[8] we have a good sense of the story not simply as a matter of literary gossip but as a strong shaping influence on his life and work.

The entire story need not be our chief concern here. We need to imagine the young, idealistic, and unemployed poet arriving in France with no object of affection. Living with Gellet-Duvivier, he took a special pleasure in visits made to the family of M. André Augustine Dufour, where he probably met one Marie Anne (Annette) Vallon, a young woman from Blois, four and a half years his senior, and the youngest of six children of Jean and Françoise Vallon, whose father had died and whose relationship with her mother was not at all close. There were problems, not unusual for young people in love at any time, but problems nevertheless. She was older; he was an English Protestant radical and she a French Roman Catholic Royalist. He had no job, little money, and still no positive sign of receiving his Lowther inheritance.

Psychologizing is easy, especially nowadays, but the temptation is strong. We have a young English radical, feisty in his opposition to established institutions, devoted to the beauties of nature, and feeling the first evidences of a poetic talent. He is caught up in the initial stages of a great revolution, yet alone, without parents, without the sister who had become so much a focal point in his life, without any desire to be the minister or lawyer his relatives wanted him to be. Such a man meets an older woman, described by Legouis as outgoing, generous, some of her letters revealing an "irrepressible, exuberant sensibility,"[9] a woman stronger in her devotion to the monarchy and its symbols than to things intellectual and artistic. And, given her relationship to her stepfather and estranged mother, she "was hardly less left to herself than William."[10] Psychologize or not, they fell in love not gradually but impetuously. Legouis's words may sound melodramatic today, but they are persuasive. Wordsworth and Annette "loved each other unreservedly from the time of their stay at Orleans." The poet's "love for her was an exalted, blinding

---

[8] *Wordsworth in a New Light*, pp. 5–6. See also Harper, *Wordsworth: His Life, Works, and Influence* and *Wordsworth's French Daughter* (Princeton, N.J.: Princeton University Press, 1921).

[9] *Wordsworth and Annette Vallon*, p. 7.

[10] Ibid., p. 9.

passion, in the presence of which all else vanished."[11] How often the
lines in the Vaudracour and Julia story in the 1805 *Prelude* seem to
capture a memory of the falling in love, the affair that followed, the
child that was born. The fact that the story was published separately
in 1820 and removed from *The Prelude* in 1832 lends even greater
credence to the autobiographical element: Young Vaudracour in a
"town of small repute in the heart of France" "vowed his love / To
Julia" and "he beheld / A vision, and he loved the thing he saw."[12]

No long courtship but an intense love affair from the beginning,
for when Annette left the town to return to Blois, she was already
pregnant, as Julia, "without the name of wife, / Carried about her for
a secret grief / The promise of a mother." The events that followed
have always been difficult to understand: the poet's secretive visits
to Blois to see Annette, their return to Orleans as the birth date
neared, the negative reactions of both families, Wordsworth's attempt to secure money from his uncle William. Then there is the
puzzling departure of Wordsworth from Orleans before the birth,
though he heard the news in Paris. And there is the record that on
December 15, 1792, in the Cathedral Church of Sainte Croix was
baptized "Anne Caroline Wordswodth [*sic*], daughter of William
Wordsworth, Anglois, and of Marie Annette Vallon." Paul Vallon was
godfather, Madame Augustin Dufour was godmother, and an absent
Wordsworth was legally represented by André Augustin Dufour.[13]

Why Wordsworth's seeming abandonment of mother and child?
Why his failure to return for a marriage he and Annette had dreamed
of in the midst of their affair? There are obvious reasons, of course,
but they have seldom been persuasive to romantic sensibilities.
France had declared war on England on February 1, 1793, and
Wordsworth, we are told, attempted to return to Blois several times,
but was warned of the dangers. Political and personal frustration
obviously tormented him. "He had indeed entered Paris," says
Moorman, "at perhaps the most critical of all the great moments of

---

[11] Ibid., p. 18. Stephen Gill, Wordworth's best biographer, offers in *Wordsworth: A Life* the salutary reminder about the actual evidence of the relationship, speaking of the tendency of so many "to slide from conjecture into statement of fact" (p. 58).

[12] 1805 *Prelude* 9.556–935.

[13] *Wordsworth and Annette Vallon*, p. 27.

the Revolution. Louvet's speech, accusing Robespierre of aiming at a dictatorship and of having instigated the September massacres, caused a momentary reaction against the Jacobins, even in the Paris sections; resolute political action on the part of the Girondins could have saved the situation." His uncles refused to sanction a longer stay in Paris, yet he returned to London with the hope of a return to France.[14]

Annette had remained in love with Wordsworth, expressing her desire for marriage although, as Legouis perceptively puts it, out of motherly love more than wifely passion. Meanwhile she remained actively engaged in the Royalist cause and a woman under surveillance by the new government—at the end of the Directory and into the first months of the Consulate—and noted on the police list as "Widow William at Blois; gives shelter to the Chouans."[15]

What seems clear is that passion faded as Wordsworth returned to London and Annette pursued her political activities. The love affair more and more seemed like a passionate episode in a young man's life that may have triggered guilt for a time, may even have figured the abandoned mothers and children of his poetry, but less and less occasioned thoughts of a marriage. The record reveals only increasing physical remoteness. Although Dorothy wrote, William did not. Dorothy and he visited Annette and Caroline for four weeks in August 1802, a pleasant visit, we gather, but one that offered further confirmation of affection but not love, of a recognition that their true kinship now lay in their deep hatred of Napoleon dramatized especially on August 15, 1802, the date of the tyrant's birth and the proclamation of his consulship for life. Wordsworth did not attend his daughter's wedding on February 28, 1816, to Jean-Baptiste Baudouin. They were to see each other only once more some eighteen years later and long after Wordsworth's love match and marriage to Mary Hutchinson. Wordsworth, along with his wife and sister, met Annette and Caroline in the Louvre on October 2, 1820, with respect, but with no great emotion, the poet presenting mother and daughter with an attractively bound two-volume 1815 edition of his poems. Annette died in Paris in 1841; Caroline, in 1862.

---

[14] *William Wordsworth: A Biography*, 1:203.
[15] *Wordsworth and Annette Vallon*, p. 54. See also Gill, *Wordsworth: A Life*, p. 340.

Back in London, shaken by the violent turn of the Revolution, at odds with himself after a love affair cooled, a child apart, his uncle still angry and unresponsive, even forbidding him to see his sister, he threw himself into the publication of *An Evening Walk* and *Descriptive Sketches*. The sense of poetic vocation grew as well as an awareness that successful publication might bring money and recognition from his uncles. The poems were published in 1793 in two small quarto volumes by Joseph Johnson of St. Paul's Churchyard. The very few reviews that followed were mostly negative, calling attention to weakness and artificiality of language. But some noted the poet's fine eye for natural detail and his new and vivid imagery.[16] Wordsworth might have been more encouraged had he been aware that Coleridge, then a Cambridge undergraduate unknown to him, had been greatly impressed by the poems. Of the *Descriptive Sketches*, Coleridge would comment, "seldom, if ever, was the emergence of an original poetic genius above the literary horizon more evidently announced."[17]

But Wordsworth was unaware of Coleridge's admiration for *Descriptive Sketches*. He was at this time at odds with the world around him and with himself, discouraged by relatives in any clerical ambitions he might have had, frowned on by his uncle in Norfolk. His correspondence with William Mathews at this time is especially pertinent as we study the quest for vocation. Writing to Mathews on May 23, 1794, he refers to *An Evening Walk* and *Descriptive Sketches* and to his more recent poem *Guilt and Sorrow, or, Incidents upon Salisbury Plain*. "But," he says, "as I had done nothing by which to distinguish myself at the university, I thought these little things might shew that I could do something. They have been treated with unmerited contempt by some of the periodical publications, and others have spoken in higher terms of them than they deserve. I have another poem written last summer ready for the press, though I certainly should not publish it unless I hoped to derive from it some pecuniary recompence."[18]

---

[16] N. S. Bauer, *William Wordsworth: A Reference Guide to British Criticism, 1793–1899* (Boston: G. K. Hall, 1978), pp. 1–2.

[17] Samuel Taylor Coleridge, *Biographia Literaria*, ed. James Engell and W. Jackson Bate, 2 vols. (Princeton, N.J.: Princeton University Press, 1983), 1:77.

[18] *EY* 1:120.

He had been unable to secure a traveling tutorship he had wanted in London. He was reading in all kinds of radical literature, from Godwin to Paine. The course of the Revolution in France cooled his revolutionary ardor, although that ardor found a fresh outlet in his support for some kind of English revolution and in a remarkable piece of political prose—not published at the time—directed against one Richard Watson, an absentee bishop of Llandaff, who, shortly after the execution of Louis XIV, preached a sermon entitled "The Wisdom and Goodness of God in Having Made Both Rich and Poor," deploring the events in France and singing a song of praise for all things in the English *status quo*.

Significant for Wordsworth at this time was a trip to the West of England, including a visit to Stonehenge, with his fellow-student at Hawkshead William Calvert, whose brother Raisley was to play a significant role in improving the poet's rather desperate financial situation. After a therapeutic month on the Isle of Wight, he walked to North Wales—a three-day journey during which he had hoped to visit Dorothy in Halifax—then on to Bristol and across the Severn River to the valley of the Wye River. It was here, a few miles above the magnificent ruin of Tintern Abbey, a setting to be movingly invoked five years later in the poem, that he found a time of physical, mental, and spiritual refreshment as he dreamed of fulfilling his political idealism and his hopes for a poetic career. Then northward again (he continued to be an astonishing walker) to the Clwyd Valley—where his old friend and earlier walking companion, Robert Jones, lived—arriving there in late 1793. It was, on the one hand, a journey of the body, but also, on the other, a journey of the creative spirit ever alert to sights and sounds. The little girl from Conway in "We Are Seven," the tinker Peter Bell, the ravaged souls of Salisbury Plain—these and so many others he had encountered on this poetic journey.

After exploring Wales, Wordsworth spent several weeks in Cumberland in the Lake District, visiting William and Raisley Calvert in Keswick, then another old friend, John Spedding, in Armathwaite, and then moving to the coastal port of Whitehaven for Christmas holidays with his uncle Richard. Wordsworth may have loved nature deeply, but he certainly valued the company of good friends.

Notable is a final reunion in February 1794, after many separations, of William and Dorothy at the home of the Rawsons—their cousin Elizabeth Threlkeld and her husband—where they stayed for six weeks. In April, in spite of the objections of grandparents, brother and sister went by coach to Kendal, then walked to Grasmere, on to Keswick, further west to Cockermouth (their childhood home now deserted and in disrepair), and to coastal Whitehaven, where their uncle Richard died in June 1794. It was a reunion significant for Wordsworth's literary life as Dorothy ministered to his every need—copying and editing poems, keeping house, and, perhaps most of all, bolstering his sagging spirits.

This may be a good occasion to at least introduce the matter of the Dorothy–William relationship, a topic we will have occasion to return to from time to time. And we will talk about it with no special psychological expertise and certainly with no taste for the gossipy or sensational, but, in keeping with the purpose of this study, to understand the relationship as it informs a literary life. Why introduce the topic which has attracted some readers from the beginning, but certainly since F. W. Bateson's *Wordsworth: A Reinterpretation*, with its strong suggestion of incest?[19] Probably because the escape of William and Dorothy at this time evoked the anger of relatives, especially uncle Christopher Crackanthorpe's wife. After expressing her puzzlement at her aunt's disapproval and dismissing the charge of financial extravagance, Dorothy comes to the heart of the matter: that, as she said, she is in "an exposed situation." In a letter of April 21, 1794, she writes, "I affirm that I consider the character and virtues of my brother as a sufficient protection." With great resolve she continues her unembarrassed *apologia*:

> I am now twenty two years of age and such have been the circumstances of my life that I may be said to have enjoyed his company only for a *very few* months. An opportunity now presents itself of obtaining this satisfaction, an opportunity which I could not see pass from me without unspeakable pain. Besides I not only derive much pleasure but much improvement from my brother's society.[20]

William and Dorothy were unquestionably, some might say excessively, close as brother and sister, but there is no existing

---

[19] (London: Longmans, 1954).
[20] D. W. to Mrs. Christopher Crackanthorpe, April 21, 1794. *EY* 1:117.

evidence of a sexual relationship. Contemporary feminist criticism—Susan Levin and Anne Mellor are notable—while arguing for the almost total domination of Dorothy by her brother, makes no such claim. Such criticism sees Dorothy as typical of neglected women writers, of women—Thea Tessman in Ibsen's *Hedda Gabler* comes to mind—who neglect their own natural gifts to support, edit, assist in any way the work of strong male forces. While urging greater attention to the quality and variety of Dorothy's writing, especially the journals and the poetry, Levin locates her squarely in a nineteenth-century women's tradition, working with an "awareness of the great Western myths of masculine power, of authority and fulfillment—helping, in fact, to create one such myth." "Her writing," continues Levin, "exists as a positive articulation of a negative situation. . . . She often appears as a negative cataloguer of irrelevant detail, a person strangely fixated on the world around her." Dorothy's is a writing of "refusal," especially of refusal "to make connections," "to engage the world in the usual manner."[21] Hers is Carol Gilligan's "different voice"[22] or Anne Mellor's "feminine" Romanticism. For Mellor "Masculine Romanticism," with *The Prelude* as her major example, "has traditionally been identified with the assertion of a self that is unified, unique, enduring, capable of initiating activity, and above all aware of itself as a self."[23] On the other hand, "Dorothy's sense of self is fluid, relational, exhibiting the permeable ego boundaries Chodorow attributed to the social construction of the feminine gender in those Western cultures in which females are assigned the role of primary infant caregiver, of mother." And "Dorothy's *Journals* linguistically represent a self that is not only relational, formed in connection with the needs, moods, and actions of other human beings, but also physically embodied."[24]

Dorothy's life from the beginning was male centered. An orphan with four brothers, she loved them all, but especially William. Catherine Macdonald Maclean early on, and more recently Robert Gittings and Jo Manton, have written tellingly of the relationship from

---

[21] *Dorothy Wordsworth and Romanticism*, pp. 3–4.

[22] *In a Different Voice: Psychological Theory and Women's Development* (Cambridge, Mass.: Harvard University Press, 1982).

[23] *Romanticism and Gender*, p. 145.

[24] Ibid., pp. 156–157.

its earliest days.[25] From the beginning Dorothy lacked a strong self-image. Gittings and Manton cite her celebrated letter to her dear Halifax friend Jane Pollard. "You expect to find me an *accomplished* woman and I have no one acquirement to boast. I am still as was your old friend Dolly Wordsworth. . . . I have nothing to recommend me to your regard but a warm honest and affectionate heart."[26]

After her father's death—she missed his funeral on a wintry day—she saw male guardians, Richard Wordsworth from her father's side and Christopher Cookson from her mother's. Never a writer by profession, she loved to read, had read *Clarissa* as a teenager, the *Odyssey*, Goldsmith, Milton, Shakespeare. As already suggested, living with the Cookson grandparents after the death of mother and father only intensified her loneliness; they were grumpy, unencouraging guardians. She was genuinely close to her brothers, but especially to William, and from the beginning, although not without creative talent herself, she seemed eager to serve him and to further his poetic vocation. We recall how she eagerly prepared his clothes as he readied himself for the trip to Cambridge to begin his studies. And there is the sense of isolation, so touchingly described by Gittings and Manton, when he leaves: "He left, the northern wind closed in, and she was alone."[27]

She was not an imposing figure, "active, impulsive, short and slight, only five feet high, the 'diminutive Dolly' as she called herself. She had a slight cast on one eye, which, however, did not spoil the sweetness of her countenance, and she radiated calm . . . a thoroughly normal woman."[28] She was fond of her grandparents' unmarried son, William Cookson, who tutored her with warmth and wisdom. At the end of the Cambridge long vacation of 1788, she and William walked with the Hutchinsons—Mary and William would later marry—to their favorite sites, Brougham Castle and the Penrith Beacon. She delighted in the marriage of her uncle Reverend William Cookson and Miss Dorothy Cowper, and lived with them at

---

[25] Catherine Macdonald Maclean, *Dorothy and William Wordsworth* (New York: Octagon Books, 1972); Robert Gittings and Jo Manton, *Dorothy Wordsworth* (Oxford: Clarendon, 1985).

[26] D. W. to Jane Pollard, July 10 and 12, 1793. *EY* 1:103.

[27] *Dorothy Wordsworth*, p. 15.

[28] Ibid., pp. 18–19.

Forncett St. Peter while her brother pursued his university studies. Living in the Forncett rectory, she took great delight in the activity of the place, the comings and goings of interesting people like William Wilberforce, who drew her to the excitement and fervor of working with the poor and with the whole anti-slavery movement.

Yet, as Gittings and Manton argue, she stops writing about love and lovers with the exception of her famous declaration, " 'it would be absurd at my age (30 years) to talk of marriage.' Beyond this there is nothing, in letters, journals, or poems."[29] "Dorothy," they contend, "knew her own nature. . . . Yet with all her lovable qualities, there is no sign that she ever aroused or expressed physical desire, nor that she felt this a loss. An admiring and perceptive man noticed the 'unsexual' character of her body, gait, and manner, while delighting in her friendship."[30]

It might be said that Dorothy lived a life of service, extending friendship to individuals, nurturing the children of both family and friends, encouraging and actively supporting the writing of her brother and others. At the same time—and Susan Levin and Anne Mellor, among others, have done much recently to call this matter to our attention—she was not without talent herself, as a poet of some note, as a charming, engaging, and informative letter writer, and, most important, as a remarkable journal keeper. One needs only to roam through her several journals to discern the sharp eye for detail whether in a description of a person, a scene, or a landscape; a deep love of human beings and of the natural settings in which they live; a sense of commitment to the good and happy life. While formal churchgoing was apparently not a matter of great concern to either Dorothy or William in their younger days, she never quite forgot the lessons of her aunt's religion, a kind of Congregationalism that broadened into Unitarianism and cut through dogma and elaborate ritual practice to the simple Christian injunction of loving God and neighbor.

The journals have, of course, brought her whatever artistic celebrity she has achieved, the first begun at Alfoxden in January 1798 and continued until the following May; the second written in Ham-

---

[29] Ibid., p. 27.
[30] Ibid., p. 28.

burg later in the same year; the remarkable Grasmere journal kept
from May 1800 to January 1803; a long journal of the trip she and
William took to Scotland in 1803; a journal of a tour to the Continent
in 1820 and a second journal of a tour in Scotland in 1822; and a final
journal of a tour to the Isle of Man in 1828. Catherine Maclean
observes, "All she describes seems to take on a life. This is partly
because she lives with the things she describes, so that they become
real to her, and she respects their life"; and, although Maclean
seems extreme in her judgment that Wordsworth "was faced with
the problem of downright plagiarism, or with the necessity of making
use of words less true," there is little question of Dorothy's impact
on some of the poems.[31] Perhaps Anne Mellor's distinction between
the male and female imagination is useful in dealing with this matter: "we might say that Wordsworth finally replaces (feminine) nature with the productions of the (masculine) imagination,"
substituting for his direct encounter with the physical world "a linguistically mediated memory of them, mediations which confine his
consciousness to a solipsistic subjectivity, one that is specifically
troped as male."[32]

It is often true, as Wordsworth says of Dorothy in "The Sparrow's
Nest," that "She gave me eyes, she gave me ears," but Wordsworth's
special gift of internalizing what she saw and heard, of translating
the interaction of the inner and outer life, of seeing into and beyond
the life of things, made his own experience or the reordering of experiences recorded by Dorothy a different kind of artistic endeavor.
Dorothy's journal looks toward the world around her. She can convey
in a simple, brisk, unpretentious manner the sights and sounds of a
day. Consider the 1802 Grasmere journal entry with its special picture of the poetic life:

> On Saturday, January 23rd, we left Eusemere at 10 o'clock in the
> morning, I behind Wm., Mr. Clarkson on his Galloway. The morning
> not very promising, the winter cold. The mountains large and dark,
> but only thinly streaked with snow; a strong wind. We dined in Gris-
> dale on ham, bread, and milk. We parted from Mr. C. at one
> o'clock—it rained all the way home. We struggled with the wind, and

---

[31] *Dorothy and William Wordsworth*, p. 27.
[32] *Romanticism and Gender*, p. 20.

often rested as we went along. . . . We were afraid of being bewildered in the mists, till the darkness should overtake us. We were long before we were on the right track, but thanks to William's skill we knew it long before we could see our way before us. There was no footmark upon the snow either of man or beast. We saw 4 sheep before we had left the snow region. The Vale of Grasmere, when the mists broke away, looked soft and grave, of a yellow hue. It was dark before we reached home. We were not very much tired. . . . We talked about the Lake of Como, read in the *Descriptive Sketches*, looked about us, and felt that we were happy. We indulged dear thoughts about home— poor Mary! we were sad to think of the contrast for her."[33]

Or there is the celebrated April 15, 1802 entry, so closely associated with the poet's "I wandered lonely as a Cloud":

It was a threatening, misty morning, but mild. We set out after dinner for Eusemere. . . . When we were in the woods beyond Gowbarrow Park we saw a few daffodils close to the water-side. We fancied that the lake had floated the seeds ashore, and that the little colony had sprung up. But as we went along there were more and yet more; and at last, under the boughs of the trees, we saw that there was a long belt of them along the shore, about the breadth of a country turnpike road. I never saw daffodils so beautiful. They grew among the mossy stones about and about them; some rested their heads upon those stones as a pillow for weariness; and the rest tossed and reeled and danced, and seemed as if they verily laughed with the wind, that blew upon them over the lake; they looked so gay, ever glancing, ever changing. The wind blew over the lake to them. There was here and there a little knot, and a few stragglers a few yards higher up; but they were so few as not to disturb the simplicity, unity, and life of that one busy highway.[34]

Keeping in mind Mellor's description of the male imagination and comparing in this case the closeness of the journal entry and the poem, one might conclude that Wordsworth was not only reminded of previous experiences by the sharpness of Dorothy's observation and the vividness of detail in her recording, but also imaginatively

---

[33] *Journals of Dorothy Wordsworth*, ed. Ernest De Selincourt, 2 vols. (Hamden, Conn.: Archon Books, 1970), 1:100–101. All references to the journals are to this edition.

[34] Ibid., 1:131–132.

prodded to organize, shape, and especially to re-create a moment of
transcendence, of internalizing the natural beauty of a scene in such
a way that the whole experience became a source of emotional
strength. She was an important part of a literary life.

The letters are, of course, invaluable in what they tell us not only
about Wordsworth the man and the poet, but also of the relationship
between brother and sister, always close, especially after they settled in Grasmere, always intense as they live, talk, and work together
in the most intimate settings. There is for many modern readers the
sense that the language of the letters is too intense, that Dorothy's
letters to her friends speak much too exuberantly about her devotion
to her brother; but, in fact, such language was not unusual for nineteenth-century correspondence of this kind.

On the one hand, Dorothy in her letters to her friend Jane Pollard can wax rhapsodical:

> You can have no Idea how much I wish to introduce him to you, I am
> sure you would be pleased with him, he is certainly very agreeable in
> his manners, and he is so amiable, so good, so fond of his Sister! Oh
> Jane the last time we were together he won my Affect[ion] to a De-
> gree which I cannot describe: his Attentions to me were su[ch] as the
> most insensible mortals must have been touched with, there was no
> pleasure that he would not have given up with joy for half an Hour's
> Conversation with me.

With a kind of awe she recalls that "I have paced that walk in the
garden which will always be dear to me from the Remembrance of
those long, long conversations I have had upon it supported by my
Brother's arm. Ah! Jane! I never thought of the cold when he was
with me." And in the very same letter, retreating from what in addition to sisterly love seems a bit of hero-worship of her brother, she
stands back with an elaborate and powerful distinction: "I am as
heretical as yourself in my opinions concerning Love and Friendship;
I am very sure that Love will never bind me closer to any human
Being than Friendship binds me to you my earliest female Friend,
and to William my earliest and my dearest Male Friend."[35]

This is not to deny the depth of Dorothy's devotion, or her deci-

---

[35] June 16, 1793. *EY* 1:95–96.

sion to make Wordsworth's literary life her own work of art, or the closeness of her own life with every dimension of her brother's even to the point of the macabre wedding day events that saw her taking to her bed with illness as Mary and William went off to be married and rushing to embrace William as he returns for the post-wedding celebration. Nor is it to be unaware of their association even after Wordsworth's obviously happy marriage to Mary Hutchinson in 1802. Dorothy clearly loved Mary as a sister, and that love was reciprocated as they lived in the same house, and as she and William continued local and more extended tours, often while Mary and the children remained at home.

Wordsworth, always the man–poet romantic in his imaginings but still in need of a certain stability, found in Dorothy that point of reference from his earliest days—a point perhaps as strong as his brother John whom he loved dearly, but, because of John's career as a mariner, saw less often—yet one that served, in the midst of his most exuberant poetic commitments, as his touch with a reality going back to childhood days in Cockermouth and happy vacations from Hawkshead and Cambridge. Dorothy was not just family, but also a soul mate, a literary companion. Yet the relatively recently discovered and published *The Love Letters of William and Mary Wordsworth* seems to offer the strongest evidence of the poet's strong and passionate feelings for his wife.

"O Mary," he writes in a Saturday, August 11 (1810) letter, "I love you with a passion which grows till I tremble to think of its strength." And, stressing the uniqueness of their relationship, he writes, "Every day every hour every moment makes me feel more deeply how blessed we are in each other, how purely how faithfully how ardently, and how tenderly we love each other." Stressing the word "love," he says that he is "persuaded that a deep affection is not uncommon in married life, yet I am confident that a lively, gushing, thought employing, spirit-stirring, passion of love, is very rare even among good people."[36]

Enough for the William–Dorothy subject for now. At the end of their Keswick interlude, William took Dorothy to visit her Barker cousins at the seaside town of Rampside in Barrow on the Furness

---

[36] Ed. Beth Darlington (Ithaca, N.Y.: Cornell University Press, 1981), p. 136.

coast, a visit and a location that will become crucial for one of Wordsworth's later poems, "Elegiac Stanzas." Returning to Keswick, now
twenty-four years old, he found himself alone and without money.
At Windy Brow he visits his friend William Calvert and finds his
younger brother, Raisley, gravely ill with consumption. Touched by
his desperate situation—Keats and his brother Tom come to
mind—he ministers to the young man until his death in Penrith in
January 1795. Providentially, young Raisley, touched by Wordsworth's concern and loving care, had willed him a handsome £900,
especially welcome because he was still without any of his father's
money from the Lowther–Lonsdale suit. Feeling reasonably comfortable financially, he headed for a fling in London. In London he
stayed with a kindred spirit, Basil Montagu, a law student at Lincoln's Inn who had lost his wife and was trying, in the midst of study,
sadness, and poverty, to raise a child called "Little Basil." They soon
became good friends, Wordsworth having offered him a loan of £300
from the Calvert legacy, and he and Dorothy often caring for little
Basil.

He soon found himself in that circle of radicals around William
Godwin, a political philosopher whose powerfully influential treatise
Political Justice, published in February 1793, advocated a kind of utopian rationalism that would ultimately generate bloodless revolution,
the breaking of all social and political barriers, and the emergence of
a society of perfect equality. As Ben Ross Schneider puts it, "Godwin's altruism was something entirely new and inspiring in the world
of Coleridge, Wordsworth, Montagu. It renewed their faith in the
goodness of mankind, and they gave up their old beliefs to become
his personal disciples."[37] Wordsworth, his own idealism shattered by
the violence and power politics that followed hard upon the hopeful
events of the early days of Revolution in France, became one of
those disciples. We get a sense of his thinking in a June 8, 1794 letter
to William Mathews. "I disapprove," he writes, "of monarchical and
aristocratical government, however modified. Hereditary distinctions and privileged orders of every species I think must necessarily
counteract the progress of human improvement; hence it follows
that I am not amongst the admirers of the British constitution."

---

[37] *Wordsworth's Cambridge Education*, p. 224.

Berating "the infatuation profligacy and extravagance of men in power, and secondly, the changes of opinion respecting matters of Government which within these few years have rapidly taken place in the minds of speculative men," he envisions "that a more excellent system of civil policy might be established amongst us."[38]

Wordsworth's friendship with Montagu brought the poet to the attention of one John Pinney, a student tutored by Montagu in the law, a person of some wealth who had come to admire the promise of Wordsworth's poetry. The Pinney family—the father was a successful Bristol sugar merchant with plantations in the West Indies—offered Wordsworth and Dorothy the use of their country house, Racedown Lodge in Dorset, still standing today, a secluded brick structure in the country, near Crewkerne. Here Dorothy, William, little Basil Montagu, and a natural daughter of their Myers cousins, found a pleasant setting, a home, and the promise of some income.

Wordsworth first met Coleridge in Bristol where Southey and he were preaching the utopian scheme of Pantisocracy. Coleridge had early on expressed an admiration for Wordsworth's poetry, and Wordsworth, at this point emotionally shaken on several counts, perhaps responded to his new acquaintance's reaction. Coleridge will make a more dramatic entrance into his life a bit later, but he is already a key figure in our drama as we see the first signs of one of the major literary relationships, one that triggers periods of great creativity in both figures. As Melvin Rader has written, "It was precisely at this most strategic of all times [after the 1795 crisis] that Coleridge extended aid. At the very period when Wordsworth was yearning for light, a friend appeared with a wealth of philosophical knowledge and an eager proselytizing spirit. During 1797–1798 the two poets were 'in as close intimacy as man could be with man.' "[39]

As Wordsworth attended Coleridge's lectures in Bristol, we can imagine him responding in somewhat the same way as Hazlitt did on hearing Coleridge preach for the first time—with a combination of awe and astonishment at the range of his knowledge and his capacity for profound thought. Coleridge had, of course, already written poetry of genuine distinction himself; indeed, he had already

---

[38] *EY* 1:123–124.

[39] *Presiding Ideas in Wordsworth's Poetry* (New York: Gordian Press, 1968), p. 2.

invented in "The Eolian Harp" and "Reflections on Having Left a Place of Retirement," the kind of conversation poem that M. H. Abrams has dubbed the "Greater Romantic Lyric" and that Wordsworth would soon find attractive for participating with Coleridge in a "lyrical dialogue."[40]

Life at Racedown had been a period of quiet after conflict for Wordsworth. In a setting of great peace he turned again to the writing of poetry, not the loco-descriptive work of a few years earlier, but harsher story-poems touched with deep feeling and set close to rugged natural settings—*The Ruined Cottage*, eventually to become part of *The Excursion*, and some of what were to be the *Lyrical Ballads*, poems of the marginalized, the abandoned, the suffering. The encouraging and supportive presence of Dorothy, their great devotion to the various pleasures of nature, reading in Plato and other idealistic philosophers he had not encountered at Cambridge, along with a growing disenchantment with the excesses of the empirical psychology of Locke and Hartley—these and other factors played a major role in the developing quiet. His stuffy melodrama *The Borderers* acted out his confusion and ultimate dissatisfaction with Godwinist rationalism.

In this closet drama, filled with echoes of Shakespearean tragedy, the hero, Marmaduke, gentle, peace-loving chief of a group of Borderers during the reign of Edward III, is seduced by the Iago-like villain, Oswald, into bringing about the death of the venerable Baron Herbert, whose daughter Idonea he loves. The year is 1265, the time of the Battle of Evesham. Oswald, "the reasoner," uses perversely Godwinian premisses to justify his wrath and desire for revenge. Avoid "the fools of feeling" of the world, he counsels, and he applauds the action of Marmaduke in throwing off "the tyranny of the world's masters, with the musty rules / By which they uphold their craft from age to age." Marmaduke, he advises, has followed "the only law," "the immediate law, / From the clear light of circumstances flashed / Upon an independent Intellect." Oswald is discov-

---

[40] "Structure and Style in the Greater Roman Lyric," in *The English Romantics: Major Poetry and Critical Theory*, ed. John L. Mahoney (Lexington, Mass.: D. C. Heath, 1978), pp. 655–659; Paul Magnuson, *Coleridge and Wordsworth: A Lyrical Dialogue* (Princeton, N.J.: Princeton University Press, 1988).

ered in the finale, and Marmaduke is condemned to be a wanderer.[41] Yet, as Schneider argues, two key premises of Wordsworth's nature poetry were very much a part of the rationalism with which he had become disillusioned: "that the will of God is more easily discoverable in Nature than in Revelation" and "that all men are equal—not just morally equal but psychologically equivalent. He always believed that any two individuals would react in the same way to the same stimulus. But for him the stimulus was Nature's 'voices,' not pleasure, pain, emulation, or benevolence as it would have been under the old dispensation."[42]

Dorothy and William were visited at Racedown by Mary Hutchinson, his childhood schoolmate, and by his friend Basil Montagu, whose son was living there. In a very real sense, his literary life resumes as he begins to write poems again, faithfully copied by Dorothy. But the great Racedown episode was the arrival of Coleridge on June 6, 1797, just after Mary had left to return home. And what an arrival it was, as the oft-cited lines of Wordsworth later recall: "We have both a distinct remembrance of his arrival—he did not keep to the high road, but leapt over a gate and bounded down the pathless field, by which he cut off an angle."[43] He stayed three weeks, then invited the Wordsworths to come to his cottage in Nather Stowey, still a peaceful, clean, and attractive village not far from Bristol, and Charles Lamb came along with them.

---

[41] Ed. Robert Osborn (Ithaca, N.Y.: Cornell University Press, 1982).

[42] *Wordsworth's Cambridge Education*, p. 236.

[43] M. W. and W. W. to Sarah Coleridge, November 7, 1845. *LY* 7.4:719.

3

Enter Coleridge: Poetic Plans and Counter-Plans

"Now for fourteen years of my Life, and those 14 the very Life of my Life—and thro' a strange variety of States, Situations and Circumstances—I am conscious myself of having felt the most consummate Friendship, in deed, word, and thought inviolate, for a man whose welfare never ceased to be far dearer to me than my own, and for whose fame I have been enthusiastically watchful, even at the price of alienating the affection of my Benefactors, and this during years, in which I stood single in my reverential admiration."

Coleridge, *Notebooks*, 1810

"One of the first things we heard from him was the death of one [Coleridge] who had been, he said, his friend for more than thirty years. He then continued to speak of him, called him the most *wonderful* man that he had ever known, wonderful for the originality of his mind & the power he possessed of throwing out in profusion grand central truths from which might be evolved the most comprehensive systems."

Robert Perceval Graves to Felicia Hemans
August 12, 1834

"In this idea originated the plan of the 'Lyrical Ballads'; in which it was agreed, that my endeavors should be directed to persons and characters supernatural, or at least romantic, yet so as to transfer from our inward nature a human interest and a semblance of truth sufficient to procure for these shadows of imagination that willing suspension of disbelief that constitutes poetic truth. Mr. Wordsworth, on the other hand, was to propose to himself as his object, to give the charm of novelty to things of everyday, and to excite a feeling analogous to the supernatural by awakening the mind's attention from the lethargy of custom, and directing it to the loveliness and the wonders of the world before us."

Coleridge, *Biographia Literaria*

IT WAS TRULY A MEETING of minds and spirits. The Wordsworths were enthusiastic about the company of Coleridge, and eventually met his wife, Sarah, and son, Hartley. They rented a large house a few miles away, Alfoxden (a hotel today), at the edge of the Quantock Hills, and they never returned to Racedown.

These were joyous days as the friendship and poetic plans of the great trio began to develop and to flourish. Coleridge's oft-quoted "We are three people, but only one soul"[1] captures nicely the spirit of the time. The bond between poet and sister needs no rehearsing, but the deepening friendship and mutual admiration of Wordsworth and Coleridge was a great boon in nourishing Wordsworth's creativity. Two contemporary critics of note have called attention to the power of interaction in shaping the work of both poets. Paul Magnuson, already mentioned, views the relationship as inspiring what he called a "lyrical dialogue" with poet responding to poet, poem to poem. His reading results in "a recognition that Coleridge's poetry was the prime influence on Wordsworth's from the first days of their association until the winter of 1799–1800, when Wordsworth began to describe himself as a self-generated poet."[2] And he has, he says, in studying the dialogue, followed the suggestion made to Cottle, with which Wordsworth perhaps agreed, that their poems may be read as "*one work* . . . as an Ode in one work."[3] William Heath, focusing on the period after the *Lyrical Ballads*, notes that "between March 19th [1802], when Coleridge arrived at Town End in Grasmere, and July 29th, when Wordsworth and his sister left Grasmere

---

[1] Moorman, *William Wordsworth: A Biography*, 1:343–344.
[2] *Coleridge and Wordsworth*, p. 10.
[3] Ibid., p. 16.

for Calais, Wordsworth had written at least twice as many poems as appeared in the whole *Lyrical Ballads* of 1798." And, as if to highlight his argument, he concludes rather dramatically that, if we include important work on *The Prelude* and *The Excursion* during the period, "the four-month effort was the last great period of concentrated and artistically successful composition in a career that was to continue for forty-eight years more."[4] The poetic life indeed!

Wordsworth, we know, was already taken by the power of Coleridge's mind and talk, and Coleridge, by Wordsworth's poetic promise. It is hard to forget the extraordinary tribute of Coleridge: "Wordsworth is a very great man—the only man to whom *at all times & in all modes of excellence,* I feel myself inferior."[5] And as for Wordsworth's many tributes to Coleridge, there are few more moving than the one recorded by the Reverend R. P. Graves on the occasion of the poet's communicating the news of Coleridge's death: "the most *wonderful* man that he had ever known."[6]

And yet, although they might be called soul brothers, they could not have been more unlike in appearance and temperament. Hazlitt recalls that they were both relatively tall men, but Wordsworth was thinner, more gaunt, with sharp, even penetrating, eyes, high forehead, long nose, calm and stately in bearing. Coleridge was plumper, "inclining to the corpulent," with a forehead "broad and high, light as if built of ivory, with large projecting eyebrows, and his eyes rolling beneath them like a sea with darkened lustre. . . . His mouth was gross, voluptuous, open, eloquent; his chin good-humored and round; but his nose, the rudder of the face, the index of the will, was small, feeble, nothing-like what he has done."[7]

The spring of 1797 was indeed a very productive one for both poets. Wordsworth reminisces with his biographer-nephew, Christopher:

---

[4] *Wordsworth and Coleridge: A Study of Their Literary Relations in 1801–1802* (Oxford: Oxford University Press, 1970), p. 5.

[5] S. T. C. to Robert Southey. See W. Jackson Bate, *Coleridge* (Cambridge, Mass. and London: Harvard University Press, 1987), p. 38.

[6] Quoted in Rader, *Presiding Ideas in Wordsworth's Poetry,* p. 1. See extract of a letter from Robert Percival Graves to a friend on the occasion of Coleridge's death, July 25, 1834, in Christopher Wordsworth, *Memoirs of William Wordsworth,* 2:291.

[7] See Hazlitt's descriptions in *The Complete Works of William Hazlitt,* ed. P. P. Howe, 21 vols. (London: J. W. Dent, 1930–1934), 17:109, 117–118.

This was a very pleasant and productive time of my life. Coleridge, my sister, and I set off on a tour to Linton, and other places in Devonshire; and in order to defray his part of the expense, Coleridge on the same afternoon commenced his poem on The Ancient Mariner; in which I was to have borne my part, and a few verses were written by me, and some assistance given in planning the poem; but our styles agreed so little, that I withdrew myself from the concern, and he finished it himself.[8]

The reminiscence is important in helping us to understand the creative burst of these months and the kind of poetry Wordsworth was to write. Overt political activity subsides; the break with Annette and Caroline now seems a firm reality. At the same time the company of Dorothy and Coleridge becomes a source of stability in his life. As they roamed one of their favorite terrains—one thinks of the landscape of the Quantock Hills and the seascape of the Bristol Channel—they talk of poetry, even plan Coleridge's *Rime of the Ancient Mariner*, although, as Wordsworth said, after having made suggestions and supplied some lines, he left the actual composition to Coleridge. John Jordan concludes that "Coleridge liked the idea of some joint publication," that "Wordsworth was simply dedicated to writing poetry," and that "the project that started from 'The Ancient Mariner' and became the *Lyrical Ballads* did not for a time have a predominant position in their fluctuating plans."[9]

Yet, more than anything else was the dream of a new kind of poem, a dream to be articulated more fully in what would become the "Preface" to the second edition of the *Lyrical Ballads*, the manifesto of both poets, although essentially the work of Wordsworth. It was to be a poetry free, natural, true to the people, language, and settings he knew best—children untouched by the corruption of the larger world; mendicants who draw their sustenance from the kindness of others and who in turn evoke that same kindness; rustics who, in the midst of poverty and suffering, seem almost like the children of the Beatitudes, blessed in spirit. It was, as Jordan puts it, "a much more sophisticated kind of description based on an almost

---

[8] *Memoirs of William Wordsworth*, 1:16.

[9] *Why the "Lyrical Ballads"? The Background, Writing, and Character of Wordsworth's 1798 "Lyrical Ballads"* (Berkeley: University of California Press, 1976), p. 20.

mystical awareness of an interaction in observation between the scene and the observer, so that the quality of the experience became the significant thing, and the feeling gave importance to the action."[10]

Wordsworth did not, of course, have to invent such characters *ab ovo*, did not have to indulge in some kind of Olympian romantic primitivism. From his earliest days he had known the wonders of sea, sky, mountains, and lakes, a world of nature relatively unspoiled. And while he was certainly not one of them as far as social class and association, he had seen every variety of man, woman, and child wherever he walked. Harold Bloom argues that the "poet of naturalism, separated by organic growth from his own past, looks around him and sees the moving emblems of a childlike consciousness in the mad, the outcast, and the dreadfully old."[11]

Wordsworth had known the impact of agrarian reform, of the dark side of industrial development, the enclosure of land and the closing out of farmers from their sources of livelihood. Kenneth Maclean

---

[10] Ibid., pp. 163–164.

[11] *The Visionary Company: A Reading of Romantic Poetry* (Ithaca, N.Y.: Cornell University Press, 1971), p. 182. See Hardwicke Drummond Rawnsley, *Reminiscences of Wordsworth Among the Peasantry of Westmoreland* (London: Dillon's, 1968). In his introduction, Geoffrey Tillotson compares the aloof later Wordsworth with the engaged younger poet. "Wordsworth," he writes, "had identified himself with Goody Blake as a human being complete. He tells us all the important things that a present-day social worker would have elicited by his questionaire" (p. 7)!

Rawnseley remembers "Rudsworth" as one who did not associate closely enough with humble, rustic folk to know their faults. And he recalls the remarks of a former woman-servant at Rydal Mount, later to become a lodging-house keeper in Grasmere. She remembers the poet "went bumming and booing about, and she, Miss Dorothy, kept close behind him, and she packed up the bits as let 'em fall, and tak 'em down, and put 'em on paper for him. And you ned', the good dame, 'be very well sure as how she didn't understand nor make sense out of 'em, and I doubt that he [Wordsworth] didn't kna much about them either himself, but, however, there's a gay lock o' fawk as wad, I dar say" (p. 12).

Still another "half-farmer, half hotel-keeper," recalls Rawnsley, saw Wordsworth "scores o' times. But he was a lonely man, fond o' goin' out wi' his family, and saying nowt nobbit a bit noan of 'em. . . . He never followed nowt nobbut a bit o' skating, happen . . . but his hobby, ye mun kna, was potry. It was a queer thing, but it was like eneuf cause him to be desolate; and I'se often thowt that his brain was that fu' of sic stuff, that he was forced to be always at it, whether or no, with or fair, mumbling to hissel' along t' roads." Yet, says Rawnsley, witnesses saw something special: " 'He was a man of a very practical eye, and seemed to see eveything,' was the feeling" (p. 32).

notes that by "the last decades of the eighteenth century English farming was the wonder of the world."[12] Yet, he says, the new phenomenon of the gentleman farmer, while it brought improvements, also brought the enclosures "which did so much to bring an end to rural living for that part of the population which probably derived most benefit from a life on the land—the yeomen, the small farmers, and the country laborers."[13] Maclean says that from 1700 to 1760, 270,845 acres, mostly arable, were enclosed by 152 Parliamentary enclosure acts. From 1761 to 1801, 2,428,721 acres were enclosed through 1,479 such acts, while from 1802 to 1804, 1,705 such acts enclosed 1,610,302 acres. "In 1801," he records, "a general enclosure bill, strongly supported by the new Board of Agriculture, was passed to facilitate and cheapen the entire procedure." The small farmer virtually disappeared, and large capitalistic farms became the order of the day.[14]

The dream of a new kind of poetry! The "Preface" to the second edition of the *Lyrical Ballads*, along with its subsequent additions and the supplementary essay of 1815, is in so many ways a remarkable document. It is remarkable not so much because it is revolutionary as because, both to satisfy his publisher and to enlighten his readers, Wordsworth is advancing a rationale for his experiment, discussing subjects, themes, characters, language that are part of the eighteenth-century poetic climate, and giving them a more coherent shape in a wide-ranging and spirited argument.[15]

There is, lest we forget, a quite classical/neoclassical dimension to the argument.[16] He has not abandoned (and here we use the Abrams categories) the mimetic in favor of the expressive. Indeed, if he is doing anything, he is trying to reconcile the two while advancing certain strong ideas about the living, organic qualities of nature, the importance of mind in shaping the materials of experience, the

---

[12] *Agrarian Reform: A Background for Wordsworth* (New Haven, Conn.: Yale University Press, 1950), p. 7.

[13] Ibid., p. 12.

[14] Ibid., p. 14.

[15] Don Bialostosky sees the "Preface" as a "constitution" for "literature," and speaks of Wordsworth's role in "founding the enterprise that constitutes us as students and teachers of literature" (*Wordsworth, Dialogics, and the Practice of Criticism*, p. xv).

[16] See Clancey, "Wordworth's Classical Undersong."

need for a freer, more direct, and natural expression. More fundamentally, he is advancing new ideas about artistic freedom, about
the vitality of the inner life, while exhibiting a subtle anxiety about
this new faith. It is an early manifestation of a tension almost always
present and never quite resolved in the poetry or the life, a tension
that enriches Wordsworth as man and poet.

On the one hand, Wordsworth sees these poems as having a
"worthy purpose" (1.98).[17] With Aristotle as precedent, he regards
poetry as "the most philosophic of all writing: it is so: its object is
truth, not individual and local, but general, and operative." Unlike
the biographer and the historian, the poet "writes under one restric-
tion only, namely, the necessity of giving immediate pleasure to a
human Being possessed of that information which may be expected
of him, not as a lawyer, a physician, a mariner, an astronomer, or a
natural philosopher, but as a Man" (1.139). He has been, he ex-
plains, more narrowly mimetic in a great many of his poems; his plan
of imitation is direct; he will, in effect, represent men in action, men
close to nature and hence more genuine in their emotions and forceful in their expression.[18]

Recognizing the importance of a poet-reader engagement rooted
in a supposition that the poet "will gratify certain known habits of
association," Wordsworth hopes that the "reader will not censure me
for attempting to state what I have proposed to perform." For he is
convinced that in these poems readers "will, no doubt, frequently
have to struggle with feelings of strangeness and awkwardness; they
will look round for poetry, and will be induced to inquire by what
species of courtesy these attempts can be permitted to assume that
title" (1.123). There is, of course, the qualification lest he be seen
as advancing a program for a poetry of naked realism, of journalistic
accuracy. He will "throw over" this rustic scenario "a certain colour-

---

[17] All quotations from Wordsworth's *Lyrical Ballads* are from *Lyrical Ballads and
Other Poems*, ed. James Butler and Karen Green (Ithaca, N.Y.: Cornell University
Press, 1992). Where the Cornell University Press edition of Wordsworth (general
editor Stephen Parrish) is not used in this study, I have used *Poetical Works*, ed.
Ernest De Selincourt and Helen Darbishire, 5 vols. (Oxford: Oxford University
Press, 1940–1949). See my earlier reference to the Norton edition of *The Prelude*
and later references to materials in the Wordsworth Library.

[18] See W. J. B. Owen, *Wordsworth as Critic* (Toronto: University of Toronto Press,
1980), pp. 1–30.

ing of imagination, whereby ordinary things should be presented to the mind in an unusual aspect" (1.123). Yet there seems a kind of uncertainty, a need to explain the experiment while ensuring that certain traditional notions of imitation, imagination, and emotion are not being overturned. Hence, certain of the ballads of humble and rustic life have a freshness of language and imagery, a cast of characters relatively free from the intimidations of polite society and ready to speak and act with a naturalness and spontaneity. Yet, at the same time, Wordsworth feels a need to anchor the movements of the inner life in the solid ground of the "real," to draw certain conclusions for the reader that ensure his desire to communicate a purpose even when that reader may find, perhaps then and even more so now, a quality of undecidability about situation and language. Jordan sees the event as less important than "the feeling observer, who—despite the 'I'—is not simply William Wordsworth, but rather observing humanity, 'the mind of Man.' " Empathy is the key.[19]

We need perhaps to linger here over several of the ballads of humble and rustic life to note this pronounced tension, this more complex agenda. We need to raise the kind of question that seems vital in a literary life: Do these poems behave as well as their author would have them in his statement of purpose? Wordsworth himself, in remarkably candid language, challenges his contemporary readers, and, by implication, the reader of today, that "in judging these Poems he would decide by his own feelings genuinely, and not by reflection upon what will probably be the judgment of others" (1.155), recognizing that "in order entirely to enjoy the Poetry which I am recommending, it would be necessary to give up much of what is ordinarily enjoyed" (1.157).

"Goody Blake and Harry Gill"—we are assured in the subtitle that it is a true story—at one level dramatizes the corruption of the wealthy and the unfortunate plight of the oppressed poor who perish despite their essential goodness. An ever-present and -guiding narrator paints the scene, introduces us to the characters, re-creates the tragedy by beginning at the end. There is a hurried tone to the sequence of questions that open the ballad. Harry Gill, the sinister capitalist cattle farmer, is elegantly appareled, bearing all the signs

---

[19] *Why the "Lyrical Ballads?"* pp. 5–6.

of his wealth. But something is immediately apparent to the narrator, indeed to anyone who views the man. "Oh! what's the matter? what's the matter? / What is't that ails young Harry Gill? / That evermore his teeth they chatter, / Chatter, chatter, chatter still" (1–4). Harry is obviously a neighborhood phenomenon, a walking emblem of greed. The omniscient narrator, having pulled us rather forcefully into his scenario, proceeds to paint the backdrop of humble and rustic life. Harry, a "lusty drover," "stout of limb," "cheeks . . . red as ruddy clover," "voice . . . like the voice of three" (17–21), was—the tense shifts abruptly to the past—the epitome of the wealthy landowner. Enter Goody Blake, a weaver, old, poor, shabbily clad, a woman who works day and night and yet cannot contend. Living alone, she is remote from the security of a village green: "On a hill's northern side she dwelt, / Where from sea-blasts the hawthorns lean, / And hoary dews are slow to melt" (30–32). Yet she is happy with survival, even takes pleasure in the warmth of summer. Even the coming of winter cold challenges her endurance, encourages her ingenuity, makes her fend for herself, finding a "lusty splinter" here, a "rotten bough" there, "Enough to warm her for three days" (51–55).

But when "the frost was past enduring" (57), this hardy woman can no longer use her wits, and must survive at any cost. It is at this point that high melodrama develops, the decision to gather her wood from Harry Gill's hedges. Gill had, of course, been on the lookout and, noting her activity, plots his response. Standing "behind a rick of barley" (73), Harry watched, heard a voice, stood ready. As the stricken woman gathers her wood, Harry "started forward with a shout, / And sprang upon poor Goody Blake" (87–88). The melodrama heightens as "fiercely by the arm he shook her, / And cried, 'I've caught you then at last!' " (92–93). The male capitalist prevails for the moment as Goody loses her bundle of wood. Yet creature of nature that she is, she appeals to its power as a source of revenge. In a scene of raw power we see "her wither'd hand uprearing"—she seems like a primitive savage—as "Harry held her by the arm." Her prayer—"God! who art never out of hearing, / O may he never more be warm!" (97–100). For a rare moment, melodrama gives way to tragedy. Harry hears the curse, and from that time forward, his fate is ghastly: "His face was gloom, his heart was sorrow" (107); "Yet still his jaws and teeth they clatter, / Like a loose casement in the wind, / And Harry's flesh it fell away" (115–117).

The narrator remains the reader's guide to the end, returning to echo his earlier pedestrian "His teeth they chatter, chatter still," and to add, in case it was not already apparent, the moral of the tale: "Now think, ye farmers all, I pray / Of Goody Blake and Harry Gill!" (126–128).

"Simon Lee" dramatizes the plight of an aging huntsman, again with a determined narrator who serves as our guide, philosopher, and, we hope, friend. Another subtitle provides assurance that we have a true story, not a fickle romance. Indeed, we are reassured that we are being provided "With an incident in which he [Simon] was concerned." We are introduced to Simon in his last stages, a man who served his master well, but who, outliving the master, is reduced to a bare subsistence. Another Wordsworthian "survivor"! He is no longer the huntsman of Ivor-Hall in Cardigan, Wales, the man who for twenty-five years was "A running huntsman merry," who joyfully sounded the horn. No man could match his "glee," and "he all the country could outrun." And now years later, "His cheek is like a cherry," and he still rejoices, "For when the chiming hounds are out, / He dearly loves their voices!" (14–47).

But time has taken its toll. Simon's strength is gone, his master, family, and friends dead, Hall of Ivor empty. Only he and his wife survive, but survive they do. Reality surrounds them; age has undermined romance. With the journalistic detail of a medical report, the narrator sketches Simon's appearance: "And he is lean and he is sick; / His little body's half awry, / His ancles they are swoln and thick; / His legs are thin and dry." His one prop is his aged wife, Ruth; his only shelter is a "moss-grown hut of clay" on a scrap of land enclosed from the heath when he had the strength. Together husband and wife can do little; their time is short. A Beckett-like figure, "the more he works, the more / Do his weak ancles swell" (33–59).

Enter the narrator with a vengeance, assuring the reader that he is aware of his patience and his need to know the upshot of his story. If the reader, he counsels, has "Such stores as silent thought can bring," there is a tale to be made from the further events he will recount, grim events indeed. Recalling a final encounter with Simon "doing all he could / About the root of an old tree, / A stump of rotten wood" and the futility of his effort, he "with a single blow" severs the "tangled root" (73–94). Simon, like the old Cumberland beggar of the *Lyrical Ballads,* has evoked the kindness and sympathy latent in a fellow human being. We are left with a final image, of a tearful but grateful Simon whose thanks outdoes any that the narrator has ever known. "Alas! the gratitude of men / Hath oftner left me mourning" (103–104).

"The Thorn" introduces us to another survivor, Martha Ray, interestingly the name of Wordsworth's friend Basil Montagu's mother. Geoffrey Hartman regards it as "Wordsworth's most experimental poem; the spot appears first as something in nature (stanzas 1–7) but then as something in the narrator: an idea that bodes forth its own dark symbols."[20] Wordsworth in various notes brings the air of realism to the fore again. The Isabella Fenwick note recalls the walk with Dorothy and Montagu and "my observing, on the ridge of Quantock Hill, on a stormy day, a thorn which I had often passed in calm and bright weather without noticing it." He had wondered about the scene at the time and about the possibility of making "this Thorn permanently an impressive object as the storm has made it to my eyes at this moment." His answer is to fictionalize within the framework of realism, to touch it with feeling. In the Advertisement of the *Lyrical Ballads* of 1798, Wordsworth tells us that he is not the speaker, that there is a "loquacious narrator," described at greater length in the "Preface" to the 1800 edition. Once more we sense a curious need to reassure readers, to guide their responses, to point out a moral. The poem, we hear, should have had an introduction, but he never found himself in a mood to write one well. Hence, he introduces a retired sea captain as speaker, a man living in a village or town where he was not a native. Credulous, talkative, idle, such men become superstitious. In a feat of psychologizing, Wordsworth sees such men as having "adhesive" minds but "a reasonable share of imagination, by which word I mean the faculty which produces impressive effects out of simple elements, but they are utterly destitute of fancy, the power by which pleasure and surprise are excited by sudden varieties of situation and accumulated imagery." Such

---

[20] *Wordsworth's Poetry,* p. 141.

men "cleave to the same ideas," and their conversation is swayed "by turns of expression, always different, yet not palpably different." The poem will move slowly, yet, through the meter, will appear to move swiftly. Language will convey passion to such readers as are unaccustomed to sympathize with men feeling in that manner or using such language. Nor should the reader dismiss the intensely felt repetition of certain phrases as mere tautology. "Poetry is passion: it is the history or science of feelings." The struggle to find a language adequate to strong feeling is powerful; hence, human beings cling to the same words to articulate their feelings. Then, sounding like a contemporary language theorist, he speaks of the beauties of the "highest kind of repetition and apparent tautology," the reason being "the interest which the mind attaches to words, not only as symbols of the passions, but as *things*, active and efficient, which are of themselves part of the passion."

How interesting to find a language stark enough, turbulent enough, to capture the tragedy of the story. There are moments of trust in the medium, in the power of word and image to dramatize, to enact, as he suggests, the very subject that holds his attention. There is the ring of the true story again, the incident reimagined and rendered poetically to give it vitality, larger meaning. No conventional description, however, but vivid nouns and adjectives, strong similes:

> There is a thorn; it looks so old,
> In truth, you'd find it hard to say,
> How it could ever have been young,
> It looks so old and grey [1–4].

Ironically, given the story to follow, the thorn is anthropomorphized—"Not higher than a two years' child / It stands erect this aged thorn." It is "a mass of knotted joints, / A wretched thing forlorn. / It stands erect, and like a stone / With lichens is it overgrown" (1–11). Yet all nature seems to conspire "To bury this poor thorn for ever" (22).

Still guided by our shipman-narrator, we are taken to a place where the thorn may be seen. Then "to the left, three yards beyond, / You see a little muddy pond"(28–29). Painstaking detail draws our attention to the central sight of the poem—indeed, we wonder why the poem is not differently titled—: "A beauteous heap, a hill of moss, / Just half a foot in height" (36–37). The narrator skillfully builds suspense as he describes the hill in great and vivid detail, again ironically postponing the shock to follow. The hill has "All lovely colours" (38). "Ah me!" he exclaims, "what lovely tints are there! / Of olive green and scarlet bright"; and then, almost teasingly, follows his description of the hill with the odd and strangely prophetic simile, "like an infant's grave in size / As like as like can be," only to put us off with "But never, never any where, / An infant's grave was half so fair" (45–55).

Now that the garrulous, not completely superstitious narrator has had his way with us, we are introduced to "A woman in a scarlet cloak" who sits by the moss, the pond, the thorn on the mountain, coming at all times of day and night to sit between hill and pond to moan " 'Oh misery! oh misery! / Oh woe is me! oh misery!' " (63–66). Still the narrator will not be completely straightforward in his storytelling. He cannot explain her sorrowful cry, but invites the reader, while Martha is in her hut, to move to the place, for "I never heard of such as dare / Approach the spot when she is there"(98–99).

Then follows Martha's story, or at least such details as the narrator can recount. Some twenty years ago she had been betrothed to one Stephen Hill, who on the day fixed for their wedding went to church with "another maid" (124). Distraught, with child, she retreated to the mountain for six months. The narrator and "Farmer Simpson" talked of the episode on a Christmas Eve, with Simpson speculating that the unborn child brought a calm to the troubled woman. No one knows, however, the outcome of the story—"if a child was born or no," "if 'twas born alive or dead." Some recall that she would climb the mountain, and sit by the thorn "in a scarlet cloak" (148–179). That much the mariner can verify, recalling in an eerie scene a stormy day when he climbed the height with his telescope and thought "I saw / A jutting crag." Then, in a scene of great visual power, he recalls, "off I ran, / Head-foremost, through the driving rain, / The shelter of the crag to gain" only to find, to his shock and horror, not a crag but "A woman seated on the ground" (181–198).

The rest is silence. The mariner offers no theory of his own; he is a creature of habit, of superstitious curiosity, recalling rumors that

Martha had hanged or drowned her baby and buried it beneath the now red-spotted hill of moss. He cannot believe the rumors in spite of calls for her punishment and attempts to prove a body lies beneath the hill of moss, attempts that are thwarted when "the beauteous hill of moss / Before their eyes began to stir; / And for full fifty years around, / The grass it shook upon the ground!" (236–239). The mariner ends with his one certainty, the moss-laden thorn and the memory that often "When all the stars shone clear and bright, / That I have heard her cry, / 'Oh misery! oh misery! / Oh woe is me! oh misery!' " (250–252).

Wordsworth's fascination with children and with the special kind of insight they possess—the unrefined knowledge, the sense of kinship and closeness to God, the lack of impatience with discontinuities—is another vital part of his concerns in the *Lyrical Ballads*. On the one hand, no poems have been more parodied; on the other, none seem more in keeping with his belief that such creatures represent a state of singular blessedness—close to nature, uncontaminated by the workings of sophisticated thinking, in tune with the presence of divine power in the world.

Try as one may, however, there is no avoiding in "We Are Seven" a strongly optimistic Wordsworth, with his conviction that besides a faith that looks through death, there is actually a time of life when death is not a reality but, rather, a new phase of life that, instead of separating, unifies more deeply. The cocksure narrator, believing firmly in the reality of death and its power to separate and to sever, is undermined in spite of himself as he recounts his meeting with the eight-year-old girl. Is he smug or self-critical, we wonder, as we try to establish the tone of the opening stanza. Simple, quick, feeling "its life in every limb" (3), what should she know of death? "Rustic" in manner, "wildly clad," eyes not just fair, but "very fair," she makes the narrator "glad" (9–12). We are almost persuaded of his unqualified admiration until a somewhat peevish, inquisitorial sequence begins. How many sisters and brothers? he questions. Seven, she quickly replies. And where do you all live? he continues. Well, two live in Conway (in Wales), and two have gone to sea. And two are dead, buried in the churchyard near the house where I live with my mother.

Immediately the puzzled narrator begins a mathematics prob-

lem: If two are dead, then it is clear that you are only five. But the
child is oblivious to the question or at least to the answer, replying
only, " 'Seven boys and girls are we; / Two of us in the church-yard
lie, / Beneath the church-yard tree' " (30–32). There is an immediacy, a simultaneity, a unity in her continuing use of the personal
pronoun "we," "us," to stress the relationship of the living and the
dead, of life and death. But the narrator persists in subtracting two
from seven, only to meet with a similar obliviousness to his attempts
to arrive at a logical conclusion. " 'Their graves are green, they may
be seen' " close to " 'my mother's door,' " and often " 'upon the
ground I sit— / I sit and sing to them' " (36–44).

At last—after three unsuccessful tries—the girl offers an intuitive, non–mathematical answer to the increasingly strident questioning: " 'O Master! we are seven' " (64). The answer, however,
only heightens the narrator's frustration and he repeats, " 'But they
are dead; those two are dead! / Their spirits are in heaven!' " (65–
66), realizing the impossibility of communication between a child
for whom all things are one and an adult who knows all too well the
sense of the many.

Childhood optimism, the sense of a radiant unity untarnished by
the things of the world, becomes an early and vital theme of the
Lyrical Ballads. In the Isabella Fenwick note to the poem, Wordsworth assures the reader of meeting the little girl near Goodrich
Castle in 1793. In the 1802 "Preface" he explicates the poem as
dramatizing "the perplexity and obscurity which in childhood at-
tends our notion of death, or rather our utter inability to admit that
notion," and in the Fenwick note to the *Immortality Ode*, he recalls,
"Nothing was more difficult for me in childhood than to admit the
notion of death as a state applicable to my own being." The seemingly silly squabble between adult and child is already a revelation
of the early and continuing tension in the poet between the hope
for a perpetual bliss and the incursions of a harsh reality.

"The Idiot Boy" is still another of the ballads dealing with children as God's chosen ones. The opening of the poem has a special
kind of narrative beauty which frames a potentially bathetic story.
Time, place, sounds, sights—all are caught crisply in the opening
stanza:

> 'Tis eight o'clock,—a clear March night,

> The moon is up—the sky is blue,
> The owlet in the moonlight air,
> He shouts from nobody knows where;
> He lengthens out his lonely shout,
> Halloo! halloo! a long halloo! [1–6].

An insistent narrator queries a mother about her decision to send her boy on a horseback journey, and little by little we learn of Johnny's mission. The boy's mother, Betty, cares for their gravely ill neighbor, Susan Gale. Her husband, a woodsman, is away from home for a week, and Johnny is chosen to summon a doctor from the town. An enchanted figure, he needs no "whip or wand, / For Johnny has his holly-bough, / And with a hurly-burly now / He shakes the green bough in his hand" (58–61). A child of nature, "full of glee" (92), "The owlets hoot, the owlets curr, / And Johnny's lips they burr, burr, burr, / And he goes beneath the moon" (114–116).

At home Betty and Susan wait for Johnny's return, but in vain. Fearing the worst, Betty sets out, is turned away by a grumbling doctor whom she questions, and then moves on, close to despair. Meanwhile, the narrator suggests possibilities for the reader to entertain as the suspense of his story builds. Perhaps Johnny is climbing cliffs to catch a star for home; perhaps he has turned himself around as he rides as a ghostly adventurer; perhaps he is hunting sheep; perhaps he is "with head and heels on fire, / And like the very soul of evil, / He's galloping away, away, / And so he'll gallop on for aye, / The bane of all that dread the devil" (343–346).

Their servant for fourteen years, the narrator pleads with the Muses that he may know the story; in a flash he sees the boy, like a figure in romance, feeding his horse and anticipating the arrival of his mother. Their reunion follows, and it is joyous in the extreme. Betty clings to her son, "And Johnny burrs and laughs aloud, / Whether in cunning or in joy / I cannot tell; but while he laughs, / Betty a drunken pleasure quaffs, / To hear again her idiot boy" (387–391). No recriminations, says Betty; her son has done his best. And Susan Gale, without a doctor's ministry, was healed and appears to the delight of all: "Oh me! it is a merry meeting / As ever was in Christendom" (440–441).

As they travel home, Betty would know of Johnny's adventures

in detail. Yet the boy's only answer, as the narrator assures us, is
" 'The cocks did crow to-whoo, to-whoo, / And the sun did shine so
cold' " (460–461). So enveloped in nature and moonlight and music
had he been that realities vanished, and he was one with a spirit he
felt within and saw without.

The child is again a central concern in "Anecdote for Fathers."
Here a father records an experience with a child even more frustrating, for the adult, than the girl of "We Are Seven." Here the child
should be even closer, more intimate, more ready to please; he is
Edward, son of the narrator, five years old, with "face . . . fair and
fresh to see," "limbs . . . cast in beauty's mould." Most important,
the father confides to the reader, "And dearly he loves me" (2–4).
It is a day of delight on "Kilve's delightful shore," of a pleasant
father-son walk, of a father's memories "of former pleasures" (8–9).
It is a day of lavish, almost extravagant delights, a time "With so
much happiness to spare, / I could not feel a pain" (15–16).

The drama thickens, however, as the adult mind finds former
pleasures of Kilve's shore and present delights of Liswyn farm almost
equally compelling. Almost on a whim, he asks his Edward which he
prefers. To his surprise, especially since he had done his own rather
full comparison, his son's response is spontaneous, seems almost ca-
pricious. In a "careless mood" he replies, " 'At Kilve I'd rather be /
Than here at Liswyn farm' " (35–36). But why, asks the father pee-
vishly, would you exchange " 'sweet Liswyn farm / For Kilve by the
green sea,' " " 'For, here are woods, and green-hills warm' " (40–43)?
Respectfully but firmly the boy remains silent as the father repeats
his "Why?" three times. Eager not to offend his parent, he looks up,
spies a bright, broad, and gilded weathervane, and finds a perfect if
not reasonable or convincing answer. The answer—in favor of
Kilve—is based not on a present delight but on an absence. " 'At Kilve
there was no weather-cock; / And that's the reason why' " (55–56).

If the boy's sudden and spontaneous reply is puzzling at one
level, so is the father's sudden resolution of his question, his problem. One highly subjective response triggers an equally subjective
resolution. Edward's father has learned not something as profound
as the reasons of the heart; he has learned, rather, of the unaware,
intuitive response of a child to the wonders of the world. He has
come to terms not so much with the limitations of adult reasoning

as with the unpredictable response of Edward, with answers based on little more than a *je ne sais quoi* operation of the mind at the expense of certain obvious realities of the world around him. And so his final wish to his "dearest, dearest boy," is that "my heart / For better lore would seldom yearn, / Could I but teach the hundredth part / Of what from thee I learn" (57–60).

Even though, thanks especially to Geoffrey Hartman, we associate the imagination–nature tension with the so-called greater poems of Wordsworth, there is operating in these humble, rustic ballads a fascination with these primitives—the little girl, the idiot boy, Simon Lee, Goody Blake, Martha Ray, and many others not considered in depth here—who at one and the same time are un-self-conscious exemplars of certain primal instincts, of the inner life operating within the constraints of polite society, of nature, and also teachers of the so-called children of light. As Hartman has put it, "One part of him said, leave nature and cleave to imagination. The other part, fearing that imagination could not be cleaved to, indeed that it would take him beyond human-heartedness even out of this world, answered, cleave to nature and leave vision and romance, those errors of the childhood of poetry."[21]

The old Cumberland beggar is viewed by a somewhat pensive, preachy narrator who has known him since youth, as more than a mere wandering beggar. He, in Bloom's terms, "moves on like a natural process," is "the irreducible natural man."[22] Sitting and eating his food in solitude, he evokes from passersby, not conscience-money, but a sharing deeply felt. The horseman "does not throw / With careless hand his alms upon the ground, / But stops, that he may safely lodge the coin / Within the old Man's hat" (26–29). The tollgate woman stops her work, "And lifts the latch for him that he may pass" (36). The post-boy, speeding behind the sauntering beggar, warns him of his approach, and, that failing, "Turns with less noisy wheels to the road-side, / And passes gently by, without a curse / Upon his lips, or anger at his heart" (41–43).

The poem turns preachy at this point, addressing "Statesmen!" and urging them to "deem not this man useless" (67). Yet what

---

[21] Ibid., p. xiv.
[22] *Visionary Company*, p. 178.

follows is an image of power and grace, one of the great images of the early poetry which sees in rustic figures not just primal instincts, not just good men and women, but also emblems of greater significance, creatures at one with "a spirit and pulse of good, / A life and soul to every mode of being / Inseparably link'd" (77–79). Such creatures humanize nature, nourish imagination, bring human beings out of selfish concerns into a deeper unity.

The earliest of the ballads, according to the Fenwick note, "Lines left upon a Seat in a Yew-tree which stands near the lake of Esthwaite, on a desolate part of the shore, yet commanding a beautiful prospect" seems, on the one hand, to capture Wordsworth's ideal of humble and rustic life, and, on the other, to be one of several different poems that move beyond what Coleridge regarded as the "not seldom matter-of-factness," the at times naked realism, the journalistic baldness, the syrupy sentimentalism. These poems are committed to the same ideals of directness of expression, the language of real men and women, and the closeness of the human and natural, yet the execution seems superior. Language is crisper, clearer; imagery fresher, less conventional. As if to throw the reader off the track—or even, as Michael Mason suggests, to parody—the opening lines evoke the *Siste viator* motif of the classical epitaph.[23] The language of the lines further participates in the ploy, offering in the remoteness of the place, "Far from all human dwelling," without "sparkling rivulet" or bee on "barren boughs," some of the tone and flavor of the diction he addresses in the "Preface." Even with the emerging in-feeling of a gentle wind stirring "the curling waves" and lulling "thy mind / By one soft impulse saved from vacancy," there remains the sense of mock imitation (1–7).

The poem then turns to realistic detail as the narrator speaks of knowing well the man who created the bower with its circling stones and "mossy sod" (9). A man of "No common soul" (13), he had turned from the world to find solace in nature and solitude. On this seat "he loved to sit" alone except for "a straggling sheep, / The stone-chat, or the glancing sand-piper" (22–24). Yet he would look beyond his initial meditation on the stark scene as "An emblem of his own unfruitful life" (29). And as he gazes beyond—the speaker

---

[23] *Lyrical Ballads* (London and New York: Longman, 1992), pp. 112–113.

invites the reader to share the gaze, "how lovely 'tis / Thou seest"—
the scene became "Far lovelier, and his heart could not sustain /
The beauty still more beauteous" (31–34). In imagining he enriches,
widens his pleasure, moves beyond himself.

In a wonderfully climactic scene, one that resonates as a kind of
adult version of the later "There was a Boy," Wordsworth sketches
the death of the hero. Thinking of "those beings, / to whose minds, /
Warm from the labours of benevolence, / The world, and man himself, appeared a scene of kindred loveliness," he "would sigh, / Inly
disturbed" at his own visionary isolation and self-absorption. Here
"He died,—this seat his only monument" (35–43).[24] And, with early
moralizing still very much in evidence, the poet issues a closing
warning to his traveler/listener/reader, one "whose heart the holy
forms / Of young imagination have kept pure" (44–45), a warning
that states more directly what is and will be a continuing Wordsworthian tension between the creations of the mind and the tug of
mortality. The man who sees only himself, who revels in the vagaries
of his own mind, who in his pride has "contempt / For any living
thing, hath faculties / Which he has never used; that thought with
him / Is in its infancy" (48–51). His eye is on himself, the least of
nature's works. Only that true knowledge that leads to love can bring
one to "revere himself / In lowliness of heart" (59–60).

Suggested here is a key problem associated with the *Lyrical Ballads* of 1798 and 1800—namely, the extent to which the poems are
faithful to the ideals set down in the "Preface" concerning people
who live close to the land, the language of real men as the proper
language of poetry. While we have seen these ideals carried out in
the poems we have been discussing, there are others in the *Lyrical
Ballads* that strike us by a certain widening of the range of subject
matter, with the lyric mode dominating the narrative, with a language still to some extent natural, even conversational, but richer,
crisper, more vivid, with an imagery rooted much less in convention
and much more in the phenomena of the natural world that sur-

---

[24] Stephen Parrish cites De Selincourt's interesting observation that the conclusion (final paragraph) develops "a distinctively Wordsworthian theme: 'revulsion
from the intellectual arrogance and self-sufficiency of Godwinism' (PW, I, 329)."
See *The Art of the Lyrical Ballads* (Cambridge, Mass.: Harvard University Press,
1973), p. 66.

rounded a poet immersed in the sights and sounds of the Lakes. Interestingly, the additions to the original Advertisement and "Preface" are helpful in understanding a somewhat different kind of poem that appears in the 1798 and especially the 1800 editions of the *Lyrical Ballads,* a poem that will, it seems, trigger a kind of crossroads situation as Wordsworth contemplates the direction of his work and the course of his career. On the one hand, he remains committed to the poetry of nature—of sea, lake, mountain, sky that surround and, indeed, envelop him; to the people and situations associated with these locales, especially the ordinary, the suffering, the young, the ignored; to a kind of expression that communicates directly and honestly. On the other hand, there is the continuing sense that poetry is the "spontaneous overflow of powerful feelings" (1.126), that the poet is "a man who, being possessed of more than usual organic sensibility, had also thought long and deeply" (1.127). There is also that vital modification, later in the "Preface," that poetry, far from glandular response, takes its origin from "emotion recollected in tranquillity" (1.149). And there is the description of the poet as "a man speaking to men: a man, it is true, endowed with more lively sensibility, more enthusiasm and tenderness, who has a greater knowledge of human nature, and a more comprehensive soul, than are supposed to be common among mankind." Such a poet is "a man pleased with his own passions and volitions . . . delighting to contemplate similar volitions and passions as manifested in the goings-on of the Universe, and habitually impelled to create them where he does not find them" (1.138). More self-conscious, more ready and able to find analogies, images of the inner life within and without, the poet is also a person of great sympathy, with the power to be, more than a mere recorder, an actual participant in what he describes. Mere description and imitation are mechanical; the true poet would "bring his feelings near to those of the persons whose feelings he describes, may, for short spaces of time, perhaps, [would] let himself slip into an entire delusion . . . modifying only the language which is thus suggested to him by a consideration that he describes for a particular purpose, that of giving pleasure" (1.138).

James Averill, in studying the Wordsworthian spectator in the narrative poems and the suffering to which he responds, sees connections with the manner of the eighteenth-century Poets of Sensibility as well as the work of Richardson, Steele, and Sterne. "By making himself the pathetic object," he says, "Wordsworth collapses the distance between the pitying observer and the suffering he contemplates. The source of emotion and the emotion itself are both located in the self." "Wordsworth," he continues, "finds in human suffering the 'freedom and power' which press the mind back upon itself. The pathetic, like the sublime, makes him aware of his own passions and volitions."[25] The poetic vocation and the poetic life!

"Lines Written in Early Spring," still one of the *Lyrical Ballads*, moves us toward a more lyrical, personal mode and voice. The episode recounted is a simple one; the manner of telling equally simple. As Wordsworth recalls some forty years later, it is rooted in a personal experience. The complexity of sweet-sadness is felt by a speaker in a lonely grove where "I heard a thousand blended notes" (1). He is not simply a detached observer here, but a participant caught up in an especially beautiful natural scene—a grove—and is pensive, perhaps in a maudlin way, as he juxtaposes Nature's linking her beauties to "The human soul that through me ran" to a reflection on "What man has made of man" (6–8). Yet the struggle of a solemn didactic voice with a personal, active, spontaneous voice is won ever so slightly by the latter. There is the obvious linking of speaker and nature; more notably there is the fellow-feeling as the periwinkle wreaths spread throughout the tufts of primrose, the faith "that every flower / Enjoys the air it breathes" (11–12). Similarly, while the speaker cannot "measure" their thoughts as "The birds around me hopped and play'd," "the least motion which they made, / It seem'd a thrill of pleasure" (13–16). Yet hesitancy follows—the familiar Wordsworthian struggle—"if" followed by "if." If this belief is "of my creed the plan," if it is "Nature's holy plan," then, playing on the earlier refrain, "Have I not reason to lament / What man has made of man?" (21–24).

"A Whirl-Blast From Behind the Hill" is a poem alive in every sense—fresh language, quick iambic rhythms, startlingly original conception. Suddenly, as the speaker sits in an "undergrove / Of tallest hollies, tall and green" (5–6), a natural setting becomes a

---

[25] *Wordsworth and the Poetry of Human Suffering* (Ithaca, N.Y.: Cornell University Press, 1980), pp. 30–54.

magical place as "A whirl-blast" "Rush'd o'er the wood with startling sound" (1–2). A calm follows, hailstones fall, and the bower, ordinarily a place of quiet, rings with the skipping and hopping of withered leaves. With a certain anticipation of "I wandered lonely," the fairy scenario unfolds, a scene of pure magic:

> There's not a breeze—no breath of air—
> Yet here, and there, and every where
> Along the floor, beneath the shade
> By those embowering hollies made,
> The leaves in myriads dance and spring,
> As if with pipes and music rare
> Some Robin Good-fellow were there,
> And all those leaves, that jump and spring,
> Were each a joyous, living thing [15–23].

One senses here, even as visual and aural elements seem to predominate, not just a spot of space but a spot of time—no breeze, no air, simply sounds of nature, the kind of intuitive moment increasingly central to Wordsworth's developing poetry. Geoffrey Hartman has made reference to images of place, of deep bowers of rich silence as early as the *Lyrical Ballads*, indeed, as early as *An Evening Walk* and *Descriptive Sketches*. "He is," says Hartman of Wordsworth, "somehow more vulnerable to apocalyptic starts and self-recognition."[26] In both *Evening Walk* and *Descriptive Sketches*, the poet–walker "seeks the 'hiding places' of power," says Hartman. But while in *An Evening Walk* "it is the natural lapse of time that reveals them,"[27] in *Descriptive Sketches* "the poet records a defeat of eye which eventually leads him through nature beyond it," the transcendent "still mainly visual."[28] Indeed, the latter poem "prefigures Wordsworth's inner preparedness for a break with nature; his imagination is increasingly forced back on itself, and beginning to recognize its autonomy or supernatural vigor."[29]

The lines "To My Sister" represent still further the widening of Wordsworth's devotion to nature, the eschewing of the narrow real-

---

[26] *Wordsworth's Poetry*, pp. 100–101.
[27] Ibid., p. 103.
[28] Ibid., pp. 110–111.
[29] Ibid., p. 116,

ism, the prosaic detail, the excessive moralizing of many of its companion pieces. It is another example of one side of the tug-of-war involving the claims of the self and those of the larger world of people and things beyond the self. The dialogue form still seems somewhat contrived, mechanical as brother invites sister to share the joys of "the first mild day of March" (1), as vivid description gives way a little too facilely to sentimental moralizing. Yet there are clear evidences of the strongly emotional poet encountering nature, of a poetic language escaping the bounds of convention on the one hand and of journalistic detail on the other. The ballad quatrain, at times breaking out of the dangers of a singsong rhythm, dominates.

What is notable is not just the setting, but also the speaker's vivid realization of setting. There is, of course, the startlingly simple opening: "It is the first mild day of March / Each minute sweeter than before." The music of nature, direct and unadorned, is the first sound heard: "The red-breast sings from the tall larch / That stands beside our door" (1–4). But the pleasure is again not merely visual or aural. There is a clear sense of an animate nature feeling and being felt. "There is a blessing in the air," but not simply the verbal blessing of religion. It is, rather, one "Which seems a sense of joy to yield / To the bare trees, and mountains bare, / And grass in the green field" (5–8). It is a blessing that comes from the interaction of the individual with a spirit of nature and its many manifestations, a one life of living things.

The poem, albeit a dialogue, fails to maintain the quality of such lines, too often falling into a preachy sentimental primitivism. Your work is done, says the narrator, Edward, to his sister, "Come forth and feel the sun." Put on your rural clothes; bring no books, "for this one day / We'll give to idleness" (12–16). Yet there is a return to the emerging theme of nature as process. In a somewhat rhapsodical outburst, there is the image of this day representing a new beginning. Love is "now a universal birth," not simply an individual passion, but one that moves "From heart to heart" and then "From earth to man, from man to earth." "It is," says Edward, "the hour of feeling" (21–24). And then toward the close of the ballad, in lines somewhat anticipatory of *Tintern Abbey*, Edward offers his sister a cue and a hope for the future. "Tuned to love," their souls shaped "from the blessed power that rolls / About, below, above," they will this

one day give to the stillness during which the spirit is ready for
intimations of something transcendent (31–35).

Perhaps two of the most quoted of the ballads carry us forward
in the tradition we have been examining. Both allow Wordsworth to
indulge himself in the dialogue-ballad. "Expostulation and Reply"
introduces us to two characters: Wordsworth, who is clearly the "William" figure, and William Hazlitt, generally thought to be the "Matthew." Matthew, the child of reason, of books, of what Keats was to
call "consecutive reasoning," encounters a blissfully passive William
enjoying nature and natural living as he sits in solitude on an "old
grey stone" (1), the primal scholar's desk, by Esthwaite Lake. Life
"was sweet, I knew not why" (14) for William, and, without rancor,
he unfolds for a rather critical Matthew the reasons for his seeming
inactivity. His mood, he says, is one not of idleness but of "wise
passiveness" (24), a state more intuitive than rational, more spontaneous than self-conscious. The eye must see; the ear must hear; the
body must feel. William is persuaded "that there are powers / Which
of themselves our minds impress," that, echoing the Bible on the
lilies of the field, come without our seeking (21–22).

William turns the tables in the companion piece. In a charmingly
mocking way, he apes Matthew's earlier approach. Get rid of your
books; clear your mind; pay attention to the lovely beauties of nature; learn the richest wisdom. While the ballad refrain is unfortunately obtrusive, there are nicely realized images of the beauties
experienced by William. Again, language and imagery seem to be in
tune with the ideals of the "Preface"—the language of real men,
without "gaudy and inane phraseology," free from the confinements
of conventional poetic diction. The poetry of life! Wordsworth is
clearly a good observer:

> The sun, above the mountain's head,
> A freshening lustre mellow
> Through all the long green fields has spread,
> His first sweet evening yellow [4–7].

The linnet's song is sweeter and wiser than that of any book, "And
hark! how blithe the throstle sings! / And he is no mean preacher"
(13–14).

Three interesting and crucial stanzas follow, vital for their expression not only of the man-nature link, but also of the peculiar character of the linking process. Nature's wealth is ready "Our minds and hearts to bless." Hers is a "Spontaneous wisdom breathed by health, / Truth breathed by chearfulness" (18–20). Then there is the oft-cited quatrain underlining, with a kind of enlightened anti-intellectualism, the special character of nature's education:

> One impulse from a vernal wood
> May teach you more of man;
> Of moral evil and of good,
> Than all the sages can [21–24].

It is an education of the heart—immediate, uninterrupted by the processes of logic, penetrating to ultimate meaning. The penultimate quatrain comes close to capturing a major tenet of Wordsworthian faith at this time:

> Sweet is the lore which nature brings;
> Our meddling intellect
> Mishapes the beauteous forms of things;
> —We murder to dissect [25–28].

The wise counselor, having answered the rational, industrious Matthew, again mimics the imperative quality of his early expostulation, here urging "a heart / That watches and receives" (31–32), inner calm, faith in the power of observation to receive Nature's gifts. Geoffrey Hartman advances interesting comments on the two poems. "For those who followed Wordsworth," he argues, "this was religion in a new dress, the dress of feeling. Religion was once more opened to all, as in the primitive Christianity of St. Paul." Wordsworth, he continues, "does not deny the supernatural but says nature is already so much. Why multiply entities, or suppose special intervention, when nature is supernatural in its powers to renovate man?"[30]

So much, for the time being, for the Wordsworth-Coleridge dream of a new kind of poetry, of a new kind of poet. It is important to keep in mind that idealism was not the only motivating factor for Wordsworth's involvement in the publication of the *Lyrical Ballads* of 1798. Always preoccupied with financial matters, and eager to

---

[30] Ibid., pp. 153–154.

accompany Coleridge on a trip to Germany, he and Coleridge (who had received a handsome £1500 annuity from Tom and Josiah Wedgewood) negotiated with Joseph Cottle for publication of eighteen poems, fourteen by Wordsworth and four by Coleridge. With the Alfoxden lease not renewed because of the suspicions of neighbors, they were ready to depart in the spring of 1798. But the passion for foreign travel needed one final satisfaction, a sentimental return to the valleys and hills of Wales that had offered such consolation on his first return to England after his traumatic days in France. On July 10, 1798, he and Dorothy crossed the Severn River and began a three-day walk up the River Wye Valley as far as Goodrich Castle and then back again. One can imagine, from his prenote, an exuberant young man returning to a favorite spot in nature as a source of consolation but also of inspiration for the days ahead. Even lovers of the poem are inclined to forget that the poem which has come to be called *Tintern Abbey* is hardly about that ruin at all. The lines were composed "a few miles above Tintern Abbey, on revisiting the banks of the Wye during a tour, July 13, 1798," and they are set down at the climax of what was apparently a trip of great joy. "No poem of mine," he writes categorically in the Fenwick note, "was composed under circumstances more pleasant for me to remember than this." Its composition, very much in the manner described by his Lake District neighbors and by his sister and other friends, took place not as he sat at a desk with quill in hand but, rather, as he walked back to the ferry and then back to Bristol. It was spoken aloud: "Not a line of it was altered, and not any part of it written down till I reached Bristol." It was probably the last poem of the 1798 collection and, for the literary life of Wordsworth, the crucial poem of his so-called early work.

And what a remarkably different poem it is, so much so that we wonder why, apart from expediency, it was included in the collection. It is not a ballad, not a narrative, not a celebration of childhood. It is not written in octosyllabics, in singsong rhythms. Coleridge would call it a conversation poem; M. H. Abrams, a Greater Romantic lyric; Robert Langbaum a poem of experience.[31] Its form is blank verse, free flowing, conversational; its rhythms are unpredictable like

---

[31] See chap. 2, note 29.

the rhythms of the human heart in conversation with itself or with a silent listener; its language, while in keeping with the Wordsworthian ideal of the language of real men, nevertheless has a more formal and stately quality, idiomatic, relaxed, and yet controlled; its images are drawn from nature, yet are seldom so narrow in scope as to sound journalistic or photographic.

Yet, with all the above said, it is perhaps the first quintessentially Wordsworthian poem, the first poem that points up the vital connection between poem and life, the struggle to articulate human ideals, tensions. It might be seen as tracing the growth of a poet and the course of a poetic life. This is not to say that the "Lines" betray the ideals of the "Preface"; rather they broaden those ideals in such a way that the merely particular gives way to the universal. Hartman's words seem apt: "An aspect of inner life is vividly rendered here without the artifice of a fictional or displaced perspective: without allegory or personification or atomism. There is complete respect for ordinary experience as well as for its extraordinary potential."[32] It is not that they are totally at odds with the stories of Simon Lee, or the Cumberland beggar, or the Idiot Boy, or the little girl, or the deserted woman. It is that they, as at times we have seen in the poems "To My Sister" or "Lines Written in Early Spring," turn for their subject to the individual speaker or voice exploring an inner conflict or tension, either apparent or suggested, and in the process telling the story of a life.

The poem is in a sense a work of crisis, a crisis always lurking below the surface in Wordsworth and only to be fully revealed in the more overtly didactic poems of 1807, *The Excursion*, and many of the later works. It is, to use the most dangerous of all psychological catch-phrases, a crisis of confidence as the poet wages a kind of tug-of-war between, on the one side, an emerging faith in the goodness of the individual, the truth of the imagination, and the harmony of the human heart with nature and, on the other side, an ever-looming awareness of the conditions of mortality, of reality itself. The tug-of-war is much less evident in the narrative poems of humble and rustic life, where Wordsworth is more the ventriloquist utilizing the

---

[32] *The Unremarkable Wordsworth*, Theory and History of Literature 34 (Minneapolis: University of Minnesota Press, 1987), p. 11.

child, the Cumberland beggar, the natural goodness of Goody Blake. Somewhat less evident are what Hartman calls "antiphonal poems" celebrating the joys and beauties of nature, the freedom and power of the imagination to create moments of transcendence. This is in no way to discount the salutary warning of Jerome McGann about relying only ori Romanticism's "self-definition" in the face of the diversity of post-1798 cultural history, and his contention that "Romantic poetry incorporates Romantic Ideology as the drama of the contradictions within that ideology."[33] Nor is it to underplay the sage readings of Marjorie Levinson, who sees the poem originating "in a will to preserve something Wordsworth knows is already lost," and suggests that "while the narrator of 'Tintern Abbey' can transcend his subject, it is clear that he cannot redeem it."[34] Both McGann and Levinson—and, indeed, other New Historicist readers—help to dramatize the tension that is so central to my argument: the tension between the claims of the individual imagination and the intense demands of history, of time, of the great world beyond the poetic mind. Yet Wordsworth is no prisoner of his time, and *Tintern Abbey* no merely poetic rendering of an historical moment. Its deeply personal voice, its sense of past joy and present loss, its somewhat problematic affirmation in the face of loss, is clearly a voice that is tempered but not determined by political dreams gone wrong, by young love unfulfilled, by the presence of a listener who eventually draws the speaker from imaginative exploration to the keenest sense of the challenges of time.

Time is at the heart of the poem. The presentness of the present rings in the opening twenty-two lines. "Five years have passed; five summers with the length / Of five long winters!" The reader is almost lulled into a supra-sensory state with a certain trance-like repetition—"again I hear / These waters, rolling from their mountain-springs / With a soft inland murmur." Repetition with variation catches us up in the magic of the scene; hearing gives way to sight: "Once again / Do I behold these steep and lofty cliffs, / Which on a wild secluded scene impress / Thoughts of more deep seclusion; and connect / The landscape with the quiet of the sky." Now emphasiz-

---

[33] *Romantic Ideology*, p. ix.
[34] *Wordsworth's Great Period Poems*, p. 37.

ing touch and sight, it seems like only yesterday "when I again repose / Here, under this dark sycamore, and view / These plots of cottage-ground, these orchard-tufts." Still the speaker would hold us with his "Once again," now with sight, and smell, and sound—or their absence—stressed in the free-flowing "hedge-rows, hardly hedge-rows, little lines / Of sportive wood run wild; these pastoral farms, / Green to the very door; and wreaths of smoke / Sent up, in silence, from among the trees" (1–19).

Quickly time past enters, but with no great regret on the part of the speaker. Five years may have elapsed; "lonely rooms" and "the din / Of towns and cities" have been his venue, but there is little if any sadness, for the "forms of beauty" he now views have been close to him, have brought special gifts. The ultimate gift is, of course, memory, or perhaps imagination, that power of mind so central to Wordsworth, a power to rescue moments of past splendor and revivify them, to recapture "sensations sweet, / Felt in the blood, and felt along the heart," sensations that trigger a sweet restorative power at times of despair and have "no slight or trivial influence / On that best portion of a good man's life; / His little, nameless, unremembered acts / Of kindness and of love." But the ultimate gift—and it is one more and more at the center of Wordsworth's faith—is a deeply spiritual one involving interaction between an active mind and an animate nature. David Perkins speaks of moments in Wordsworth's poetry when there is a "linking of man and nature," moments when "the love felt . . . becomes a religious emotion," "when the human soul seems linked to nature" as its "true home."[35]

Difficult to articulate in psychological terms, it is "another gift," a "blessed mood," one in which a certain freedom dominates, a suspension of consecutive reasoning or dogmatic belief in favor of a controlling power. While we have had indications in the early poems of nature as a beauteous arena for human action, as a force in the life of sensitive human beings, of a spontaneity of mind that cuts through the winding ways of logic, this is the most comprehensive and richest combination of all of these into a kind of new collage. The language of the poem reflects this slow transformation—from

---

[35] *The Quest for Permanence: The Symbolism of Wordsworth, Shelley, and Keats* (Cambridge, Mass.: Harvard University Press, 1959), p. 62.

relatively sharp, straightforward nouns and verbs, from fairly crisp
adjectives and adverbs, to a more ambivalent, almost philosophical
language; from recognizably decisive voices to a more hesitant, if
ultimately confident, voice. It is a voice, a language, a tone, a style
that is clearly different, clearly at a new level of density, a combination of elements that will characterize the style of Wordsworth in
many of the other ballads of 1800, the Lucy poems, *The Prelude*, and
the poems of 1807. One might say it is Wordsworth at the height of
his poetic power. We notice the style in this second movement of
the poem, but most especially as he sums up the greatest of all the
blessings he has experienced in his five years away from the banks
of the River Wye:

> that serene and blessed mood,
> In which the affections gently lead us on,
> Until, the breath of this corporeal frame,
> And even the motion of our human blood
> Almost suspended, we are laid asleep
> In body, and become a living soul:
> While with an eye made quiet by the power
> Of harmony, and the deep power of joy,
> We see into the life of things [41–49].

Seeing into the life of things, intuiting value at moments of unsus-
pected openness to the life-giving powers in nature—these are part
of a strong pull in the poet toward a secular faith, or, to borrow a
phrase from M. H. Abrams, a natural supernaturalism that is at the
root of his prayer of reminiscence, "O sylvan Wye! Thou wanderer
through the woods, / How often has my spirit turned to thee!" (57–
58).

The time sequence of the poem changes still again as, having
returned to the banks of the Wye and recalled the blessings it
brought him in the past, he stands again in the present and hopes
for the future. Those blessings, never doubted, are nonetheless difficult to phrase, and hence have a kind of shimmering edge of pleasing vagueness. Standing on the banks of the Wye, "with gleams of
half-extinguish'd thought, / With many recognitions dim and faint, /
And somewhat of a sad perplexity, / The picture of the mind revives
again." The scene now offers hope for the future.

In a mini-autobiographical section he charts the course of his spiritual growth in nature, from the "coarser pleasures" and "glad animal movements" of childhood to the adolescent rapture of a time when nature was "all in all," "when like a roe / I bounded o'er the mountains, by the sides / Of the deep rivers, and the lonely streams, / Wherever nature led." The poet, like poets and artists of all ages, finds words inadequate, and yet struggles with words to articulate that condition of the spirit in very early youth. "I cannot paint / What then I was," he exclaims. Then, in a feat of extraordinary proportions, he sees himself as a youth hunted by a nature dazzling with beauties, a nature alive, active: "The sounding cataract / Haunted me like a passion: the tall rock, / The mountain, and the deep and gloomy wood, / Their colours and their forms, were then to me / An appetite; a feeling and a love, / That had no need of a remoter charm, / By thought supplied, or any interest / Unborrowed from the eye" (59–84). No metaphysics is required for the youth caught up in the rapturous forces of nature; he surrenders, unaware of or unconcerned about the pressing realities of the great world beyond.

In the fashion of a brilliant short-story teller or autobiographer, he shifts the mood of this section dramatically but deftly. The tone shifts from exuberant to elegiac: "That time is past, / And all its aching joys are now no more, / And all its dizzy raptures" (84–86). Hail and farewell! The archetypal Wordsworthian crisis is dramatized while he is still in his twenties. The tug-of-war described earlier is not a development of old age, but is evidenced even in a poem of seeming affirmation. At one level it is an obvious crisis; age brings loss of youthful closeness to nature. And this crisis is dealt with by recognizing how one's response to nature, while changing, may mature, deepen, enrich. There is little of the sweet-sadness of the closing lines of Keats's "To Autumn," with its images of ripeness and fulfillment, but also of "gathering swallows twittering in the skies." Rather, after that early elegiac hesitancy, there is quick recovery and an almost militant tone. At the core of the recovery is, along with sections of *The Prelude*, perhaps the most searching and powerfully expressed statement of Wordsworth's image of and confidence in the power of nature to nourish the spirit. He "would believe" that "other gifts" have brought "abundant recompence" for the loss.

First, he has moved beyond the view of nature of "thoughtless youth" to hear "the still, sad music of humanity." He has felt in greater depth what was hinted at in only the broadest terms in the humble, rustic poems, that sense of a living, organic nature that links all living things:

> A presence that disturbs me with the joy
> Of elevated thoughts; a sense sublime
> Of something far more deeply interfused,
> Whose dwelling is the light of setting suns,
> And the round ocean, and the living air,
> And the blue sky, and in the mind of man,
> A motion and a spirit, that impels
> All thinking things, all objects of all thought,
> And rolls through all things [94–102].

And in a final act of faith he affirms his continuing, if changed, love of nature, his belief in the collaboration of the things of the sense and the things of the mind in the creation of a nature that is "The anchor of my purest thoughts, the nurse, / The guide, the guardian of my heart, and soul / Of all my moral being" (110–111).

So much for the consolations of a full and rich appreciation of the spiritual, even religious power of nature in one's life. So much for Wordsworth's quick qualification of the elegiac strain that accompanies his first sense of loss. The poem seems to have reached some kind of conclusion; the symphony seems to have rounded to its triumphant moment.

But it is not the end. There must be a final, uniquely Wordsworthian problem. What if? What if I did not believe in what I have just affirmed? What if my solitary commitment to nature were not enough, were too risky? Is trust in the mind's power to build values enough? Is the poetic life enough? There has always been something peculiarly awkward about the negatives of the opening lines of this epilogue. "Nor perchance, / If I were not thus taught, should I the more / Suffer my genial spirits to decay." How to read these curious words and those that follow. Several readers find no problem in the invocation of Dorothy's presence, see it as completing the natural with the human. For Hartman, "It becomes a vow, a prayer, an inscription for Dorothy's heart, an intimation of how this moment can

survive the speaker's death."[36] Yet for me there are interesting possibilities for seeing the lines as a hedge, as an interesting illustration
of a growing need in Wordsworth for someone or something to supplement his love of nature. The crisis pulls him strongly toward his
sister. Hers is not merely a presence after 111 lines of solitary rumi-
nation. It is a dominating presence which the language and the insistent rhythms convey.

He will not lose joy in age, for Dorothy, scarcely a year younger,
"art with me, here, upon the banks / Of this fair river." No ordinary
sister, she is "my dearest Friend, / My dear, dear Friend," "My dear,
dear Sister!" And she is with him at this very moment of affirmation,
and "in thy voice I catch / The language of my former heart, and
read / My former pleasures in the shooting lights / Of thy wild eyes."
Not only does he see himself in Dorothy, but prays, knowing the
power of nature: "May I behold in thee what I was once" (112–121).

What seems almost like a Romantic pact climaxes the poem. And
there is a growing emphasis on the "we" rather than the "I," a growing sense of a more communal experience. If I should not be here to
"hear thy voice" or "catch from thy wild eyes these gleams / Of past
existence," you will remember that "We stood together," and not
forget "That after many wanderings, many years / Of absence, these
steep woods and lofty cliffs, / And this green pastoral landscape,
were to me / More dear, both for themselves and for thy sake!"
(146–160). Love of nature leading to love of man or woman? Or love
of nature needing support beyond the solitary ego, the feeling mind?
Interesting questions emerge from this major poem so central to
Wordsworth's early literary life, so central to understanding a poet
who at age twenty-seven has known the ecstasy of natural communion, the disappointment of democratic hopes and youthful love, and
who would cling to an early faith while sensing the need for something more to bolster the journey of the spirit in a world of loss.

---

[36] *Wordsworth's Poetry*, p. 28.

4

To Germany: Poetic Solitude and Return

"I am not, however, afraid of such censure, insignificant as probably the majority of those poems would appear to very respectable persons; I do not mean London wits and witlings, for these have too many bad passions about them to be respectable even if they had more intellect than the benign laws of providence will allow to such a heartless existence as theirs is; but grave, kindly-natured, worthy persons, who should be pleased if they could. I hope that these Volumes are not without some recommendations, even for Readers of this class, but their imagination has slept; and the voice which is the voice of my Poetry without Imagination cannot be heard."

W. W. to Lady Beaumont
May 21, 1807

"There is scarcely one of my Poems which does not aim to direct the attention to some moral sentiment, or to some general principle, or law of thought, or of our intellectual constitution. For instance in the present case, who is there that has not felt that the mind can have no rest among a multitude of objects, of which it either cannot make one whole, or from which it cannot single out one individual, whereupon may be concentrated the attention divided among or distracted by a multitude?"

W. W. to Lady Beaumont
May 21, 1807

"Mr. Wordsworth is the most original poet now living. He is the reverse of Walter Scott in his defects and excellences. He has nearly all that the other wants, and wants all that the other possesses. His poetry is not external, but internal; it does not depend upon tradition, or story, or old song; he furnishes it from his own mind, and is his own subject.

William Hazlitt, *On the Living Poets*

THE PLAN OF THE Wordsworths and Coleridge to visit Germany finally seemed settled. The first edition of the *Lyrical Ballads* had brought some money, probably about thirty guineas, but essentially the Wordsworths' financial situation was precarious. while Coleridge had the security of the Tom and Josiah Wedgwood annuity of £150. Their lease of the Alfoxden house had been canceled because of the silly suspicions of neighbors about dubious political activities, and they were literally homeless. On September 14, 1798—before the first edition of the *Ballads* appeared—they were on their way to Germany with a man named John Chester. Arriving in Hamburg on September 18—their ideal image was not matched by the reality of the city—they stayed for a while at Der Wilde Mann, a small inn. Although the city appeared to them dirty, unfriendly, and pervaded by a kind of sadness, there was a special pleasure in meeting and talking with the great German poet Friedrich Klopstock and visiting Remnant's English bookshop, where they bought a copy of Percy's *Reliques of Ancient English Poetry* and Gottfried Burger's poems. Wordsworth is never far removed from his vocation.

Unable to find lodging with a German family—one of their great plans in their decision to visit Germany was to learn the language—and to keep up with the most modest standard of living in the great city, they decided to move to the more romantic south of Germany, specifically the attractive town of Goslar at the foot of the Harz mountains. Unfortunately again, instead of having the opportunity to savor the natural beauties of the area, they found themselves in the midst of record-breaking cold—we are told it was the coldest weather of the century—indoors, with no local library, Wordsworth experiencing persistent pain, and brother and sister feeling the suspicious glances of townspeople who mistook them for lovers. This was a time when, out of touch with family and friends, they were

never closer—we have little if any correspondence from the period—a time that fueled those speculations of Bateson-like students
of Wordsworth who saw the relationship as intimate if not definitely
sexual.

If the Wordsworths were unhappy in Goslar, Coleridge, along
with Chester, could not have had a more congenial German experience. They had gone to Ratzeburg, near Hamburg, and then on to
the university at Göttingen. Coleridge, unlike Wordsworth, learned
German well, and his extensive study in German philosophy brought
him under the spell of Kant, Schelling, and others who were to have
such a marked influence on his philosophy, aesthetics, and practical
criticism. It is this philosophizing side of Coleridge that ultimately
weans him away from the poetic life, although he wrote some his
great tragic poetry in the years when he was producing his brilliant
work in philosophy, aesthetics, and theology. It is also this philosophizing side that proved less attractive to Wordsworth, who was now
more than ever committed to the life of the poet.

Coleridge had taken as one of his roles in life to be the encour-
ager of Wordsworth to complete the planned epic poem *The Recluse*,
so many fragments of which had already appeared in various shapes
and sizes. The epic, we recall, was to be on the whole predicament
of the poet living in solitude, and was to have a section called *The
Excursion* and an introductory piece, a prelude, in which he would
trace and examine special moments in his coming-of-age as man and
poet. Coleridge continued the prodding on this trip, but again
Wordsworth's procrastination—or perhaps his general feeling of in-
adequacy or even dissatisfaction with such a project—put the poem
low on his list of priorities.

Unquestionably, the period was one of great emotion, of both
aloneness and loneliness, of closeness to his sister, of a deepening
commitment to writing about himself and a certain anxiety about
this kind of commitment in the light of the public and social demands on a poet to be a philosopher and a teacher. The first edition
of the *Lyrical Ballads* had been published by Cottle after he left for
Germany, and the reception of this new kind of poetry was, at best,
mixed. The five hundred copies sold slowly, and the reviews were
not encouraging. Some critics liked the experimental quality of the
language; others admired the simplicity and emotion of some of the

poems. Southey, however, a force to be reckoned with, ranked Wordsworth with the great living poets, but complained about the uninteresting subjects of "The Idiot Boy," "The Thorn," "Goody Blake and Harry Gill," and had kind words only for *Tintern Abbey*. And Charles Burney expresses his doubts about the social and political ramifications of some of the poems including *Tintern Abbey*.[1] Cottle himself, the pragmatic publisher, cites a major problem: "The ordinary people, whoever they are, never read his poems, and still don't. He is the poet of the Lake District, but you won't find Lake District poets reading his stuff."[2] At least for a time, the so-called educated reader was not impressed with poetry about peasants, even when the poet professed to be communicating his own feelings or to be dramatizing the freshness and honesty of natural people in natural settings.

Whatever the fate of these early poems, Wordsworth was determined to continue, not perhaps in exactly the same vein, but rather broadening the base of his settings, characters, and language. Maybe the kind of observation made by a serious and concerned critic like Hazlitt brought courage. Hazlitt remarked, after Dorothy had shown him some early manuscripts, that "I saw touches of truth and nature . . . and the sense of a new style of poetry came over me. It had something to me of the same effect that arises from the turning up of fresh soil, or the first welcome breath of spring."[3] If Hazlitt's words were encouraging, the financial returns were not, with Cottle remaindering a large number of first-edition copies, transferring the copyrights to Longmans, and, when he found they were worthless, returning them to Wordsworth and Coleridge.

Whatever the balance sheets revealed, however strong the urging of Coleridge to get on with *The Recluse*, Wordsworth pressed on with his "new poetry," a poetry of the mind, the imagination, of human beings in close rapport with nature, a poetry celebrating life and freedom, yet powerfully conscious of death and loss. The voice is increasingly personal. The settings continue to be natural but wonderfully wide ranging, picturesque without being photographic, sub-

---

[1] Bauer, *William Wordsworth: A Reference Guide*, pp. 1–3.

[2] Quoted in Davies, *William Wordsworth: A Biography* (New York: Athenaeum, 1980), p. 104.

[3] *Complete Works of William Hazlitt*, 17:117, 14.

lime without being melodramatic. Above all, the poetry seems to reveal a Wordsworth as confident as we are likely to find, even though there is nothing pollyannish or utopian about his vision. Indeed, it is in Germany where, in addition to writing shorter lyrics, he begins his *magnum opus*, his prelude to *The Recluse*, his attempt to examine the growth of his mind by rescuing imaginatively moments of vision that have shaped his personal and poetic life.

Two poems immediately catch our attention as we anticipate the publication of a second volume of lyrical ballads. The first, "There was a Boy," composed between early October and late November or early December of 1798, first published in the *Lyrical Ballads* of 1800, and eventually incorporated into *The Prelude*, is an astonishing poetic feat, the first of two poems about magical boys.[4] As with Lucy, we are unsure of who the boy is even when Wordsworth, in the later Isabella Fenwick note, mentions William Raincock of Rayrigg as one who demonstrated the musical virtuosity celebrated in the poem. Many have seen the boy as Wordsworth himself, as they have seen Lucy as Dorothy, and there is evidence to make the reader pay attention to such theories. But character identification is hardly our purpose here, and, for that matter, rarely does such identification illuminate the poem in the most satisfying ways. What we have is a poem alive with possibilities, wonderfully undecidable and yet equally close to the marrow of a particular human experience. We sense a confident poet at work here, if not a completely confident human being. We sense a trust in the medium as the poem stands by itself without an obtrusive mediator. We sense a greater closeness between speaker and subject; indeed, there are moments when barriers seem to fall apart and we wander in two worlds, conscious of only one.

The speaker starts, in keeping with the voice of earlier ballads, as a storyteller—"There was a Boy"—but immediately enlists the aid of the boy's landscape to verify what is to follow, to bear witness to the magic of the twelve-year-old: "ye knew him well, ye cliffs / And Islands of Winander!" It is as if boy and nature are congenial friends. And *congenial* seems not only an appropriate word in our context, but an increasingly important variant of that forceful Words-

---

[4] 1850 *Prelude*, 5.364–397.

worth-Coleridge word *genial*, suggesting a joyous, life-giving relationship.

What follows immediately is a remarkable cameo worthy of the best short-story writer—story, setting, suspense, sound. Everything collaborates for some thirty stunning lines. First we see the boy standing alone at "evening" as he did "many a time" for the speaker, a time "when the stars had just begun / To move along the edges of the hills, / Rising or setting . . . / Beneath the trees, or by the glimmering lake." The poem builds in excitement—run-on lines, a collage of iambs and trochees—as we witness the boy as musician of nature, "with fingers interwoven, both hands / Press'd closely palm to palm and to his mouth / Uplifted, he, as through an instrument, / Blew mimic hootings to the silent owls, / That they might answer him."

Without hesitating to anticipate or explain hyperbole, we are enveloped in a Stravinsky-like music, for the boy's music evokes the response of the owls, creates a kind of polyphonic but ultimately joyous effect as one responds to the other. How different the language, the treatment of nature from what one expects in the poetry of sensibility so important in Wordsworth's poetic life. There is little contrived, little conventional in setting and description; it has the ring of brisk Anglo-Saxon English, concrete, vivid. And while the music is always present, it is always varied; the poem respects no formal boundaries. The owls do not simply respond in predictable owl-fashion: "And they would shout / Across the wat'ry vale, and shout again, / Responsive to his call." Hard *q*, *scr*, *ech*, *joc* sounds contribute alliteratively to the strange music—"quivering peals, / And long halloos, and screams, and echoes loud / Redoubled and redoubled, a wild scene of jocund din!" (How different from the "and that was all" responsiveness of nature to a similar speaker and situation in Frost's "The Most of It."[5])

Surely this scene suggests a naturalistic version of the "wild ecstasy" Keats's speaker beholds on the Grecian urn, yet the narrator here calls attention in the symphonic feast to "a pause / Of silence such as baffled his best skill." The boy hangs "listening" at such moments. In the 1815 "Preface," Wordsworth deals with a poetic

---

[5] *The Poetry of Robert Frost: The Collected Poems Complete and Unabridged*, ed. Edward Connery Latham (New York: Holt, Rinehart and Winston, 1975).

source for this unusual image of hanging. Taking the celebrated "half way down / *Hangs* one who gathers samphire" from the Dover Cliff scene in *King Lear*, he attributes the image to "a slight exertion of the faculty which I denominate imagination." The samphire gatherer does not "literally hang," but "presenting to the senses something of such an appearance, the mind in its activity, for its own gratification, contemplates them as hanging" (3.31). The imagination of the magic boy incorporates the beauty of the scene into his heart with an immediacy no philosophical pondering can achieve; the scene—rocks, woods, even the heavens—is reflected in his mind as surely as it is "received / Into the bosom of the steady lake." Boy and nature seem one.

Our poet/short-story writer undermines the brilliance of the scene, the beauty of the lad, with a surprising closing. Unlike Keats's nightingale, this boy was born for death, death when he was ten years old, suggesting some rude interruption of the boy's magical association with everything around him.

The poem continues to surprise us as, eschewing the kind of narrative rationalization that climaxes, for example, Housman's "To an Athlete Dying Young," the narrator here renders himself naked to his readers. We watch him as he feels and dramatizes the event, as he proceeds "at evening" through the beauteous vale where the boy "was born," down the churchyard slope above the village school, standing "near his grave / A full half-hour together . . . / Mute." We are puzzled by this final posture of the speaker. Why mute for half-hour after half-hour? Is the memory of a schoolboy so deeply wrenching? Is the death of still another Lycidas an occasion for wonderment? Or is the poet again haunted by mysterious juxtaposition of a world of youthful, imaginative joy with the inevitability of death?

"Nutting" is a poem not just of the same chronological period, but also of the same psychic phase of the poetic life in Germany in 1798–1799. There is one major difference, in that the voice turns even more fervently inward. The narrator is totally involved in his own experience and in communicating it directly, although, as in *Tintern Abbey*, there is a somewhat abrupt appearance of a listener, a maiden who receives three lines of seemingly paternal, or should we say fraternal, advice at the end.

It is a lush, rich, powerful account of a traumatic event that took place on an otherwise calm, innocent nutting expedition. The same narrator who can build a superlative narrative of the boy now matches that performance in probing his own experience. He tells such a good story, lean, crisp, well paced, even tinged with a nice humor and self-mockery. There is a lovely matter-of-factness in "It seems a day" followed by the full reinforcement of "One of those heavenly days which cannot die." He clearly must mean us to smile as he describes himself setting out on a much-desired nutting expedition, leaving the cottage "With a wallet o'er my shoulders slung, / A nutting crook in hand," "a Figure quaint" attired "More ragged than need was" (1–7).

Like a nineteenth-century Adam, he forces his way "Among the woods / And o'er the pathless rocks," finally coming upon his own Eden or Bliss, "one dear nook / Unvisited" (12–15). The scene shimmers with youthful fantasy; the language explodes with a never-ending range of possibilities, from the natural lushness of the setting to the seductive sexual suggestions of a young man eyeing a prize untouched by other hands. It is a "dear nook"; it is "unvisited"; it is a place "where not a broken bough / Droop'd with its wither'd leaves, ungracious sign / Of devastation," where "the hazels rose / Tall and erect, with milk-white clusters hung. / A virgin scene!" (15–19). The suspense builds, and along with it a steamy eroticism, as we are led from the temptress nature to the tempted boy. The boy-speaker seems totally un-self-conscious as he describes his response in great physical and psychological detail. This is a boy alive, feeling, unrestrained by societal pieties. He delays his ultimate pleasure to savor the preliminaries. The lines "A little while I stood, / Breathing with such suppression of the heart / As joy delights in" capture this sense of prolonging the expectation, with the sounds of "breathing and suppression" brilliantly contributing (19–21). The delay is enhanced by the further delay in the narrator's account. Fearing no "rival," he "eyed / The banquet" or—still waiting—he sits and plays with the flowers, a pleasure "known to those, who, after long / And weary expectation, have been bless'd / With sudden happiness beyond all hope" (22–27). Almost unconsciously, he reveals in his language his special pleasure in the virginity of the place, its aloneness, its being unseen by any other human being, its eternality as "fairy water-breaks do murmur on / For ever" (30–31). And sound works brilliantly in the following lines that describe his posture, with deftly positioned *s* sounds and the onomatopoetic "murmur and the murmuring sound" creating a special music. It is the aloneness of Lucy, the perfect rapport of speaker and setting.

Then, as in "There was a Boy," but even more shockingly, our expectations are undermined. We expect the erotic preparations to culminate in lovemaking of great tenderness, and yet, as in a thriller, we are turned in other directions. The speaker—it is difficult to determine motivation, either exuberance or cruelty—describes his action with great vehemence. Iambs of increasing intensity give way to powerful spondees:

> Then up I rose,
> And dragg'd to earth both branch and bough, with crash
> And merciless ravage, and the shady nook
> Of hazels, and the green and mossy bower,
> Deform'd and sullied, patiently gave up
> Their quiet being [41–46].

We image the boy on a rampage. Yet just as abruptly the violence of scene and language is tempered—is it satiation or sudden awareness of what has happened?—as a more regular iambic rhythm catches an image of the speaker pausing in the midst of his ravishing and "Exulting, rich beyond the wealth of kings." Remembering a moment of awareness, of recognition, of fear, "I felt a sense of pain when I beheld / The silent trees, and the intruding sky" (49–51). It is a moment of richly complex emotion. On the one hand, there is the sense of loss witnessed by the "silent trees" and "intruding sky." On the other hand—and for the first time, we become aware of a listener, a "Maiden"—there is the discovery of "a Spirit in the woods" and the counsel to the woman to "move along these shades / In gentleness of heart; with gentle hand / Touch" (52–54). David Ferry sees the human being as "a destroyer and disturber of the calm of things because he alone knows that he must die, and also that they must die." Mysteriously, Ferry argues, he is the "agent of time," and delights in that role. Yet, "he grieves for what he has done, since peace and quietness, protection from destruction are what he himself desires most, and therefore in ravaging the glade he has ravaged the object of his own desire."[6]

In both poems nature proves an arena not only of life and joy, but also of death and destruction. It is an arena where passionate intensity breeds wild action and spontaneous response, but also tranquil reflection. As the speaker of "There was a Boy" stands "mute" and the speaker of "Nutting" becomes aware of "a spirit," we sense in the Wordsworth of the *Lyrical Ballads* period the pull of reality, of violence, loss, and death. And at the same time we feel a richer awareness of the mystery of nature, its power, and its limits.

Clearly, the so-called Lucy poems take on richer meaning when read in conjunction with "There was a Boy" and "Nutting." They are mysterious pieces, and whether Lucy is Dorothy or Mary or, indeed, anybody in particular is much less important than what she is in the evolving cast of characters of the *Lyrical Ballads*. Hartman is surely right in seeing the Lucy poems as lyrics of passage; I see them, in company with others of the period, as bridge poems between the poetry of humble and rustic life, where the anchor of reality always seems to keep a firm hold on the imaginings of speakers, and the poetry of imagination, where reality is often a springboard for the creations of the mind. If ever Wordsworth achieved something close to a full faith in nature and imagination, it is in the poems of the years before 1810, but more specifically in the poems of the period before 1807. Understanding Wordsworth involves understanding the drifts and directions of his poetry, for here we see most clearly the unclear, the tensions of a life and career where the pull of mind is matched by the pull of reality; the pull of a benevolent, shaping nature is matched by the pull of a fearsome, powerful nature; where the joy of unity is matched by the sadness of separation and loss.

We return to the Lucy poems. Here, whether we have the biographical critic's real person or Hartman's "Wordsworth's nearest approach to a personal myth,"[7] death and loss are the primary realities.

---

[6] *The Limits of Mortality: An Essay on Wordsworth's Major Poems* (Westport, Conn.: Greenwood Press, 1978), p. 27.

[7] *Wordsworth's Poetry*, p. 157.

Lucy is surely a more intense version of the girl in "We Are Seven," the boy in "There was a Boy." She has the quality of utter purity, utter aloneness, utter closeness to nature. She is seen, as many critics have noted, almost exclusively from the vantage point of the poems' speakers, from the impact that her loss brings. Anne Mellor argues that Lucy and other female figures in Wordsworth's earlier poems "do not exist as independent self-conscious human beings with minds as capable as the poet's." They are "rarely allowed to speak for themselves."[8]

She dwells "among th' untrodden ways" with "none to praise" and "very few to love" (1–4). Yet it is her very aloneness that irradiates her for the speaker. Yes, "A Violet by a mossy Stone," but also "Half-hidden from the Eye!" Yes, "Fair as a star," but "when only one / Is shining in the sky" (5–8). The last stanza of this lyric underlines her "unknown" or hidden life and, for that matter, death. But her death, the death of a beautiful maiden unsullied by the world, dramatizes more fully the power that woman, that mythic force, exerted in the speaker's life: "The difference is to me!" (12).

We are not primarily concerned with the exact chronology of the Lucy poems, so we move to a second and even shorter Lucy lyric. Again the utter simplicity masks the profundity of feeling; the delicate naturalness of language hides the range of implication. The first Lucy lyric introduced us to the maid, described her majestic aloneness, and expressed the speaker's response to her seemingly untimely death. The second lyric brings us even closer to the phenomenon of Lucy's death. The brilliant alliteration of the opening lines—"A slumber did my spirit seal; / I had no human fears"—suggests the tug-of-war theme again (1–2). A confident speaker seems shielded from human anxieties by the bliss of sleep; the mind is its own place. Continuing alliteration reinforces the silence of the speaker's world, the idealizing activity of his mind: "She seem'd a thing that could not feel / The touch of earthly years" (3–4). Lucy is dead, we say in utterly prosaic words. But the poet struggles to convey her return not to a river's bank or a sky. She has become an element in a larger scheme of things. "No motion has she now, no force; / She neither hears nor sees" conveys a kind of terror. There

---

[8] *Romanticism and Gender*, p. 19.

is no suggestion of absorption into a heavenly paradise, a beatific vision, only something like the starkness of a hard reality we might find in modern poets like Frost and Stevens: "Roll'd round in earth's diurnal course / With rocks and stones and trees" (4–8).

How different the monologue of Nature in "Three years she grew in sun and shower." Nature is a benevolent, if somewhat dominant, personification, almost an image of the Creator. No distant, remote Deity here; rather, a loving Lord who spies his creation after three years of sun and shower had breathed a special kind of loveliness on her. He—Nature is clearly masculine—will take her to himself. Knowing Lucy, he has an assurance of her continuing presence as an enduring beauty not to be touched by hard realities. Past gives way to future tense; the lighter, swifter movement is replaced by a slower, more relentless rhythm enforced by an abundance of long vowel sounds. Reality has intruded on dream; "She shall be mine, and I will make / A Lady of my own" (5–6). We hear the conversational rhythms of the monologue, the happy combination of simple and somewhat more elaborate language as Nature plots his patriarchal course of action for the growth and education of Lucy. In a stanza filled with rich images of music and dance, Nature continues his bequest of gifts of exuberance and calm. She will know "vital feelings of delight" which "Shall rear her form to stately height, / Her virgin bosom swell, . . . / While she and I together live / Here is this happy dell" (31–36).

Nature has spoken: Let Lucy be everything I have determined. There is a Genesis-like tone as one gift after another has been bequeathed, and the Creator sees his work done. But the narrator returns to add an undercutting finale. Lucy dies, and we wonder not about the fact of death, but about its place in the rhetoric of the poem. In what ways are we prepared? Or are we? Has Lucy been so caught up in Nature that she seems part of his eternality? Is the "happy dell" a world of imagination where no tragedy can enter? Did the speaker see her as beyond the limits of mortality? Bateson contends that "it is at least possible that the dangerous relationship with Dorothy was now solved, subconsciously, by killing her off symbolically. Lucy, who had been loved so dearly, was dead. The guilty possibilities were evaded by the removal, subconsciously, of the

guilty object."⁹ Whatever the answer, the poem again has the somewhat sudden turn, the ring of reality, the return motif. Death is
something Lucy seemed beyond, but it took her to itself and left a
forlorn speaker with "This heath, this calm and quiet scene; / The
memory of what has been / And never more will be" (41–42). The
Lucy poems have a finality about their endings. Beautiful, joyous,
close to nature is the girl, but she is still a child of Mother Earth and
still subject to the claims of reality, the ultimate claim being death
itself.

The other Lucy poems of the second volume of *Lyrical Ballads*
continue—perhaps less successfully—the theme of death and loss.
So also does the sequence of Matthew poems—generally believed
to be based on Wordsworth's beloved schoolmaster at Hawkshead—
which, on the one hand, celebrates the natural wisdom and learning
of this teacher and, on the other, eulogizes his death. The dialogue
of "The Fountain" sees a young narrator and a seventy-two-year-
old Matthew lying "beneath a spreading oak," a "mossy seat." The
narrator is delighted as "from the turf a fountain broke, / And gur-
gled at our feet," and urges a mutual celebration (5–8). Matthew
recalls days of joy at this site. Observing the fountain and the
streamlet that flows from it, he poeticizes the scene, creating what
amounts to an early version of a continuing Wordsworthian archetype: the stream, the flowing water of experience. To this flowing
water he attributes a kind of immortality. It knows nothing of the
pull of mortality. "How merrily it goes!" " 'Twill murmur on a thousand years, / And flow as now it flows" (22–24).

Matthew, however, knows the stays of age as he, almost anticipating the Coleridge of "Dejection," with "eyes . . . dim" and
"childish tears" and "heart . . . idly stirr'd" (28–29), hears now the
sound of the past. He knows the reality of the present, and yet,
although he mourns loss, he does not despair. The wise mind
"Mourns less for what age takes away / Than what it leaves behind"
(34–35). The encounter of narrator and Matthew turns curiously
mysterious as Matthew speaks of days almost over, of the love of
many, and of singing "my idle songs / Upon these happy plains"
(59–60), but also of "but by none / Am I enough belov'd" (54–55).

---

⁹ *Wordsworth: A Re-Interpretation*, p. 153.

The narrator is quick to console, if only by providing the answer of imagination, of substitution—"And Matthew, for thy children dead / I'll be a son to thee" (61–62). But Matthew cannot imagine, and quickly replies, "Alas! that cannot be" (64), content to wander on singing "those witty rhymes / About the crazy old church-clock, / And the bewilder'd chimes" (70–72).

Death and loss are realities for the beloved schoolmaster, and "The Two April Mornings" is a vivid dramatization. Narrator and Matthew walk "while bright and red / Uprose the morning sun" (1–2), bright light again suggesting the vividness of youthful faith and hope. Matthew stops, looks, utters with a kind of Christian stoicism, "The will of God be done!" (4). Curious about the response of the "blithe" schoolmaster on so brilliant an April morning, the narrator wonders "what thought / . . . So sad a sigh has brought?" (13–15).

Matthew stops a second time, and—a sharp reminder of the counter-image of skewed light in Wordsworth's poetry—notices, as he looks toward the eastern mountain top, "Yon cloud with that long purple cleft" (21). It triggers remembrance of another April morning—thirty years ago. On a day bright and beautiful he fished to his delight, only to come later to his daughter Emma's grave in the churchyard. With memories of the death of the boy in "There was a Boy"—Emma was nine, he was ten; he a whistler, she a singer—we hear his mourning. As he leaves the yard, he meets a "blooming Girl, whose hair was wet / With points of morning dew," perhaps an anticipation of the solitary reaper. On the one hand, "To see a Child so very fair, / It was a pure delight!" (42–47). Yet how quickly the joy gives way to a "sigh of pain" as, looking at her and probably remembering Emma, he "did not wish her mine!" (52–55). The awareness of death, of loss, tempers any earthly joy, and the narrator leaves us with an astonishing image, really a picture that might embody Wordsworth himself. Matthew has died, and yet the narrator cannot erase the emblem of the man standing at that moment recounting the pain of loss "with his bough / Of wilding in his hand" (59–60).

"Michael" is the uniquely pastoral Wordsworthian poem of the 1800 *Lyrical Ballads*, a poem true to the naturalistic ideals of the "Preface" and yet in remarkable ways breaking out of the trap of photographic realism and heavy didacticism. Michael, like Matthew, becomes another almost emblematic figure—indeed, almost a biblical figure in a narrative with more than a few biblical overtones. Old, venerable, devoted servant of the land, loving husband of Isabel and father of an almost miraculously late-arriving child (Luke), he is, like so many of his predecessors in the Wordsworthian *dramatis personae*, a survivor. His story is briskly and unceremoniously told, longer than the folk ballad, leaner and terser than the earlier pastorals. Like "There was a Boy" and the Matthew and Lucy poems, it may more than the more rustic pieces embody what Wordsworth meant by that curious term "lyrical ballad," an engaging story touched by the feelings of the narrator. Unlike the classic folk ballad, which is prized for its objectivity and its lack of narrative intrusion of any kind, the lyrical ballad is truly a Wordsworthian invention, a poem, as he says in the "Preface," where the "feeling gives importance to the action."

"Michael" was the last poem included in the *Lyrical Ballads* of 1800. The narrator, as in so many such poems, is companionable but not overbearingly so. His description of a setting still accessible to the traveler of today is vivid. The rhythms are iambic, but not monotonously or cloyingly so; the meter, as is increasingly the case in the developing poet, is more open, a free-flowing blank verse that not only advances the story, but also pleases the reader. There is clearly a gathering immediacy in the opening lines, a sense of an encounter between venturesome traveler and an imposing nature:

> If from the public way you turn your steps
> Up the tumultuous brook of Green-head Gill
> You will suppose that with an upright path
> Your feet must struggle; in such bold ascent
> The pastoral Mountains front you, face to face.
> But, courage! for beside that boisterous Brook
> The Mountains have all open'd out themselves,
> And made a hidden valley of their own [1–8].

One notes a starkness, an almost Frostian, modernist dimension to the setting. The narrative sharpens further and continues in its minimalist mode. Our attention is directed to a bare stage, so bare that the passerby might almost miss what the narrator considers vital: "Beside the brook / There is a straggling Heap of unhewn stones; / And to that place / A Story appertains" (16–18).

That story unfolds with ballad-like simplicity, a familial story of husband-father, wife-mother, and son, a story, the narrator recalls, from his earliest days when he cared less for books, but knew "the power / Of Nature, by the gentle agency / Of natural objects led me on to feel / For passions that were not my own, and think / At random and imperfectly indeed / On man, the heart of man, and human life" (28–33). Such a narrator/poet speaks of a tale that seems to anticipate what he had in mind for his epic *The Recluse* and to reveal in curious ways the crossroads at which Wordsworth stands at the time of the *Lyrical Ballads* and the kind of poetic-career questions he faces.

That crossroads has already been observed in the curious dual thrust of the "Preface" to the *Lyrical Ballads,* with its image of the poet of humble and rustic life struggling with the image of the intensely personal poet intrigued by the workings of the inner life and by its analogies in nature, and increasingly committed to poetry as the re-creation of strong feeling. The crossroads metaphor, often a jejune one, has a peculiar aptness for the Wordsworth of the turn of the century as a whole range of questions occupies him: Yes, I do want to be a poet, but what kind of a poet? Shall I, in my desire to resuscitate the stale conventionalism of contemporary poetry, stay close to the soil, to the settings of my most beloved locales—the Lakes, the mountains, the Bristol Channel Coast, the whole range of spectacular settings in which I lived and moved? Shall I follow through on my rejection of the trite diction of current poets and find a simpler, more unadorned vocabulary? Or shall I pursue the urgency of the inner life, the strong need for the mind to express its deepest longings, its love of nature as a revelation of a deeper spiritual power, its sense of the ecstasy of childhood unity with the divine and the deep sense of loss that comes with age?

Tintern Abbey has already shown a movement toward the poetry of the inner life; the 1800 volumes, with the Lucy pieces, "There was a Boy" and "Nutting," show more of this. It is fair to say that, if not completely consciously, then with a clear sense of a stronger pull of the inner life, Wordsworth is turning toward a more personal poetry, a more individualized speaking voice which we hear under the impact of strong inner forces. Such a poetry reveals a fascination with the workings of the mind, specifically of the imagination, especially in its encounters with nature, in its powers to shape, create. In Germany, and we will talk about this large matter presently, it was the poem on the growth of his own mind—*The Prelude*—that preoccupied him as he struggled to locate these reservoirs of power in his psychic life that brought him to his present maturity, as he, in effect, prepared his artistic credentials for the epic poem *The Recluse*.

So the tale of Michael unfolds with both the rustic world and the terrain of the feeling poet staking claims. On the one hand, the narrator offers his prelude to the story, "a history / Homely and rude" meant "For the delight of a few natural hearts." On the other, "with yet fonder feeling," he will proceed with an even more specific audience, "Of youthful Poets, who among these Hills / Will be my second Self when I am gone" (35–39). He would, it would seem, inaugurate a tradition of poets who would continue to convey in their work the gospel of nature in the language of true feeling.

And, on one level, "Michael" is a simple pastoral story, in some ways a Lake District parable of the Prodigal Son. Grasmere Vale is the setting; the characters include the eighty-year-old Michael, "An old man, stout of heart, and strong of limb," whose "mind was keen, / Intense, and frugal, apt for all affairs." No mere shepherd, "he had learn'd the meaning of all winds, / Of blasts of every tone" (42–49). Mountains, valleys, streams, and rocks were not mere phenomena of nature to him, but sources of "The pleasure which there is in life itself" (79).

Enter Isabel, his wife, some twenty years younger, "a Woman of a stirring life, / Whose heart was in her house" (83–84), working faithfully at spinning wool. The only other inhabitant of the house was Luke, a son born in their age. Together they lived and worked in peace and happiness, with the lamp providing light for the evenings and giving the house its name, The Evening Star.

Love was pervasive in The Evening Star, but Luke brought special joy to the aging Michael, whether the father rocking the infant's cradle or making a "perfect Shepherd's Staff" (193) for the five-year-old or climbing the heights with the ten-year-old now a companion. From Luke "there came / Feelings and emanations, things which were / Light to the sun, and music to the wind." Michael's "Heart seem'd born again" (210–213).

The poem moves to the present again with almost biblical overtones—"Thus in his Father's sight the Boy grew up: / And now when he had reached his eighteenth year, / He was his comfort and his daily hope" (214–216). But the tranquillity of daily pastoral life is shattered by the world of business. Michael must pay almost half of his resources to satisfy a financial forfeit of his brother's son. Rather than sell a portion of his land, he forgives the brother's son and resolves to send the now eighteen-year-old Luke to another relative to "repair this loss" (262). All is ready, but in keeping with the religious overtones of the poem, there must be a covenant. Visiting the beginnings of a sheepfold "Near the tumultuous brook of Green-head Gill / In that deep Valley" (332–333), Michael rehearses for Luke the history of the land, then proposes that Luke symbolically begin the sheepfold. "This was a work for us; and now, my Son, / It is a work for me. But lay one stone, / Here, lay it for me, Luke, with thine own hands" (395–397). With blessings on his son and a promise to maintain the land and keep up the covenant, he bids farewell to Luke. Luke bravely departs, and initially prospers in his venture, writing to his parents "loving letters full of wondrous news" (442). While Michael labors at the sheepfold, Luke turns to evil ways and is forced to leave the country.

Michael, now too aged to lift a single stone, nevertheless works the land, still another Wordsworthian emblem. Shortly after, Isabel dies, and the land passes into a "Stranger's hand" (484). Only the oak and the unfinished sheepfold remain "Beside the boisterous brook of Green-head Gill" (491), another spare setting as we imagine the inroads of industry ravaging the land, the old order of nature and things natural passing to the modern era of progress and development. Marjorie Levinson's New Historicist reading of *Michael* makes more explicit the thesis she advanced about *Tintern Abbey*. "Wordsworth's sheepfold," she argues, "is explicitly offered to the reader as a historical landmark testifying to an earlier and more satisfying way of life; at the same time, the narrator persuades us that the passage of that historical moment has brought about a finer tone in social bonding."[10]

The Wordsworths, disappointed with their experience in Germany, left Goslar in February 1799 and headed for England. Landing

---

[10] *Wordsworth's Great Period Poems*, p. 37.

in May, William and Dorothy headed north to Sockburn in Durham, Yorkshire, to visit their old friends the Hutchinsons. Disillusioned by the French Revolution and, like his new hero Burke, contemptuous of the smug theory of Enlightenment philosophy;[11] troubled by financial worries—Richard harassing him to repay a debt or Basil Montagu unable to return money he owed to the poet—and by physical ailments, Wordsworth was nevertheless happy to be home. That happiness increased when Tom Poole brought Coleridge to Sockburn on October 26, 1799 for a great reunion—a scene to reckon with, not quite the menagerie of Shelley, Byron, and company in Switzerland in 1816, but certainly (as we might say today) a group of Bohemians getting together after a separation. Even John Wordsworth, on leave between his many voyages for the East India Company, was there after attending the funeral of his uncle Kit Cookson, a funeral not attended by Wordsworth, who still smarted from the way he had been treated as a boy.

But it was also a scene of conflicting emotions—Dorothy, still the devotee of her brother; Wordsworth, now in love with his childhood friend Mary Hutchinson; Coleridge, with his pregnant wife, Sarah Fricker, and now in love with Sara Hutchinson. Hunter Davies's fancied sketch of this congenial group, with the exception of Coleridge's wife, enjoying each other and the beauty of their surroundings, is not far-fetched. Using Sarah Coleridge as his point of reference, he proceeds:

> She didn't go in for all this nocturnal wandering, these romantic musings, poetry readings under the trees, by the lakeside or behind rocks. It's hard to believe how the sixsome paired off, if they ever did— Dorothy was very fond of Coleridge, who was especially fond of Sarah Hutchinson, who in turn was very fond of John Wordsworth. They were all really in love with each other, and all in love with themselves. As in the West Country, they were living an early version of a drop-

[11] James Chandler speaks of "Burke's unwitting service to the radical movement itself. Burke contributed much to the formation of an articulate radical ideology in the England of the 1790s." And about Wordsworth's connection with Burke, he contends: "So somewhere between 1793 and 1818 Wordsworth 'returned,' by way either of memory or of the printed word, to the writings that contained the untheoretical principles of this confirmed genius" (*Wordworth's Second Nature*, pp. 17, 30). Wordsworth's highest tribute is the celebrated passage added to Book 7 of *The Prelude*, 512–543.

out-life: young people who refused to take up the conventional middle-class occupations moving around, staying in cheap rented premises, living off the land and off their wits (and off pieces of writing when they could manage it), getting hand-outs from their friends or relations, endlessly discussing and arguing about their philosophical or political views.[12]

Coleridge and Wordsworth, truly kindred poetic spirits, toured the Lake country with John—from Hawkshead, where Wordsworth learned of his cherished Ann Tyson's death three years before; to Rydal, and finally to Grasmere, for the poet a final resting place. The peace of the valley, the majesty of the surrounding mountains, the soothing charm of the lakes—all of these touched him deeply, and, when he found a house that pleased him, he wrote to Dorothy to describe this paradise and to offer a plan for living there. On December 17, 1799, brother and sister, like a knight and his lady, set out from Sockburn on what has become a legendary journey. First on horseback, then on foot, they battled a raging snowstorm so fierce that they did not reach Kendal for three days. And from Kendal, where they purchased household needs, they pushed on to Grasmere, arriving there on December 21, 1799 at what was then the Dove and Olive Branch, now Dove Cottage. The house (still welcoming visitors today, thanks to the National Trust) was simple, but comfortable and certainly picturesque. Guides today still direct visitors to the kitchen and Dorothy's bedroom on the first level, to a second level where there are Wordsworth's bedroom, a living room, and two guest rooms. And there is the garden just above the house, a place of great pleasure for brother and sister and still nicely kept today. The modern visitor marvels at how such a house could have hosted so many guests for such long stays, and yet the spirit of the place was always one of welcoming.

The summer of 1800 saw Wordsworth, with the encouragement of Coleridge, going on with the publication of a second edition of the *Lyrical Ballads*, with many poems from the German sojourn and others written since his return and with the *Rime of the Ancient Mariner* moved from beginning to end and the full and famous "Preface" added. Cottle had sold off the bulk of the first edition of five hun-

---

[12] *William Wordsworth: A Biography*, p. 104.

dred copies as remainders and, of course, at a loss. As mentioned earlier, the 1799 reviews were mixed, but sales jumped with a new distributor, and the remaining stock was sold.

The above is not to suggest that an audience was waiting expectantly for more Wordsworth poetry. The poet's own brilliant assessment of the state of English taste at the time and the implications for the poet are worth noting briefly. "For a multitude of causes," he writes in the 1800 "Preface," "unknown to former times, are now acting with a combined force to blunt the discriminating powers of the mind, and, unfitting it for all voluntary exertion, to reduce it to a state of almost savage torpor"—a combination of "the great national events which are daily taking place, and the increasing accumulation of men in cities, where the uniformity of their occupations produces a craving for extra-ordinary incident, which the rapid communication of intelligence hourly gratifies." In response to the violence of war and the routinization of industrialism, "the literature and theatrical exhibitions of the country have conformed themselves" (1.129).

Indeed, Longmans publishing house, in bringing out a new two-volume edition, reprinting 750 copies of the first and a thousand of a companion to be published separately, had no illusions about a best-seller. The advance of £80, though hardly munificent, was in keeping with Wordsworth's own realism as evidenced by the epigraph to this edition and the ones that followed in 1802 and 1805— *Quam nihil ad genium, Papiniane, tuum!* His celebrated letter to the British statesman Charles James Fox, appended to a gift of the two volumes, reveals an acute awareness of poetry and the poet in an age of increasing mechanization. Recommending to Fox's attention "Michael" and "The Brothers" as poems in which he has portrayed "the domestic affections" of a vanishing class "now almost confined to the North of England," he argues that such "affections will always be strong amongst men who live in a country not crowded with population, if these men are placed above poverty." Praising Fox as one who holds sacred "the property of the Poor," he recommends his own poems as written "with a view to shew that men who do not wear fine cloaths can feel deeply." "The poems," he says, "are faithful copies from nature" and "may excite profitable sympathies in many kind and good hearts, and may in some small degree enlarge our feelings of reverence for our species, and knowledge of human nature."[13]

Like Wordsworth and Coleridge, Wordsworth's brother John had a sense that the *Lyrical Ballads* were different, that they did not aim for mere popularity, and that their full effect might not be felt for a time. "I do not think," he writes to Mary Hutchinson on March 9, 10, 1801, "that W[illiam's] poetry will become popular for some time to come; it certainly does not suit the present taste."[14] And in another letter to Mary on February 25, 26, 1801, he suggests that "in time" the poems "will become popular but it will be by degrees." The small numbers who will be pleased "will be pleased in a high degree and they will be *people of sense* this will have weight-& people who neither understand or wish to understand will buy and praise them."[15] Again writing to Mary on March 9, 10, 1801, "my brother's poetry has a great deal to struggle [against] but I hope it will overcome all—it is certainly founded upon Nature—and that is the best foundation."[16]

Yet comments, reviews, and opinions notwithstanding, Wordsworth widened his range in the second and later editions of the *Lyrical Ballads*, worked hard on the new poems, as he had on the poems in Germany, and continued his intense commitment to the writing of *The Prelude* which he had begun in Goslar. Coleridge distanced himself from the project more and more, although he continued to be a staunch advocate and a vigorous promoter of Wordsworth's reputation as a new and promising poet. It might be said that Wordsworth became a poet in the full sense at this time, not just in the grandiose terms that emerge from Romantic discourse, but in the sense of being a poet who writes as he lives and lives as he writes. More and more he sees his work as a career in and out of time and, most interesting, takes the lead in what the I have called elsewhere a new defense of literature.[17] That defense is

---

[13] W. W. to Charles James Fox, January 14, 1801. *EY* 1:315.

[14] See *The Letters of John Wordsworth*, ed. Carl Ketcham (Ithaca, N.Y.: Cornell University Press, 1969), p. 103.

[15] Ibid., p. 95.

[16] Ibid., p. 103.

[17] See *Whole Internal Universe*, pp. 99–111. See also Clifford Siskin, *The Historicity of Romantic Discourse* (New York: Oxford University Press, 1988).

rooted in a conviction that art is not a merely ornamental vehicle for bearing the great truths of experience, but, historically anchored to be sure, a relatively independent creation rooted in the imagination's power to embody in metaphor and symbol the workings of the inner life in themselves or in their encounters with the external world. Is it any wonder that Wordsworth's poetry has found the remarkable range of critical appraisal it has today, from the historicizing, to the psychologizing, to the deconstructive, and beyond?

Wordsworth at the crossroads, then, chose the road of *Tintern Abbey*, with the voice of his speakers struggling to articulate personal and public encounter in a language and imagery that, however ambiguous, draws the reader to the intensity of the struggle. The section on the poet in the 1802 addition to the "Preface" to the *Lyrical Ballads* seems to capture vividly a new sense of purpose. "What is a Poet?" That is the question. Is he a reflector of consensus? Is he an elegant restater of the persisting truths of the tradition? Or is he a person responsible only to himself, free from societal connections? These continue to be bedrock questions for artists in any age, and Wordsworth, on the surface at least, seems to opt for freedom. At a deeper level, however, he is still engaged in the tug-of-war we have been following even in his early career, but the claims of the self seem to be prevailing. The poet "is a man speaking to men," a person "with more lively sensibility, more enthusiasm and tenderness," and "a greater knowledge of human nature and a more comprehensive soul." He is one "pleased with his own passions and volitions, and who rejoices more than other men in the spirit of life that is in him." He delights "to contemplate similar volitions and passions as manifested in the goings-on of the Universe," and is "habitually impelled to create them where he does not find them" (1.138).

5

The Poetic Life as Epic: The Prelude

Sometimes it suits me better to invent
A tale from my own heart, more near akin
To my own passions and habitual thoughts;
Some variegated story, in the main
Lofty, but the unsubstantial structure melts
Before the very sun that brightens it,
Mist into air dissolving!
. . . .
But from this awful burthen I full soon
Take refuge and beguile myself with trust
That mellower years will bring a riper mind
And clearer insight.

> 1850 *Prelude*

Friend of the wise! and teacher of the good!
Into my heart have I received that lay
More than historic, that prophetic lay
Wherein (high theme by thee first sung aright)
On the foundations and the building up
Of a Human Spirit thou hast dared to tell
What may be told, to the understanding mind
By vital breathings secret as the soul
Of vernal growth, oft quickens in the heart
Thoughts all too deep for words!

> Samuel Taylor Coleridge, "To William Wordsworth:
> Composed on the Night after his Recitation of a
> Poem on the Growth of an Individual Mind"
> (January 1807)

For one of the keys to the understanding of the human predicament is the recognition that there is, for the human individual, no reality—no comprehensible and useful reality, at any rate—other than that of an object as *perceived* by the human eye and the human mind—no abstract reality, in other words, detached from the eye of the beholder. All that we see around us may be considered to some extent as a part of ourselves, the reflection of our own astigmatisms, our own individual perspectives, and—sometimes—our intuitions. Unless it is taken that way, we cannot recognize its reality, or we know it to be real.

George Kennan, *Sketches from a Life*

Although *The Prelude* was not published until after the poet's death in 1850, after long years of rethinking, refeeling, re-editing by Wordsworth and by relatives and executors, its origins are clearly in the years when the Wordsworths were living at Alfoxden near Coleridge, when the *Lyrical Ballads* was being composed and published. We linger briefly over these remote beginnings, conversations with Coleridge concerning a long philosophical poem to be called *The Recluse*, "containing views of Man, Nature, and Society . . . as having for its principal subject the sensations and opinions of a poet living in retirement."[1] Whatever the motivation—"the burden of the past" or "the anxiety of influence"—there were early spurts of poetic energy toward a master work, but the poem, despite the constant urging of Coleridge and other friends, was never completed. Gill's terse reminder is instructive: "Only two things are certain. The philosophical poem conceived in 1798 was to be entitled *The Recluse*. It was never completed, nor did Wordsworth ever publish a poem called *The Recluse*."[2]

A middle section of the epic, *The Excursion*, to be discussed later, was published in 1814. Somewhat ironically, as a test of his qualifications, he was led to write an introductory poem, a prelude, recording the origin and development of his poetic powers, and that poem

---

[1] Preface to the 1814 *Excursion* in *Prose Works* 3:5.
[2] *Wordsworth: A Life*, p. 144.

has become his masterpiece. What, according to the preface to *The Excursion*, was to be the "Ante-chapel" to "the body of a Gothic church" became the church itself. Its evolution, a matter of considerable debate among readers and critics, admirers and non-admirers of the several versions, stretches over a period of some fifty years—1799 to 1850—and the edition was published after Wordsworth's death. Known to his family and friends as "the poem to Coleridge" and described by Coleridge himself as "a Poem on the Growth of an Individual Mind," the title was finally chosen by his wife, Mary.[3]

And a remarkable poem it is, as man-poet struggles to define himself, to locate himself in both literary and larger worlds. It is also another example of the poet's moving in new directions. Having committed himself to a poetry of real men and women speaking a natural language of feeling, here, as in *Tintern Abbey* especially, we find a poetry of the inner life written by a poet struggling to find his essential self, to explore those psychic moments from earliest childhood that have made him what he is. We are reminded of Lawrence Lipking's fine phrase about the poet's life as that which "has passed through a refining poetic fire."[4] A debate has developed, especially during the last twenty-five years, concerning which of the two major versions—1805 or 1850—is the greater aesthetic success, but this book is really not a part of that exchange.[5] For me, the debate only reinforces my continuing argument that Wordsworth's poetry enacts dramatically a tension present in his life and work from the beginning; that the theory of two Wordsworths, as William Galperin has most recently argued, will simply not bear up under careful examination of the poems themselves.[6] Indeed, the evolution of *The Prelude* is itself witness to a poet anxious about his deeply naturalistic faith and yet concerned about the pull of the social, political, and religious dimensions of a larger reality.

Liberal or conservative, naturalistic or orthodox religious, the poem is epic to be sure—but, as noted by many, modern epic. Mov-

---

[3] See Dorothy Wordsworth, *Journals*, 1:96.

[4] *Life of the Poet*, p. 7.

[5] See "Waiting for the Palfreys: The Great *Prelude* Debate," *The Wordsworth Circle*, 17, No. 1 (1986).

[6] *Revision and Authority in Wordsworth: The Interpretation of a Career* (Philadelphia: University of Pennsylvania Press, 1989).

ing beyond the classical mythology of Homer and Virgil or the Christian vision of Milton, it is spacious spiritual autobiography, the epic rendering of a poetic life. The setting for the beginning of the work is Goslar; the date, late 1798; those present at the creation, Wordsworth and Dorothy. Whether one speaks of a two-book *Prelude* of 1799, a thirteen-book version of 1805, or the posthumously published *Prelude* of 1850, there is an ever-looming thesis: the dawning of a consciousness, the evolution of a soul, the exploration of a powerful bond between spirit and nature. Chronologically and psychologically our starting point is the lean, brilliant two-book *Prelude* begun in Germany during that bitterly cold winter when brother and sister were isolated from everything but their own intensely personal devotion to each other—a version that captures in miniature the progression from childhood paradise to the first flickerings of loss. And we arrive finally at a poem in which that excursion into the inner life becomes part of a larger world—Revolution in France, the noise and turbulence of London, and the shattering of youthful political and social idealism.

The play of what Herbert Lindenberger has called "the resources of both the inspiration and the conscious will"[7] is evident from the beginning. Wordsworth is widening his engagement with nature, his confidence in nature's education of the human heart, and he is also responding to a quite conscious need to be the personal poet of "prophetic utterance" engaged in a massive epic plan.[8] That tension is evident in the development of Wordsworth's poetic plan as *The Recluse* becomes increasingly an effort of will, one never to be realized, and the introductory *Prelude* becomes his preoccupation.

Yet even in the structure of *The Prelude* itself the tension is revealed, as the original plan—the first four books and the present conclusion plus some selected passages—gives way to a much larger work in which the personal voice is enveloped in social commentary, political rhetoric, even sentimental piety. Extremely fertile are Lindenberger's observations that "what goes on in the poem is a constant flight from the subjectivity of private experience to the

---

[7] *On Wordsworth's Prelude* (Princeton, N.J.: Princeton University Press, 1963), p. 112.

[8] Ibid., p. xiii.

assertion of publicly communicable and valid truths"[9] and that this public tone "eventually becomes the basis for a new rhetoric, one that left no room for introspection and that could quite comfortably take up the public role which his later duties of poet laureate demanded."[10] Jerome McGann, some twenty years later, points to one pronounced way of dealing with aspects of the problem not only in Wordsworth but in Romanticism in general. Complaining about the "Romantic ideology," simplistic and naïve in the extreme, he asks for a criticism that will "return poetry to a human form—to see what we read and study as poetic works produced and reproduced by numbers of specific men and women."[11] And while McGann himself has his own ideological biases, he has clearly led the way to the New Historicist impulse in such contemporary theorists as James Chandler, Marjorie Levinson, Alan Liu, and Clifford Siskin, emphasizing the importance of locating Wordsworth in the complexities of the French Revolution and its political ramifications. This impulse, which I often find extreme in its argument that evasion is the source of the sublimation in the poetry, nevertheless needs our continuing attention.

It is important to study the posture of the speaker as the poem opens. The voice is, of course, epic; the tone and language, elevated. The Muse is not some classical god or goddess, not the Holy Spirit, but another power. The speaker is not some remote, austere Bard, but a self-conscious poet speaking naturally, openly, vulnerably. He seems most in tune with the natural forces around him, a "free" man having "escaped / From the vast city, where I long had pined / A discontented sojourner."[12] But freedom is not an unmixed blessing as he savors the delight of "this gentle breeze." What to do with it? Where to find a vantage point? Adam and Eve-like, he observes that "The earth is all before me" and "shaken off, / That burthen of my own unnatural self." Still, the unshackled ego, the gift of freedom felt in nature's warm breezes, would go for naught unless the speaker "felt within / A correspondent breeze" beginning gently and with a "virtue" or power that is "quickening" and now felt as "A

---

[9] Ibid., p. 5.
[10] Ibid., p. 9.
[11] *Romantic Ideology*, pp. 159–160.
[12] See my earlier reference (chap. 1, note 4) to the Norton edition of *The Prelude*.

tempest, a redundant energy," a powerful, even extravagant force. The breeze without and the breeze within are now co-conspirators, collaborators, "congenial powers" that break up a "long-continued frost" and bring "vernal promises" of things to come.

As the interaction of mind and nature continues to be examined, scenario is important. As "poetic numbers" come, as the poet assumes a priestlike stance—"A renovated spirit singled out"—he comes on an autumn day "To a green shady place, where down I sate / Beneath a tree," a place warmed "from a sun / Two hours declined toward the west," a place of "A perfect stillness." In a mystical mood, the poet "mused" for a time, not rising "till the sun / Had almost touched the horizon; casting then / A backward glance upon the curling cloud / Of city smoke"—again, that recurring image of light fading.

The poet, now "a Pilgrim resolute," returns to "the chosen Vale" of Grasmere, resolved to create, to—as David Simpson would have it—"figure the real."[13] As Milton did, in quest of what to write about, he welcomes the "light" that "Dawns from the east," only "to disappear / And mock me with a sky that ripens not / Into a steady morning." The mind struggles for some noble theme in the midst of "unruly times," "Unmanageable thoughts." He has "that first great gift, the vital soul," and does not lack "general Truths" or "external things," yet a subject matter continues to elude him as he eliminates one possibility after another—a Miltonic romance, a chivalric tale, the adventures of Mithridates, Odin, Sertorius, Dominique De Gourges, Wallace (1.1–220).

Yet, even with a rich fund of material, "Sometimes it suits me better to invent / A tale from my own heart, more near akin / To my own passions and habitual thoughts" or to feel a "yearning toward some philosophic song / Of Truth that cherishes our daily life." To write about oneself while staying in touch with a larger reality—this is the inevitable dilemma for the poet at a turning point. To write now or to wait in the hope "That mellower years will bring a riper mind / And clearer insight"—which way to move? With more than a touch of self-indictment—"Thus my days are past / In contradic-

---

[13] *Wordsworth and the Figurings of the Real* (Atlantic Highlands, N.J.: Humanities Press, 1982), p. xi.

tion"—and with sharp echoes not only of the Parable of the Talents but more sharply of *Lycidas*—"Ah! better far than this, to stray about / Voluptuously through fields and rural walks" and "Like a false steward who hath much received / And renders nothing back"—he is driven to write about himself, remembering and inspired by the music of the Derwent River of his boyhood (1.221–269).

Vivid early memories of purely physical bliss follow hard upon the large questions about the poetic life. Five years old, the child "Made one long bathing of a summer's day; / Basked in the sun, and plunged and basked again," stood alone, like some primitive, "Beneath the sky, as if I had been born / On Indian plains, and from my mother's hut / Had run abroad in wantonness, to sport / A naked savage, in the thunder shower" (1.290–300). His imagination caught by the idea of his origins, his development, he begins the process of rescuing from his past certain islands of light that shaped his spirit. The first two books form a crucial unit as he describes his non-academic, poetic *paideia*, his awe in the presence of nature, the development of his imagination, and the interaction of mind and nature. It is this interaction that is distinctive and that has been noted by critics early and late. William Hazlitt, Wordsworth's contemporary, described the poet's *Excursion* as "less a poem on the country, than of the love of the country," as "not so much a description of natural objects, as of the feelings associated with them." He does not simply present his reader with "a lively succession of images and incidents, but paints the outgoings of his own heart, the shapings of his own fancy."[14] Geoffrey Hartman seems to echo Hazlitt as he says that "Wordsworth cannot be said to discover nature as such but rather the reality of the relation between nature and mind."[15]

It is as if for the Wordsworth of this time life can be captured and recounted only imaginatively, that events must and can be rendered only poetically. Indeed, it is as if there is at root an essential literariness to the life. Imbedded in all this is a theory of biography, of autobiography: that no life can stand by itself for the artist, that

---

[14] "Observations on Mr. Wordsworth's Poem The Excursion," *Complete Works of William Hazlitt*, 4:112.
[15] *Wordsworth's Poetry* p. 170.

it needs the realities, of course, but it needs, much more urgently, the organizing, coloring powers of mind to dramatize them, to see and feel their complexities and nuances. "Of course," says Lipking, "poets share the human lot. But the great poet also makes his own destiny; he makes it, precisely, with poems."[16] And for Wordsworth in the late 1790s and early 1800s, there was just enough egotism, just enough faith in the literary imagination to outweigh—some would say, evade—the persistent and insistent claims of the great world beyond.

The opening book is, of course, constructed around a series of "spots of time," moments when the mind enters into a deeper union with a spirit in nature, moments which literally possess a "renovating virtue," a power to make us new and, in the process, to nourish. These are not the sentimental episodes of popular Romanticism, a day by the ocean, a walk in the sun, a joyous exploration of a starry sky. For every joy there is a corresponding fear; for every moment of exhilaration there is a corresponding doubt and anxiety. The poem not only rescues, but also revivifies those moments as the poet recalls, "Fair seed-time had my soul, and I grew up / Fostered alike by beauty and by fear" (1.301–302). These are moments when the mind is its own place, when it intuits value, when seeing gives way to vision. There is the night when, roaming the mountains, he plunders a nest only to feel that "when the deed was done / I heard among the solitary hills / Low breathings coming after me" (1.321–323). Or there is the bravado of the boy stealing a boat on a summer evening, rowing out under cover of darkness as "my boat / Went heaving through the water like a swan" (1.375–376). Long after his youthful terror and his hasty return to the shore, his mind for days "Worked with a dim and undetermined sense / Of unknown modes of being" (1.392–393). Or there is the excitement of a youthful ice-skating episode as the skater wheels wildly, to the point of dizziness, only to stop short, "yet still the solitary cliffs / Wheeled by me— even as if the earth had rolled / With visible motion her diurnal round! / . . . Till all was tranquil as a dreamless sleep" (1.458–463). These "spots of time" are deeply physical, yet in each episode sensation precedes vision, form penetrates image.

---

[16] *Life of the Poet*, p. ix.

Interestingly, the intensely vital, sharply narrative and dramatic voices yield to a more public, almost oracular, voice that would offer a lesson learned from the episode that for some readers speaks eloquently for itself. After the nest-robbing scene, Wordsworth, with no dramatic difference between the 1805 and the 1850 versions, proclaims the power of "a dark / Inscrutable workmanship that reconciles / Discordant elements, makes them cling together / In one society" (1.342–344). That same, more public voice intervenes after the boat-stealing experience, and addresses the "Wisdom and Spirit of the universe! / Thou Soul that art the eternity of thought" as a force that "from my first dawn / Of childhood didst . . . intwine for me / The passions that build up our human soul" (1.401–407). The skating scene is climaxed by an apostrophe to "Ye Presences of Nature in the sky / And on the earth! Ye Visions of the hills!" and to their "ministry" (1.464–468). The active, intense pre-teenager, absorbed in the sights and sounds, lakes and mountains, sea and sky in his childhood haunts, already has intimations of something transcendent, already is maturing in his response to nature's physical pleasures and in how they "by invisible links / Were fastened to the affections" (1.611–612). The poet of 1798–1799, conscious of a listening Coleridge prodding him to get on with his epic mission, hopes his *Prelude* will be a spur "To honourable toil," yet is not too afraid to indulge himself, to express a sadness in putting aside "recollected hours," "visionary things," "sweet sensations that throw back our life, / And almost make remotest infancy / A visible scene, on which the sun is shining," to wish that "This labour will be welcome, honoured Friend" (1.626–647).

Book 2 moves from childhood to adolescence and an even deeper awareness of a reality beyond the physical, and especially of the growing power of mind. It is an awareness of "Two consciousnesses, conscious of myself / And of some other Being" (2.32–33). The poetry enlivens so many youthful pleasures already mentioned— trips to the islands of Windemere, holidays and journeys on horseback to the stone circle at Swinside, to Furness Abbey, and the peace of the inland valley, strawberries and cream at the White Lion Inn in Bowness, the return over the lake to Hawkshead as "the calm / And dead still water lay upon my mind" and "the sky, / Never before so beautiful, sank down / Into my heart, and held me like a dream!" (2.170–174).

Pleading ignorance of technical psychological explanation, the kind Coleridge would be familiar with, the narrator will not "parcel out / His intellect by geometric rules," will recognize the "Hard task, vain hope, to analyse the mind" (2.203–228). He will, instead, appeal to the infant's delight in the pleasures of a mother as a paradigm of the deeper pull of the child toward a force in nature, a capacity both to receive and to give, "Working but in alliance with the works / Which it beholds." Significant for the argument of this study, Wordsworth records the first dawning of a "Poetic spirit," in only a few chosen ones "Through every change of growth and of decay, / Pre-eminent till death" (2.259–265). Early on in his spiritual autobiography, the poet is sharpening the problem of sustaining a creative spirit, a kinship with the maternal, life-giving forces of nature in the light of the toll taken by time.

In the midst of this account of his deepening education in the workings of nature comes Wordsworth's great tribute to the power of imagination, not as "analytic industry," but rather as "creative agency." As in the prose, so in the poetry Wordsworth's discussion is always less technical, but no less insightful, no less powerful in what it attributes to the mind. Mind is free, with a direction of its own, yet conscious of "the regular action of the world." But it is not subdued by that world. Again the play of faith in the workings of the inner life and the presence of the world beyond is evident. He celebrates imagination as "A plastic power," "a forming hand, at times / Rebellious, acting in a devious mood." It is "at war / With general tendency, but, for the most, / Subservient strictly to external things / With which it communed." Still, the seeming tension, even contradiction, continue as he speaks of imagination as "An auxiliar light . . . which on the setting sun / Bestowed new splendour." It holds in its power and bestows further blessings on "birds," "breezes," "fountains," even the "midnight storm" (2.359–376).

Arguments about 1839 and later textual revision granted, the poet's faith in nature remains essentially unchanged over a period of forty-five years. In 1805 the speaker celebrates the "joy" of seeing "in all things" one life (2.429–430). In 1850 there is joy in being part of a creation that "looked / Towards the Uncreated with a countenance / Of adoration, with an eye of love" (2.412–414). Yet a comparison of a five-line section that follows shows no change whatever: "If, mingling with the world, I am content / With my own modest pleasures, and have lived / With God and Nature communing, removed / From little enmities and low desires, / The gift is yours" (2.428–432).

With the essential features of Wordsworth's coming-of-age established—the development of a richly imaginative life close to nature, a life seemingly sufficient in itself—the poem moves toward a collision of private and public. And collision it is, for after a certain initial seductiveness in the lure of a great university, the excitement of a country nearby exploding with the enactment of democratic ideals, the distractions of a great city, there follows a certain emptiness, even despair at the failure of any of these to correspond to the cravings of the mind. And yet they are always reckoned with, always seen as part of a larger, insistent reality.

Books 3–8 deal with the years at Cambridge, years of disappointing formal education. One gets the sense of high expectations as the young man from the Lake District goes up to university after leaving the Hawkshead School he loved so dearly: "My spirit was up, my thoughts were full of hope." With a touch of self-mockery, he sketches his own self-importance in the midst of friends a few years his senior—"to myself I seemed / A man of business and expense, and went / From shop to shop about my own affairs" (3.18–27).

There is a remarkable candor in his poetic self-dramatization, his sense of being an outsider in a world of sophistication: "I was the Dreamer, they the Dream; I roamed / Delighted through the motley spectacle. / . . . Migration strange for a stripling of the hills, / A northern villager." And yet, as suggested earlier, he is caught up in the world of Cambridge and not always unwillingly so. As "weeks went roundly on," he seems to have enjoyed the "invitations, suppers, wine and fruit." With the "Evangelist St. John" as "my patron," and "Trinity's loquacious clock" a neighbor to his "nook obscure" above the college kitchen, and the "pealing organ" his nightly musical companion, he felt at least in part a citizen of a new community. Yet sparer images of community give way to the richer, more pregnant revision of 1850, an image of the poet's aloneness in the midst of everything. We imagine the young student looking from his bedroom to the antechapel "where the statue stood / Of Newton with his prism and silent face, / The marble index of a mind for ever / Voyaging through strange seas of Thought, alone" (3.30–63).

It is in the last two lines of the Newton image, added in 1838–1839, that we find a genuine insight into the hustle and bustle of the lines that follow, lines that capture the "College labours," the "loyal students," "hardy recusants," "honest dunces," "Examinations, when the man was weighed / As in a balance," "excessive hopes," "small jealousies" and that set down squarely the poet's attitude: "Such glory was but little sought by me, / And little won," and "more than all, a strangeness in the mind, / A feeling that I was not for that hour, / Nor for that place" (3.64–82).

And yet these years must not be seen as ones of either personal or social deprivation, for, if they brought disappointment about Cambridge, they also brought a deepening sense of the natural beauties around the university and of the sublime settings experienced on summer vacations in Hawkshead or in France and Switzerland. It was close to nature that his real education took place, and he describes it in what amounts to religious terms, or, as David Ferry puts it, in mystical terms.[17] "I looked for universal things; perused / The common countenance of earth and sky: / Earth, nowhere unembellished by some trace / Of that first Paradise whence man was driven" (3.109–112).

Nature continues to be more than the things of the earth, isolated phenomena, detached beauties for the young man roaming the countryside. In both the 1805 and the 1850 texts, mind and nature are linked to form one life, a life rich and full. "To every natural form, rock, fruit or flowers, / Even the loose stones that cover the high-way, / I gave a moral life: I saw them feel, / Or linked them to some feeling: the great mass / Lay bedded in a quickening soul, and all / That I beheld respired with inward meaning" (3.130–135). How categorical the faith expressed in both 1805 and 1850 versions. Reassuring Coleridge that his theme to this point has been "What passed within me," he nevertheless feels confident that the poet's life is fit subject for "heroic argument" (3.175–184).

---

[17] Ferry sees Wordsworth moving beyond the "sacramental" to the "mystical," a "total rejection of mortal things, even of those things which perfectly demonstrate order" (*Limits of Mortality*, p. 159).

Yet all is not solemn for the young poet. College anxieties brought him closer to fellow students. When lonely "if a throng was near / That way I leaned by nature; for my heart / Was social, and loved idleness and joy" (3.232–236). Still, the imagination had its moments. The sense of "illustrious men" of the past was strong. Chaucer, Spenser, and Milton were his continuing classmates in whose company he felt a special pleasure. A remarkable chapter in Don Bialostosky's *Wordsworth, Dialogics, and the Practice of Criticism* contrasts the mystification of "Great Books" education in Alan Bloom's *The Closing of the American Mind* with Wordsworth's early idealization of Cambridge and his growing delight in a personal, individual kind of learning in which the mind is exercised and enlarged.[18] Wordsworth sounds almost like an educational philosopher at this point, an adviser to teachers and administrators as he ruminates on the importance of putting youthful energy to use. "Youth," he pleads, "should be awed, religiously possessed / With a conviction of the power that waits / On knowledge, when sincerely sought and prized / For its own sake" (3.390–393).

Book 4 opens almost jubilantly as the poet recalls the return to a Lakeland summer vacation. It is, however, epic jubilant, as speaker, setting, language, and imagery combine—"I overlooked the bed of Windemere, / Like a vast river, stretching in the sun" (4.5–6). He is home at last—Hawkshead—his "old Dame," Ann Tyson, and other mothers perusing him with pride, bracing walks, circling the lake. It is a special time of the day—here again Wordsworth's fascination with half-light as symbol of the erosion of childhood ecstasy: "The sun was set, or setting"; "evening soon brought on / A sober hour, not winning or serene." Yet, though dark and cold the air, it was as the face of a beloved's "is sweetest then / When sorrow damps it"; everything is touched "if the heart have fulness in herself." It is "the immortal soul with Godlike power" that touches the beauty of nature, enriches it, gives it deeper meaning. Whether 1805 or 1850, the text is the same, as an almost mystical experience is recorded. The poet seems like a blessed figure: "Gently did my soul / Put off her veil, and, self-transmuted, stood / Naked, as in the presence of her God" (4.142–152). Nature is still central for Wordsworth, but as

---

[18] Pp. 255–266.

part of a larger scenario, as a divine presence. In David Ferry's searching words, "nature can be for man a kind of symbol of eternity, for the absence of death, and can seem to such a person as Wordsworth to possess and exemplify an order superior to his own, because it can never be the victim of the final act of personal disorder, individual death."[19]

Ferry has, of course, made the classic argument for Wordsworth's love of aloneness, his hostility to whatever, human or otherwise, turns man's attention away from the beauty and life-giving power of nature. Yet despite Ferry's skepticism about the poet's axiom that love of nature leads to love of man, there is certainly persuasive evidence to the contrary in this summer-vacation episode. We read of "A freshness also found" "In human Life," of his missing the presence of an old man, the presence of babies and of growing girls. The ways of "plain-living people"—the quiet woodsman, the shepherd, his "grey-haired Dame" working, reading her Bible, attending church—all of these seem to hold his attention and to generate in him a "human-heartedness." Here is that inevitable and characteristic Wordsworthian conflict as the preciousness of his inner life is challenged by signals of "mortality" from "the world of death," "Deep, gloomy," and "severe" (4.191–252).

Nowhere is the mind-reality struggle more succinctly and yet powerfully expressed than in the image of men too long separated "from our better selves" "by the hurrying world," and of the bliss that comes not with loneliness, but aloneness or "Solitude." He recalls such a time when after a day of "strenuous idleness," as light turns to dusk and all is "still," he spies on his way home—the poet-storyteller is strongly in evidence—"an uncouth shape" with long arms, "pallid his hands," mouth that looked "ghastly in the moonlight," "companionless." Watching and hearing the mutterings of a discharged veteran of the American wars, he greets the man and hears the grim story of his service and his return home. Like the Good Samaritan, the poet will not pass him by as others have, but beckons, "Come with me." Commending the lost soul to the care of a cottager, and pleading with the man not to wander in the public road, he hears the soldier's plaintive "My trust is in the God of

---

[19] *Limits of Mortality*, p. 28.

Heaven, / And in the eye of him who passes me!" (4.352–459), and offers thanks to his benefactors.

From the opening pages of this study I have stressed that, contrary to the popular view of Romanticism in general and Wordsworth in particular, books are an important part of the poet's life. From his early days in his father's library, to his training at Hawkshead School and the extracurricular reading while at Cambridge, books are not the "dull and endless strife" expressed by the speaker of "The Tables Turned." While the young poet in a range of poems sets formal education against learning close to nature, the rhetoric of such binaries always seem clear. The human heart is shaped by both nature and books. To this point nature has been his primary teacher, yet man has "wrought, / For commerce of thy nature with herself, / Things that aspire to unconquerable life." Yet, unlike the speaker-poet of Shakespeare's sonnets, this speaker feels that books "must perish" or at least become obsolete. Why, he questions, must the spirit "lodge in shrines so frail" (5.1–49)?

In the midst of his puzzlement over the fragility of books, he recalls the wistful smile of a friend who had also felt the wonder. The poet recalls a quiet summer noon when, in a rocky cave by the ocean, he sat reading *Don Quixote* and musing on the matter so intensely that he fell asleep and dreamed. It is a haunting dream of an Arab—"A lance he bore, and underneath one arm / A stone, and in the opposite hand, a shell, / Of a surpassing brightness." Puzzled, the dreamer questions the Arab, and learns that the stone is Euclid's *Elements*, geometry, a science of measurements, exactitude. The other, the shell "Is something of more worth," and, holding it to his ear at the Arab's behest, he hears and understands, although in an "unknown tongue," a "loud prophetic blast of harmony; / An Ode, in passion uttered, which foretold / Destruction to the children of the earth, / By deluge, now at hand." Reassured that all would happen as predicted, he hears that the Arab will bury the two books, the stone of reason, the shell of poetry. Eager to stay close to the Arab, the poet cannot keep pace as the knight gives a troubled look back over the wilderness, half of which is covered with "A bed of glittering light." Asked the meaning, he replies that it is "the waters of the deep / Gathering upon us" (5.78–140). Armageddon, or the violent reverberations from France, or perhaps a poetic evasion of history?

Waking in terror, he sees the sea and the book he had been reading. Not a spot of time, but a memory, the dream often became a reality for the poet.

Books often prove more formative and influential than the educational theories that proposed to train the young. Wordsworth matches his infant prodigy, the product of "unnatural growth," worthy of "pity," against his Winander boy already considered earlier. Trained far from the theorists, if trained at all, this boy is nature's own, participating in her beauty, sharing her life, and finally taken to her by death. Time takes its toll, but the poet will still contend with it, will still find ways to affirm that the reality of death can be overcome. Turning to the village church, he imagines it "forgetful of this Boy" and of children who were "real," his own classmates, "yielding not to the happiest upon earth." With a prayerful wish, he pleads for such creatures, asks for blessings on them: "May books and Nature be their early joy, / And knowledge, rightly honoured with that name— / Knowledge not purchased by the loss of power!" (5.293–425). Fine ingredients for the poetic life!

Almost abruptly, the scene shifts to another memory, this one of a day in the Vale of Esthwaite at twilight when he spied on the opposite shore a heap of garments, apparently those of a swimmer, that, after a long watch, still lay unclaimed. Reality followed imagining the next day in a ghastly scene as crowds gather and searchers probe until "At last, the dead man, 'mid that beauteous scene / Of trees and hills and water, bolt upright / Rose, with his ghastly face, a spectre shape / Of terror." Yet, says the poet, the scene brought "no soul-debasing fear," for, since he had roamed "the forests of romance" in a literary life, the spectacle has been tempered by books and has received a "decoration of ideal grace; / A dignity, a smoothness, like the works / Of Grecian art, and purest poesy" (5.426–459). It is an effect approaching the catharsis of Greek tragedy. Fictions of all kinds nourished his childhood and gave him friends among their writers. Fiction makers, often seen as charlatans by the "ape / Philosophy," are for Wordsworth leaders in a new defense of literature; they "make our wish, our power, our thought a deed, / An empire, a possession" (5.525–529). Theirs is not DeQuincey's literature of knowledge, but a literature of power. And it is a "visionary power," attending "the motions of the viewless winds" and "Embodied in the mystery of words" (5.595–597).

Summer vacation ended—natural beauties, "Frank-hearted maids," "nights of revelry" only memories—he returns to Cambridge, although he is still the reluctant student unwilling to compete for honors or to follow the college regimen. He lived "more to myself," and felt "The Poet's soul was with me at that time," with hopes still unrealized for the completion of *The Recluse*, but with his sense of a literary life more sharply defined. His pleasure was more in his imaginative environs than in the academic and social whirl. By winter night he walked "the College groves / And tributary walks," and by "the single tree," an echo of the *Immortality Ode*, "Often have I stood / Foot-bound uplooking." Spenser himself could hardly have had "more tranquil visions in his youth" (6.1–94). It was a time of reflection, of speculation about language, about geometry, about ultimate causes, "Supreme Existence," "God" (6.115–141).

This is also the time when, after a nine-year separation, his sister Dorothy is "restored" to him, a "gift." Together they visit the beauteous environs of Brougham Castle near Penrith, and, like characters in a poetic drama, peer through Gothic windows at a landscape "by the light of morning beautiful." It was also the time when that other "maid," Mary Hutchinson, whom Wordsworth first met in infant school days, enters the drama. It is a splendid cast of characters; even Coleridge, far away "in search of health / And milder breezes," in his absence seems a part (6.198–241). Wordsworth's concern for his friend and fellow poet is genuine, something to keep in mind as we look ahead to the painful break between the two friends in 1810.

A third summer vacation brings him and his friend Robert Jones to Europe for walking and climbing the Alps. His motives are deeply personal—"But Nature then was sovereign in my mind"—and also political—"Europe at that time was thrilled with joy, / France standing on the top of golden hours, / And human nature seeming born again" (6.339–341). For Alan Liu, "a tourist in Wordsworth's mold is a historical man who, as soon as he spots scenery, thinks himself primitive and original." His vigorous New Historicist reading contends that the Book 6 account of the 1790 tour, "read in its own context, is a sustained effort to deny history by asserting nature as the separating mark constitutive of the egotistical self," that the purpose of the book is "to prevent the self from looking through nature to underlying history."[20] Yet Wordsworth and Jones, arriving in France the day before the anniversary of the fall of the Bastille and the king's acceptance of a new constitution, seemed to catch the spirit of the great Fête de la Fédération in Paris, seeing "How bright a face is worn when joy of one / Is joy for tens of millions" (6.348–349). Moving south in France, then to Switzerland, Italy, and Germany on a trip already described in our earlier recounting of the poet's *Descriptive Sketches*, he found "benevolence and blessedness / Spread like a fragrance everywhere" (6.357–358) and strength, "To feed a Poet's tender melancholy / And fond conceit of sadness" (6.365–367). Joining groups, breaking bread together, dancing "round and round the board," "we bore a name / Honoured in France, the name of Englishmen, / And hospitality did they give us hail, / As their forerunners in a glorious course" (6.400–405).

On to the convent of the Grande Chartreuse, a place of "awful *solitude*" later to be violated by the forces of revolution. Wordsworth, still young and relatively innocent of the darkest revolutionary impulses, dramatizes in additions to the poem Nature's cry of "Stay, stay your sacrilegious hands!" but responds with "Honour to the patriot's zeal!" "spare / These courts of mystery" (6.419–451).

On that very day, Jones and he first caught sight of Mont Blanc with the magnificent Vale of Chamouny below. The power of history is met by the mysterious forces of nature, and Wordsworth is captivated, as Shelley later would be, by the mountain. The physical sight is overpowering, sublime, yet the deeper lesson of human brotherhood is eagerly read from the book of nature. It is the Simplon Pass episode, describing vividly "how different a sadness Would issue." Eager to realize the imagination's dream of crossing the Alps, the travelers and their guide, following a band of muleteers, begin their symbolic climb. It is as if physical energy and effort struggle to match the power of the imagination's picture. A brief stop for a meal is a prelude to the final ascent, but they become separated from their fellow climbers. Puzzled, frustrated, they meet a peasant who informs them *"that we had crossed the Alps"* (6.560–591).

As in his earlier recording of apocalyptic experiences, the poem

---

[20] *Wordsworth: The Sense of History*, pp. 12–13.

rises to more formal statement, in this case a lyrical, rather than a technical, tribute to the power of Imagination. Psychological terminology is inadequate; only metaphor and symbol can catch some of its ultimate mystery. It is, says the poet, an "awful Power" that "rose from the mind's abyss / Like an unfathered vapour that enwraps, / At once, some lonely traveller." Previously "lost," he now celebrates his creative power, the moment "when the light of sense / Goes out, but with a flash that has revealed / The invisible world" (6.594–602). Rising to an even more formal level of discourse, he, in 1850 as in 1805, takes on the poetic mantle to proclaim:

> Our destiny, our being's heart and home,
> Is with infinitude, and only there;
> With hope it is, hope that can never die,
> Effort, and expectation, and desire,
> And something evermore about to be (6.604–608).

The return to the foot of the mountain is the return to the real, the familiar. Indeed, the descent reveals a landscape on the order of Thomas Weiskel's Romantic sublime—"The immeasurable height / Of woods decaying," "The stationary blasts of waterfalls," "Winds thwarting winds," "Black drizzling crags that spake by the way-side / As if a voice were in them," "Tumult and peace, the darkness and the light"—all of these (Milton comes to mind) "Characters of the great Apocalypse, / The types and symbols of Eternity" (6.624–640). As Weiskel has it, "In both Kant and Wordsworth the sublime conducts us, as it were, to the frontiers of the 'invisible world,' but leaves us as soon as that world is consciously represented or given any positive content."[21]

The mystical moment ended, the journey continues to Lake Locarno, Como whose beauty is as quickening—with no difference in 1805 and 1850 texts—as "when God, the giver of all joy, is thanked / Religiously, in silent blessedness" (6.685–686). At Gravedona, mistakenly rising at the tolling of the church clock to moonlight, they become lost, and, sitting on a rock, wait for the light. They keep a Gothic vigil in a mysterious darkness. Still expectant, hopeful, ideal-

---

[21] *The Romantic Sublime: Studies in the Structure and Psychology of Transcendence* (Baltimore and London: The Johns Hopkins University Press, 1986), p. 43.

istic, he returns home, with threats of war stirring and yet with no overt social or political involvement on his part. The spirit of youth was his, and "new delights / Spread round my steps like sunshine o'er green fields" (6.777–778).

Recalling at the beginning of Book 7 the "Six changeful years" that have passed since the two-part *Prelude* of 1799 and its preamble of 1798, and again apologizing to Coleridge for his many delays, he recalls how sitting at home at twilight he feels a revival of joy, a desire to sing again. Twilight deepens, yet in its midst he spies a "glow-worm" "Clear-shining, like a hermit's taper seen / Through a thick forest." The silence touches him no less than the power of sound before; the collision of sound and touch is intriguing, and once again skewed light plays its role in the framing of a vision of experience in which joy and sorrow, loss and gain, impotence and creativity are intertwined. And still again, wonderfully synaesthetic images reverse the previous process. Now a nocturnal joy and geniality envelop a grove and spur it to toss in sunshine "its dark boughs aloft." The wind of inspiration has prevailed, and, lethargy and procrastination conquered, he reassumes his role as poet (7.1–45).

Bidding farewell to Cambridge with a routine B.A., he is happy, but still anxious about his choice of life. Like so many young men and women in any age, he is eager to know how to put his gifts to use and yet needs time to plot a course of action. And like so many, he goes to the big city, London. How different the reality from the dreams "Of your green groves, and wilderness of lamps / Dimming the stars, and fireworks magical, / And gorgeous ladies, under splendid domes, / Floating in dance, or warbling high in air / The songs of spirits!" Or of the great public sights—"The River proudly bridged; the dizzy top / And Whispering Gallery of St. Paul's; the tombs / Of Westminster; the Giants of Guildhall" (7.122–136). The poet now addresses the city: "Rise up, thou monstrous ant-hill on the plain / Of a too busy world" (7.149–150). And what a world it is, the "thickening hubbub" (7.211) of Chaos in *Paradise Lost*.

How struck he was by the performances of lawyers in the London courts or of statesmen like William Pitt the Younger, prime minister from 1783 to 1806. Yet there is no higher tribute to a public figure than that paid to Edmund Burke in the 1832 addition to the poem.

Burke, the great English standard bearer against the Revolution in France, certainly could not have brought joy to the younger poet, alive as Wordsworth was with Rousseauistic enthusiasm for the toppling of the *ancien regime*. James Chandler has relatively recently taken issue with the approaches of M. H. Abrams, Geoffrey Hartman, and others to the intellectual and political development of Wordsworth. Like Marjorie Levinson, Alan Liu, and other New Historicists, Chandler calls attention to Wordsworth's early experience of the Revolution and his interest in the political philosophy of Rousseau and Godwin. "By the time he wrote his contributions for the *Lyrical Ballads*," he contends, "Wordsworth had participated intellectually, socially, and politically in what was already recognized as the most momentous of modern revolutions."[22]

Now it is "Genius of Burke! forgive the pen seduced / By specious wonders," a tribute to the statesman whose *Reflections* saw the true underpinnings of a destructive spasm of change, the true motives of self-serving rebels. Wordsworth's rhetoric is that of the poet in search of a figurative rendering of a tribute. He sees Burke, "old, but vigorous in age,— / Stand like an oak whose stag-horn branches start / Out of its leafy brow, the more to awe / The younger brethren of the grove." And he celebrates Burke as he proclaims not just the beauty of individual freedom, but the stability and time-tested qualities "Of Institutes and Laws, hallowed by time," the glory of tradition, of moderate reform tempered by that tradition, "and with high disdain, / Exploding upstart theory, insists / Upon the allegiance to which men are born" (7.511–530). As early as his celebrated letter to Richard Watson, Bishop of Llandaff, a radical turned reactionary of the first order, Wordsworth had interested himself in and supported the dream of democracy in France. It is Chandler who has done most in plotting the impact of Burke, who has argued for him as the "presiding genius"[23] of *The Prelude*, even though "for a long time Wordsworth was unable to make any acknowledgement of his early adult thought."[24] Chandler views Burke as Llandaff's "surro-

---

[22] *Wordsworth's Second Nature*, p. 8.
[23] Ibid., p. xxi.
[24] Ibid., p. 11.

gate" in the letter, but further argues that "somewhere between 1793 and 1818" the poet turned away from the rationalism of Rousseau and Godwin to what he called the "second nature" of Burke.[25]

London is a city of contradictions. Now there is the echo of the Westminster Bridge sonnet as the mind collaborates with the external scene to create a richer reality, "the peace / That comes with might; the deep solemnity / Of nature's intermediate hours of rest, / When the great tide of human life stands still." Then there is half the city breaking out "Full of one passion, vengeance, rage, or fear" of "executions," "a street on fire, / Mobs, riots, or rejoicings." There is Bartholomew Fair: "What a shock / For eyes and ears! what anarchy and din." To the young poet it is a "blank confusion" for "thousands upon thousands of her song," yet, in spite of noise and turbulence, "The Spirit of Nature was upon me there" (7.650–770). London, for all its corruptions, has a kind of living, organic quality, like that of Nature itself, a power to mend those whose minds and hearts can encounter her spirit.

Book 8's very title, "Retrospect—Love of Nature Leading to Love of Man," has occasioned wide-ranging discussions among readers and critics not just of *The Prelude*, but also of the man and the poet himself. From those who read the title straightforwardly as reflecting a special progression from naturalism to humanism in Wordsworth, from a love of things of nature to a love of humankind, to those like David Ferry who question the facile progression and ultimately argue that Wordsworth was repelled by human beings in general and found his chief comfort only a mystical aloneness, the arguments have been wide-ranging. Fearful of taking an easy middle ground between the two positions, I nevertheless see an alternative position very much in keeping with the development of my thesis from the beginning: that is, that there existed from the beginning in

---

[25] Ibid., pp. 20–30. James Heffernan offers a different and interesting point of view on Burke and Wordsworth: "Burke's influence on Wordsworth's interpretation of the Revolution must certainly be recognized. Yet Burke's ideology cannot explain why Wordsworth invokes the myth of paradise to describe the way the world appeared to him and his fellow enthusiasts at the outbreak of the Revolution." See his "History and Autobiography: The French Revolution in Wordsworth's Prelude," in *Representing the French Revolution: Literature, Historiography, and Art*, ed. James A. W. Heffernan (Hanover, N.H.: Dartmouth College, University Press of New England, 1992), p. 50.

Wordsworth's life as translated into his art a deep tension between, on the one hand, the claims of a profound personalism, a deep love and nourishment of individual consciousness in the presence of the sights and sounds of nature and, on the other, the growing awareness of the claims of the outside world, the world of men, events, and institutions. It is, of course, to reject the easy and sentimental view that Wordsworth allied himself with the masses, with the beggars and children and war veterans who served as emblems of certain powerful qualities in human nature. There is little, if any, evidence of such alliances in the poetry. Wordsworth from the beginning was a relatively remote person, deeply devoted to nature, happy when close to presences of divinity whether in the remoteness of the Lake District or the uncharacteristically quiet moments of London and the larger world. Yet the more one reads, and *The Prelude* continues to be spiritual autobiography, the more one senses first evidences of the indispensability of friendship, the demands of the oppressed, the weak, the young, the need for some form of human community.

In this connection it is interesting to study in some depth the progression in Book 8 from love of nature to the love of man. Addressing Helvellyn on Grasmere Fair Day, he attributes a watchful eye to the mountain as he "with unshrouded head" oversees the "crowd," the "village green," "a little family of men, / Shepherds and tillers of the ground—betimes / Assembled with their children and their wives, / And here and there a stranger interspersed" (8.1–17). It is a day of excitement, with heifers lowing, merchants negotiating and selling, the lame and the blind begging and singing, speechmakers proclaiming, and "the loveliest of them all, / Some sweet lass of the valley," selling "Fruits of her father's orchard / . . . blushing restlessly." Here the little are great, the meek are blessed as "all things serve them" (8.37–63).

Nature and city are shapers of the poetic spirit, but it is to the natural setting of his Lakeland birthplace that he pays his ultimate tribute, writing of the almost paradisaical places of his childhood, "imperial bowers" that "leave behind a dance of images," and then of a time when the "common haunts of the green earth" and the "ordinary interests of man" summoned him as man and poet. Then comes a time when his affections move beyond immediate relatives and friends so that he could experience "Love for the human creature's absolute self" and could feel that "Shepherds were the men that pleased me first" (8.117–128). But these were not the shepherds of some Golden Age, those of Arcadia or Arden, but rather "of a life / Intent on little but substantial needs (3.161–162). In his mind's eye, he catches such a shepherd in and out of season, in weather fair or foul, most notably in a haunting image:

> suddenly my eyes
> Have glanced upon him distant a few steps,
> In size a giant, stalking through thick fog,
> His sheep like Greenland bears; or, as he stopped
> Beyond the boundary line of some hill-shadow—
> His form hath flashed upon me, glorified
> By the deep radiance of the setting sun:
> Or him have I descried in distant sky,
> A solitary object and sublime,
> Above all height! like an aerial cross
> Stationed alone upon a spiry rock
> Of the Chartreuse, for worship [8.264–275].

Such experiences ennobled man for the poet, "And thus my heart was early introduced / To an unconscious love and reverence / Of human nature" (8.277–279).

The 1805 and 1850 versions alike offer the grateful prayer of the poet, "But blessed be the God / Of Nature and of Man" (8.301–302). Yet nature remains his pre-eminent concern. Loitering in a grove by Coniston Water, shaded from the light of day, he watches admiringly "the golden beams of light / Flung from the setting sun, as they reposed / In silent beauty on the naked ridge / Of a high eastern hill" (8.463–466). Responding prayerfully, he praises the beauty of the scene, but in the spirit of emotion recollected in tranquillity, or, perhaps more accurately, emotion anticipated in tranquillity. Wherever he breathes his last, he will imagine this scene of light illuminating darkness, will look back, although the valley has darkened, and see the lingering power of the setting sun.

London is now regarded as a "Grave Teacher, stern Preceptress" (8.530), a place that awakened him to the larger world. No noise, voice, or folly of the great city could undermine a new "trust in what we *may* become" (8.650). Here he learns of his ignorance and, above all, of the self-indulgence and limitations of a solitary life, a young man of "vain conceits" and "dreams." Still playing on his fascination with light and darkness, he now sees a divinity in the scene, as the light is only enhanced by the darkness, and the mind is haunted, aroused, fascinated by the tension, the play of opposites. Like Adam, he feels "yet in Paradise / Though fallen from bliss, when in the East he saw / Darkness ere day's mid course, and morning light / More orient in the western cloud, that drew / O'er the blue firmament a radiant white, / Descending slow with something heavenly fraught" (8.650–664). Here he sees a unity, one spirit. In 1850, as in 1805, with the gift of such a vision, such an awareness of light in darkness, the soul feeds "On the pure bliss, and takes her rest with God" (8.675).

Wordsworth as narrator, again using the motif of the river, now brings his story to France, to his first visit, his sense of the place, his exposure to revolutionary fervor everywhere, his meeting with Michael Beaupuy and conversion to the spirit of change, his later disillusionment and near despair when the Revolution turned selfish and violent. Even as the river winds and turns and returns "Seeking the very regions which he crossed / In his first outset," so, he assures Coleridge, has his mind moved to this point in his poem. Or, as the climber, having gained the "aerial Down," catches his breath and surveys the scene he has just mastered, so has he reached a crucial point and would now assess his feelings. But "Now we start afresh / With courage, and new hope risen on our toil." On to new themes "how much unlike the past" (9.1–22).

The scenario moves from the literary side of London to the excitement and allure of France (he had known it first on his earlier trip with Jones), to Paris and its monuments—the Field of Mars, Montmartre, the Pantheon, sites of great revolutionary moment—as well as its other side "Of Tavern, Brothel, Gaming-House, and Shop, / Great rendezvous of worst and best" (9.54–55). Though he savors the experience, collecting a rock from the Bastille as a remembrance, it is LeBrun's painting of Mary Magdalene, with its power and sublimity, that especially catches his attention. Alan Liu is especially attentive to LeBrun's work, noting that "it bears interesting resemblances to a famous 'sublime' painting that Wordsworth probably did not see until 1806 but . . . read about in Reynolds's *Discourses* between July and December, 1804, possibly during his autumn work on Books 9 and 10: the Wilton-Beaumont version of Richard Wilson's *Destruction of Niobe's Children* (Pl.17)." "The *Repentant Magdalene*," argues Liu, "is like Wilson's painting in exposing beauty not to a Claudian but to a Salvadorean or Burkean setting—a landscape that suggests violation by rough forces."[26]

Wordsworth is a man trying to find a meaning in the midst of all the excitement, reading the literature of Revolution, listening to news reports, trying without success to find "A chronicle that might suffice to show / Whence the main organs of the public power / Had sprung" (9.101–103). As one so committed to what is "felt in the blood and felt along the heart" as a basis for faith and belief, he finds the "affections left / Without a vital interest" (9.106). But a "patriot" he did become, attracted by the courage and idealism of young military men like the earlier-mentioned Michael Beaupuy with whom he associated. Yet, looking back now, he recalls "universal ferment," a growing sense of men deceived, a mockery of "the past and that to come!" Seeing a land of passionate intensity, "like a plain / Devoured by locusts," men like Beaupuy were heading for the "borders of the Rhine" to join the Austrian and Russian forces ready to restore the monarchy (9.123–185). A Babel of wild rhetoric deafened him, and yet "in their weakness strong, I triumphed" (9.261–262).

The bravest saw the imperialist designs of the extreme radicals and were disillusioned, among them Beaupuy, the one who initially caught Wordsworth's fancy as he talked of reform, help for the poor and oppressed, and the opportunity to bring about a rule of the people instead of monarchic tyranny. It was along the banks of the Loire where Beaupuy died fighting, the poet remembers, that he spied the "hunger-bitten girl" and exclaimed with hope, " 'Tis against *that* / That we are fighting" (9.509–518).

Dramatically Wordsworth recalls the sad story told by Beaupuy and others at the time. It is the tale of Vaudracour and Julia (recorded at length in 1805, barely a cameo in 1850 after being published as a separate poem in 1820) and their tragic wooing, loving, and parting. As we read the poetic drama, we hear at many points Wordsworth's own unhappy story of himself, Annette, and Caroline.

---

[26] *Wordsworth: The Sense of History*, p. 371. See my "Reynolds and Wordsworth: The Development of a Post-Enlightenment Aesthetic," *European Romantic Review*, 3 (1992), 147–158.

Wordsworth sets before us a haunting picture of revolutionary force as Book 10 opens. Using his continuing favorite image to suggest the fading or the shading of beauty, he reimagines his leaving Orleans with its unspoken memories of Annette and his daughter. A beautiful day is "fading with unusual quietness" as he casts "a farewell look" and heads for the "fierce Metropolis" (10.10–11). The king is deposed and imprisoned on August 14, 1792, to be executed, and the invading armies of Austria and Prussia are turned back and retreat to the Rhine. The Republic is proclaimed, but only after "Lamentable crimes" (10.41) in the massacres of September 2–6, 1792. In a spectacular scene given the sharpest literary overtones, he conjures up images of upheaval and calm:

> For the spent hurricane the air provides
> As fierce a successor; the tide retreats
> But to return out of its hiding-place
> In the great deep; all things have second birth
> The earthquake is not satisfied at once;
> And in this way I wrought upon myself,
> Until I seemed to hear a voice that cried,
> To the whole city, "Sleep no more" [10.80–87].

Macbeth's world lives for the poetic imagination; history is not so much evaded as rendered dramatically.

Robespierre is charged and countercharged—Wordsworth followed events in the pamphlets of the time—only to achieve supreme power in July 1793. The Englishman would devote himself to the cause of opposition with a confidence in "One nature, as there is one sun in heaven" (10.158), in the "sovereign voice . . . within the soul, / Arbiter undisturbed of right and wrong" (10.183–184). Chandler is again a strong voice for the Burkean conservatism of Wordsworth, the importance of tradition, the power of social ties, the suspicion of theory. It is, he says, the "second nature" of Burke, the "moral wardrobe of the naked shimmering nature" of Rousseau that increasingly attracts the poet and in a way makes him "a more thoroughgoing traditionalist than Burke himself."[27]

---

[27] *Wordsworth's Second Nature*, p. xxii. James Heffermam again offers a different view: "For Wordsworth, revolutionary France briefly embodied the power to change the world radically, to make it universally just, free, and happy. In re-creating his

Back in England he expresses his strong allegiance to the Girondins killed or driven to suicide in the Paris debacle, dramatizing the ultimate and destructive radicalization of the Revolution, the blood-violence that, in the name of national security, turns against anyone not totally loyal. Dark, sinister forces take no prisoners; "Friends, enemies, of all parties, ages, ranks, / Head after head, and never heads enough / For those that bade them fall" (10.361–363).

Looking back to a time when the love of nature consumed him, he prays, with little significant difference between the 1805 and the 1850 texts, to the "great God" (1805, 10.385), "Power Supreme" (1850, 10.420), about the other, more selfish side of the love of man. In the midst of violence he understands the roots more clearly, confiding to Coleridge his dream or nightmare of the atrocities committed in the name of revolutionary humanism. Yet there were "Bright sprinklings of all human excellence" (10.484) in the midst of the savagery, as he recalls that hopeful first trip to France now controlled by a violent Robespierre and groaning "Under the vengeance of her cruel son, / As Lear reproached the winds" (10.505–507). Poet again turns to poet for his allusion.

Still confiding in Coleridge, he tells of his delight in the downfall of the power politicians on a special day for him. As he walks over the sands adjoining the estuary of the river Leven—he had been visiting cousins, at Rampside, a village facing Peele Castle— "beneath a genial sun" (10.516), he gazes at childhood haunts, paying a special visit to Cartmel Priory and the grave of his favorite Hawkshead teacher, William Taylor. Standing by that grave in the priory churchyard, the poet feels that Taylor would, like any caring teacher, have felt a sense of pride in knowing that the young student who in his class "Began to spin, with toil, my earliest songs" was now "not destitute / Of promise" (10.549–552). And his personal

---

experience of this power, Wordsworth foreshadows its violence and brutality from the beginning, but nowhere does he repudiate power itself. Instead, by inbedding the history of the French Revolution within a history of his own life, he sought to show why the power released by the Revolution had to pass from the world of politics where he 'was and must be of small worth' (10.192), to the world of poetry, where he could demonstrate his spiritually redemptive force" ("History and Autobiography: The French Revolution in Wordsworth's *Prelude*," *Representing the French Revolution: Literature, Historiography, and Art* [Hanover, N.H., and London: University Press of New England, 1992] p. 58).

joy in the vocation of poet is matched by the news he hears from travelers that "Robespierre is dead!"

Book 11 of the 1850 version—Book 10 of 1805—brings the French interlude to a conclusion. The Reign of Terror, closed by the guillotining of Robespierre and many of his followers, is followed by authority putting on a "milder face" (11.2). Disillusioned by the aberrations of the revolutionaries, he still holds to a trust in the people and to a faith that events in France might lead to a peaceful transition in England where the Pitt government had become increasingly repressive.

Returning to his own role, he takes the reader back to his early summer 1792 enthusiasm for the Revolution in some of his best-known and oft-quoted lines: "Bliss was it in that dawn to be alive, / But to be young was very Heaven!" For the youthful and idealistic poet of the time, "the whole Earth, / The beauty wore of promise." The goal of universal freedom was within reach for active partisans like Wordsworth and even for the more contemplative, but that goal was no longer in some distant "Utopia" but "in the very world, which is the world / Of all of us,—the place where, in the end, / We find our happiness, or not at all!" (11.105–144). Yet revolutionary dreams did not come true as "become oppressors in their turn, / Frenchmen had changed a war of self-defence / For one of conquest" (11.206–207). It was a time of attractive schemes, the kind Burke was to criticize so savagely, and of easy Godwinian rationalistic optimism. Wordsworth's continuing sense of the claims of the individual and those of the larger world is heightened, as he records his own initial response to schemes of betterment building "social upon personal Liberty" (11.240). Filled with expectation and hope, he pursued some ideal image of humankind and of human experience.

Anticipating the Solitary's loss of revolutionary hope in *The Excursion*, the poet describes his youthful confusion as he, "Sick, wearied out with contrarieties, / Yielded up moral questions in despair" (11.304–305). Plagued with this "strong disease," he turned from Godwinism to mathematics, with its freedom from "the disturbances of space and time." But, ever a presence in his life, Dorothy is his point of stability, his salvation. She "preserved" him as "a Poet," sustained him even through the cataclysm of a pope crowning Napoleon as emperor. In a curious, even grotesque variation on the image of skewed light, here the sun "That rose in splendor" not so much darkens as is transmogrified, "And, turned into a geegaw, a machine, / Sets like an Opera phantom" (11.306–369). Youthful dream has turned to nightmare.

Coleridge is very much a presence in the closing lines of Book 11, as Wordsworth reminds him that this story of the struggles of a young mind is clearly for his ear; on his way home from Malta, Coleridge is in Sicily. Though democracy flourished there after Timoleon drove the tyrant Dionysus the younger away, it is now a colony of the kingdom of Naples, and Wordsworth sees Coleridge mourning this fall from greatness as he mourns the ravages of upheaval in France. Courage will come, however; for "There is / One great society alone on earth: / The noble Living and the noble Dead" (11.392–394). He grieves for Coleridge far away, and plaintively, in half–light, pleads, "Oh! wrap him in your shades, ye giant woods" (11.417).

Restoration and renovation are the dominant themes of the final books, paradise regained through many agencies—the religious power of nature, the love and ministration of his sister and his wife, but, most of all, the continuing power of the "spots of time." He will not allow his epic song to end unhappily. It must conclude joyously. Nature has been a powerful restorative after his dark cynicism—"Ye motions of delight," "ye breezes and soft airs," "Ye waves," "ye groves"—and he pleads for the poetic gifts of a voice and a music as harmonious as hers "that I might tell / What ye have done for me." A brilliant image of light captures the power as "The morning shines, / Nor heedeth Man's perverseness; Spring returns,— / I saw the Spring return, and could rejoice" (12.9–33).

Recalling Mary Hutchinson at this point—they had married on October 4, 1802—as one who had escaped the tyranny of the senses, whose mind was not perplexed by "barren intermeddling subtleties" (12.155), he remembers his own previous purity of mind and responsiveness to the power of nature. And, in the midst of his despondency, he feels "visions of imaginative power," and stands in the presence of Nature, "as now I stand / A sensitive being, a *creative* soul." The poetic life has been preserved.

Written in 1799, the celebrated "spots of time" passage amplifies these "visitings." Recent New Historicist readings of the passage—indeed, of the concluding books in general—have taken issue with the traditional interpretation of Hartman and even with some of their own. Hartman contends that Wordsworth's "trust in Nature remains a trust in the human mind, which finds inexhaustible rewards in the world, and is renewed by natural rather than supernatural means."[28] James Chandler, with Burke as his hero, historicizes Wordsworth's restoration, seeing the "spots of time" as representing "the triumph not only of mental discipline, but also of discipline–as–tradition, a discipline grounded on what Burke calls prejudice." That Wordsworth could not destroy his traditionalism, Burke's "second nature, not even in the name of nature itself is 'proved' in *The Prelude* by the eventual emergence of the spots of time."[29] Alan Liu, accepting Chandler's basic premise that the doctrine of the "spots of time" was "indeed an ideology against ideology," goes on to suggest "that the influence behind such ideology was not only Burke's philosophy of prejudice applied against a specific French philosophy but also a pre-philosophical exercise of denial—an effort by the Imagination to contain the phenomenal event that most seized imagination at the time of composition."[30]

These and other interpretations have enriched the way we read the poem, with its account of the growth of the poet's mind and life. And yet it is the image of growth and development itself that commands even greater attention. The passage is a powerful account of how these "spots," these spatio-temporal experiences, "retain / A renovating virtue"—a re-creating, making-new power felt as early as childhood when "The mind is lord and master—outward sense / The obedient servant of her will" (12.209–223). To the earlier nest-robbing, boat-stealing, ice-skating episodes is now added another, even eerier episode, that of the Penrith Beacon. With one of his father's servants, Wordsworth, scarcely five years old, rode on horseback to the area around the Beacon, an eighteenth-century watchtower where lookouts stood at the ready for an invasion from across the channel. Becoming lost, he wanders and comes upon a clearing where a murderer had been hanged. "The gibbet-mast had mouldered down, the bones / And iron case were gone," yet on the ground

[28] *Wordsworth's Poetry*, p. 259.
[29] *Wordsworth's Second Nature*, p. 198.
[30] *Wordsworth: The Sense of History*, p. 395.

the initials of the murderer were carved. Spying them, he fled, only to experience a collage of scenes—"A naked pool that lay beneath the hills, / The beacon on its summit, and, more near, / A girl, who bore a pitcher on her head, / And seemed with difficult steps to force her way / Against the blowing wind." Ordinary phenomena, to be sure, but years later, the creative imagination, in rescuing them, finds a kind of sublimity rendered only as a "visionary dreariness" (12.208–262).

In lines following this episode, he articulates an ultimate faith. Both the 1805 and the 1850 versions affirm the power of mind and imagination to mold reality, to make value, to recover moments of childhood vision that can sustain us in age. Yet there are the same continuing qualifications, the same recognition of the demands of being human. He is "lost," yes, as he meditates on the "mystery of man," but sees "In simple childhood something of the base / On which thy greatness stands." Sounding like Coleridge, he is confident "that thou must give, / Else never canst receive." Saint Paul-like, seeing in a glass darkly, he speaks of the past returning, "the hiding-places of man's power / Open." But he sees only "by glimpses now" and is deeply conscious that "when age comes on, / May scarcely see at all." Hence his writer's commitment to give "as far as words can give, / Substance and life to what I feel, enshrining / Such is my hope, the spirit of the Past / For future restoration" (12.273–286). Hence his larger quest to find permanence in change.

Almost as an afterthought comes another remembrance intensely personal, an occasion for some sense of guilt. It is a poetic rendering of "One Christmas-time"—December 19, 1783, to be specific, and we have earlier recounted the story—as Wordsworth and his brothers, Richard and John, anxiously await the horses that will bring them home from Hawkshead School for family holidays. "Scout-like," he stands on a crag—on "a day / Tempestuous, dark, and wild." On December 30, before their return to school, their father died, and the poet and his brothers, "orphans then, / Followed his body to the grave," his death seeming a "chastisement" for their undue anxiety. In both 1805 and 1850 he speaks of bowing low to God "Who thus corrected my desires" whenever he recalls the episode. And the remembrance continues to be powerful.

Restoration of faith and renovation of spirit continue to be dominant themes in Book 13 (Book 12 of the 1805 text). Nature is the great benefactor, her gifts "emotion" and "moods of calmness." Out of the interchange come genius and a search to know the truth. At first "Benighted," but "the dawn beginning now / To re-appear," he now has a new faith in "A Power / That is the visible quality and shape / And image of right reason" calming the passions, the "busy dance / Of things that pass away" (13.1–31).

Separating himself—his words seem almost like an anticipatory rejoinder to the New Historicist—from "what the Historian's pen so much delights / To blazon—power and energy detached / From moral purpose," he finds "in Man an object of delight, / Of pure imagination, and of love" (13.42–50). Burke-like, he trusts a knowledge rooted in feeling that has stood a test of time, that sets the present against the larger perspective of the tradition, that eschews theoretical schemes—Adam Smith's *Wealth of Nations* is regarded as an "idol" (13.77)—that could not withstand the test of human experience.

Pausing in his recollections, setting down the course of a poet's life, he resolves to write about "a mere mountain chapel" and its "simple worshippers," about "substantial things," "rapture, tenderness and hope." His chief theme will be "No other than the very heart of man / As found among the best of those who live" (13.230–42). Wordsworth is clearly working out a poetic creed, a conviction that "the inner frame is good," that "Nature" has "power / To consecrate" the exterior of creatures and "to breathe / Grandeur upon the very humblest face / Of human life" (13.281–287). To Coleridge he affirms a confidence in his poetic gifts.

This new resolution triggers an almost mythic memory of a similar theme of commitment and dedication as he crossed Salisbury Plain in July or early August 1793, returning from the Isle of Wight to Wales without resources, separated from Annette, and unhappy as he saw the British fleet off Portsmouth preparing for a campaign against the French that went against all his ideals and hopes. Mythic to be sure, he envisions Time fleeing backward and beholds, "Our dim ancestral Past in vision clear." There are hordes of men, the rustle of spears. He "called on Darkness—but before the word / Was uttered, midnight darkness seemed to take / All objects from my sight." The desert is eerily lit by flames, "the sacrificial altar fed /

With living men—how deep the groans!" Roaming the plain, he sees "circles, lines, or mounds," evidences of the ancient Druids and their temples and observatories. In his waking dream he sees "long-bearded teachers, with white wands / Uplifted, pointing to the starry sky" (13.320–346).

Imagining a relationship with Coleridge at the time—they did not know each other well until 1797—he hears his friend praising the shaping capacity of his mind. He further recalls his vision of a "new world," one to be made real for others, a Burkean world "ruled by those fixed laws / Whence spiritual dignity originates," "The excellence, pure function, and best power / Both of the object seen, and eye that sees" (13.370–378). Once again the poet's quest for a reconciliation of subject and object.

Book 14 (13 in the 1805 version) again violates chronology in the interests of artistic form and vision. It revolves, of course, around the climbing of Mount Snowdon in Wales during the walking-tour Wordsworth and Jones made from June to August 1791. Its original position gave it a kind of final, climactic effect in the February 1804 five-book *Prelude*, and it takes the same position with the same effect in the 1805 and 1850 texts. It is in so many ways Wordsworth at his symbolic best, as landscape becomes the vehicle for describing his most deeply felt and envisioned convictions about his renovation, about the imagination as the nurturing power in his life, about the nature of art in general.

The episode seems to belong to the part of Wordsworth's literary life to be discussed when we consider the sonnets, songs, *Immortality Ode*, and other poems. On the one hand, he seems, at least on the surface, at his most confident about the power of mind to make meaning, about the life-giving power of nature and its guarantee of hope for immortality. On the other, reverberations of loss, of fading of vision, of death are there as well.

Wordsworth and Jones, like the boy in "Nutting," leave their hut at daybreak, move westward "to see the sun / Rise from the top of Snowdon" (14.5–6). As always the quest is for light, brightness as a guarantee of the mind's quest for immortality, eternality. Yet quickly juxtaposed against the quest for the sun is a brilliant, vividly realized picture of the darkness before the dawn, the mist that hides the light:

> It was a close, warm, breezeless summer night,
> Wan, dull, and glaring, with a dripping fog
> Low–hung and thick that covered all the sky;
> But, undiscouraged, we begin to climb
> The mountain–side. The mist soon girt us round" [14.10–15].

Again, with memories of the excited anticipation of the boy in "Nutting," we watch the excitement of the climber. Suddenly the poet becomes the painter, sketching a mystical setting—"at my feet the ground appeared to brighten, / And with a step or two seemed brighter still." More brightness around him, and then, suddenly, "The Moon hung naked in a firmament / Of azure without cloud, and at my feet / Rested a silent sea of hoary mist." Light illuminates darkness. Silence prevails "save that through a rift— / Not distant from the shore whereon we stood, / A fixed, abysmal, gloomy, breathing-place— / Mounted the roar of waters, torrents, streams, / Innumerable, roaring with one voice / Heard over earth and sea, and in that hour, / For so it seems, felt by the starry heavens" (14.35–62).

The vision faded, later the poet sees a meaning. It is, in the 1805 text, the symbol of a mind "that feeds upon infinity, / That is exalted by an under-presence, / The sense of God, or whatsoe'er is dim / Or vast in its own being" (13.70–73); and in the 1850 text, it is "the emblem of a mind / That feeds upon infinity, that broods / Over the dark abyss," "a mind sustained / By recognitions of transcendent power" (14.70–75). Seldom do we find Wordsworth, in either the poetry or the prose, speaking in such philosophical, almost Coleridgean, fashion. It is the mind's "mutual domination which she loves / To exert upon the face of outward things, / So moulded, joined, abstracted, so endowed / With interchangeable supremacy, / That men, least sensitive, see, hear, perceive, / And cannot choose but feel" (14.81–86).

In the spirit of the "Ode to Duty," Wordsworth continues. His story is modest, of "A humbler destiny," of "thorny ways" (14.136–138). Love is his chief source of strength—"That gone, we are as dust" (14.170). But there is "a still higher love," one "that adores, but on the knees of prayer, / By heaven inspired"—in 1805 proceeding "More from the brooding soul, and is divine" (13.165), and in 1850, in more overtly Christian terms, "Bearing in union with the purest, best, / Of earth-born passions, on the wings of praise / A mutual tribute to the Almighty's Throne" (14.185–187). This spiritual love is inseparable from imagination, largeness of mind—in the poet's words, "Reason in her most exalted mood" (14.192). Returning to the river motif, he honors imagination as source as he has traced his life from its dim origins to the bright light of childhood, losing sight of it for a time only to recover and greet it again. Out of this progression has come in the 1805 version "The feeling of life endless, the one thought / By which we live, infinity and God" (13.183–184) and in the 1850 text a "Faith in life endless, the sustaining thought / Of human Being, Eternity, and God" (14.204–205).

The poem closes with tributes to others, to those who have kept him in touch with the world of people and events around him. There is, of course, Dorothy, who helped him to temper his love, to move beyond the self. To his soul, too often "A rock with torrents roaring," she "didst plant its crevices with flowers" (14.251–253). So also Mary, "an inmate of the heart, / And yet a spirit, there for me enshrined / To penetrate the lofty and the low" (14.269–271). And then there is the memory of Raisley Calvert whose humaneness and concern and gratitude brought the inheritance at a time of financial crisis that "cleared a passage for me, and the stream / Flowed in the bent of Nature" (14.370–371). And, of course, there is always his listener, Coleridge, a man placed on earth "to love and understand, / And from thy presence shed the light of love" (14.278–279).

The poet looks ahead, perhaps to the completion of the envisioned but never completed longer poem *The Recluse*, to a plan of action that may excuse him "For having given this story of myself" (14.393). Rounding to a conclusion, he engages Coleridge, reminding his friend that the later portions of his poem were touched by loss, "under pressure of a private grief, / Keen and enduring" (14.421–222)—certainly the death of his beloved brother John. But Coleridge's presence is a "comfort" along with this poem, "this offering of my love" (14.426–431).

Wordsworth will end affirmatively this account of his spiritual life, this progress-of-the-soul poem. He and Coleridge will later take on the mantles of prophets as they look ahead to "a few short years of useful life," a "race" to be run (14.432–434). Again, reimagining another age, another people who may fall back to "old idolatry," "servitude," "ignominy and shame," he foresees the poets partici- pating in a redemptive act, namely, the deliverance of that people from such a fate. The poetic and prophetic vocations become one: As priests of a new gospel, they will minister to a flawed world. Wordsworth, the poet and yet the human being who knew childhood loss, failed love, dashed hopes for political change, death of family and friends, sends forth his homily as the poem ends:

> Prophets of Nature, we to them will speak
> A lasting inspiration, sanctified
> By reason, blest by faith: what we have loved,
> Others will love, and we will teach them how;
> Instruct them how the mind of man becomes
> A thousand times more beautiful than the earth
> On which he dwells, above this frame of things
> (Which, 'mid all the revolutions in the hopes
> And fears of men, doth still remain unchanged)
> In beauty exalted, as it is itself
> Of quality and fabric more divine [14.436–456].

6

Varieties of Poetic Experience: The 1807 Poems

"Upon this I shall insist elsewhere; at present let me confine myself to my object, which is to make you, my dear Friend, as easy-hearted as myself with respect to these Poems. Trouble not yourself upon their present reception; of what moment is that compared with what I trust is their destiny, to console the afflicted, to add sunshine to daylight by making the happy happier, to teach the young and the gracious of every age, to see, to think and feel, and therefore to become more actively and securely virtuous; this is their office, which I trust they will faithfully perform after we (that is, all that is mortal of us) are mouldered in our graves."

W. W. to Lady Beaumont
May 21, 1807

Blessings be with them, and eternal praise,
Who gave us nobler loves, and nobler cares,
The Poets, who on earth have made us heirs
Of truth and pure delight by heavenly lays!
Oh! might my name be numbered among theirs,
Then gladly would I end my mortal days.

Wordsworth, *Personal Talk*

"*Poems, in Two Volumes* was important to Wordsworth because these two unpretentious octavos, unbuttressed by prefatory theorizing, were, in fact, a decisive statement of poetical independence, both to the world and to Coleridge. . . . It would seem that whatever became of *The Recluse*, Wordsworth was determined to shape a career and to present his own poetical identity to the public. . . . But now Wordsworth was putting forward poems that belonged entirely to the years after he made his decision to return to the Lake District, poems, moreover, which were the most challenging he had ever published."

Stephen Gill, *William Wordsworth: A Life*

WORDSWORTH'S LITERARY LIFE does take a different course after the publication of the second edition of his *Lyrical Ballads*, moving more decisively toward a new poetry of consciousness. He had, of course, achieved a reputation of sorts even when his treatment of rustic characters and settings was criticized or parodied. Certainly, the ideas of the 1800 "Preface" triggered response; certainly, Coleridge took serious note of his work, indeed, even engaged in what more than one critic has called a dialogue with that work![1] And there is the story that even the Queen bought a copy of *Lyrical Ballads* and gave it to a friend. In the public literary arena, only the *Edinburgh Review* ignored the poems.

After the outburst of creativity that produced a second edition of the *Lyrical Ballads* in 1800, there was a period of quiet, at least on the surface. Never the complete solitary, Wordsworth made new and good friends in Catherine and Thomas Clarkson, who lived near Ullswater in Grasmere. It is a time of visits from many friends outside of Grasmere, old London friends such as John Marshall, husband of Dorothy's friend Jane Pollard. In September of 1801 he takes the first of several trips to Scotland, to attend Basil Montagu's wedding. And November brings another visit from Mary Hutchinson (one of several over the succeeding few years), and a visit of Mary, Dorothy, and William to Greta Hall in Keswick to bid farewell to a physically weak, opium-addicted, and emotionally troubled Coleridge, who, unable to face another raw Lake Country winter, was leaving for London. Indeed, this was the time when, despite little

---

[1] Note the varying dialogic approaches of Magnuson (*Coleridge and Wordsworth*) and Bialostosky (*Wordsworth, Dialogics, and the Practice of Criticism*).

obvious evidence of a developing love affair, Wordsworth and Mary Hutchinson, who had known each other since school days at Dame Birkett's school in Penrith, grew closer and decided to marry.

The Hutchinsons had come to Penrith from County Durham, where Mary's father had lived all his life, a successful tobacconist of the same stock, same shopkeeper trade as Wordsworth's mother's family. There were eight children, all of whom were orphaned at a young age, so Mary and William had much in common. The families kept in touch even when Tom Hutchinson, a brother eager to buy land and searching everywhere for a suitable location, finally settled in Yorkshire. Hunter Davies speculates interestingly that the "trips by John and William to Yorkshire, referred to by Dorothy in her *Journals*, therefore have deeper significance, when you realize that William must have been courting Mary."[2] Whatever the exact situation, the relationship, unlike the passionate affair with Annette, seemed calm, slow to develop, and much in keeping with that side of Wordsworth that sought a balance for his strong emotions, a source of permanence to complement his youthful trust in the workings of the imagination.

Dorothy's anxieties about her brother's visits to Mary and about the implications of marriage for his poetic career notwithstanding, Wordsworth and Mary were formally engaged and planned a simple autumn wedding. With Dorothy reassured that she would live with her brother and sister-in-law after the wedding, there was still one important matter to deal with. Annette and Caroline were still on his mind, and Wordsworth, formerly the political radical and gallant lover and now the more sober, concerned poet about to marry and to take on new responsibilities, wanted to deal with what he considered his obligations.[3] With the death of Sir James Lowther, Lord Lonsdale, his heirs agreed to settle the long-disputed, twenty-six year-old debt to the Wordsworth children, a sum of £8,500, £3,825 pounds of which was invested for poet and sister by their brother Richard. Wordsworth and Dorothy were now ready for the voyage to Calais and some sort of reunion with Annette. They stopped first at

---

[2] *William Wordsworth: A Biography*, p. 144.

[3] See the reference to the exchange of letters between the Wordsworths and Annette in Dorothy's *Journals*: 1.102, 114, 116, 117, 127, 147, 154, 156, 157, 166, 167, 183, 133.

Keswick, then visited the Clarksons at Eusemere and Mary at Gallow Hill. From London they took the Dover coach over Westminster Bridge and arrived in Calais on August 1, 1802.

If it was a reunion, it was a curious, but certainly definitive one. During a four-week stay Wordsworth saw a different person, older, a Royalist French woman committed to her country. And he was a different person as well—a man, engaged to a childhood friend, an Englishman devoted to his country and his democratic ideals, a poet whose profession was now the center of his life. We imagine friendly polite conversations, with Dorothy always kind and attentive to Annette and Caroline. Wordsworth was clearly touched by the presence of his French daughter and was willing to offer support, but he seemed uninterested in marriage and family. Both lover and beloved must have realized they were not in love, and certainly not suited for marriage; after the long visit, Annette returned to Blois and William to London. They would meet only once more, some eighteen years later in the famous reunion in the Louvre. Annette always maintained a Wordsworth connection, however. Remaining unmarried, she called herself either Madame William or Veuve William while her daughter was christened as Anne Caroline Wordswodth (*sic*). The trip had been the right thing to do. Wordsworth had taken care of the amenities as a responsible man should, but the whole episode must have left him with more than a touch of sadness, even guilt, as he prepared for his marriage to Mary.

Wordsworth and Dorothy returned to London on September 11, 1802, staying at Montagu's apartment, and enjoying a reunion of the five Wordsworths, their first since childhood days. Wordsworth and Mary were married at Brompton Church near Scarborough, Yorkshire on October 4, 1802. From everything we know, it was a good and happy marriage—a family of three sons and two daughters, a Wordsworth increasingly orthodox in religion and politics— and the relatively recent edition of their love letters confirms the depth of their love in good times and bad.[4]

---

[4] Typical of their expressions of love is Wordsworth's letter to Mary on August 11, 1810: "O Mary I love you with a passion of love which grows till I tremble to think of its strength; your children and the care and the longings of absence—when I am moving about in travelling I am less unhappy than when stationary, but then I am at every moment, I will not say reminded of you, for you never I think are out

I have already alluded to the curious and intense relationship of Dorothy and William from their earliest days, so I will not return to it in any detail except to sketch briefly the frequently told stories about Dorothy's behavior on the wedding day—how emotionally upset she appeared to be, how she slept wearing the wedding ring the night before the ceremony, how she became ill and could not attend the church, how she rushed into his arms when her brother returned for breakfast after the wedding. Yet the three return to Grasmere after the festivities, as Hunter Davies aptly puts it, "a strange trio indeed."[5]

These are busy times and no mystical images of a solitary poet will do. Wordsworth's financial situation certainly improved as he and Dorothy began receiving the Lowther money. He also attracted a new, enthusiastic, and wealthy patron in Sir George Beaumont, painter of note and one of the founders of the National Gallery. It was Beaumont who, living at the time with Coleridge at Greta Hall in Keswick, and knowing how the two poets wanted to live near each other, bought a plot at Applethwaite on the slopes of Skiddaw in Keswick and, through Coleridge, presented it to Wordsworth. The land went unused, however, as Coleridge, concerned about his health, went to Sicily and Malta; but Wordsworth did become a voting freeholder of Cumberland.

Travel was a vital part of the poet's life. On August 15, 1803, shortly after the birth of his first child, John, Wordsworth, along with Dorothy and Coleridge, set off on a six-week tour of Scotland, a lively and important trip described engagingly in Wordsworth's *Memorials of a Tour in Scotland, 1803* and Dorothy's journals. They savored the delights of natural scenery, but enjoyed almost as much the company of people, the attraction of literary sites. They visited Gretna Green, then Burns's house, a dreary Glasgow, and what they regarded as a disappointing Lowland and a delightful Loch Lomond and the Highlands, Rob Roy's birthplace. Then they toured the Border country with Sir Walter Scott who read to them his still-unpub-

---

of my mind 3 minutes together however I am engaged, but am every moment seized with a longing wish that you might see the objects which interest me as I pass along, and not having you at my side my pleasure is so imperfect that after a short look I had rather not see the objects at all."
   [5] *William Wordsworth: A Biography*, p. 159.

lished *Lay of the Last Minstrel* at Melrose Abbey, a prelude to many Scott visits to the Lake country in the years ahead. Hunter Davies pays particular attention to what he describes as this last "wandering tour." Wordsworth, of course, traveled for the rest of his life, and the images of that journey enriched his future years, but, says Davies, "he felt his visionary experiences were becoming rarer even before Scotland. . . . As he approached thirty–five, certain changes appeared to be taking place in his character and in his attitude to life."[6] The trip nevertheless remained a splendid one, as Dorothy's journal offers many of her unusually splendid cameos which are to be recaptured and rendered poetically in Wordsworth's poetry.

One might offer an anthology of such intertextuality at this point, but the work of Anne Mellor and others has been most influential in enabling readers to see and understand the uniqueness of journal entry and poem, the special genius of Dorothy and William. I select a few notable examples, however, as they illuminate the poet's literary life, dramatize the poet's turning the stuff of daily experience into art.

There is, for example, a note of Sunday, September 11, 1803, a note that proves the ultimate source of the poet's "Stepping Westward." The sharp eye for natural detail, the crispness of the language of description, the general verve of the journal keeper—these and other qualities stand out.

> We have never had a more delightful walk than this evening. Ben Lomond, and the three sharp–crested mountains of Loch Lomond, which we had seen from the garrison were very majestic under the clear sky; the lake was perfectly calm, the air sweet and mild. I felt how much more interesting it is to visit a place where we have been before than it can possible be the first time, except under peculiar circumstances. The sun had been set for some time, when, being within a quarter of a mile of the ferryman's hut, our path leading close to the shore of the calm lake, we met two neatly dressed women without hats, who had been probably taking their Sunday evening's walk. One of them said to us in a friendly soft tone of voice, 'What, you are stepping westward?' I cannot describe how affecting this expression was, in that remote place, with the western sky in front, *yet*

---

[6] Ibid., pp. 161–162.

glowing with the departing sun. William wrote the following poem in a remembrance of his feelings and mine.[7]

Or there is her account of seeing Rob Roy's grave when descending into Glengyle at the head of Lake Ketterine, and passing through Macfarlane's grounds and seeing the burial place of the MacGregors. It is a rich and lush scene, yet the human element with all of its implications touches her.

> As we descended, the scene became more fertile, our way being pleasantly varied, through coppices or open fields, and passing many farm-houses, through always with an intermixture of uncultivated ground. It was harvest time, and the fields were enlivened [might I be allowed to say pensively?] by many small companies of reapers. It is not uncommon in the more lonely parts of the Highlands, to see a single person so employed.

Interestingly enough, Dorothy quotes from her brother's "The Solitary Reaper," noting how the poem was inspired by a sentence in another journal-like document, Thomas Wilkinson's *Tour in Scotland*, as if to note the workings of the poetic imagination.[8]

Then there are her accounts of the rains along the Firth of Forth, her delight in the city of Edinburgh. There is her modest, and, for students of the association of journal and poetry today, most intriguing description of walking along the banks of the Tweed to Nidpath Castle. The castle, she writes,

> stands upon a green hill overlooking the Tweed, a strong square-towered edifice, neglected and desolate, though not in ruin; the gardens overgrown with grass, and the high walls that fenced in broken down. The Tweed winds between green steps, upon which and close to the river-side, were many sheep pasturing; higher still are the grey mountains. But I need not describe this scene, for Wm. has done it far better than I could, in a sonnet which he wrote the same day; at least, the last five lines of his poem will impart to you more of the feeling of the place than it would be possible for me to do.[9]

Dorothy, it would seem, is not only the good journal-keeper, but also a strong commentator on how she saw herself and her work in relation to poetry, specifically her brother's poetry.

---

[7] *Journals*, 1:367–368.

[8] Ibid., 1:139–380.

[9] Ibid., 1.387–388. The poem is "Degenerate Douglas! Thou Unworthy Lord."

An interesting letter of October 14, 1803 to his kindly patron, Sir George Beaumont, sheds light on the inner conflict so central to every phase of Wordsworth's literary life. Beaumont, we remember, had purchased for Wordsworth the charming spot of land, Applethwaite, near Keswick, so that the poet, Coleridge, and Southey, could be close together as artists and fellow Lakers. It was a plan never realized, and Wordsworth, grateful but unable to build, procrastinates for some eight years before writing a letter of thanks. He is grateful for "two elegant drawings," is anxious about the possibility of a French invasion, is concerned about certain physical, although they seem more than physical, problems that have impeded his writing of late. "I do not know," he writes, "from what cause it is, but during the last three [y]ears I have never had a pen in my hand for five minutes, [b]efore my whole frame becomes one bundle of uneasiness. . . . [T]his is a sad weakness; for I am sure, though, it is chiefly [o]wing to the state of my body, that by exertion of mind [I] might in part control it."[10]

Living at Dove Cottage brought more than its share of personal and public joys and concerns—the mixed-blessing visit of Hazlitt (he had become notorious for his harassment of women) and their growing political separation after Napoleon's crowning and Wordsworth's organizing the local Grasmere Volunteers against threats of a French invasion after his return from Scotland; the birth of his children; the visit of Scott and their journey with Humphrey Davy from Patterdale and their climbing of Mount Helvellyn together. He toured the Lakes with Scott, and Scott's observation in a letter to a friend is revealing and helpful for one studying a literary life of the poet. "Wordsworth," observes Scott, "wrote in particular in such a character as exists only in romance, virtuous, simple, and unaffectedly restricting every want and wish to the bounds of a narrow income in order to enjoy the literary and poetical leisure which his happiness consists in."[11]

No event of these busy years touched Wordsworth more than the accidental death of his brother John. John Wordsworth was almost three years younger than William, part of that family of five orphaned

---

[10] *EY* 1:407–408.

[11] Quoted in Christopher Wordsworth, *Memoirs of William Wordsworth*, 1:167.

at early ages and eventually separated in various ways. Since school-days the two had not really seen much of each other, William remain-ing close to his childhood haunts; John, a sailor traveling to far-off places. John was certainly closer to William than were the other brothers; indeed, although he was at sea for long periods, he was a vital part of the Wordsworth circle when at home. At the beginning of 1800 he had come to live at Dove Cottage, much to William's delight, and William accompanied him part of the way to Penrith on his way to sea again on the *Abergavenny East-Indiaman* in the spring of 1801. He enjoyed walking in a fir-grove near Dove Cottage, so much so that he made a path affectionately called John's Grove or Brother's Grove by his family. He was an astute critic and a firm supporter of his brother's poetry.

At the end of 1804 John was given command of the ship, a ship on which he had lost money in the past, but, with a good cargo now, there was promise of a profitable voyage. The rest is well known. The ship was caught in a storm on February 5, 1805 after leaving Portsmouth, and, upon striking rocks on the Bill of Portland, it sank with some 300 crew and passengers, John included, perishing. Much can be said and much has been written about the impact of the news on Wordsworth and his family, but nothing captures that impact quite so powerfully as a stark, pregnant statement in the poet's Feb-ruary 1805 letter to his friend Beaumont: "I trust in God that I shall not want fortitude; but my loss is great and irreparable."[12] Loss and disillusionment, already having scarred his spirit with the violent failure of the French Revolution, are now a vital reality for Words-worth, and, with a two-month leave of absence from poetry, that reality pulls him more and more to it, challenging his faith in the healing power of nature, the power of imagination and feeling, the ministry of solitude. He makes what amounts to a commitment to the memory of John, asking his brother Richard to secure for him anything from the wreckage of the ship—only a sword was recov-ered—that might remind him of his brother.

In a March 12, 1805 letter to Beaumont, Wordsworth moves be-yond loss to raise bedrock questions of faith and religion. Never a devotée of organized religion or a regular churchgoer in his early

---

[12] W. W. to Beaumont, February [ca. 23] 1805. *EY* 1:548.

years, he was nevertheless a believer in a divine presence, a transcendent spirit. Now certain questions take on a strident tone. Why was John, an ebullient, vigorous, generous man taken so cruelly? Is God just in punishing the virtuous and leaving a family so grief-stricken? Why, he writes to Beaumont, "have we sympathies to make the best of us so afraid of inflicting pain and sorrow, which yet we see dealt about so lavishly by the supreme governor?" And he continues:

> Why should our notions of right towards each other, and to all sentient beings within our influence differ so widely from what appears to be His notion and rule, if every thing were to end there? Would it not be blasphemy to say that upon the supposition of the thinking principle being destroyed by death, however inferior we may be to the Great Cause and Ruler of things, we have *more of love* in our nature than he has? The thought is monstrous; and yet how do we get rid of it, except upon the supposition of *another* and a *better world*, I do not see.[13]

These are sentiments of great power, of tormented questioning for the burgeoning poet of the first decade of the nineteenth century, sentiments that must be reckoned with by those who would point to certain mystical expressions of strong faith and hope. Wordsworth prays, in the same letter to Beaumont, for "strength and power," and images of strength and power appear more prominently in the richly human poems of 1807. John's death was clearly a major event in a period generally associated with most of Wordsworth's greatest poetry, most notably with *The Prelude*, begun in Germany in 1798 and completed in May 1805 (although, of course, not published until after his death). But it was, in spite of its concrete rendering of the power of death and loss, only part of a larger pattern. The temptation for the biographer, even the literary biographer, especially when he lacks specific psychological training and expertise, is to talk about his subject's growing older, about mid-life professional and personal crises, about turning points in a life or career. The irony is that such a temptation is understandable and that the speculation it triggers is not entirely without merit. After all, at this point in our story Wordsworth is moving toward thirty-five, is married, and has a son, John, born on June 18, 1803; a daughter, Dorothy—or Dora—on

---

[13] *EY* 1:556.

August 16, 1804; and another son, Thomas, born on June 16, 1806. He was to have two other children, Catherine—born September 6, 1808; and William—or Willy—born on May 12, 1810. Given family responsibilities and the lack of any substantial income from his work, he thought continually about money. He has known personal sorrow, and has experienced the disappointments as well as the joys of publication, including hostile as well as favorable reviews of his work. His early radical fervor has abated somewhat, and he is comfortable with the friendship of men like Beaumont, Scott, and Davy, clearly Establishment types. Surrounded by women who cater to his every need, he finds a certain peace and security in his domestic life.

After the seclusion of Dove Cottage, Wordsworth treated himself to a London spring holiday in 1806. He stayed for two months, first with his brother Christopher, a rising Church of England man; then with Beaumont in Mayfair at Grosvenor Square. Then it was on to Windsor and, now a respectably married man and a poet, he visited his uncle Canon Cookson and had his portrait painted by Henry Eldridge. And there were, of course, visits to Lamb, Godwin, and other literary friends.

Homesick after the London stay, he returned to the Lakes, and moved into the farmhouse at Coleorton in Leicestershire, lent to him by Beaumont. His attempts to reconcile Coleridge and his wife failing, Coleridge and his son Hartley joined him, and a regular routine of work was established. Interestingly, all the Wordsworths attended the local church at Coleorton, visiting twice on Sundays although critical of the preaching. Never, as already mentioned, a scrupulous churchgoer previously, he now seemed to move toward a more serious approach to religion as still another anchor of stability—an approach, as we shall see later, that will culminate in his strong association with and support of the Established Church.

In the spring of 1807 William and Mary went to London, staying a month while Dorothy and the children remained at Coleorton, and then returned with Scott for the summer. After spending part of the winter at Stockton-on-Tees, at the house of John Hutchinson, he returned to Grasmere in the spring of 1808. A period of enormous activity and travel, of the vicissitudes of birth and death, of success and failure, was closed, and he was once again at his geographical and spiritual home.

It is such a backdrop that enables us to come to terms with a period of great poetic productivity. Following the unproductive year of 1801 came a remarkably prolific period from December of 1801, with Wordsworth writing much of the first two books of *The Excursion* and the bulk of the poems published in early May 1807 in his celebrated *Poems in Two Volumes*.

While it has become a commonplace to associate the 1807 poems with *Tintern Abbey* and *The Prelude* as high points of Wordsworth's career, the contemporary reaction was at best mixed, at worst sharply negative. The reviews were directed at Wordsworth's poetry itself or at the poetry as the center of a more general attack on the Lake poets. Anonymous reviews in the *Critical Review*, *Le Beau Monde*, and the *Literary Annual Register* were unabashedly negative. Francis Jeffrey in the *Edinburgh Review* was kinder to the *Lyrical Ballads*, regarding the 1807 poems as succeeding only when Wordsworth moves away from his system outlined in the "Preface," and complaining of the poet's attempts to bring a certain loftiness of tone to banal subjects. For Jeffrey, writing in the *Edinburgh Review* of April 12, 1808, the rustic pieces of George Crabbe seem true to life while Wordsworth's characters in poems like "The Thorn" are "aberrations from ordinary nature." Byron was, by comparison, tolerant in a July 3, 1807 review in *Monthly Literary Recreations*, seeing the poems as less successful than the *Lyrical Ballads*. While Wordsworth often dresses commonplace ideas in silly language, he says, some of the poems have a natural beauty. Most savage and sweeping were the indictments of James Montgomery in the *Eclectic Review* for January 4, 1808. Another praiser of some of the innovations of the *Lyrical Ballads*, Montgomery sees the 1807 poems as dealing with trifles. The sonnets are obscure and heavy, and even the *Immortality Ode* is savaged because of its preaching of pre–existence. The only kind words are reserved for Wordsworth's talent for natural description in poems like "Resolution and Independence."[14] Wordsworth played the part of the brave artist, but he was clearly hurt, and, putting aside a new long poem, *The White Doe of Rylstone*, and his work on *The Recluse*, he published no new poems for seven years.

There are, of course, many strategies to follow as one confronts

---

[14] Bauer, *William Wordsworth: A Reference Guide*, pp. 7–9.

the task of dealing with more than one hundred poems in this 1807 collection. One is the purely chronological, and that approach is not without merit, pointing up as it might the month-by-month, year-by-year progress of a career. Another is thematic, focusing on the continuity of themes from the *Lyrical Ballads*, or perhaps the abandonment of some, or the emergence of other new concerns. Still another strategy would be to employ a specific critical methodology, a more traditional approach, or perhaps one that employed New Critical close-reading techniques or even one that employed the possibilities of contemporary theories like New Historicism, Deconstruction, dialogics. Attractive though these approaches might be, the danger is apparent. Telling the story of a literary life might become secondary to the power of certain theoretical premises. Biography might give way to something quite different.

What I would like to do is play the critical pragmatist, using the rich resources of traditional and modern theoretical emphases to illuminate a rich body of poetry. In a sense, I take my cue from an intriguing suggestion by Don Bialostosky in his recent book on Wordsworth and the practice of criticism. A student, although not an uncritical one, of the dialogical method of Mikhail Bakhtin, he extends Bakhtin's emphasis on the dynamic of competing voices in the novel—and, by implication, in poetry—into the arena of critical practice. "This orchestrated display of diverse languages creates a dialogue among socially specific ways of 'conceptualizing the world in words' (DN 292) and represents them as they co-exist with, supplement, contradict, or address one another in people's consciousnesses."[15] And Bialostosky would extend the dialogic reading of poetry to the business of criticism. Listening to the several voices in *The Prelude* which critics like James Chandler, Alan Liu, Susan Wolfson, and others have enabled him to hear, he says, "the interaction of the many voices these readings reveal within Wordsworth's voice makes a stronger claim on my interest than the self-indulgent single voice of the ideologue to which McGann would reduce them."[16] Earlier in the same work, he movingly urges that "we students of literature must find new ways to assimilate and respond to what our

---

[15] *Wordsworth, Dialogics, and the Practice of Criticism*, p. 65.
[16] Ibid., p. 73.

colleagues make for our objects of inquiry, and we must reflect on what it means for us always to meet those objects in the company of those colleagues."[17]

I will continue to focus sharply on Wordsworth's poetic life, seeing that life not so much rigidly determined by its surrounding biographical and historical milieu as colored, enriched, illuminated by it. And while the poems will to some extent take on lives of their own, they will become not simply self-referential constructs illustrating the play of language but also artistic struggles to empower language and perhaps catch the complexities in the developing life and career of a writer.

It is difficult to attribute anything like definitive meanings to the poems of these years. They simply do not suggest a clear movement to a new level of understanding, to some fuller statement of an essential Wordsworthian Romantic faith. The picture is much too complex; the poems, too varied in spirit and manner; the continuing conflict of belief and doubt, too apparent to allow for any easy biographical theorizing. There are, to be sure, still evidences of the humble, rustic strain of the *Lyrical Ballads*; "The Sailor's Mother," "Alice Fell, or Poverty," and "The Emigrant Mother" are clear cases in point. More notable, however, is the personal, self–conscious, lyrical voice of the song, sonnet, or ode, a voice still direct and natural, but not narrowly realistic, a language and imagery still free from the "gaudiness and inane phraseology of eighteenth–century poetic diction." To return to our earlier metaphor: Wordsworth, it would seem, saw himself at a personal and literary crossroads at the time of his writing *Tintern Abbey*, a poem rather different from most other poems in the *Lyrical Ballads* collection. And at the time he seems to have chosen the voice of *Tintern Abbey* as he turned to the Lucy poems, "There was a Boy," "Nutting," to the early books of *The Prelude* and certainly to the 1807 *Poems*, our present stop in the literary life. While a Bakhtinian assembly of voices is frequently present, each conditioned and conditioning, there seems to be a dominant voice close and responsive to the living, vibrant forces of the natural world. They are poems frequently lending themselves to historicization yet consistently concerned with the inner life and with the direct, spon-

---

[17] Ibid., pp. xx–xxi.

taneous expression of the workings of that inner life. Their rhythms are thoroughly and variously musical; their language and imagery, crisp and clear. One might simply say that they are better poems, the work of an artist in command of his medium, but the charge of *je ne sais quoi* subjectivity is easily justified here.

So we are left with the sense that they are poems with a difference, although the most important reveal the same tension evident in Wordsworth's poetry from the beginning. But the tension is more complex, less bluntly articulated, especially in those poems where joy seems to dominate, where light seems to prevail, where hope for a never-ending happiness seems to be heard in ringing tones—so much so that the reader is almost lulled into a blissful unawareness of the more somber organ tones of loss, doubt, yearning for stability.

We proceed to what I trust are representative poems in which there is a clear sense of direct encounter seemingly unencumbered by the need for the anchor of security, of a commitment to and trust in the power of mind/imagination to shape meaning and value.[18] "My heart leaps up" might be seen as the seminal poem of this group.[19] Brief, spontaneous in expression, terse in its profoundly simple language and imagery, it is a lyric of celebration of something fundamental in Wordsworth's poetry, something primal—"natural piety" is the obvious expression often too glibly seen in orthodox religious terms—something that can be one's "all and all," that can link the spirit of the human being to a larger pervasive spirit that infiltrates all living things. In some ways it has the time sequence of *Tintern Abbey*, although it is a very different poem in form. The first two lines celebrate a recurring experience for the speaker as he utters, "My heart leaps up when I behold / A Rainbow in the sky" (1–2). Recurring, we say. The emotion goes back to "when my life began," to childhood ecstasy; it continues to the present with the assuring, "So is it now I am a Man" (3–4).

Short though it is, the poem then takes an interesting turn from affirmative to optative. The speaker seems to will the continuation of the ecstasy he celebrates with a semi–religious "So be it when I

---

[18] See Owen Barfield, "Symptoms of Iconoclasm," in *Saving the Appearances: A Study in Idolatry* (New York:: Harcourt, Brace & World, 1965), pp. 126–132.

[19] All quotations from the 1807 poems are from *Poems in Two Volumes, and Other Poems, 1800–1807*, ed. Jared Curtis (Ithaca, N.Y.: Cornell University Press, 1983.)

shall grow old," with the hint of uncertainty or anxiety that it may not, and the grim alternative he sets for himself if it should not: "Or let me die!" (5–6). The confidence that opens the closing three lines, a confidence rooted in Wordsworth's early and continuing faith that "The Child is Father of the Man" is again followed by the optative "And I could wish my days to be / Bound each to each by natural piety" (7–9). Confidence, to be sure—strong confidence, one might say—but with just the suggestion of doubt about the future when the child becomes the man, when boyish oneness with nature is threatened by the onrush of adult anxiety.

Two other poems of 1802 focus on a speaker's rapture at the sight of a butterfly. In one the speaker, coming upon a butterfly at rest, commands gently "Stay near me—do not take thy flight! / A little longer stay in sight!" (1–2). Delight is clear, but so is a certain fear that the butterfly—in which he finds "much converse," much to evoke memories of other times, other places, much that makes it "Historian of my infancy!"—may fly away (3–4). It as as if the creature's connections with the past are more important than the beauty it brings to the present moment. There is a pleading tone to the address that follows—"Float near me; do not yet depart!"—and again a strangely grotesque quality to the reason for such pleading: "Dead times revive in thee," albeit those times are a "solemn image" of My Father's Family" (5–8).

The second stanza breaks loose from any notalgic undermining as the speaker imagines a childhood episode with his "sister Emmeline"—often identified as Dorothy.[20] With memories of the boy in "Nutting," he creates a vivid scene—active verbs and nouns predominate—of how they "chased the Butterfly," he a "very hunter" rushing "upon the prey," "with leaps and springs / I follow'd on from brake to bush." But she, a more gentle spirit in the sport, "feared to brush / The dust from off its wings" (12–18). It is a poem of drama, of humor, of energy, of peacefulness, of ecstasy as felt in childhood. And yet there is that slight nuance of "once upon a time," of something gone, not to return, but also of confidence in the power to rescue and re-create those special moments.

---

[20] See the Fenwick note to the poem: "My sister and I were parted immediately after the death of our mother, who died in 1778, both being very young."

The second "To a Butterfly" poem is equally, if not more, engaging, yet its voice, its scenario are more ambivalent. Written, according to the Fenwick note, in the orchard at Town-End, Grasmere, it captures a special moment, or perhaps thirty moments, a time held in suspension by the poet-director as he addresses the absolutely still butterfly–"I've watched you now a full half-hour / Self-pois'd upon that yellow flower" (1–2). The fascination is with the creature's perfect stillness: "How motionless! not frozen seas / More motionless!" Again the speaker, imaginative always, projects himself with the creature into a new and equally pleasurable future: "and then / What joy awaits you, when the breeze / Hath found you out among the trees, / And calls you forth again" (5–9). Like Coleridge, forced to remain at home in the lime-tree bower, his prison, while his friends roam the beauteous countryside, Wordsworth creates the new scenario for the butterfly.

The second stanza offers a scene of beauteous Romantic community, as the speaker draws the motionless butterfly into a more active engagement, sharing family secrets, welcoming the creature into their company. "This plot of Orchard-ground is ours; / My trees they are, my Sister's flowers" (10–11). Soar, fly, enjoy, but "Stop here whenever you are weary, / And rest as in a sanctuary." Be one of us, says the speaker, imagining a kinship and joy among living things— "Come often to us, fear no wrong; / Sit near us on the bough!"

The speaker's voice seems confident of the power of nature, the strength that comes from emotional commitment and imaginative trust. "We'll talk of sunshine and of song; / And summer days, when we were young." It is a happy prospect weakened only by a slightly sad, nostalgic touch in the suggestion of those days as "Sweet childish days, that were as long / As twenty days are now!" (10–19). Childhood moves into age, and the pull of reality begins to intensify.

"Written in March While Resting on the Bridge at the Foot of Brother's Water" is a nearly perfect lyric. The speaker, interestingly described as "resting" by that small lake near the foot of Kirkstone Pass, describes a scene of bustling activity with sounds and sights of a vitally alive nature contributing to a certain carnivalesque scene. Wordsworth's Fenwick note describes the poem as composed "extempore." The verbs contribute greatly to the effect, as do the rhyme and meter. There are two ten-line stanzas, each stanza beginning with a bustling *a, a, b, b* opening followed by a line longer by a foot with a *c* rhyme that seems to set a quieter tone. The meter moves from iambic to spondaic to anapestic, its very irregularity suggesting the activity it imitates. Note the activity of the four-line opening of the first stanza: "The Cock is crowing / The stream is flowing, / The small birds twitter, / The lake doth glitter," followed by the more resposeful fifth line in the exact middle of the stanza: "The green field sleeps in the sun," a line that seems to gather cock, stream, birds, and lake into a larger unity bathed in light. The second half of the stanza proceeds similarly if somewhat less energetically: "The oldest and youngest / Are at work with the strongest; / The cattle are grazing, / Their heads never raising," again closing a five-line unit with a longer, somewhat resposeful final line, with the falling rhythm of three trochees followed by the rising rhythm of an iamb, and the "one" of line ten rhyming the "sun" of line five: "There are forty feeding like one."

The same pattern is clear in the second stanza: varied rhythms, crisp and simple language and imagery, strategic use of rhyme and meter. But the poem is more than a demonstration of technique and virtuosity. What stands out are the almost unrelieved joyous spirit, the trust in the power of images, the humanization of nature in springtime. The stanza opens with a fairly standard image, "Like an army defeated / The Snow hath retreated" and moves to the more decisive, longer middle line in which, to proclaim to everyone the arrival of spring, "The Ploughboy is whooping-anon-anon." The closing quintet sees not only humans rejoicing, but every phenomenon of nature taking on human qualities to join with the Ploughboy: "There's joy in the mountains; / There's life in the fountains; / Small clouds are sailing, / Blue sky prevailing; / The rain is over and gone."

"To the Cuckoo" carries further the exuberance of the 1807 collection, treating the beauties of natural settings with vividness; but it moves beyond mere delight in the beauty of those settings and creatures to a deeper awareness of a spiritual dimension in them available only to those who see clearly, feel deeply, imagine freely. This poem, like so many in the collection, evidences a strong belief in a divine presence that underlies and animates the natural world, that speaks through its creatures, that energizes those who see and listen, that sustains the spirit even when it seems elusive. Words-

worth's remarks about the poem in the 1815 Preface are most instructive for readers: "This concise interrogation ['Shall I Call thee
Bird,' etc.] characterizes the seeming ubiquity of the voice of the
cuckoo, and dispossesses the creature almost of a corporeal existence" (3.22).

The poem is, in fact, a "now-then" poem, although a confident
voice seems to control it. It is both a greeting and a question, or a
greeting, a question, a memory, and an affirmation. The greeting is
straightforward: "O blithe New-comer! I have heard, / I hear thee
and rejoice" (1–2); the speaker is struck by the happy sound and
associates it with other such sounds. It is this "now-then" sequence
that triggers the question. Are you a "Bird" or really "but a wandering Voice?" (1–4). We are reminded of the speaker in Keats's
"Nightingale," regarding that bird not just as the one he is hearing
in Hampstead Heath in May 1819, but also as a voice heard in "ancient days by emperor and clown," "in the sad heart of Ruth," in the
world of "magic casements." The sound is not that of a single cuckoo
but also of all birds' songs, of all sound that conveys a sense of the
beautiful in life and nature, that brings a vision into the life of
things. Enthusiastic, the speaker issues his address of welcome, a
welcome rooted in his gratitude for the tale of "visionary hours"
(11). Shelley says of the skylark soaring to the heavens, "Bird thou
never wert"; Wordsworth says something similar: "No Bird; but an
invisible Thing, / A voice, a mystery" (14–15). That voice in
"Schoolboy-days" made him "look a thousand ways: / In bush, and
tree, and sky" (17–20) and continues to enliven his days albeit a
little less vitally. It is memory, the imaginative recapturing of the
past, that allows him to "beget / That golden time again" (27–28).

Several poems from the *Poems Written During a Tour in Scotland*
focus on special people and places who embody or convey the joy so
prized by Wordsworth at this time. They are, like the cuckoo, magical creatures and places once seen, or perhaps noted by Dorothy in
her journals and then remembered, which embody the otherworldli-
ness that seems to entrance the poet at special moments, that removal from the "light of common day" and entrance imaginatively
into the fairy-land of imagination.

There is, of course, "The Solitary Reaper," with its ballad-like
mood and its richly dialogic manner, as the speaker invites the lis-

tener, perhaps us as readers, to "Behold her, single in the field, / Yon solitary Highland Lass!" cutting and binding the grain and singing a "melancholy strain." There is the further invitation not just to "behold," but also to listen to her song: "O listen! for the Vale profound / Is overflowing with the sound,' the long *o* sounds lulling us into the world of the bird (1–8). How nicely the sound of the song—there is a rich confluence of *s* sounds—is played off against the quiet of the setting as the speaker elevates the quality of the Maiden's song:

> No Nightingale did ever chant
> So sweetly to reposing bands
> Of Travellers in some shady haunt,
> Among Arabian Sands:
> No sweeter voice was ever heard
> In spring-time from the Cuckoo-bird,
> Breaking the silence of the seas
> Among the farthest Hebrides [9–16].

The song puzzles the speaker, and he wonders about its subject, "old, unhappy, far-off things, / And battles long ago"; or "Some natural sorrow, loss, or pain, / That has been and may be again" (19–24). Indeed, as Don Bialostosky notes, the listener is "urged to share the speaker's experience and even to help explain its meaning."[21] But the subject matter seems less important than the singer "singing at her work, / And o'er the sickle bending" (27–28). Whatever the subject, the singer and the music draw the speaker—"I listened, till I had my fill"—and as he moves on, up the hill, back to his journey and the real world, "The music in my heart I bore, / Long after it was heard no more" (30–32). The internalization of a scene of beauty, a song of rich melancholy; the power of the memory of the song to touch one long after; the speaker's concern with its "significance for others," with both personal and "social renewal"[22]—these are the special joys of mind, of ecstatic union recaptured and memorialized in poetry.

The poetry remains fundamentally Wordsworthian in its love of people who live close to the earth, who possess a special natural

---

[21] *Wordsworth, Dialogics, and the Practice of Criticism*, p. 145.
[22] Ibid.

wisdom, who speak a language pure and direct, and yet again, as in so many of the 1807 poems, the base of subject matter and expression is broader, less concerned with journalistic accuracy, photographic realism. "Stepping Westward" is a wonderfully disarming poem for the reader accustomed to the moods, characters, and workings of eighteenth–century poetry. Its opening, as we have already seen, is evoked by Dorothy's *Reflections* and the story of her and William walking by the side of Loch Ketterine after sunset on their way to a hut where they had been entertained before. One of two neatly dressed women, out for their Sunday evening walk, spoke in a charmingly friendly way— "*What, you are stepping westward?*"—their question becoming the first line of the poem.

The speaker answers this endearing question with an unqualified "*Yea.*" Wordsworth's familiar light-dark imagery, especially the imagery of half-light, emerges as the speaker compares the "wildish destiny" of staying in this place, "In a strange Land" with the prospect of advancing, "With such a sky to lead him on" (1–7). The steady, iambic rhythms carry the poem forward, as the speaker sees and feels "The dewy ground was dark and cold," notes "Behind, all gloomy to behold," and with great gusto exclaims, "And stepping westward seemed to be / A kind of *heavenly* destiny" (8–11).

In the idiomatic manner so characteristic of Wordsworth's best poetry, the speaker "liked the greeting," associating, as he did, the song of the cuckoo with "a sound / Of something without place or bound" (12–16). The soft voice and simple courtesy of the woman are not simply aural or visual; the greeting "was felt" (21), internalized, and, as with so many such experiences for Wordsworth, served as nourishment to his psychic life. Indeed, the episode takes on an almost symbolic quality as the speaker, breaking sequential time barriers, recalls "while my eye / Was fixed upon the glowing sky, / The echo of the voice enwrought / A human sweetness with the thought / Of travelling through the world that lay / Before me in my endless way" (21–26). The conflation of the sweetness of the "*you are stepping westward?*" question with the image of a more symbolic journey through the uncertain days of a lifetime leaves readers with a powerful sense of the ability of mind and imagination to nourish the spirit and bring strength to the human being.

We need not linger over one of the most popular, the most familiar, the most anthologized of the poems in this Scotland sequence of the 1807 poems, but we also must not neglect the part it plays in the drama of the poet at the top of his power, writing in a great variety of lyric modes uncluttered by Romantic primitivism and celebrating the joys of the life of feeling, the pleasures of living close to nature and people and phenomena shaped by nature. The background of the poem in the beautiful entry in Dorothy's *Journal* for April 15, 1802 has already been discussed. Curiously, it is a poem that combines Wordsworth's and Dorothy's observation of the daffodils on the banks of Ullswater in March 1802, Dorothy's brilliant journal entry, Mary's composition of lines 21–22 with their emphasis on the "inward eye," and stanza two added in 1815; and yet, ultimately, it is not a journal entry, not an emendation, but a poem crafted and shaped finally by the artist. It is also one of Wordsworth's most brilliant demonstrations of "emotion recollected in tranquillity," of the internalization of a natural scene and its consequent moral force in the interior life.

"I wandered" is, in keeping with its scene, a rhythmic, thoroughly musical poem, a poem of joy in the midst of nature recalled, with less immediacy perhaps but perhaps with more power. It is a poem that renders obeisance to the capacity of the imagination first to shape into a harmony the details of a brilliant spring scene and, more important, to re-create that scene later—and, who knows, perhaps again and again—and with the re-creation to bring nourishment and happiness to a human being who had described himself in the opening lines as "lonely as a cloud."

Wordsworth's ability to paint a scene has rarely been matched. The reader imagines the "lonely" narrator being stunned by a dazzling ballet on that memorable day when he comes upon "a crowd, / A host, of dancing daffodils" as he sees them "dancing in the breeze" (3–6). But this is no simple ballet for the narrator-director, for his attention is immediately focused on the dancing waves beyond the shore and on a kind of wondrous competition between flowers and waves. But there is no real competition as the daffodils "Outdid the sparkling waves in glee" (8).

As the narrator recalls, and the repetition of the verb suggests, he was caught in this moment of sudden wonder, unthinking, unreflective. "I gazed—and gazed." He took no further step beyond the spectator's delight in the ballet competition to wonder about "What wealth the show to me had brought" (11–12). It is only now, away from the scene, lying blissfully "on my couch," inactive in the worldly sense— indeed, "In vacant or in pensive mood"—that the daffodils "flash upon that inward eye / Which is the bliss of solitude." It is only now that the inward eye of imagination, as it does so often in *The Prelude*, not only recovers the past, but relives it as well in a special way—sympathetically, actively, spiritually. Presence is not the vital factor. Absence is a blessing, for now the mind can do its work uncluttered by the demands of humdrum reality. The rhythmic iambic couplet closes the poem on a note of blissful return: "And then my heart with pleasure fills, / And dances with the Daffodils" (13–17). The speaker, through the power of imagination/memory, is caught up in another world, shares its pleasures, participates in its activities apart from the harsh demands of the world he inhabits in his day-to-day routine.

The sonnets are a veritable feast in the great banquet of the 1807 poems, beautifully crafted, if in any tradition that of Milton with an octave of *a, b, b, a, a, b, b, a* rhymes followed by a sestet of *c, d, c, d, c, d*, but, more notable, a pronounced tendency for the octave to flow, at time exuberantly, into the sestet with no elaborate break. They are sonnets, personal and lyric to be sure, but at times public and rhetorical in their keen sense of an audience; with an enormous variety of subjects—political, biographical, social, historical, and most notably personal—these sonnets emerge for an audience either unfamiliar with or not sympathetic to a form that had been somewhat out of fashion in the eighteenth century. They are poems, like so many in the two volumes of 1807, in which the poet, writing with what seems to be a striking confidence in his medium and its power to catch truth in a feeling-oriented way, conveys his concerns, hopes, dreams, disappointments; expresses neither a sentimental optimism nor a bleak pessimism, but, rather, that mix of both, that continuing tension between an immediate grasp of the real and a sense of its slipping away. The best sonnets are those that do not fit categories like joyous or sad, but that capture, as Keats's consistently do, the exquisite intertwining of both.

So many of the sonnets have, as some important New Historicist criticism has pointed out, a kind of deliberate specificity about them—a particular date, event, person is recorded—and yet their success lies in particular in their ability to send out not only immediate, but also more wide-ranging signals, more reverberating possibilities.[23] Take, for example, the often–quoted, frequently anthologized "Composed Upon Westminster Bridge, September 3, 1802." Dorothy's vivid journal entry for July 31, 1802 and Wordsworth's own words in the Isabella Fenwick note—"Composed on the roof of a coach on my way to France Sept. 1802"—associate the poem with the trip of Dorothy and William to France to meet Annette and Caroline. The sonnet is a classic Wordsworthian "spot of time." There is a perfect immediacy about the expression, a concentration on securing a single effect, the rare calm and peace that comes over a great city as the night dies and the day begins to dawn, that brings the sensitive soul to an awareness of a presence that pervades natural phenomena.

Far from being a poem about Westminster Bridge, or the Thames, or even London itself—it actually offers a most uncharacteristic view of the city—it is an evocation of nature and her power. Dorothy's journal entry for July 31, 1802 is memorable in its capturing of the scene:

> It was a beautiful morning. The City, St. Paul's, with the river and a multitude of little Boats, made a most beautiful sight as we crossed Westminster Bridge. The houses were not overhung by their clouds of smoke, and they were spread out endlessly, yet the sun shone brightly, with such a pure light, that there was even something like the purity of one of nature's own grand spectacles.[24]

Wordsworth moves beyond recording to response, beyond detail to organization of detail into flashingly new and original images.

---

[23] David Ferry, speaking of this phenomenon, describes "the special way in which all these considerations have led us to read the poem. It is often as if the 'surface' meanings of the poems were a beautiful and intelligible message, apparent at once, and as if hidden in that message there were clues to a 'deeper' meaning, still more beautiful though in some way at odds with the message one had read at first." For Ferry, "Westminster Bridge" illustrates "the sort of poem which has a satisfactory meaning 'with relation to a fixed time and place' and an equally wonderful, quite different meaning when understood 'under the aspect of eternity' " (*Limits of Mortality*, pp. 12, 14).

[24] *Journals*, 1:172–173.

There is a sudden, idiomatic quality to the opening line as the speaker utters categorically, "Earth has not anything to shew more fair," and then, excluding those men and women afflicted with what he called the "savage torpor" of the age in the *Lyrical Ballads* "Preface," he proceeds, "Dull would he be of soul who could pass by / A sight so touching in its majesty" (1–3).

The speaker then creates a scene of that brief time in the life of the city when the gods seem to breathe, when it takes on a spiritual dimension. The language seems to bear out Wordsworth's claim that there is no essential difference between the language of prose and the language of poetry, that poetry organizes and charges language with emotion. We note the large number of monosyllabic words—words of real people, as Wordsworth might say—the deceptively simple simile that frames the scene, the splendid use of sound, especially *s* alliteration and long vowel sounds to create the slow, solemn mood of silence. "This City now doth like a garment wear / The beauty of the morning" (4–5), the city now humanized in wearing the special bright beauty of sunrise. With "smokeless air" for a few brief moments, one can see clearly "silent, bare, / Ships, towers, domes, theatres, and temples lie / Open unto the fields, and to the sky" (4–8). And it is not just the things of man that are bathed in morning light, for "Never did sun more beautifully steep / In his first splendor valley, rock, or hill" (9–10).

To this point the speaker has been shaping a scene. As the sonnet rounds to a conclusion, he injects himself increasingly. Never had he seen or felt "a calm so deep" (11), that calm never more flashingly dramatized than in the nature-humanized image, "The river glideth at his own sweet will" or more prayerfully approached than in his "Dear God! the very houses seem asleep; / And all that mighty heart is lying still!" (12–14). Here is the moment of seeing into the life of things, of feeling at one with a presence that rolls through all things.[25]

"It is a beauteous Evening, calm and free"—largely because of the Isabella Fenwick note recording that "This was composed on

---

[25] Ferry sees the final line suggesting "that the city is not merely sleeping but dead, its heart stilled," that Wordsworth "looks at London and sees it as a corpse and admires it as such, welcomes a death which is the death of what the city has come to stand for in his symbolic world" (*Limits of Mortality*, p. 18).

the beach near Calais in the autumn of 1802" or the entry in Dorothy's journal for August 1802, "The weather was very hot. We walked by the seashore almost every evening with Annette and Caroline, or William and I alone. . . . It was also beautiful, on the calm hot night . . . Caroline was delighted"—has been routinely associated with Wordsworth's love affair with Annette Vallon, the birth of a child, Caroline, Wordsworth's failure to marry Annette, and the trip of Dorothy and William to France to visit Annette and Caroline. All of the above is fine, of course, but the poem, like the "Westminster Bridge" sonnet, is never limited by biographical data, never constricted by specific time, event, situation. It is at once an evocation of the power and eternality of nature by the adult speaker and a reassuring Wordsworthian address to the listening child that her intuitive awareness of divinity matches the most searching philosophic argument.

The octave juxtaposes the silent beauty of the setting—*s* alliteration, long *e* and *o* sounds—with the explosive assertion of its power—hard consonant sounds "Being," "motion make," "like thunder." There is a brilliant simplicity in the opening; the poet seems to be writing with an absolute confidence in his poetic vocation: "It is a beauteous evening calm and free." Suggestive generality is followed by a sharp detail, a simile to describe the quiet of the moment: "The holy time is quiet as a Nun / Breathless with adoration" (2–3); and an even more specific detail to capture the beauty of the sunset while underlining the controlling motif of silence: "the broad sun / Is sinking down in its tranquillity; / The gentleness of Heaven is on the Sea" (3–5).

Such a portrait of the beauteous evening changes abruptly, surprisingly so, as the speaker, alerting his companion, counsels, "Listen!" and then describes the breaking of the silence. From a personification that appears often in his treatments of nature—"the Mighty Being is awake" (6)—to the onomatopoeic capturing of the power of the Being which "doth with his eternal motion make / A sound like thunder—everlastingly" (7–8), Wordsworth conveys an almost mythic image of a Nature alive, powerful, eternal.

Turning to the child, and seemingly aware of the dominance of his own vision and the level of his adult abstraction, he pauses to reassure her, using traditional religious symbols, but in a sense undermining their absoluteness with his suggestion that truly religious experience is rooted in an inward awareness of an ultimate presence. For the child lies "in Abraham's bosom all the year," worships at the "Temple's inner shrine" with the uncluttered, unspoiled awareness of a youthful spirit, "God being with thee when we know it not" (13–14). Truly the Child is Father of the Man.

Among the sonnets, and still in a more private, personal vein, is a seventeen-line poem not often considered in discussions of Words-worth's poetry. The scenario reveals a speaker beholding Hesperus, the evening star, neither "Spirit who from Heaven hath flown" "Nor Traveller gone from Earth the Heavens to espy!" The light is skewed, nuanced, as Hesperus is "First admonition that the sun is down!" and "yet it is broad day-light." Clouds pass away, and at last the sky is "all his own" (1–8).

The brilliance of the "most ambitious Star!" startles the speaker for a moment. More important, it triggers an "inquest"; he imagines that, like the star, he "might step beyond my natural race," that, like Keats in "When I Have Fears," he "might one day trace / Some ground not mine," and, that wish being granted, "My Soul, an Appa-rition in the place, / Tread there, with steps that no one shall re-prove!" (9–17). Wordsworth is clearly caught up in the world of the star, in the possibility of escaping the bonds of mortality to become a spirit treading the magic grounds of paradise.

Wordsworth was quite capable of escalating the intensity of his poetic voice in the sonnets, of moving beyond personal expression and the articulation of inward consciousness to deal with public con-cerns, although ultimately his deepest personal concerns, the impor-tance of individual freedom, the beauty and sacredness of nature, underlie his ideals of nationhood, the responsibilities of leaders, the spread of peace and justice. Here merge the personal voice and the prophetic voice of the poet/critic of contemporary culture and soci-ety. The power of the voice is especially caught in the sounds, the leanness of the language, the wonderfully interrupted rhythms.

We need not linger long over perhaps the most popular, certainly most often-quoted sonnet. There is an immediacy to its opening, a sharp movement to the theme, no coyness, hesitancy, false propri-ety. Actually less than a line drives home the point: "The world is too much with us"—with the quick reinforcement of how and why in "late and soon, / Getting and spending, we lay waste our powers: / Little we see in Nature that is ours; / We have given our hearts away, a sordid boon!" (1–4). Wordsworth seems to return again to the "savage torpor" motif of the *Lyrical Ballads* "Preface," to the notion that men and women have destroyed—the military metaphor of laying waste is a powerful one—their most basic capacities to feel and to imagine in the presence of their natural surroundings.

The second quatrain, or at least most of it, combines the plaintive with the deliberate, as it reinforces more vividly the charges of the first, the accusation that we have sold out to the world, given our hearts, our best selves, away. The scenes, rooted in nature, are powerfully erotic, suggesting not wily, studied seduction but wild abandon, orgiastic exhibitionism, anything that can lure men's hearts. First there is "This Sea that bares her bosom to the moon"; then the suggestion of a kind of starved sexual energy moving toward climax, "The Winds that will be howling at all hours / And are upgathered now like sleeping flowers," both followed by a restatement of the theme: "For this, for every thing, we are out of tune" (5–8). Then the sestet opens with a four-monosyllabic-word epilogue, an epilogue that indicts author and readers even more savagely than what has gone before. Bad enough, we imagine the speaker suggesting, that we are unresponsive to the love-offerings of nature, but worst of all, "It moves us not" (9). We do not care; we are dulled, unaware. Then, in the very middle of the first line of the sestet, following a pronounced caesura, the voice of the speaker, which has ranged from anger to sadness to this point, explodes with a guttural apostrophe, "Great God," followed by nearly unrelieved enjambment as he, in high melodrama, exclaims almost blasphemously, "I'd rather be / A Pagan suckled in a creed outworn" (9–10); I'd rather abandon every traditional religious belief, every pious dogma if I might return to the primitive awe, reverence, amazement, worship of nature's beauties, might locate the psychic myth-making power within, if I might, Gloucester-like, see feelingly. "So might I," he says, just a bit calmer, but still caught up in the intensity of his response, "Have glimpses that would make me less forlorn" (12). The glimpses—an interesting, pregnant word in the context, suggesting the shadings of powerful images rather than mere sight or sound—would relieve the sadness and anger that he feels. And what glimpses they are, evoking a world and a time when it was possible to believe in myth, in the imaginative view of reality, in the presence of the divine in the midst of the vicissitudes of everyday reality. Standing on the pleasant lea, a pagan convert, he might forget the "Getting and spending" and "Have sight of Proteus coming from the sea; / Or hear old Triton blow his wreathéd horn" (13–14). It is a powerful sonnet, a sonnet keenly attuned to a culture out of tune with the vivifying energies of nature, the comforting visions of myth, yet confident of the power residing in the inner life, in the creations of mind, in a natural supernaturalism.

The much-cited "London, 1802" also comes to mind as the private voice becomes more public, as the voice of England present summons England past. It is as if the poet's inner vision is challenged, even disrupted, by national politics. Again, the Miltonic sonnet form, with its lack of any elaborate division between octave and sestet, its greater freedom of movement, is clear. The vocative quality of the opening—"Milton! thou should'st be living at this hour"— suggests a cry for help, for a country devoted to the ideals of freedom, for men able to speak the truth in the face of violent controversy. "England hath need of thee" (1–2), thinking of Milton's commitment—another time, another place—to the ideals of the Puritan Revolution, ideals of a reformed Church, free of the corruptions of clergy, ideals of a society where an active citizenry can speak and write and publish without fear of repression, where virtue is seen not as repression or mere avoidance of evil, but as the active exercise of the best instincts of the human being.

The sonnet proceeds in an almost headlong manner as the speaker offers his bill of particulars in the form of brilliant figures of speech. England is "a fen / Of stagnant waters" (2). Using synecdoche most effectively, he surveys the perversion of English ideals— "altar, sword, and pen, / Fireside, the heroic wealth of hall and bower, / Have forfeited their ancient English dower / Of inward happiness" (3–6), and concludes with his vision of what is wrong and how it can be changed. Bluntly he argues, "We are selfish men" and pleads with Milton prayerfully, as an ancient people would plead with their champion, "Oh! raise us up, return to us again; / And give us manners, virtue, freedom, power" (6–8). Let Church, State,

Literary Establishment, Family recapture these ideals that once were realities but now are only faint shadows.

Turning even more directly and personally to Milton in the sestet, he prizes Milton's splendid isolation "like a Star and dwelt apart," with "a voice whose sound was like the sea" (9–10). Curiously, the speaker, appropriating the figure of Milton for himself and his own poetic vocation, sees him as heroic in Wordsworthian terms. A fighter for freedom, a spokesman for a free and reformed Church and State, a towering man of letters, "So didst thou travel on life's common way, / In cheerful godliness." At the same time he could put down his pastoral garb, his epic pen, his vision of the fall and ultimate redemption of mankind, while "thy heart / The lowliest duties on herself did lay" (12–14).

And it is not just England or Milton that dominate the imagination of the inspired poet of this first decade of the century. The young radical, who roamed the streets of Paris or Orleans in 1791 with freedom in his blood, with change and democracy as his fondest hopes for the world, knew well before his so-called period of decline the forces of moderation, of reaction, of changing in order to reform. The stirring opening words that open the sonnet "Great Men have been among us" summon as witnesses great Commonwealth freedom-fighters like Algernon Sidney, Andrew Marvell, James Harrington, Sir Henry Vane the Younger, and "others who call'd Milton friend." These men were first "Moralists," then statesmen; they were, as Burke might put it, not theorists but men who "could act and comprehend." They were not self-serving demagogues, but men who "knew how genuine glory was put on." Burke seems to loom large as the catalogue of political wisdom continues in the octet. Milton and those who espoused his ideals "Taught us how rightfully a nation shone / In splendor"; they demonstrated, as Burke was to declare eloquently to his fellow members of Parliament concerning the English need to conciliate the American colonies, "what strength was, that would not bend / But in magnanimous meekness" (1–9).

With hardly a pause, the sestet turns at the halfway point in line nine to France. The speaker finds such men in France as he did in England. Spondees deliver a throbbing message. Fertile personifications deliver a savage critique—"Perpetual emptiness! unceasing change!" Skillful synecdoches, prefaced by the relentless "no," offer a vision of ghastly, chaotic France, now ruled by license, not by wisdom: "No single Volume paramount, no code, / No master spirit, no determined road; / But equally a want of Books and Men!" (11–14).

The public voice continues to be heard, especially in the sonnets, a voice that continues to celebrate the ideal of freedom, to berate the betrayal of the Revolution in France, to offer prophetic warnings to his fellow Englishmen. The voice is frequently conscious of another and kindred presence—Wordsworth, of Dorothy—in "Composed in the Valley near Dover, on the Day of Landing" with its vivid contrast of Europe "in bonds" and the freedom of England: "My Country! and 'tis joy enough and pride / For one hour's perfect bliss, to tread the grass / Of England once again, and hear and see, / With such a dear Companion at my side" (11–14). That public voice eulogizes François Dominique Toussaint, surnamed L'Ouverture, the son of a black slave who, as governor of Haiti, fought against Napoleon's reestablishment of slavery and was imprisoned in 1802. Creating an almost Christ-like portrait, he sees Toussaint as "the most unhappy Man of Men" (1) and urges an imprisoned, suffering hero to "Wear rather in thy bonds a cheerful brow" (7), to take comfort and pride both in the legacy of opposition to tyranny he has left behind and in "Powers that will work for thee; air, earth, and skies," allies and friends, "exultations, agonies, / And love, and Man's unconquerable mind" (9–14).

A less frequently discussed, but powerful sonnet, "September 1, 1802," originally called "The Banished Negroes" when published in *The Morning Post*, February 11, 1803, is a plea on behalf of the oppressed, as Wordsworth and Dorothy see dramatized the driving of all blacks from France. There is a special power, but never a stridency, about the poem. The depth of the speaker's feeling is enough; the image of the woman is more powerful than any political tract; the depth of the speaker's concern nuances any images of an aging revolutionary Wordsworth turning reactionary or conservative.

As is the case with so many of the 1807 poems, especially the sonnets, there is a wonderfully straightforward, almost repertorial quality in the simplicity of the opening. We can imagine the scene, the ship, Dorothy and William returning from Calais. "We had a fellow-Passenger who came / From Calais with us, spotless in array"

(1–2). She has been expelled humiliatingly from France, and there is a peculiar ambivalence about her as Wordsworth observes her. She is "A Negro Woman like a Lady gay" (3), "silent as a woman fearing blame," "Dejected, meek"; but this is only part of the portrait that Wordsworth etches brilliantly in rich detail (4–5). He is obviously moved by the woman, struck by the different signals her expressions send out to him, but, more important, to the world at large. Unembarrassed, proud, resolute, "She sate, from notice turning not away" (6).

The last five lines continue the episode, sharpening the image of the somewhat laconic woman. No mere token sympathy, no sentimental idealization, the lines burrow to the soul of a woman whose expression prevails over any intellectualization of her situation, and mock any image of a defeated, despairing outcast. Creating something like an emotional jolt, the speaker dramatizes the woman—"driv'n from France / Rejected," declaring her situation "Nor murmur'd at the unfeeling Ordinance" (10–14). The word *feeling* continues to have a peculiar Wordsworthian cast to it, as if the plea is not just for intellectual recognition as the beginning of reform, but also, and more crucial, for emotional persuasion.

The thesis of this overview of the 1807 poems in Wordsworth's literary life has been that even in his most buoyantly confident poems of this collection there are evidences of a dark side, of a tension between a faith in and commitment to the power of mind/imagination to shape values and a deepening awareness of the unavoidable demands of a reality beyond. Several poems in the collection offer a stronger, even more notably marked awareness of a need for anchors of emotional support—political, social, philosophical, religious—in which one can find a security, a point beyond the ego, a faith to live by when the sharpness of vision wanes, the rapport of spirit and nature becomes less vital, the phenomena of death, sorrow, loss invade the joyous environs of youthful ardor and confidence.

I have, in following Wordsworth's poetic life, already alluded to the events of the 1790s and early 1800s that confronted him with the dark side: failed love, political disillusionment, uncertainty about a career, the death of his brother John. My strategy has been to respect the demands of history and biography, even in such a committed poetic life, and yet not to fall into the trap of a cause-and-effect story. The literary life I am tracing has tried to keep certain representative poems as central—from early efforts in loco-descriptive poetry such as *An Evening Walk* and *Descriptive Sketches*, to the great ventures of the *Lyrical Ballads* and *The Prelude*, through the present consideration of that varied collection rather innocently called *1807 Poems*—and has, in following that strategy, found rich opportunities for letting the poems speak for themselves, first as creative efforts and then as embodiments of a rich, complex, even mysterious life.

There are several poems of the first order in the *1807 Poems* that seem to stand out from their companion pieces. They seem to dramatize, seldom with any overt didacticism, the theme of loss and death and also new counter-themes of hope and duty and the need for some firm societal, political, philosophical representation of these counter-themes. I mean in no way to suggest that these poems have not achieved abundant and exemplary treatment elsewhere through the years, only that such poems, some brilliantly figurative, reveal a poet not simply aware of the nuances of experience, but also more somberly aware of a too optimistic trust in his early years and of a need for new virtues, new sources of strength to deal with the harsher realities that come with age. I take four of these as excellent examples; chronologically they range from 1804 to 1806.

Not enough attention, I believe, has been paid to "The Small Celandine," one of three celandine poems. "To the Small Celandine" and "To the Same Flower" celebrate the seldom-noticed flower, noted for its beauty but especially for its power to close or open according to the degree of light and temperature in the air, a power seen by Wordsworth as its capacity to protect itself from wind and cold. "The Small Celandine," the third poem. with essentially the same subject, deals with the flower in more metaphorical—indeed, symbolic—terms, creating, as is often the case with a Wordsworth interested in ballads, a kind of mini-drama that shimmers with interpretive possibilities.

The mini-drama begins innocently enough; one might say calmly, blithely. The narrator offers us a lesson about the flowers: "There is a Flower, the Lessor Celandine, / That shrinks, like many more, from cold and rain." But the celandine has a special distinction, however: its endurance, resilience, survivability. It seems to have some special, inner strength that ensures "the first moment that the sun may shine, / Bright as the sun itself 'tis out again!" (1–4). And, as if to reassure readers that this is more than a botany lesson, the narrator speaks of many a personal observation to dramatize the celandine's self-sufficiency, its ability to shelter itself from the harsh forces of nature: "When hailstones have been falling, swarm on swarm, / Or blasts the green field and the trees distress'd, / Oft have I seen it muffled up from harm, / In close self-shelter, like a Thing at rest" (5–8).

The drama builds as the narrator in a sense undermines his earlier eulogy. A stanza moves from the everyday power of the flower to a somewhat alarming episode "lately," "one rough day," when he passed the flower and "recognized it, though an alter'd form." There is a degree of suspense; yes, we hear that one recent day he saw the flower differently. Yes! But altered how? What follows is a grotesque scarecrow-like image of the flower "Now standing forth an offering to the Blast, / And buffeted at will by Rain and Storm" (9–12). Darkness visible.

To this point the speaker is reasonably remote, recording the flourishing, then the decline and fall, of the resilient flower. As the drama continues, the narrator enters more fully and intimately into it, carrying on an interior monologue and recording it for us. And it is a puzzling monologue, not decisive, ambivalent in a variety of ways. We hear that "I stopp'd." We wonder what is suggested by his telling us what he "said with inly-muttered voice." What does "muttered" suggest? An innocent observation? wistful remark? sarcasm? sadness? Whatever the mood, there is a decisiveness about one thing: that the flower *must* grow old. "It doth not love the shower, nor seek the cold: / This neither is its courage nor its choice, / But its necessity in being old" (13–16). And age changes, takes its toll on beauty: "Stiff in its members, wither'd, changed of hue" (19). "Decay" is its lot.

The internalization of the scene intensifies as the account of the interior monologue closes and the narration resumes. The narrator records his response to the tragedy he has just described, and it is a frustratingly ambivalent one: "And, in my spleen, I smiled that it was grey" (20). What can his state of mind be as he smiles at the

predicament of the withered celandine? Does he smile with a grim
delight that the flower's demise matches his own? Is the flower a
symbol of himself, the decay a symbol of his own? Or is his smile
one of sadness, a sense of "You too" or perhaps "You and I both"? We
are left puzzled with this startling episode and a shaken speaker's
response.

Shaken though it may be for a time, there is a recovery and a
stolid translation of the episode into a somewhat definitive "To be a
Prodigal's Favourite—then, worse truth, / A Miser's Pensioner—
behold our lot!" There is a parable-like quality to his interpretation
of the flower's passage from resilience to decay, followed by a now-
familiar prayerful closing, "O Man! that from thy fair and shining
youth / Age might but take the things Youth needed not!"

We have already had occasion to discuss Sir George Beaumont as
one of a limited cast of characters in Wordsworth's early life. Friend
and benefactor, Beaumont was a painter of minor distinction, and it
is one of his paintings that occasions a most revealing poem in a
vein similar to that of "The Small Celandine." Wordsworth's Isabella
Fenwick note on background is instructive, although, again, such
background does not make the poem any more powerful. Beaumont
had done two pictures of Peele Castle, one of which he gave to
Wordsworth's wife, Mary. The castle is relatively near Barrow-in-
Furness in North Lancashire. On the Isle of Man just off the coast
of Rampside stands the battered but imposing ruins of the castle
that was once the residence of the Princess of Mona. Christopher
Wordsworth, his uncle's biographer, records that Wordsworth spent
a four-week college vacation there at the home of his cousins the
Barkers in August and September 1798. We can imagine how blissful
those days must have been for a young idealist shaken by personal
and public sadness. We can further imagine his response to Beaumont's painting (still at Coleorton and exhibited in 1982 at a Wordsworth Museum exhibition in Grasmere). Though not a painting of
the first order, it is nevertheless an imposing rendering of Peele
Castle in a storm—with a touch of Burke's sublime—the castle
standing firm in the midst of black clouds, turbulent seas, powerful
winds.

As the poem opens, the speaker, with memories of the peace of
a youthful summer vacation, seems alarmed at what he considers the

frightening character of Beaumont's vision. The reader may be struck by how Wordsworth, the year now being 1806, his brother John recently drowned in the tragic shipwreck, responds. There is the sense that, as in "The Small Celandine," the subject, here Peele Castle, becomes a metaphor for the self, its present state, its response to the picture, its resolve for the future. Again we have a "then-now" poem as the speaker in relatively regular iambic pentameter quatrains (*a, b, b, a*) views the work. Again there is an element of strategic surprise as the initial viewing of the painting and the first seven stanzas that follow seem concerned less with the painting than with memories of a different time that the scene evokes. It is not the immediate emotional impact of a castle torn by tempest but, rather, a quiet, companionable memory. "I was thy Neighbor once, thou rugged Pile! / Four summer weeks I dwelt in sight of thee: / I saw thee every day; and all the while / Thy Form was sleeping on a glassy sea" (1–4). Images of more blissful days, cloudless, windless, unchanging, filled with light, dominate the next two stanzas as the speaker revels in memories of an existence untrammeled by change: "Whene'er I looked," he addresses the Castle, "thy Image still was there; / It trembled, but it never pass'd away" (7–8). He feels that at the time "the mighty Deep / Was even the gentlest of all gentle Things" (11–12), and, with a wish that he had Beaumont's gift of painting, he affirms that he would have touched the scene imaginatively, would have, in the spirit of Addison's pleasures of the imagination, brought a unique dimension to it: "The light that never was, on sea or land, / The consecration, and the Poet's dream" (15–16). He would have seen not Beaumont's stormy vision of the Castle, but one "Beside a sea that could not cease to smile; / On tranquil land, beneath a sky of bliss" (19–20), "A Picture had it been of lasting ease, / Elysian quiet, without toil or strife" (25–26).

Then, as in the drama of "The Small Celandine," there is a turn in the rhetoric of the poem, a strangely stern indictment of what he would have done then "in the fond delusion of my heart" (29). With "no more" sounding a new knell, of submitting "to a new control," of a "power ... gone, which nothing can restore," there is the revelation that "A deep distress hath humaniz'd my Soul" (33–36). There is the immediate suggestion of "loss" of a "mind serene," of his sadness at the death of his brother John, Beaumont's friend; and, indeed, that loss is something that cannot be ignored in a careful and thorough reading of the poem (39–40). Yet to see these and subsequent lines as merely the account of a brother's death and the grief it occasions is to miss a key part of this poem, of the group we find ourselves discussing here, of the *1807 Poems*, perhaps even of Wordsworth's poetry generally—namely, the way in which a particular sadness can be seen in the larger context of the clash of joy and sorrow, gain and loss, optimism and pessimism, and the ways in which the poet confronts such clashes.

Yes, there is brief mention or at least suggestion of John, his dearest brother, of his death "whom I deplore" (42), but it is brief indeed. Beaumont the painter is addressed; Beaumont's sublime painting is analyzed. And the analysis now, unlike the one earlier in the poem, is decidedly positive, an object no longer to "blame," but to "commend"—"passionate," but "wise and well." And, with an image that evokes the identification of speaker and scene, an image with a "spirit" "Well chosen," an image, like the later, withered state of the small celandine, with which the speaker seems to identify, he admires "That Hulk which labours in the deadly swell, / This rueful sky, this pageantry of fear!" (43–48). The identification and the admiration, indeed love, intensify with a related image: "And this huge Castle, standing here sublime, / I love to see the look with which it braves, / Cased in the unfeeling armour of old time, / The lightning, the fierce wind, and trampling waves" (49–52).

One might say that the poem speaks beautifully for itself to this point, being rather than meaning, articulating metaphorically rather than ruminating philosophically. Yet, as in "The Small Celandine," the speaker feels a need to draw conclusions, highly personal ones, to sum up—indeed, to offer a certain amount of self-indictment—as he says farewell to an earlier poetry of the self, of the imagination, and welcome to what can only be called a more stoic life. "Farewell, farewell the Heart that lives alone, / Hous'd in a dream, at distance from the Kind!" Farewell to a kind of happiness "to be pitied; for 'tis surely blind." Hello to "fortitude, and patient cheer," for "Not without hope we suffer and we mourn" (57–60).

The pull of the individual and the social, the imagination and the senses, the personal and the public, freedom and restraint has seldom been more graphically dramatized in Wordsworth's poetry to date, and seldom has the tug-of-war pulled more toward conservative values. One need not look to the so-called later Wordsworth for clear and artistically engaging enactments of the essential struggle of his imagination from the beginning.

If we describe the previous two poems as artistically engaging in their search for more stolid values, for a firmer anchoring in the real, we cannot say the same about still another "quest for security" poem, the *Ode to Duty*. Here tensions seem resolved in advance; the past is to a great extent rejected, as the speaker prays for "confidence of reason," for endurance. The Isabella Fenwick note is especially instructive in pointing up the turn outward, to a point of security beyond the self. "We should," he says, "be rigorous to ourselves and forbearing, if not indulgent, to others, and, if we make comparisons at all, it ought to be with those who have morally excelled us."

But it is not just a new remorse about early individualism, a new conservatism that catches the attention. The choice of the somewhat stiff form of the classical ode (the Fenwick note tells us that the poem is "on the model of Gray's Ode to Adversity, which is copied from Horace's Ode to Fortune"); the Senecan Stoic motto ("Not only consciously good but so habituated by training that I not only can act rightly but cannot act otherwise"); the regular use of rather colorless abstractions ("O Duty," "dread Power," "Stern Lawgiver"); the singsong rhythms—all point to a more anxious Wordsworth. The poet now seems more eager to see poetry as a vehicle for instruction, a record of conversion, a new act of faith in a life characterized by virtues of restraint and a continuing measuring of self against a code of classical ethics.

There is, apart from the reverential tone, a kind of awkwardness of both diction and rhythm in the opening of the poem: "Stern Daughter of the Voice of God! / O Duty! if that name thou love / Who art a Light to guide, a Rod / To check the erring and reprove" (1–4). That awkwardness continues, even as the rhythms become more regularly iambic, and the speaker criticizes his earlier life when he "too blindly" reposed his trust in "freedom" (25–28). He would "supplicate for thy control," following his prayer with the jarring inversion, "Me this uncharter'd freedom tires" and the stolid, "I long for a repose which ever is the same" (37–40). There is deep resignation in the concluding stanza, a sense of almost precious guilt and a plea for a new code of virtue, "guidance" for his "weakness," "The confidence of reason," "the light of truth" (59–64).

Although it has been the object of parody, of criticism by Sara Hutchinson and Coleridge, there are few starker, almost modern poems than *Resolution and Independence*. While it does tread the delicate line between mawkish sentimentality and somber realism, it seems nevertheless to tip the balance toward the latter. Coleridge uses particular stanzas to illustrate nicely his reservations about the "INCONSTANCY of the *style* . . . the sudden and unprepared transitions from lines or sentences of peculiar felicity (at all events striking and original) to a style, not only unimpassioned but undistinguished."[26]

The poem returns to the humble and rustic motifs of the *Lyrical Ballads*, to some extent to the language of that life. The seven-line (*a, b, a, b, b, c, c*) stanza, with a somewhat free iambic pattern, carries forward the narrative, or should I say the drama, with a good deal of energy. There is, indeed, some of the someberness of the early poems combined with the lyric brightness of the more joyous 1807 poems. But what is most striking is the poem's taking its place with the texts already considered which, on the one hand, portray the sadness that is part of the fabric of real life and which, on the other hand, commend virtues of endurance and survival. Paul Magnuson, whose "dialogic reading sees a Coleridge-Wordsworth canon as a single work," argues that " 'Resolution and Independence' is the sequel to Coleridge's [verse letter] and turns as abruptly from its depression as other moments in the 1802 dialogue turn from their preceding moments."[27]

There is a charming, joyful three-stanza opening. "All nature seems at work," as Coleridge's "Work Without Hope" puts it. Sound and sense combine, as a symphony of light and music develops—sun, wind, rain, bird-song, water-noise. "All things that love the sun are

[26] Coleridge, *Biographia Literaria*, ed. James Engell and W. Jackson Bate, 2 vols. (Princeton, N.J.: Princeton University Press, 1983), 2:121–126.
[27] *Coleridge and Wordsworth*, p. 309.

out of doors; / The sky rejoices in the morning's birth" (8–9). Focusing on the self in the midst of this feast of the senses, a "Traveller," "I heard the woods and distant waters, roar; / Or heard them not, as happy as a boy" (15–18). There is almost perfect rapport: "The pleasant season did my heart employ"; all the ways of the world seem "so vain and melancholy" (19–20).

Such a spirit is characteristic of many of the 1807 poems. But, as seen already in "The Small Celandine," "Elegiac Stanzas," and the *Ode to Duty*, the spirit is challenged, not openly or brashly, but almost innocently, by the appearance of a flower, a painting, or a person that seems to undermine the mood, the joyous vision, and to offer a counter-image. Stanzas four and five offer the first omens, the first hints of how joy and sorrow are intertwined. Yes, the speaker suggests, joy is the order of this special morning, but to be human is to know that "As high as we have mounted in delight / In our dejection do we sink as low" (24–25). Happy as he is on this morning, there is "another day" coming, one of "Solitude, pain of heart, distress, and poverty" (34–35).

Conflicting moods, so typical of the mature Wordsworth, begin to dominate the poem as we hear the speaker, Job-like, wrestling with his situation. On the one hand—"a happy Child of earth am I"—he echoes the sentiments of "Expostulation and Reply" and "The Tables Turned" in expressing his confidence that "all needful things would come unsought / To genial faith, still rich in a genial good," a confidence in the creative power of mind (38–39). On the other hand, there is the almost biblical questioning: "But how can He expect that others should / Build for him, sow for him, and at his call / Love him, who for himself will take no heed at all" (40–42). Chatterton, Burns, poets in general are his witnesses, beginning in "gladness," ending in "despondency and madness" (48–49).

At the very moment of crisis emerges the leech-gatherer, a figure from Wordsworth's gallery of rustics, yet not a figure, but a natural phenomenon, stark, "unawares," "The oldest man he seem'd that ever wore grey hairs" (55–56). In a full stanza he lingers over this phenomenon, seeing the man "As a huge stone is sometimes seen to lie / Couch'd on the bald top of an eminence; / Wonder to all who do the same espy." Large, seemingly immovable, awesome and mysterious in its presence, the image generates another image, simile giving birth to simile. How did such a stone get to such a height? How did such a creature reach such an age? The stone "seems a thing endued with sense: / Like a sea-beast crawl'd forth, which on a shelf / Of rock or sand reposeth, there to sun itself" (64–70). In images that have a Frostian ring, the old man's body, reminding us of the celandine or of Peele Castle, "was bent double, feet and head / Coming together in life's pilgrimage; / As if some dire constraint of pain, or rage / Of sickness felt by him in times long past, / A more than human weight upon his frame had cast" (73–77).

Enter the speaker more immediately, struck by the old man's presence, greeting him—"This morning gives us promise of a glorious day" (97)—and questioning him about his identity and occupation. Rustic though he be, he answers in "a stately speech" (103). He is a leech-gatherer, "old and poor" (107), yet the speaker sublimates him, imagining him "Like one whom I had met with in a dream; / Or like a Man from some far region sent, / To give me human strength, and strong admonishment" (117–119). His language, "discourse" it is called, hardly denotative, barely decodable, is ultimately mysterious for the speaker, "like a stream scarce heard; / Nor word from word could I divide" (114–115). Still fearful, wishful, mindful of fellow poets dead and gone, seeking comfort in his sadness, he returns to his questioning about exactly what the man does. Gathering leeches, the man answers, but there are now few to gather. What strikes the speaker, indeed, troubles him, is the man's stoic, "Yet still I persevere, and find them where I may" (133); he survives in the midst of loss and age. As so often in this cluster of 1807 poems, the speaker finds metaphors for his own sense of the slow erosion of youthful hope and joy, his reaching beyond the self and its power. This reaching out, always present in Wordsworth as man and poet, is articulated in increasingly pronounced and prayerful fashion as it is at the end of "Resolution and Independence." " 'God,' said I, 'be my help and stay secure; / I'll think of the Leech-gatherer on the lonely moor' " (146–147).

And beyond the celandine, Peele Castle, the leech-gatherer are other images of endurance in "The affliction of Margaret," "The Sailor's Mother" (a poem praised by Coleridge), and, most notably, in "Character of the Happy Warrior," a poem immediately occasioned by the death of Lord Nelson on October 21, 1805, but ultimately grounded in the tragedy of his brother John's death. This last poem celebrates all those heroic figures, public and private, "more able to endure, / As more expos'd to suffering and distress," and eulogizes the happy warrior "whose law is reason" (24–27).

Clearly the most celebrated of the 1807 *Poems* is the *Immortality Ode*. Its full title, of great importance for all who study the poem carefully, reads, "*Ode: Intimations of Immortality from Recollections of Early Childhood*," and the poem has as its suggestive epigraph the lines from another crucial poem of this collection, "My heart leaps up."

We know that the composition of the poem came in two phases and that it attracted the attention of Coleridge early, probably occasioning his own poem, some would say response, "Dejection: An Ode." In the Isabella Fenwick note, Wordsworth says that his poem "was composed during my residence at Town-End, Grasmere; two years at least passed [probably between March 27, 1802 and March 6, 1804] between the writing of the first four stanzas and the remaining part." We know from these notes and other sources that he had a great deal to say about the poem and the circumstances surrounding it, all of it helpful although not necessarily affording any magical inroads. Some may be skeptical about what he calls "particular feelings or *experiences* of my own mind on which the structure of the poem partly rests." Intriguing, however, is his comment that "nothing was more difficult for me in childhood than to admit the notion of death as a state applicable to my own being. . . . With a feeling congenial to this, I was often unable to think of external things as having external existence, and I communed with all that I saw as something not apart from, but inherent in, my own immaterial nature." And there is his further remembrance that he needed at times to follow a Johnsonian course of establishing contact with a wall or a tree to bring himself back from "this abyss of idealism to the reality." Later in life, however, he regretted "a subjugation of an opposite character, and . . . rejoiced over the remembrances."

There is also the intriguing observation on his childhood, as recorded in his nephew's *Memoirs*, that at that time his feelings were of "my absolute spirituality, my 'all-soulness' " with the consequent belief that he could not die.[28] Or there is the observation, in a Janu-

---

[28] 2:476.

ary 1815 letter to Catherine Clarkson, that the *Immortality Ode* "rests entirely upon two recollections of childhood, one that of a splendour in the objects of sense which is passed away, and the other an indisposition to bend to the law of death as applying to our particular case." So powerful is this mind-reality tension, he says, that "A Reader who has not a vivid recollection of these feelings having existed in his mind in childhood cannot understand that poem."[29] The poet directing his audience, to be sure!

Perhaps the most potent *apologia* for the poem and its difficulties is Coleridge's reinforcement of this final remark to Catherine Clarkson and his framing a large part of the discourse to be used in any real critique of the poem. The ode, says Coleridge, is, indeed, meant for a select audience, those "accustomed to watch the flux and reflux of their inmost nature . . . to feel a deep interest in modes of inmost being, to which they know that the attributes of times and space are inapplicable and alien, but which yet can not be conveyed, save in symbols of time and space."[30]

But the poem must also be read as it is, touched by the personal anguish, political turmoil, and social change of the years during which Wordsworth was composing. In so many ways it gathers together his tensions and anxieties that have been increasingly apparent, but never so vividly dramatized. Jeffrey Robinson sees Wordsworth's disappointments leading to "an enormous retrenchment and reorganization of his goals and (like other young Romantics) his interpretation of experience; in this new way he seems to have found the beginnings of equanimity." The influence of Burke, the friendship with the "religious Coleridge" "helped slowly to settle Wordsworth toward his own more conservative poetics (or as Peter J. Manning has recently suggested, to *return* him to the conservative world view in which he had been raised)." A life close to Dorothy, to his beloved nature gives him "his identity as a poet . . . and stands opposed to the fluctuation of passion—love and radical political activism."[31] The poetic fire encounters history and the writer in history. The *Ode* is in a sense a map of the inner life with

---

[29] *MY* 3.2:189.

[30] *Biographia Literaria*, 2.147.

[31] *Radical Literary Education: A Classroom Experiment with Wordsworth's "Ode"* (Madison: University of Wisconsin Press, 1987), pp. 142–143.

shadowy boundaries rendered by a poetic cartographer, shadings of loss and gain, sadness and joy, despair and hope. It is a remarkable rendering of the emotional struggle between these polarities as we have been witnessing the contest almost from the beginning.

Its beauty lies in its lack of neatness, indeed its seeming formlessness, as it roams back and forth in the psyche, looking for fixed points of reference and stability. We have a speaker now adrift, now secure; now bemoaning the loss of childhood ecstasy, now ready to march with the creatures of nature and to sing a paean of joy and hope. He is a speaker who evokes conflicting emotions just as Wordsworth does, allowing us to hear shouts of joy undermined by the organ tones of sadness as if he were a living emblem of the human experience. At times we find a passion to affirm subverted by his awareness of how difficult affirmation is. The *Ode* nuances much more richly than "The Small Celandine" and "Elegiac Stanzas," allowing for the withering effects of time on the flower, the shattering impact of wind and waves on the castle, and the need for secure anchors beyond the self, but refusing to capitulate to suffering and death.

The form of the poem relentlessly matches the ebb and flow of the speaker's emotions. An irregular Pindaric ode, with varying lengths of lines and stanzas, continuing enjambment, the poem is a classic interior monologue. One might think of it in terms of a question, an answer advanced, and, depending on one's point of view, a justification of the answer or a rationalization. The opening, introducing in regular iambic rhythms the brilliant imagery of light that Wordsworth associates with clarity of vision, is a "then-now" stanza as the speaker contrasts the way he saw the world as a child with the way he sees it as a man. Childhood is a divinity-charged existence, a time of connectedness "when meadow, grove, and stream, / The earth, and every common Sight, / To me did seem / Apparell'd in celestial light, / The glory and the freshness of a dream" (1–5). Such a state now seems remote, the rapture gone as, somewhat like Coleridge in "Dejection: An Ode," he mourns, "It is not now as it hath been of yore;— / Turn wheresoe'er I may, / By night or day, / The things which I have seen I now can see no more" (6–9).

The second stanza offers strong reinforcement. Images are more concrete and vivid, the details sharper, as the ruminating speaker re-creates the brilliance of youthful days. He is surrounded by flower, lake, sky, sun, moon, rainbow, but again, like Coleridge's speaker in "Dejection," he sees, but does not feel. And he bemoans in biblical fashion: "But yet I know, where'er I go, / That there hath pass'd away a glory from the earth" (17–18).

In the midst of the "joyous song" of the birds or "as the young lambs bound / As to the tabor's sound," he is the oddity. "To me alone there came a thought of grief" (19–22). But this thought of grief is short-lived, so the speaker assures us; a "timely utterance"—is it the poem itself or, more strikingly, the voice of memory; or, even more strikingly, the voice that commands joy to conquer sadness?—"gave that thought relief, / And I again am strong" (23–24). Sounding waterfalls, mountains, sea, wind, beast, even the happy shepherd whom he addresses gleefully, "all the earth is gay" (29). And "the fulness of your bliss, I feel—I feel it all" (40). Yet the inevitable "But" follows, the "Tree," the "single Field" that "speak of something that is gone," and the stanza concludes with two powerful questions that go to the heart of Wordsworth's life and work: "Whither is fled the visionary gleam? / Where is it now, the glory and the dream?" (51–57). Light once seen, now gone. Nature once charged with spirit, now darkly silent. Where have all the flowers gone? What has become of the ecstatic union of mind and nature? There is a deep sadness in the questions, the onomatopoeic *wh* sounds suggesting the quick breath of the wind whispering away the brightness of vision suggested by the assonantial long *o*'s and *e*'s—"visionary gleam," "now," "the glory and the dream."

Stanza five begins what seems like the second movement in the symphony, the attempt to answer the resounding questions left at the end of the previous stanza. Wordsworth's disclaimer in the Fenwick note notwithstanding—"It is far too shadowy a notion to be recommended to faith, as more than an element in our instincts of immortality"—the controlling answers and the images in which they are couched are ultimately Platonic: the ideal state, a slow forgetting of the bright forms of pre-existence, and a final passage into a world of shadows. "Heaven lies about us in our infancy!" and "Shades of the prison-house begin to close / Upon the growing Boy" (66–68), but all is not lost. There is imagination, but time is relentless, as "At length the Man perceives it die away, / And fade into the light of common day" (75–76). Almost frantically focusing on the child as "best Philosopher" (10), "Mighty Prophet!" "Seer blest!" (114), he nevertheless foresees an ending: "Full soon thy Soul shall have her earthly freight" (129).

But the poem will not end here; there will be no capitulation to age. But, we say, how can such a charting of the progress of the soul turn joyous, even wildly joyous at times. There is, of course, no completely satisfying answer for the wide range of readers who confront the poem. Douglas Bush, already noted, in the tradition of Matthew Arnold, sees Wordsworth evading the dark side of experience, the impact of original sin, and resorting to what he sees as facile optimism. Others, especially those in the Coleridge tradition of Wordsworth criticism, find the resolution very much in keeping with the Romantic affirmation of the poet. Still others in the Mc-Gannian New Historicist tradition would see it as denial.

In stanza nine, the first of the last movement of the symphony of farewell, we have the longest and most shapeless of the poem— thirty-nine lines with their own peculiar shapes and rhythms, their own language of both sharp denotation and rippling suggestiveness. It is a movement of almost simplistic affirmation undermined by a flow of richly connotative language that struggles to articulate the state of the aging spirit, only to be further undermined by a brilliantly vivid image of confident faith that prepares the way for the marching-band quality of the last two stanzas. Given the journey toward loss and age in the previous movement, the stanza chooses almost not to deal with it in any straightforward way. Just when tragedy looms large, comedy will have its day. Wordsworth will have faith regardless of his awareness of the tragedy of life.

The opening quatrain, with its singsong *abab* rhythm, has an almost too decisive optimism: "O joy! that in our embers / Is something that doth live, / That nature yet remembers / What was so fugitive!" (132–135). Yet while the optimism continues through the psychic ruminations of this lengthy stanza, it is moderated and refined by longer, even stanzaic patterns with irregular rhythms. There is a kind of measured gratitude that pervades the interior monologue, one that, while positive, will not evade intimations of sadness. Memory brings the hope of "perpetual benediction" (137), yet the remembrance is not mere nostalgia. The more mature speaker treasures not merely the light, the bright certainties of childhood, but also complex and more mysterious gifts, "those obstinate questionings / Of sense and natural things!" (144–145), gifts that are primal and enduring, capable of sustaining one in the midst of grief or doubt.

The stanza closes with the fertile metaphor rooted in Plato, or in Wordsworth's Plato. On the one hand, it envisions the movement away from the sea of light, eternity, and yet, on the other, it celebrates the capacity to return. The fast-changing rhythms and rhymes of the previous lines move toward the decisively iambic closing couplet:

> Hence, in a season of calm weather,
> Though inland far we be,
> Our souls have sight of that immortal sea
> Which brought us hither,
> Can in a moment travel thither,
> And see the Children sport upon the shore,
> And hear the mighty waters rolling evermore. [164–70].

The poem pushes on as the speaker joins in nature's celebration, and yet recognizes that "nothing can bring back the hour / Of splendour in the grass, of glory in the flower" (180–181). Yet he would rejoice in what is left, "in the faith that looks through death, / In years that bring the philosophic mind" (188–189).

The final stanza is a powerful and peculiarly Wordsworthian valediction. In still another variation of the image that goes back to his earliest poetry—shaded or skewed light—he calls attention to "The Clouds that gather round the setting sun," and records how those clouds, far from blotting out the sun or bringing grief, "Do take a sober colouring from an eye / That hath kept watch o'er man's mortality" (199–200). The enduring heart, changed by time though ultimately still the same; free in youth, solidly anchored in the reality of time and age, underlies the final affirmation: "To me the meanest flower that blows can give / Thoughts that do often lie too deep for tears" (205–206).

7

The Post-1810 Wordsworth: The Maturing of a Poetic Life

"It gives me real pain when I think that some future commentator may possibly hereafter write—This great poet survived to the fifth decennary, but he appears to have dyed in the year 1814 as far as life consisted in an active sympathy with the temporary welfare of his fellow creatures."

Henry Crabb Robinson to D. W.
November 1, 1842

"Distaste for Wordsworth's views has thus far largely precluded asking what kinds of poetry he evolved to convey them and what sorts of interest such poems might repay. The late poems deliberately no longer offer the richly represented self of, say, *The Prelude*, but once understood within their historical situation, their contexts steadily widen and their procedures gain meaning."

Peter Manning, *Reading Romantics*

Dread Power! whom peace and calmness serve
No less than Nature's threatening voice,
If aught unworthy be my choice,
From THEE if I would swerve;
O, let thy grace remind me of the light
Full early lost and fruitlessly deplored;
Which, at this moment, on my waking sight
Appears to shine, by miracle restored!

My soul, though yet confined to earth,
Rejoices in a second birth;
—'Tis past, the visionary splendor fades;
And Night approaches with her shades.

Wordsworth, "Composed Upon an
Evening of Extraordinary Splendour"

THERE HAS BEEN, almost from the beginning but especially in twenti-eth-century Wordsworth studies, a strong interest in the post-1810 or post-"Golden Decade" poet, as well as a pronounced tendency to see the later life and work as characterized by decline or, worse still, as a descent into the pious and prosaic. Such an attitude is interest-ing when we remember, first, that Wordsworth was barely forty at the time of his so-called decline and lived a full and busy life until he was twice that age, and, second, that, far from regarding the *Lyri-cal Ballads*, the 1807 *Poems*, and *The Prelude* as some kind of last gasp of creativity, he continued to write, edit, and revise poetry until the year of his death.

It may be true that few works of the post-1810 period match what some would regard as the special poetic excellence of the Golden Decade; still the enormous poetic output of 1810 to 1850— the final assembly of pieces for his epic *The Recluse* as *The Excursion* (1814), the symbolic *White Doe of Rylstone*, the remarkable sequence of River Duddon sonnets (1820) and the *Ecclesiastical Sonnets* (1822), *Yarrow Revisited and Other Poems* (1835), to name major undertak-ings—represents an effort of considerable stature in his literary life. Yet readers and critics continue the "early–later" paradigm in dis-cussing the post-1810 poems. As early as Hartley Coleridge's melo-dramatic "What a mighty genius is the Poet Wordsworth! What a dull proser is W. W. Esqre. of Rydal Mount, Distributor of stamps and brother to Rev'd. the Master of Trinity"[1] and the iconoclastic Bertrand Russell's later "In his youth he sympathized with the French Revolution, went to France, wrote good poetry, and had a natural daughter. At this period he was a 'bad' man. Then he became 'good,' abandoned his daughter, adopted correct principles, and

---

[1] *Letters of Hartley Coleridge*, ed. Grace Evelyn Griggs and Earl Leslie Griggs (London: Oxford University Press, 1936), p. 93.

wrote bad poetry," the early–late pattern, often in more sophisticated terms, is fixed.[2]

Matthew Arnold, certainly an admirer of Wordsworth, and a proponent of the Golden Decade approach, nevertheless separates himself from those whose praise for Wordsworth's philosophy would neglect his gifts as a poet. "His poetry," he says, "is the reality, his philosophy—so far, at least, as it may put on the form and habit of 'a scientific system of thought,' and the more that it puts them on—is the illusion." The young Arnold found the recluse at Rydal Mount too provincial, too uncultured for his tastes, not well read enough. Favoring the shorter poems, he sees the greatness of Wordsworth's poetry coming from "the extraordinary power with which Wordsworth feels the joy offered to us in nature, the joy offered to us in the simple primary affections and duties; and because of the extraordinary power with which, in case after case, he shows us this joy, and renders it so as to make us share it."[3]

Leslie Stephen, agreeing with Arnold on Wordsworth as philosophic poet, nevertheless praises this side of his work. His poetry, he argues, retains its power as the bright lights of other poets fade. But Stephen still holds to the image of a compartmentalized life, a before and after, a younger poet and an older philosopher. "We love him," says Stephen, "the more as we grow older and become more deeply impressed with the sadness and seriousness of life," at the time "when we have finally quitted the regions of youthful enchantment. And I take the explanation to be that he is not merely a melodious writer, or a powerful utterer of deep emotion, but a true philosopher."[4]

To Dover Wilson, Wordsworth looms more as late Wordsworth, a poet who belongs "to us all, the leaders of the Oxford Movement like John Keble, to unitarians like Stopford Brooke, to the 'saints of rationalism' like John Stuart Mill and Leslie Stephen." All creeds,

---

[2] Quoted in Edith Batho, *The Later Wordsworth* (Cambridge: Cambridge University Press, 1933), p. 312.

[3] "Wordsworth," *Essays in Criticism, Second Series: Contributions to the "Pall Mall Gazette" and Discourses in America,* in The Works of Matthew Arnold, 15 vols. (New York: AMS Press, 1903–1904), p. 00.

[4] "Wordsworth's Ethics," *Hours in a Library,* 4 vols. (New York: G. P. Putnam, 1904), 3:136.

all political persuasions turn to him "for beauty, for joy, for wisdom and for strength."[5]

Willard Sperry, somewhat in the Arnold tradition, shortens Wordsworth's career even more decisively than others. Allowing for some flashes of excellence, he nevertheless concludes that Wordsworth "could not be relied upon, after about 1806, to write poetry which bore upon its face the credentials of its greatness, and, failing inspiration, he manufactured verses," agreeing with Garrod's statement "that the last forty years of Wordsworth's life are 'the most dismal anti-climax of which the history of the world holds record.' "[6]

Even critics such as Edith Batho, a pioneer in the study of the later poems, complicate the problem of "the two Wordsworths." A wise and reasonably persuasive student of the post-1810 Wordsworth, she does not subscribe to the wholesale-decline approach. At the same time her measured praise says little about the poetry itself. She seems right, however, in her judgment, a judgment borne out by the rhythmic flow of freedom and anxiety evident in the poetry studied thus far, that "Wordsworth never lost faith in humanity. He refused to subscribe to the sentimental creed which takes no account of the actual state of humanity";[7] that the roots of evil, injustice, human sadness run even deeper than he had realized; and that "the remedies must be more profound."[8] And Michael Friedman, whose work has the ring of Raymond Williams, E. P. Thompson, David Erdman, and Carl Woodring, sees Wordsworth's genius as closely tied to "the stability of England's social and economic structures at the time when patriarchal political economy was disintegrating and England was being propelled into developed industrial capitalism." He further and strongly contends that the poet's "creativity seemed to have been linked to a strong need for the sense of an enclosing, supporting community."[9]

Carl Ketcham, in his introduction to the Cornell University edi-

---

[5] *Leslie Stephen and Matthew Arnold as Critics of Shakespeare* (Cambridge: Cambridge University Press, 1939), p. 59.

[6] "Wordworth's Decline" in *The English Romantics: Major Poetry and Critical Theory*, ed. John L. Mahoney (Lexington, Mass.: D. C. Heath, 1978), p. 698.

[7] *Later Wordsworth*, p. 149.

[8] Ibid., p. 230.

[9] *The Making of a Tory Humanist: William Wordsworth and the Idea of Community* (New York: Columbia University Press, 1979), p. 1.

tion of *Wordsworth's Shorter Poems, 1807–1820*, observes that "Really careful examination of Wordsworth's poems after about 1808 has been remarkably uncommon," almost giving the impression "that Matthew Arnold's dictum about Wordsworth's great decade, after which only a 'mass of inferiour work remains,' has been accepted, perhaps with gratitude, by all but a few dedicated Wordsworthians."[10] The major and classic studies of Geoffrey Hartman, M. H. Abrams, Harold Bloom, and others have focused chiefly on the pre-1814 poems in developing their arguments. The workings of more recent theoretical approaches such as deconstruction, New Historicism, and feminist theory have found the so-called earlier poems more hospitable. And those who have chosen to write at any length about the later works have rarely done so with exuberant praise, at times protesting almost too much about the quality of the poetry in the face of the poet's increasing political, religious, and social conservatism.

Mary Moorman, certainly a major biographer of the poet, sees problems in the post-1810 work. As she discusses Wordsworth's failure to complete his long-planned epic *The Recluse* and his emphasis on sonnets and shorter poems, she cites letters written by his family and friends indicating "that there was a mental shrinking from a task that he felt too heavy for him; a lack of inclination rather than of physical power to accomplish."[11] She cites especially Coleridge's judgment that *The Excursion* was inferior to *The Recluse* because it was "too much concerned with setting forth truths which to most people would be already self-evident."[12]

Stephen Gill, while in no way subscribing to the anti-climax theory, does point to the poetic silence following the negative reviews of the 1807 *Poems*, and Wordsworth's frustration with his inability to finish *The Recluse*; and yet, in a most telling observation on the 1817 poems, praises how "all of the 1817 poems testify to Wordsworth's creative vigour, but their tone suggests a poet aware that a moment in his imaginative life is coming to a close." He misses the "ebullience of earlier lyrics . . . , the energy that suggested the limitless

---

[10] (Ithaca, N.Y.: Cornell University Press, 1989), p. 5.
[11] *William Wordsworth: A Biography*, 2:257.
[12] Ibid., 2:266.

possibilities for poetry in the play of imagination upon the everyday."[13]

Gill's comment enforces my tracing of the course of Wordsworth's literary life, especially that phase following the period from 1797 to 1807. To speak of a movement in the poet's imaginative life as coming to a close sounds right, as does the tempering of an enthusiasm for the limitless possibilities of poetry. To speak further of the play of imagination upon the everyday is to catch a motif central to this study from the beginning. That motif—so often rehearsed in the study of the earliest poems, the *Lyrical Ballads*, and the 1807 *Poems* as a fundamental tension between, and anxiety about, the claims of the inner life as nourished by the imagination's encounter with nature and the demands of an insistent reality beyond the self—captures nicely the situation of Wordsworth in the years following the publication of the 1807 volumes.

Peter Manning, in a recent essay on Wordsworth's "Stanzas Suggested in a Steam-Boat off St. Bees Heads on the Coast of Cumberland," develops an interesting and perceptive approach to the later poetry. Noting the general lack of interest in the poems after 1807 and the way that lack of interest has "precluded asking what kinds of poetry [Wordsworth] evolved to convey them and what sorts of interest such poems might repay," he advances a fascinating strategy. Wordsworth's "final period," he insists, "should not be held in thrall to his earlier one, just because the earlier is more appealing." Wordsworth, he contends, outlived most of his fellow poets and also the period which literary historians have defined and described and in which they have placed him. "The late poems deliberately no longer offer the richly represented self of, say, *The Prelude*, but once understood within their historical situation, their contexts steadily widen and their procedures gain meaning."[14]

In a word, we do not meet a dramatically new poet in the later work; we meet one still experiencing the same tensions. The Wordsworthian poetic life is a continuum. Yet he is less quick to affirm a personal vision rooted in his inner life and in a deep rapport with a spiritual presence in nature, more ready to search for points of refer-

---

[13] *Wordsworth: A Life*, p. 325.
[14] "Wordsworth at St. Bees," p. 273.

ence in forces beyond the self, in a more ordered society, a more communal religion, a richer awareness of the limitations of mortality.

Richard McGhee's remarks on differences in the poetry after 1814 are worth noting. He sees the difference as "one of substance rather than exclusively one of degree." While "his earlier poetry embodied an existential discovery of meaning and beauty in the natural creation, his later poetry sought to escape the bounds of natural existence and penetrate to a perception of the essential values which transcend and give ultimate meaning to earthly beauty." Focusing on the comparison of the visiting Angel to the sun in the "Vernal Ode," he argues that there is no attempt at identification as there might have been in the earlier poetry. "The simile," he contends, "suggests that nature shares with infinity certain characteristics which can be revealed to mortal man only at times of twilight."[15]

William Galperin's recent study is most persuasive as he insists on "the validity of demarcating Wordsworth's career" but refuses to see the "alleged 'anti-climax' " as "a betrayal of the poet's radical or romantic vision." For him, the period of the Golden Decade "resulted instead from Wordsworth's exercise of poetic authority— yielding a revision of the earlier poetry that by turns anticipates and supersedes our contemporary, revisionist approaches to romanticism."[16]

The result of this idea of development from a literary standpoint is a drift, then a more pronounced movement, toward the quotidian, the didactic, toward a more predictable, indeed prosy diction and imagery. At the same time, there are occasions where we hear the younger poet (and the last section of this chapter will explore them), when the old skewed light, the autumnal tone, the metaphor of fulfillment leap out to engage, to provoke, to force an exploration of the rich complexity of experience. What we find is a Wordsworth growing older chronologically and artistically, but a Wordsworth still most deeply concerned with translating felt experience into the central activity of his life: poetry.

The question of "late-career art," of what Herman Broch has

---

[15] " 'And Earth and Stars Composed a Universal Heaven': A View of Wordsworth's Later Poetry," *Studies in English Literature*, 11 (1971), 641, 647–648.

[16] *Revision and Authority in Wordsworth: The Interpretation of a Career* (Philadelphia: University of Pennsylvania Press, 1989), p. 2.

called the "style of old age" or John Russell "Art Born in the Fullness of Age" is, of course, a large and mysterious one, certainly too
large for a study such as this one and perhaps not completely appropriate for a consideration of a literary life like Wordsworth's. Yet
some of Broch's and Russell's insights can be useful in helping us to
understand the phenomenon and to sharpen our arguments about
continuities in Wordsworth's career and about the inadequacies of
categories like "Golden Decade" or "early and late." Russell, taking
his cue from Kenneth Clark's lecture "The Artist Grows Old,"
speaks of "work done in old age in a distinctive, innovatory and often
problematic style by creative people in all the arts, from Aeschylus
in the 'Oresteia' in 458 B.C. to this year's music by Elliott Carter
and this year's paintings by Willem de Kooning and Francis Bacon"
and of a "late style, easier to recognize than to define, but in any
case unmistakable."[17]

Broch speaks of "the style of old age" as "not always a product
of the years; it is a gift implanted along with his other gifts in an
artist, ripening, it may be, with time, often blossoming before its
season under the foreshadow of death, or unfolding of itself even
before the approach of age or death; it is the reaching of a new level
of expression." "Every true artist," argues Broch, "aware that he
must form his own universe, is in some ways a rebel, willing to shat-
ter the closed system into which he is born. But he must realize that
revolution is not enough, that he must also build anew the essential
framework of the world."[18] In this paradoxical continuity—rebelling
in order to rebuild, reforming, as Burke would have it, in order to
preserve—Broch sees a process. And the rebuilding and reforming
"is achieved by the style of old age; for this style, revolutionary by
means of its abstractness, gains a level one can only call the super-
religious."[19]

We return to the narrative of a literary life. Ironically, our celebration today of the 1807 poems hardly matches the response of Wordsworth's contemporary readers and critics. *The Critical Review*,

---

[17] "Art Born in the Fullness of Age," *The New York Times*, August 23, 1987, section
1, pp. 1, 11.
[18] Introduction, in Rachel Bespaloff, *On the Iliad*, trans. Mary McCarthy (New
York: Pantheon Books, ca. 1947), p. 11.
[19] Ibid., pp. 22–23.

Edinburgh Review (Francis Jeffrey is especially harsh), and *Eclectic Review* were, as we saw, sharply negative.[20] Though Wordsworth played the role of the brave artist, he clearly was hurt by the reception of the volumes. Two celebrated letters go a small way toward helping us to understand how he dealt with his disappointment. They also reveal some of his deepest feelings about his own poetry and poetic life, and about the larger role of poets and poetry in a society. "London wits and witlings lack the capacity to respond to poetry," he writes to Lady Beaumont, a tragic problem "because to be incapable of a feeling of Poetry in my sense of the word is to be without love of human nature and reverence for God." Even readers of good will miss the significance of his poetry, for "their imagination has slept; and the voice which is the voice of my Poetry without Imagination cannot be heard." And so he would trust in posterity.[21] Later we find him, at least on the surface, expressing indifference about

> things upon which so much of my life has been employed. I am not quite 41 years of age, yet I seem to have lost all personal interest in everything which I have composed. When I read my poems, I often think that they are such as I should have admired and been delighted by if they had been produced by another, yet, as I cannot ascertain how much of this approbation is owing to self-love, and how much to what my own powers and knowledge supply to complete what is imperfect in the poems themselves, upon the whole my own works at present interest me little, far too little. . . .[22]

The year 1810, of course, saw the culmination of a festering problem between Wordsworth and Coleridge. The two had been at odds as early as 1808, unfortunately because of misunderstandings and unspoken feelings. Wordsworth's seemingly honest concern about his friend's physical and emotional condition, plus crossed signals about Coleridge's dealings with Longmans concerning the publication of *The White Doe*, marked the beginning of the end. It seems to be the classic case of one man's insecurity and another's vanity. The final blow was Coleridge's reaction to Basil Montagu's tactless rendition of a confidence Wordsworth shared with him about their mutual

---

[20] *William Wordsworth: A Reference Guide*, pp. 7–15.
[21] W. W. to Lady Beaumont, May 21, 1807. *MY* 1.1:146.
[22] W. W. to John Edwards, March 27 [1811]. *MY* 2.1:471.

friend's erratic behavior. Montagu, hardly the most responsible of men, informed Coleridge in London that Wordsworth had "commissioned" him to pass the word that Coleridge had been a drunkard, a spendthrift, and general nuisance while living at Allan Bank. Crabb Robinson's part in bringing about a truce notwithstanding, the relationship was never the same, Coleridge recording in his *Notebooks* that his friend "had no Hope of me" and describing the comment as "this accursed analysis or rather anatomy of a friend's Character."[23]

It would be easy to argue that the emergence of a new Wordsworth begins around this time. There is a sense of deep personal disappointment choking creativity. After conflict comes a quiet of sorts after the 1807 *Poems*, with the poet in London for a holiday and little evidence of any poetic activity. Certainly, the sheer drama of public events—revolutionary failure in France, the violence of the Terror, the coming of Napoleon—took its toll as radical fervor seems to give way to greater conservatism and an uncertainty about the profession of poetry. The young poet who went to France in 1791, joined the revolutionary groups supporting the call for freedom and democracy, and felt the disillusionment that came from violence and power-politics, is still a lover of freedom and a supporter of the poor and oppressed. But, here again, the impulses of the heart and dreams of the imagination are tempered by a more vivid awareness of the claims of the real, of the possibilities and yet the limitations of reform. Let Hazlitt, Godwin, Shelley, Byron, and others think of him as traitor, he nevertheless found himself trying to effect in both his public and his poetic life a reconciliation of some kind between the needs of the human heart and the demands of the external world.

This attempt to reconcile, now more overt, now more documentable, is not different in kind from the tug-of-war we have already witnessed in the poems of affirmation qualified by doubt. The intensification of industrialism, the pursuit of the great god Mammon, the slow decline of the class system—all these deepened his social conservatism and political Toryism. And the essentially non-sectarian poet of natural religion moves increasingly toward a closer affiliation with the Established Church of England as a point of further stability. One develops a different image of the Wordsworth of these

---

[23] October 1810.

years, a more public figure, now ensconced with a family of five at Rydal Mount, having moved from a crowded Dove Cottage to a smoky Allan Bank and then to the Parsonage in Grasmere, playing the role of elder statesman, associating himself with landed gentry like the Lowther family, his father's employers, who became his models.

As many Wordsworth biographers have told the story, the most vivid acting-out of his growing conservatism was the Westmoreland election of 1818, which pitted two sons of the Earl of Lonsdale, from whom he had received a £100 annual pension and the post of Distributor of Stamps, against one Richard Brougham, the Whig politician, whom he had come to regard as a dangerous radical. The Lowthers won that election, and Wordsworth, even more firmly in the Burke tradition, saw the victory as a triumph of anti-Jacobinism. He dined with the Bishop of Llandaff at Rydal Mount, the same man who had evoked his wrath in the exuberant days of 1794 when he was concerned about absentee Professors of Divinity at Cambridge. On a personal level, he disapproved of his brother Richard marrying at age forty-six a woman twenty-five years his junior. He was especially harsh on the sybaritic DeQuincey, who fathered a child by a servant woman and continued his opium habit; Wordsworth's displeasure led to outright alienation even when DeQuincey later mended his ways and made a good marriage.

That other side of a complex Wordsworth seeking an anchor beyond the self, although always present to some degree, is now sharply pronounced. Yet that side, while often giving vent to a preachy, predictable kind of poetry, often finds its voice and its own proper language, unstable at times and rich with possibilities; and the poetry that emerges, far from a falling-off, represents a phenomenon of sorts, a Romantic poetry of age, autumnal, subtly nuanced in its charting of the poet's later psychic development. Mary Moorman's point, put perhaps a little too strongly, is nonetheless telling. She sees Wordsworth as

> never able, at any period of his life, to stand aloof from any situation once his imagination was kindled and his sense of principle aroused. ... He saw and felt with the strength and decisiveness of imaginative genius, and however mistaken he might be in the causes he espoused

in these later years, his writings in their support bear at their best the stamp of poetry, and always that of deep conviction.[24]

After the long silence, Wordsworth's first volume of new poetry was published in August 1814 and dedicated to Lord Lonsdale, "Illustrious peer," as a "token of high respect and gratitude sincere." I say "new" with the understanding, of course, that the poem was part of a master plan the poet had advanced as early as 1798, and that the first book—*The Ruined Cottage*—was completed as a separate poem in that year, with drafts of what were to be Books 2–4 originally done in 1806. I have already alluded, in considering *The Prelude*, to the plan he had unfolded for an epic poem to be called *The Recluse*, and the preface to *The Excursion* returns in detail to that plan—for a three-part work that would be "a review of his own mind . . . and how far Nature and Education had qualified him for such employment," and how as preparation "he undertook to record, in verse, the origin and progress of his own powers, as far as he was acquainted with them."

That introductory poem, although it will continue to be revised and will remain unpublished during his lifetime, has been completed and has been the inspiration "to compose a philosophical poem, containing views of Man, Nature, and Society; and to be entitled, *The Recluse*; as having for its principal subject the sensations and opinions of a poet living in retirement." *The Recluse*, originally intended to have in its first and third parts "meditations in the Author's own person," was, of course, never completed despite the notable proddings of Coleridge and the encouragement of others, whereas *The Excursion*, originally planned as the middle part, emerged as a complete work in 1814.

And an interesting work in the poet's literary life it is, in the tradition of the long philosophical poems of the eighteenth century, with a cast of characters, some might say, who embody the spectrum of Wordsworth's attitudes toward a range of subjects—the workings of the individual mind in its quest for meaning; the social, political, and religious situation; the celebration of Christian faith. Judson Lyon sees the poem growing out of conversations with Coleridge in

---

[24] *William Wordsworth: A Biography*, 2:362.

1798, especially out of Coleridge's desire that it be anti-mechanistic, and out of a "pressing need" felt by both poets "to combat the prevailing enthusiasm of their day for pure reason."[25]

The poet assures his reader that, while he announces no formal system, he hopes that the physical and spiritual adventures of his characters will help that reader "in extracting the system for himself." Curiously, the "Prospectus," which was originally planned as the conclusion of the first book of *The Recluse*, introduces the drama in epic fashion, and, for our purposes, continues the ongoing Wordsworthian motif of the mind's encounter with reality, the rhythmic claims of the free, healthy imagination in search of its own values, and the ever-present insistence of the world outside, with its limitations and demands. As "On Man, on Nature, and on Human Life, / Musing in solitude, I oft perceive / Fair trains of imagery before me rise, / Accompanied by feelings of delight / Pure, or with no unpleasing sadness mixed" (1–5), he resolves, "Whether from breath of outward circumstance, / Or from the Soul—an impulse to herself—I would give utterance in numerous verse" (11–13). Like a nineteenth-century Homer or Virgil or Milton, and knowing the "burden of the past" and the "anxiety of influence," he would, in the spirit of a "natural supernaturalism," sing of many themes: "Of Truth, of Grandeur, Beauty, Love, and Hope, / And melancholy Fear subdued by Faith." He would sing of the counter-demands of the self, "Of the individual Mind that keeps her own / Inviolate retirement, subject there / To Conscience only, and the law supreme / Of that Intelligence which governs all," pleading, Milton-like, "fit audience let me find though few!" (14–23).

His plea for inspiration is to Urania, goddess of astronomy, of love and beauty, of things within and beyond, as he unfolds the mysterious nature of his epic task, not the wrath of Achilles, or arms and the man, or man's first disobedience, but the fear-inspiring view "Into our Minds, into the Mind of Man– / My haunt, and the main region of my song" (40–41). Conscious of how self-centered and inner-directed his inner journey can become, he, as if to reassure,

---

[25] *The Excursion: A Study* (New Haven, Conn.: Yale University Press, 1950), p. 65. See also Kenneth Johnston's *Wordsworth and The Recluse* (New Haven, Conn.: Yale University Press, 1984).

would offer not "A history only of departed things, / Or a mere fiction of what never was" (50–51). He, the poet-priest, echoing the
"correspondent breeze" motif of *The Prelude*, would proclaim "How
exquisitely the individual Mind / (And the progressive powers perhaps no less / Of the whole species) to the external World / Is fitted:—and how exquisitely, too— / Theme this but little heard of
among men— / The external World is fitted to the Mind" (63–68).

Continuing his commitment to the poet's vocation to create the
taste of his audience, to rouse readers from the "savage torpor" of
societal forces, he asserts that "by words / Which speak of nothing
more than what we are, / Would I arouse the sensual from their
sleep / Of Death, and win the vacant and the vain / To noble raptures" (58–62). His plea to Urania is strongly couched and rooted in
his always but now more solidly realized world beyond, in what Keats
would describe as the "vale of soul-making," of "the tribes / And
fellowships of men," places where he "must hear Humanity in fields
and groves / Pipe solitary anguish" (73–77). The proclaiming poet,
still the exuberant artist of joyous rapture close to nature, but now
more sobered, more ripened by the passage of time and the inroads
of sorrow, will not despair or give way to cynicism. In an almost
militantly hopeful spirit he wishes that the sounds of the world will
"Have their authentic comment; that even these / Hearing, I be not
downcast or forlorn!" (81–82). He would, looking back on his earliest desire to write about humble and rustic life, mix "more lowly
matter," describe "The transitory Being that beheld / This Vision,"
and prays, "Be not this labour useless" (97–99).

As I have already suggested, *The Excursion* is dramatic in form, at
times lending itself to a Bakhtinian dialogic reading, voices in con-
cert and conflict; its characters are the Poet/Narrator, the Wanderer,
the Solitary, and the Parson. And how appropriate the form is, although the overall result is an excessively long, somewhat prosaic
piece, too often given to pious and even tedious moralizing, but
frequently marked by brilliant sections that have the ring of Wordsworth at his best. The opening scenario is a vivid reminder of his
preoccupation with light and shade—"summer, and the sun had
mounted high: / Southward the landscape indistinctly glared" (1.1–
2). And to the North there are "shadows that lay in spots / Deter-

mined and unmoved, with steady beams / Of bright and pleasant sunshine interposed" (1.6–8).

Enter the Poet in search of a cooling shade. On the moorland appears a ruined cottage and in the midst of the ruin the object of his quest: "a Man of reverend age, / But stout and hale, for travel unimpaired" (1.33–34), a Wanderer. Old and tried friends, they had often walked together through rustic settings, and the old man, a poet (albeit an unpublished one), would speak of "Abstrusest matter, reasonings of the mind / Turned inward" or "at my request would sing / Old songs, the product of his native hills" (1.65–67). Those words and songs will be remembered and recorded by the Poet/Narrator.

It is interesting to compare the readings of a more traditional Wordsworthian critic such as the early Geoffrey Hartman and a moderate New Historicist like James Chandler. For Hartman, the theme of *The Ruined Cottage* is the "humanized imagination," and the true subject of the poem is the "perfected mind of man facing a still imperfect world."[26] Chandler historicizes the poem, regarding the Pedlar's meditation as

> an important part of what makes *The Ruined Cottage* so seminal for Wordsworth's subsequent work. The poet presents an oral tale told by an experienced father figure to an immature son figure for the purpose of passing on appropriate moral habits from the former to the latter. *The Ruined Cottage* seems all that one could expect a traditional poem to be.[27]

The remembrance and recording read like a mini-biography of Wordsworth. Poet and poetry continue to be intertwined. As a six-year-old, he tended cattle on the hills, and the foundations of his mind are laid in nature and the phenomena around him. Chandler argues that we see the centrality of *The Ruined Cottage* in Wordsworth's intellectual maturing "if we view it as a transformation of the poem Wordsworth produced during his most fervently radical period, Salisbury Plain (1793–4)." For him the earlier political views "are signalled in its opening stanzas, where, echoing Rousseau,

---

[26] *Wordsworth's Poetry*, p. 140.
[27] *Wordsworth's Second Nature*, p. 161.

Wordsworth argues against the Hobbesian position that any state of civil society is preferable to the state of savage nature."[28]

There is a *Prelude*-like "spot-of-time" quality in the language and imagery, as he tells how he "many an evening, to his distant home / In solitude returning, saw the hills / Grow larger in the darkness; all alone / Beheld the stars come out above his head, / And travelled through the wood, with no one near / To whom he might confess the things he saw" (1.126–131).

The Wanderer received early on the precious gift of imagination. Books were clearly secondary in such an education, yet he read widely in legends, the stories of martyrs, and Gothic tales which nourished this power of mind. His chief inspiration was the Light, source of joy and hope, as "he beheld the sun / Rise up, and bathe the world in light"; and again, like a Pauline naturalist, "his spirit drank / The spectacle: sensation, soul, and form, / All melted into him; They swallowed up / His animal being; in them did he live, / And by them did he live; they were his life" (1.206–210). The Poet brings a notably overt religious tone to his descriptions of the Wanderer's education in nature, describing it as "a visitation from the living God" (1.212).

Urged by his mother, he teaches for a while at the village school, but his "wandering thoughts" (1.313) and "restless mind" (1.321) impel him to be on the move, and "much did he see of men" (1.341), especially those who live close to the soil and speak a natural language. So does the Wanderer-turned-Pedlar pass his days until in retirement "he lived at ease" (1.386), walking the public ways, enjoying the peace and liberty of nature. Though he was brought up in the stern Christianity of the Scottish Church, the dark side of his early experience gives way to a gospel of kindness, concern, and love; as the Poet says, "his religion seemed to me / Self-taught, as of a dreamer in the woods" (1.409–410).

Like a philosopher, wise and in tune with the human situation, he is encountered by the Poet in search of a cool drink, and, when he is refreshed, the poet listens to the long meditation of his host, one in which he mourns the loss of a devoted daughter, Margaret, "a Woman of a steady mind, / Tender and deep in her excess of love"

---

[28] Ibid., p. 160.

(1.513–514), with a caring and industrious husband and "a pretty boy" who was "their best hope, / next to the God in heaven." Their first days were ones of "peace and comfort" (1.532–534).

But "Two blighting seasons" and "the plague of war" (1.537–540) have taken their toll, and sick husband and a second child have brought poverty. Time passes, and the Wanderer goes his way, but returns later to find a desolate ruined cottage, a haggard Margaret, and a crying child. Her husband, Robert, had entered the army and gone off to distant lands in order to support his family; she has apprenticed her elder son, and now lives, knowing nothing of her husband, "her eyelids drooped, her eyes downward were cast" (1.792). Still another visit brought a starker awareness of her plight; except for her children, "She had no wish to live, that she must die / Of sorrow" (1.850–851). After nine years as widow, still, like Martha Ray in "The Thorn," waiting for a husband's return, "she died; / Last human tenant of these ruined walls" (1.915–916).

Book 1 closes with the Poet/Narrator reflecting on the tragic story of loss, of poverty, of grief, of death. The Wanderer, noting the grief and his prayer of blessing, responds in overtly Christian terms that were added to the poem in 1845:

> My Friend! enough to sorrow you have given,
> The purposes of wisdom ask no more:
> Nor more would she have craved as due to One
> Who, in her worst distress, had oftimes felt
> The unbounded might of prayer; and learned, with soul
> Fixed on the Cross, that consolation springs,
> From sources deeper far than deepest pain,
> For the meek Sufferer [1.932–939].

Instructed, the two return to the village inn, "the sun declining shot / A slant and mellow radiance, which began / To fall upon us" (1.957–959). Light tarnished, less brilliant, but still light with a sweet luster.

Book 2, essentially an account of the Poet's travels with the Wanderer, introduces another key figure and voice in the poem, the Solitary. Of Scottish parentage, dwelling "in a spot that lies / Among yon mountain fastnesses concealed" (2.155–256), a military chaplain at first vain and affected but then charmed by "A blooming Lady"

(2.187), he relinquished his ministry, married the woman, and re-tired to a rural home. "How free their love, / How full their joy!" (2.196–197), the Wanderer exclaims. But married bliss is quickly touched by tragedy, as the Solitary loses wife and children, and is left alone, praying for death and indifferent to all concerns both pub-lic and private.

This Solitary, like Wordsworth himself, was roused from grief and lethargy by "A glorious opening, the unlooked-for dawn, / That promised everlasting joy to France!" (2.212–213). Stirred by revolu-tionary hopes, he goes to France to preach "The cause of Christ and civil liberty, / As one, and moving to one glorious end" (2.221–222). Yet his radicalism, originally spirited and idealistic, was soured by the power politics and violence, and he became by turns anti-religious, rationalistic, cynical, anarchic. Tormented and world-weary, he came "among these rugged hills," "Steeped in self-indulging spleen," re-solved "that he will live and die / Forgotten,—at safe distance from 'a world / Not moving to his mind.' " (2.309–314).

At last Poet and Wanderer come upon the Solitary (still another facet of Wordsworth's multi-sided temperament), his spirit and his voice conditioned by his life and times. A passing funeral procession evokes the piety of the Wanderer but a sarcastic comment from the Solitary that the man just buried was "unblest" (2.596) and with little tribute, had departed "Like a ripe date which in the desert falls / Without a hand to gather it" (2.605–606). As they enjoy the hospitality of the Solitary's cottage, the Poet and the Wanderer hear the story of its former resident, a Grasmere pauper who in his prime served the household well. Lost in a storm while gathering turf for fuel, he is found by shepherds "breathing peaceably" (2.821), and the Solitary recalls, as the pauper is carried home, his emerging from the mist to view a magnificent sight. It is a vision of a "mighty city" (2.835) of diamond and gold, of court, canopy, and throne "Such as by Hebrew prophets were beheld" (2.867). From the simple beauty of Grasmere vale, "That which I *saw* was the revealed abode / Of Spirits in beatitude." The Solitary, like one healed in the Scriptures, exclaims, " 'I have been dead,' I cried / 'And now I live! Oh! where-fore *do* I live?' " (2.873–876), descending to the house of the injured man who died three weeks later. The Wanderer, exhilarated by the tale, urges, "Now let us forth into the sun!" (2.903).

And forth they go in Book 3, with the Solitary guiding the group through a rich body of natural scenery. The peace and security of a "hidden nook" (3.50) greets them, vivid metaphors creating a scene of quiet beauty, alliteration and assonance evoking a mood of reverence for those spots in nature where the gods breathe in a special way. It is a Wordsworthian stillness "save the water that descended, / Diffused adown that barrier of steep rock, / And softly creeping, like a breath of air" (3.69–71). The Wanderer, filled with wonder and puzzled by the Solitary's coldness, argues to the existence of a Creator from the design he finds around him—a strangely fresh theodicy, compared to the abstractions and personifications that follow.

But the Solitary feels no such conviction, sees no such evidences of a Divine Presence. As they are for that other, reality-engaged Wordsworth from the beginning, the delights of the Wanderer are for him "The sport of Nature, aided by blind Chance / Rudely to mock the works of toiling Man" (3.126–127). The dialogue intensifies as the Wanderer engages the despondent Solitary for his lack of faith in an eternal bliss. And the Solitary is gracious but firm in his response, like the speakers of "The Small Celandine" or the "Elegiac Stanzas." "Mutability is Nature's bane," he says, Hope a cheat "and when / Ye need her favours, ye shall find her not; / But in her stead—fear—doubt—and agony!" (3.458–361). No rhetorical power of Poet/Narrator or Wanderer can end the gloomy confessional as he moves from large philosophical generalizations to more intensely personal reflections, of falling in love with "One on whose mild radiance many gazed" (3.503), of a happy marriage and family. But— terrifying image that persists in the poetry—"from some dark seat of fatal power" came death to claim that family and leave him disconsolate (3.637).

Roused from dreams, pleading for solace, then looking inward, "life was put / To inquisition, long and profitless" (3.697–698). Revolutionary France reconverts him to the cause of freedom, of a society with equality for all. He feels the spirit of the Hebrew Scriptures, "and resumed / A long-suspended office in the House / Of public worship" (3.760–762), added prayer to prophecy. Yet, like the Wordsworth of *The Prelude*, his hope gives way to disillusionment when bloodletting and destruction become the order of the day. And "in Britain, ruled a panic dread of change" (3.827), with fear and repression everywhere. The Solitary, confused, at odds with himself, looks West and ships out to America—"How bright the sun" (3.880)—to New York, a city at first exciting but soon, like London, "on nearer view, a motley spectacle . . . / Of high pretensions" (3.897–898). And the quest continues further West, but again he cannot find "that pure archetype of human greatness" (3.951).

Only the inner life brings comfort, and his state of soul is brilliantly caught in a metaphor that seems like a variation on the "received into the bosom of the steady lake" of "There was a Boy":

> The tenour
> Which my life holds, he readily may conceive
> Who'er hath stood to watch a mountain brook
> In some still passage of its course, and seen,
> Within the depths of its capacious breast,
> Inverted trees, rocks, clouds, and azure sky;
> And, on its glassy surface, specks of foam
> Numerous as stars; that, by their outward lapse,
> Betray to sight the motion of the stream,
> Else imperceptible [3.967–977].

There follows the image of the stream as the course of life, from flowing energy to moments of stillness to further "traverses and toils" (3.985). Yet the Solitary would take one liberty with his image: that the course of movement and stillness, music and silence will in his case give way to a certain eternal stillness and silence, "The unfathomable gulf, where all is still" (3.991).

Enter the Wanderer, still part of the ongoing dialogic tension not only in this poem but also in the course of Wordsworth's literary life. It is and has been a tension between the poet's need to enter imaginatively into experience, to find in the workings of the inner life a basis for value, and the poet's need to find some process of anchoring, some basis of stability amidst the fickleness of earthly existence. In response to the Solitary's loss of heart, his increasing despondency, his growing cynicism and mistrust of all institutions, the Wanderer, in Book 5, plays the role of lecturer, of counselor and comforter, as bearer of the Wordsworthian gospel of trust in some power beyond the individual. That power, always a force in even the earliest poems, has become increasingly more sharply defined. It is now not simply a kind of stoic resoluteness or a pragmatic realism, but more and more a sharp religious sense, the awareness of an ordered reality outside the mind created by a Supreme Being whom we venerate by faith and good works. Indeed, that sense takes on even more sharply defined Christian outlines that would seem to correspond to the poet's growing allegiance to the Church of England.

The opening of the Wanderer's discourse seems tinged by the confidence and optimism of Pope's Deism in the *Essay on Man*:

> One adequate support
> For the calamities of mortal life
> Exists—one only; an assured belief
> That the procession of our fate, howe'er
> Sad or disturbed, is ordered by a Being
> Of infinite benevolence and power;
> Whose everlasting purposes embrace
> All accidents, converting them to good [4.10–17].

Quickly the Deistic seems reinforced by a more overtly Christian tone, as the Wanderer counsels the distraught Solitary. And this counsel is followed by a prayer more decidedly Christian to a personal God:

> Soul of our Souls, and safeguard of the world!
> Sustain, Thou only canst, the sick of heart;
> Restore their languid spirits, and recall
> Their lost affections unto thee and Thine! [4.28–31].

Yet the eighteenth-century Deistic note returns as the Wanderer, emerging with Narrator and Solitary from that "covert nook," Prospero-like, calls attention to "How beautiful this dome of sky; / And how awful! Shall the Soul, / Human and rational, report of Thee / Even less than these?" (4.32–38). God has made the Wanderer His "priest," dwelling "In such a temple as we now behold / Reared for thy presence" (3.43–45).

And if sight should fail, he may still recapture those youthful moments of vision "when, stationed on the top / Of some huge hill-expectant, I beheld / The sun rise up, from distant climes returned" or "saw him toward the deep / Sink, with a retinue of flaming clouds / Attended" (4.112–118). Here we see light giving way to darkness, but it is a darkness illuminated by the brightness of past days of ecstatic union with nature. The "fervent raptures," again echoes of the *Immortality Ode*, are forever gone, yet the Wanderer will struggle and "aspire / Heavenward" (4.123–127). Man's mortality is the source of sorrow, but a sorrow that is more than the excess of a childish complaint. In a powerful image echoing many in *Tintern Abbey*, *The Prelude*, and the *Immortality Ode*, the Wanderer comes to the heart of his ruminations, his philosophical–theological dialogue with the Solitary about loss and gain, despair and hope. "Alas!" he cries, "the endowment of immortal power / Is matched unequally with custom, time, / And domineering faculties of sense / In *all*" (4.205–208). Yet a new articulation of hope, couched in more overtly religious language, goes beyond the naturalism of the earlier poems. The victory is for "him, who, seeking faith by virtue, strives" to follow "conscience reverenced and obeyed, / As God's most intimate presence in the soul, / And His most perfect image in the world" (4.223–228).

Wanderer and Poet continue their journey, the one continuing his philosophical discourse, the other on occasion responding exuberantly and adding his own Wordsworthian reflections. In strongly biblical terms the Wanderer recounts the fall of man, now a supernatural naturalism, now not simply the loss of "splendor in the grass, or glory in the flower," but a fall "From those pure heights" of communion with the "articulate voice / Of God" (4.634–641). In the spirit of the sonnet's "Great God! I'd rather be a pagan," he records the gift of Jehovah, the gift of imagination to embody divinity bestowed on Jewish, Persian, Babylonian, Grecian, and earlier peoples.

After the long history of the imaginative quest for the divine, the Solitary, truly a student of Voltaire and child of the Enlightenment, would cynically critique the Wanderer's speech being delivered at a distance from "our native land"—Scotland—where zealots "sow afresh the weeds of Romish phantasy" (4.907–908). Yet he is touched by the anti-rationalism, the faith of the Wanderer, wondering only where to begin a new life, how to find a faith for himself. On the one hand, the Wanderer reminds him, "The Mind is free—/ Resolve" (4.1080–1081), and, on the other, he offers assurance of "One / Who sees all suffering, comprehends all wants, / All weakness fathoms, can supply all needs" (4.1090–1092). The "celestial light" of the earlier Wordsworth has found a sharper embodiment as the Wanderer offers hope to the Poet/Narrator, holds out the ultimate goal in words that remind one of the closing of Coleridge's "Self-Knowledge"—"Peace in ourselves, and union with our God" (4.1116).

The long homily concluded, the Poet is deeply touched. Evening gathers, light but really half-light touched by the first hints of on-coming darkness—"yellow radiance spread," "A dispensation of the evening power" (4.1303–1306). It is a return to reality after moments of rich intuition, imagination now incorporated into the rich realities of human life. The funeral train returns; Wanderer and Poet are welcomed into the Solitary's cottage.

A new day, a farewell to the valley, and the trio move toward a splendid vale with handsome church and monuments. Enter, as they read an account of the parish, the Pastor, the fourth of this Words-worthian *dramatis personae*. And he plays his Wordsworthian role well; he is the more overtly religious counterpart of the Wanderer, strengthening the latter's philosophy with his wisdom as minister of the Church. The Solitary, recounting the previous day's discourse, bemoans how far short of their ideals human beings fall, how little philosophy and religion succeed in their goals. The Poet/Narrator agrees that "Profession mocks performance" (5.378). And the Solitary uses the cycle of the seasons to reinforce his sense of decline and loss in human life, from spring "Hopeful and promising with buds and flowers" (5.397), to autumn "with bowers that hear no more / The voice of gladness" (5.406–407), to winter with its "desolate sway" (5.410).

The Pastor is greeted by the Wanderer with a series of sharp, staccato, somewhat Tennysonian questions—"Is Man / A child of hope? Do generations press / On generations, without progress made?" "Are we a creature in whom good / Preponderates, or evil?" "A living power / Is virtue, or no better than a name?" (5.465–472). Pressed by this barrage of questions, the Pastor, a representative of church and religion, is no Polyannish optimist, recognizing the world around him where "comprehension fails, and truth is missed," where "darkness and delusion round our path spread" (5.511–512). His is a rich religious humanism, an optimism rooted in faith "Which unassisted reason's utmost power / Is too infirm to reach" (5.520–

521). It is faith that proposes action, living in the world, and bringing to that world a watchful and alert eye. Sounding now like Vaughan, now like Herbert, the Pastor counsels, "Go forward, and look back; / Look, from the quarter whence the lord of light, / Of life, of love, and gladness doth dispense / His beams" (5.539–542). With such movement "Then will a vernal prospect greet your eye, / All fresh and beautiful, and green and bright" (5.545–546).

Well-instructed, the Wanderer poses the bedrock question. How find an "inward principle" to effect "outward argument" (5.571–573)? You have, says the Pastor, already articulated the answer in speaking of the limitations of human knowledge, the folly of human vanity. In response to the Wanderer's request, the Pastor offers specific cameos of the good and happy life. The Wordsworthian devotion to humble and rustic people and settings continues in these cameos. There are the husband and wife living in the mountains "in childless solitude" (5.692), working in quiet dignity, hearing "The voice of wisdom whispering scripture texts" (5.724). The Wanderer recalls the couple and their Spartan dwelling, especially—still again symbolic images of light and darkness—a dark, autumnal night when "destitute of other hope," he spied the light to guide him to a "friendly covert," "Joy to myself!" (5.742–752). Here he found hospitality, the beauty of a life close to nature, the example of the matron of the house praying that her comforting thoughts were more often directed to the "heaven . . . by my Redeemer taught" (5.826). Even the reluctant Solitary is touched by the rugged goodness of such men and women, recalling from his own experience a Scottish peasant growing verdant grass in the midst of rugged rock.

The essential Wordsworthian Romantic conservatism shines through in the closing sentiments of the Pastor, sentiments ultimately rooted in "The Voice of Deity, on height and plain, / Whispering those truths in stillness, which the Word, / To the four quarters of the winds, proclaims" (5.991–993). These truths are established in Burkean "solemn institutions" (5.1001), points of objective strength within which the individual mind finds its own and larger meaning. Life is not escape from the human situation, not retreat to the mind's private environs. In the Pastor's response to that most pressing question of the Wanderer, one seems to hear the later, the more secular voice of Moneta to another poet, in Keats's

The Fall of Hyperion: "Life, I repeat," says the Pastor, is "energy of love / Divine or human." But it is an energy "exercised in pain, / In strife, in tribulation; and ordained, / If so approved and sanctified, to pass, / Through shades and silent rest, to endless joy" (5.1012–1016).

Book 6, set in the security of the peaceful parish churchyard in Grasmere, is stolid, wooden in style, opening with the Wordsworthian Poet/Narrator offering loyal tribute to England and its Church. He prays for devoted servants such as the Pastor who begins an exchange with the Solitary, cataloguing emblems of such servants in almost epitaphic cameos. There is the rustic who, when his beloved had married another, mourned his loss, fell victim to fever, and ultimately died bereft. Then there is the miner-adventurer who, after years of frustrated searching, finds his fortune, only to turn to "immoderate cups" (6.242), vanishing and leaving behind only the path from his cottage to the mine called "THE PATH OF PERSEVERANCE" (6.254). Dawson of Grasmere, gifted, reserved, but a joyous man turned prodigal, allured by the seductions of the city, finally repented to his parents and was delivered from his inner turmoil "when Mercy made him / One with himself, and one with them that sleep" (6.374–375). Then there is a rustic pair, "flaming Jacobite" and "sullen Hanoverian" (6.458–459), driven from "desperate strife" (6.449) to a quiet refuge. They meet, become friends, talk, enjoy a common happiness in spite of differences, and their friendship deepens into a richness of spirit. And they memorialize that spirit with a dial upon the site of an "old yew" (6.493) as their "private monument" (6.499).

As the stories continue, a dialogue between the Solitary and the Pastor unfolds an intriguing theory of Christian tragedy. The Solitary initiates the process with his reflection that the tragic stories of Prometheus, Tantalus, Oedipus may very well be "Fictions in form, but in their substance truths" (6.545). Sounding like a forerunner of Arthur Miller in his celebrated essay on "Tragedy and the Common Man,"[29] he argues that one can exchange royalty for the humble and rustic and "here the tragic Muse / Shall find apt subjects for her

---

[29] See *Tragedy: Vision and Form*, ed. Robert W. Corrigan (San Francisco: Chandler, 1965), pp. 148–151.

highest art" and behold "the dread strife / Of poor humanity's afflicted will / Struggling in vain with ruthless destiny" (6.551–557).
The Pastor agrees that those with faith "admit / That, through all
stations, human life abounds / With mysteries," that unless faith is
tested, its power would never be seen or felt (6.562–563).

The Pastor continues his calling of the roster of saints in the
churchyard. He points to the grave of a woman at peace now, a
woman in life quick of mind and graceful in speech, but remote,
alone, and obsessed with two great passions of "avaricious thrift"
and "a strange thraldom of maternal love" (6.709–710). Still another
cameo is of a young woman and her child. Once Queen of Twelfth
Night, Ellen danced gleefully around the Joyful Tree with her secret
burden of love betrayed, a woman abandoned, a child born—echoes
of "The Thorn." She loved and cared for the child, but is stalked by
tragedy as she takes employment as a domestic servant and is forbid-
den any contact with her child, who dies shortly thereafter. After
long vigil at the infant's grave, Ellen returns to her mother's home
seeking peace in endurance and in the counsel of the Pastor, struggles valiantly, but eventually succumbs. Never, says the Pastor as he
points to the two graves, was Ellen's the scoff of the skeptic. Whenever anyone offered pity or complaint, she replied with Wordsworthian resignation, but a resignation now configured in a larger Christian
framework: "He who afflicts me knows what I can bear; / And when
I fail, and can endure no more, / Will mercifully take me to Himself"
(6.1046–1048).

In response to the Wanderer's query about another doomed resident of the valley, the Pastor recounts the tragic story of Wilfrid
Armathwaite, a man who could not live with the shame he experienced after abandoning wife and family. And yet Wilfrid died not as
an outcast forgotten by all, but "pitied among men, absolved by
God" (6.1112). To a mother's grave the Pastor then points, but only
to speak of the courage of the father/husband as he lovingly raised
their six beautiful and happy daughters, bearing witness to how "her
Spirit yet survives on earth!" (6.1191).

Book 7 opens with a uniquely Wordsworthian transition and
pause, as the Poet compares the cameos of the inhabitants of the
churchyard to what seem so like the "spots of time" in his early life.
He is "awakened" to the brilliance of the setting sun "on Snowdon's

sovereign brow, / On Cader Idris, or huge Penmanmour," to the sound of "pastoral melody or warlike air" (7.1–10). These moments were not passing fancies, but, like the "renovating virtue" of the spots, "images and precious thoughts, / That shall not die, and cannot be destroyed" (7.29–30). He continues his questioning, wondering about five graves clustered close to the village school, and the Pastor offers his story of the good priest Joseph Sympson, husband and father of three, the man of good deeds, of an active, caring mind, who loved and fostered the sense of community, ministered to the sick and poor, loved family, eschewed worldly delights. The Pastor expresses pleasure and admiration in recalling Sympson, once wild and lively, then serene and wise in his mature years. "Him might we liken," he says, "to the setting sun / . . . with an inconstant and unmellowed light" (7.230–233).

The Wanderer, as he listens, is reminded of "the Wonderful"— specifically, the Reverend Robert Walker, pastor of Seathwaite Chapel in the Duddon Valley, a man of temperance, industry, charity, and total commitment whose biography is appended to Wordsworth's Duddon sonnets. Remembering him at once, the Pastor praises the utter simplicity of his ministry, the total humility with which he went about his work. Although "the Wonderful" leaves "No cognizable vestiges" (7.358) of his priesthood, yet the good life of man or woman, however unheralded by the world, has its special and final reward. "The memory of the just survives in heaven" (7.388).

Quickly follows another story, this one of a "gentle Dalesman" (Thomas Holme), deaf, lonely, unable to hear the music of nature yet upheld "by the solace of his own pure thoughts" (7.417), he— Samuel Johnson's "single talent well employed" comes to mind— put his gifts to use, dutifully pursuing a rural life. And when his parents die, he becomes part of a second family, his books a source of delight and instruction, his work an act of devotion to others. He was, in short, a living symbol, and his death was mourned by many. Still another of these almost scriptural creatures appears: John Gough of Kendal, blind, yet a man of science and natural history, a man putting whatever talents he had in the service of others. In Miltonic fashion, the Pastor opens his tribute with an ironic apostrophe to "Soul-cheering Light, most beautiful of things! / Guide our way, mysterious comforter!" (7.482–483) and points to Gough's great power of imagination to discover "A type and shadow of an awful truth" (7.527).

And the epitaphs continue with the Pastor's tribute to Margaret Green, only daughter and last child of happy parents already with "Seven lusty sons" (7.636). Taken in childhood, "pride and soul's delight" (7.686) of her parents, she brings the ultimate consolation that she sleeps in "peaceful bed" (7.694). And then there is the flashing portrait of young Oswald, scholar, vigorous athlete lavishly graced with the gifts of "nature's hand" (7.727). Among a wonderfully extravagant series of images of his gifts, one seems especially striking: "How the quoit / Whizzed by the Stripling's arm! / If touched by him, / The inglorious football mounted to the pitch / Of the lark's flight,—or shaped a rainbow's curve, / Aloft, in prospect of the shouting field!" (7.740–444). One of ten recruits from his valley, Oswald with his comrades trains to meet the ominous threats of Napoleon, yet he, like the athlete dying young, meets a cruel and ironic fate. Ministering to his shepherd father's flock, he was seized by convulsions, suffered twelve days of torment, and died. Nature creates an almost symbolic scene at his funeral service: bright sun followed by loud thunder claps.

The eulogies ended, the Wanderer, touched by evidences of the Divine, "stood / Enwrapt" (7.893–894). The Solitary, either to conceal how his skeptical nature has been been touched or how ashamed he is of his "habitual spleen," walks toward "the sacred Edifice," "intent upon a monumental stone" (7.907–913) commemorating, the Pastor imagines, the Elizabethan knight Sir Alfred Irthing who was drawn from his military exploits and from the world "resolved / To make that paradise his chosen home" (7.938–939).

Book 8 sees the Pastor inviting all to his parsonage. Hesitating for a time, the Solitary engages the Wanderer in a discussion of the chivalric knight and the humble peasant. Rustics are for him knight-errants of sorts, not requiring fine clothes and high rank to feel deeply. The Wanderer, in sympathy with such Wordsworthian naturalism, is nevertheless saddened by the ravages of industrialism, of open land developed to the extreme, of factory smoke blotting out the white light of the sun. Labor is no longer for man, but man for never-ending labor. Here "Disgorged are now the ministers of day, /

And, as they issue forth from the illumined pile, / A fresh band meets them, at the crowded door" (8.174–176). "Gain" is the new god; "factory," the new temple; and the Wanderer's question is sharp: Is progress destructive? His answer has the ring of hope, that everything depends upon "the moral law" (8.216). The Poet/Narrator yearns for the peace and order and love of another time, but, like an older, more tempered version of the speaker of *Tintern Abbey*, the Wanderer replies not only that "That time is past," but also that there is "Nothing to speed the day, or cheer the mind" (8.275). The Solitary's voice is starker in the general lament, more frightening in its language and imagery. "Hope is none for him!" he angrily cries. Thousands "Are leagued to strike dismay" with "outstretched hand / And whining voice" (8.354–360).

Wordsworth's epic, with its many voices in dialogue, rounds to a conclusion with a sweeping overview by the Wanderer, a discourse affirming his faith in a spiritual force pervading the universe, linking all things together, and offering a hope for the future. Clinging to a confidence in the face of loss, a loss always present even in the earliest poems of a literary life, a sense of light shaded, youth faded, he again returns to the central Wordsworthian question—"Ah! why in age / Do we revert so fondly to the walks / Of childhood"—-and advances the central Wordsworthian answer, now more sharply couched in a more pronounced religious language. In youth, he says, "the Soul discerns / The dear memorial footsteps unimpaired / Of her own native vigour" (9.36–40). But childhood cannot be idealized. It must be seen as part of a journey to deeper knowledge, as a base for the wisdom of age and experience. Feeling and thought link together to become a new source of knowledge; age becomes "a place of power" (9.55). There is loss, to be sure, but the gain is rich as we are separated from the tyranny of eye and ear, the turbulence of the world, and receive "Fresh power to commune with the invisible world" (9.86).

A much different Solitary, capturing a good deal of the Wordsworthian faith tempered by experience, responds: For those, he contends, who cannot trust themselves, "nor turn to their own hearts / To know what they must do; their wisdom is / To look into the eyes of others thence / To be instructed what they must avoid" (9.144–147). Grateful for such a response, the Wanderer turns social critic as he bemoans the child uneducated or poorly educated by "the arts / Of modern ingenuity" (9.158), by the Chartrists' "Delusion which a moment may destroy" (9.198). And how splendid the time when, following Andrew Bell and the Madras plan of education (which Wordsworth will later take issue with), the country will feel a duty "to *teach* / Them who are born to serve her and obey" (9.297–298).

With the French Revolution over and England more secure; with "the discipline of slavery" (9.351) past, the time is ripe for a new virtue, a new humanized society. Amidst these Utopian dreams the Pastor's wife sets a Wordsworthian scene for all: "Behold the shades of afternoon have fallen," and "see—beyond— / The silvery lake is streaked with placid blue; / As if preparing for the peace of evening" (9.419–422). Lighting a gypsy-fire on the shore of an island on the lake, they enjoy a choice meal and the song of the Pastor's daughter, a joyous evening in a setting of repose and tranquillity.

As they return to land, they view from a green-covered hill the valley below, with the church tower, symbol of permanence and truth, presiding over a place set apart from the noise of a busy world. Each member of this visionary company, each facet and voice of the Wordsworthian spirit, finds a focus in this setting, yet all particular and narrow concerns seem blotted out in the process. The sun, no longer flashingly bright, has attained its "western bound" (9.592). In the midst of this mystical spectacle, the Pastor prays, once again with the reverence of a supernatural naturalism. It is a prayer that captures the increasingly direct and strong quest for an ultimate point of permanence that can respond and give meaning to the yearnings of the heart and the figurings of the imagination. That point, no longer the "presence" felt by the speaker of *Tintern Abbey* or the "immortal sea" envisioned by the speaker of the *Immortality Ode*, is now a more concrete embodiment of those youthful goals and hopes—"the true and only God, / And from the faith derived through Him who bled / Upon the cross, this marvellous advance / Of good from evil; as if one extreme / Were left, the other gained" (9.720–724).

The Pastor, during a service of vespers, praises the richness of the poor, the wisdom of the unlearned, and calls on the beauties of nature to witness his prayer. The group departs, silent, and "o'er the shadowy lake, / Under a faded sky. No trace remained / Of those celestial splendours" (9.758–760). As they depart, the Solitary, that continuingly questioning voice of the Wordsworthian psyche, pauses, offers thanks, bids farewell. His final words echo strongly the closing lines of the *Immortality Ode*, and yet echo them with a new and ironic confidence. " 'Another sun,' / Said he, 'shall shine upon us, ere we part; / Another sun, and peradventure more; / If time, with free consent, be yours to give / And season favours' " (9.779–783).

The Poet, now more decisive and resolute about his vocation, closes his epic with a promise that whatever renovation of spirit, healing of wounds, and reconciling of minds have ensued or may ensue, "My future labours may not leave untold" (9.795). This is not a dramatically "new" or "later" or "declining" Wordsworth, but a maturing poet now encountering the light and the shadows, the joy of the free mind and the pull of an insistent world beyond, and finding in nature and the things of humankind something of what he had gropingly experienced earlier as "a sense sublime of something far more deeply interfused." The great poetic project reaches a kind of finality; the epic reaches a conclusion. The poetic life continues, but the woods ahead are fresh and the pastures new.

Wordsworth's *Collected Poems* of 1815 was no mere republication of old material. A somewhat more pompous, egotistical figure, wounded by reviews of earlier work, Wordsworth collects his poems and organizes them around the now-famous categories ("childhood," "fancy," "imagination," "sentiment and reflection," and others), and includes a new preface and supplementary essay in which he advances important ideas on poetry, imagination, fancy, and related aesthetic concerns. At about the same time, *The White Doe of Rylstone*, delayed at the time of the 1807 reviews, appeared, a sign of Wordsworth's new image of himself as a major literary figure, one committed to poetry as a source of instruction and consolation, with imagination as its unique medium, and yet increasingly committed to a stable social order after the aberrations of Robespierre and Napoleon. Still a lover of the meadows and streams, of humankind, of liberty and justice, he seeks to express this love within a larger social framework.

Like *The Recluse*, *The White Doe of Rylstone* in its origins goes back to a considerably earlier point in Wordsworth's literary life. As early as the summer of 1807 Wordsworth envisioned such a poem, then listened to the critiques of friends like Lamb and Coleridge, tried several revisions, but did not publish the piece until 1815. Kristine Dugas, editor of the poem for the Cornell edition, speaks of the "hesitancy" and "delay"—the problem becomes increasingly evident in the later work—and speculates that Wordsworth was struggling with a variety of problems, "the difference between the representations of ideas and of actions, the problem of intention and execution, and the morality of the use of imaginative symbols."[30]

Rooted in the legend of the white doe in Percy's *Reliques of Ancient English Poetry* and greatly influenced by Wordsworth's reading in Thomas Dunham Whitaker's *History and Antiquities of the Deanery of Craven*, the poem, on the literal and historical levels, is generally loyal to the basic story, and yet it breathes a special life and originality into the events of the ill-starred uprising of Roman Catholics under the Duke of Norfolk against Queen Elizabeth in 1569. The poem, which seems unlike almost any other that Wordsworth has written up to this point, focuses sharply on the involvement in the rebellion of one Richard Norton and all his sons save Francis, and dramatizes that son's struggle to dissuade his father from the action and ultimately to save his father and the proud banner of the clan.

But all ends in tragedy, as father perishes and son is declared a traitor as he attempts to raise the banner at the shrine of the Virgin. Only the Norton sister Emily, a lovely Spenserian heroine invented by Wordsworth and the one who had embroidered the banner originally, remains to mourn the division of the family, comforted only by the visitations of the doe.

While history, especially the specter of violence and disillusionment in France, may still haunt the poet's imagination, Wordsworth seems to use it more as backdrop here, seems more interested in understanding the fate of a family and the survival of a daughter and a faithful doe. Dugas argues that the poet has changed what is essentially a story of fiction and adventure into one of imagination and love, with the *White Doe* emerging "as the supreme representative of Wordsworth's epitaphic mode," as a poem offered by a

---

[30] Introduction, *The White Doe of Rylstone; or, The Fate of the Nortons by William Wordsworth*, ed. Kristine Dugas (Ithaca, N.Y.: Cornell University Press, 1988), p. 4.

teacher to an audience capable of a reflective emotion. Such a poet-teacher would challenge the imagination of "people," not the "public"—he is still smarting from the negative reviews of the 1807 poems—and invite them into the action as co-creators.[31]

Indeed, the narrator invites the reader into the historical context, internal and external universe, recalling with his wife, Mary, to whom the poem is dedicated, happy days when they read together "How Una, sad of soul—in sad attire, / The gentle Una, born of heavenly birth, / To seek her Knight went wandering o'er the earth" (6–8). Recalling how they imaginatively shared Una's sorrow as she led her "milk-white Lamb" (14), learning "How nearly joy and sorrow are allied!" (24) and, further, how, inspired and soothed, they wandered with Una, "willing to partake / All that she suffered for her dear Lord's sake" (39-40), he speaks of how "this Song *of mine* once more could please" (41). Such pleasures for the poet, the true servant of the Muse, are not passing fancies, but have a deeper "power," a "moral Strain" (62). Wordsworth still sees himself as an artist, but also as a teacher.

In a letter of January 18, 1816 to Francis Wrangham, Wordsworth makes a telling comment about the poem and, for our purposes, also about the literary life that is central to this volume, to that peculiar chemistry of feeling that touches the activities of the world and vice versa. "The Poetry," he writes, "proceeds whence it ought to do from the soul of Man, communicating its creative energies to the images of the external world."[32] Alan Liu finds "no better index of the power of poetry we discover in the years following 1807 than Wordsworth's ability not only to free 'power' from all worldly reference but to reground such reference wholly in the Empire of the Poet."[33] As readers we are transported at the outset into the historical setting of the poem. It is "Eliza's golden time," an age of "zeal" and "faith" (1.40–42), the Sabbath day as the doe—gentle, soft, peaceful—approaches Bolton Priory for the celebration of a liturgy. The doe is bejewelled with Wordsworthian images of brightness, not so much decorative as integral to a certain symbolic quality. She is

---

[31] Ibid., p. 7.
[32] *MY* 3.3:276.
[33] *Wordsworth: The Sense of History*, p. 490.

white "as lily of June," "beauteous as the silver moon / . . . left alone in heaven," like "A glittering ship, that hath the plain / Of ocean for her own domain" (1.61–68). The speaker is awestruck by the mystery, whether she is a mortal creature "Or a Spirit, for one day given, / A gift of grace from purest heaven" (1.79–80). Let me, "beguiled / By busy dreams, and fancies wild" (1.325–326), he pleads with the Muse, have a "mortal story!" (1.336).

And the story is forthcoming, a story told rapidly in couplets, of how Emily, a creature of peace, had fashioned the banner in "vermeil colours and in gold" (2.349) in order to "fulfil / Too perfectly" her father's "headstrong will," had embroidered on the banner at his command "The Sacred Cross; and figured there / The five dear wounds our Lord did bear" (2.353–358). The Nortons, except Francis and Emily, launch the insurrection pledged to the forces of Percy. Francis, unarmed and shielded only by the power of love, tries in vain to calm the rebellion, but all his efforts to reason with his father fail. The "sacred Standard falls," and "Of that rash levy naught remained" (4.1160–1165). Francis carries out his father's last wish before execution, to bear the banner to Bolton Priory and place it at Saint Mary's shrine. Hurrying home, now a blessed figure who had "the worst defied / For the sake of natural Piety" (5.1245–1246), he is killed by the forces of Sussex. The banner is taken, reddened by his blood, and he is buried in the churchyard at Bolton Priory.

Rylstone withers away, as does the Norton name, and Emily, now a pilgrim, wanders far and wide. She too becomes a blessed creature, an emblem of Wordsworthian fortitude, "Sustained by memory of the past / And strength of Reason; held above / The infirmities of mortal love" (7.1643–1645). Lucy-like, a figure of endurance and survival so central to Wordsworth's imagination, she remained alone, "To live and die in a shady bower, / Single on the gladsome earth" (7.1656–1657).

But with Emily is the white doe, creature of love bringing peace. A sanctified pair, they remain together with no "pain or fear," return to Rylstone, and often visit the grave of Francis at Bolton Priory. The speaker's voice becomes prominent again as the poem closes. He recalls the tragedy, yet, sounding like Wordsworth, promises "A second and yet nobler birth; / Dire overthrow, and yet how high / The re-ascent in sanctity!" (7.1864–1866). At peace with herself, comforted by the presence of the doe, Emily stood apart from the world, yet always ready to minister. Often she joined the Wharfdale peasants in their prayers, and, freed from earthly constraints, she died and was buried in Rylstone Church.

Once again the familiar Wordsworthian image appears, this time to close the poem, an ending and a beginning: "Most glorious sunset!—and a ray / Survives—the twilight of this day" (7.1890–1891). The White Doe, nourished by nature, partaker of "Heaven's grace" (7.1895), survives as symbol, guarding Emily's grave and receiving the blessings of her mistress. "Thou, thou art not," proclaims the speaker, "a Child of Time, / But Daughter of the Eternal Prime!" (7.1927–1928).

Death continues to be a reality in Wordsworth's life. We remember the impact of his brother John's drowning in 1805. Now, upset by the depression of his wife after the deaths of their children, Catherine on June 4, 1812 and Thomas on December 1, 1812, he took her and her sister, Sara, off to Scotland in July 1814. In 1815 they visited London, then went on a holiday to Bury St. Edmunds. Interestingly, these trips were unusual in that they did not include Dorothy, who seems increasingly a much less important figure than his wife, a fact borne out by the love letters between Wordsworth and Mary, with their remarkable revelation of his passionate relationship with a woman of intelligence and charm.

It is also a period of family and financial concerns. During the heyday of Napoleon, Wordsworth's contact with Annette was broken, but after the fall of the tyrant, celebrated in a series of reactionary odes that irritated Hazlitt, Shelley, and Godwin, Eustace Baudoin, a friend of the Vallon family and a prisoner of war of the English, visited Rydal Mount with news of Annette and Caroline and how they had fared during the war. Baudoin's brother and a civil servant, Jean-Baptiste, became engaged to Caroline in 1814, and there were letters exchanged between Rydal and Paris, with Wordsworth offering his approval of the wedding. Dorothy and Sara planned to attend—there is no mention of William—but Napoleon's escape from Elba and his advance on Paris certainly made the trip impossible. After Napoleon's final defeat at Waterloo, the marriage took place on February 28, 1816, without Wordsworth's presence, although Caroline is listed as the poet's daughter on the wedding certificate. He had sent an annual payment of £30 to Caroline, and in 1835 had made a final settlement of £400 on his natural daughter. Annette received a small government pension from the Royalists when they returned to power. Wordsworth's final meeting with Annette followed a European tour by the poet, Mary, Dorothy, and family friend Crabb Robinson. The group lodged on Rue Chalot, the street where Annette and the Baudoins were living, and Mary and Annette met comfortably in the Louvre on October 2, 1820 with language the only problem.[34] It was apparently on this visit that Wordsworth gave his French family a pencil portrait of himself and the two volumes of his *Collected Poems* of 1815.

Among Wordsworth's most anthologized short poems is the sonnet "Surprized by joy," a title used by C. S. Lewis for one of his autobiographical pieces. The Fenwick note alerts us to its having been suggested "by my daughter Catharine, long after her death." Catharine, who died on June 4, 1812 at the age of three, was the first of two Wordsworth children to die very young. Our best estimate is that the poem was written sometime in the 1813–1814 period, at any rate at least a year after Catharine's death. We know that it came to be included in his *Miscellaneous Sonnets* from 1815.

Yet, once again, the poem, this time a work that follows the so-called Golden Decade, moves beyond the mere record of a family death, touches that record with feeling, continues the course of the poetic life. Beginning with a deep inner joy but one that demands sharing with another, some recognition from beyond, the speaker turns to "share the transport." But no sooner does he turn, "Surprized by joy—impatient as the Wind," than he becomes keenly aware of loss, of the mortality of the world beyond, of death, for she cannot participate, "long buried in the silent Tomb, / That spot which no vicissitude can find."

The poem proceeds to capture a key Wordsworthian tension, the claims of a heart's desire and imagining and the force of the processes of nature. It is not so much poetic decline as a widening of poetic awareness. "Love" brought the image of Catharine to his mind, but the power of mind has "beguiled" so as to make him "blind / To my most grievous loss." That awareness was the "worst

---

[34] Gill, *Wordsworth: A Life*, p. 340.

pang that sorrow ever bore, / Save one," the memory of the day of her death, his standing alone, "Knowing my heart's best treasure was no more." The day of "splendour in the grass, of glory in the flower" is gone, and so also is the confidence in "soothing thoughts." What is needed is perhaps the "philosophic mind," the awareness "That neither present time, nor years unborn / Could to my sight that heavenly face restore."

The year 1819 saw the publication of *Peter Bell* and *Benjamin the Waggoner*, the former described by Mary Moorman as "Wordsworth's most narrative poem,"[35] an enthusiasm not shared by Wordsworth's contemporaries. Actually written some twenty years earlier in his *Lyrical Ballads* experiment, then revised often, it was parodied mercilessly by Reynolds in *Peter Bell: A Lyrical Ballad*, but most fiercely in Shelley's *Peter Bell the Third*. Interestingly enough, the first edition, with a drawing by Sir George Beaumont and a dedication to Southey, sold out its five hundred copies in two weeks. The "public" had its say.

Two poems of the period deserve attention in catching the spirit of Wordsworth's literary life. The first, *Laodamia*, with finely crafted six-line stanzas closed by strategic rhyming couplets, reveals Wordsworth's reading in classical literature, especially his interest in an episode in Book 6 of Virgil's *Aeneid* and its pertinence for his artistic purposes. The episode concerns the response of Laodamia to the death of her husband, Protesilaus, apparently the first Greek casualty of the Trojan War. As she prays fervently to see him, Hermes, messenger of the gods, touches her with his wand, calms her fears, and brings news that he will come for "three hours' space; / Accept the gift, behold him face to face" (23–24). He appears as a spirit, however, and she reaches to embrace him. His words describe his unhappy fate—the first Greek to perish, slain by Hector. She pleads for "one nuptial kiss" (63), incurring the displeasure of Jove. The spirit of her husband, a Wordsworthian spokesman, urges discipline, control of "Rebellious passion: for the Gods approve / The depth, and not the tumult of the soul," and counsels that she "meekly mourn / When I depart, for brief is my sojourn" (74–78).

His is a message of future joy, as he appears now in "Elysian

---

[35] *William Wordsworth: A Biography*, 2:364.

beauty" (95), speaks of "happier beauty; more pellucid streams," of "Climes which the Sun, who sheds the brightest day / Earth knows, is all unworthy to survey" (104–108). Seek, he says to his wife, "Our blest re-union in the shades below" (142). Sounding almost Keatsian, he urges the quest for a higher truth and love, "That self might be annulled" (149). Yet the all-too-human Laodamia shrieks and dies as Hermes returns to recover Protesilaus. A powerful closing stanza deals with human grief as the Wordsworthian narrator, echoing quite remarkably the sentiments and using the imagery of the earlier "The Small Celandine," counsels fortitude, reminds the reader that human grief and suffering are realities to be reckoned with, but not as if mankind alone experienced decline and fall. Look to nature and its cycles; look to a spot "Upon the side / Of Hellespont (such faith was entertained) / A knot of spiry trees for ages grew / From out the tomb of him for whom she died." As the trees reach a height "That Ilium's walls were subject to their view, / The trees tall summits wither'd at the sight; / A constant interchange of growth and blight!" (167–174). The fate of the small celandine, "Stiff in its members, withered, changed of hue," is magnified.

Notable in the so-called later years is the return to the lyrical yet disciplined measures of ode, song, and sonnet. He published little in 1818 or 1819 as he worked on a sequence of sonnets on the River Duddon. At this time his reputation as the shaper of a new kind of taste developed notably among his contemporaries, even those who had reservations about many of his innovations. Coleridge, arguing that Wordsworth's more theoretical prefaces caused many of his problems, nevertheless ranked him "nearest of all modern writers to Shakespeare and Milton." Shelley and Byron, who had often targeted him for parody, acknowledge his special kind of artistic genius. Keats considered him "superior to us, in so far as he can, more than we, make discoveries and shed a light on them." Hazlitt saw Wordsworth as rescuing English poetry at this time, as "the most original poet now living," as producing "a deeper impression on a smaller circle, than any of his contemporaries."[36]

---

[36] See Coleridge's *Biographia Literaria*, 2:151. Writing to Charles and James Ollier on October 15, 1819, Shelley responds to Southey's sharply negative "assertion that I imitate Wordsworth. It may be said that Lord Byron imitates Wordsworth, or that Wordsworth imitates Lord Byron, both being great poets, and deriving from the

"Composed Upon an Evening of Extraordinary Splendour," written in 1817 and first published in 1820, is an excellent example of the continuities with variations that pervade many of the later poems of Wordsworth. There is, on the one hand, enough freedom of expression, enough interior monologue, to associate it with the irregular Pindaric ode of which his early *Immortality Ode* is representative. Yet there are a formality of structure—each stanza has twenty lines with a basic iambic rhythm and regular rhyme scheme—and an elevation and elegance of utterance that we associate with the more regular classical ode. Ketcham sees Wordsworth exploiting "the dual nature of the ode—it is a private as well as a public utterance—as a source of vital tension." "Contrasts of many sorts attract him," he argues: "personal and universal concerns; concrete impressions and general ideas; simple immediacy and the changelessly transcendental; and, as expressions of all these contrasts, the poetry of simple sincerity versus the expected formalisms of the ode."[37]

But, on a more subtle level, there is less anxiety in the speaker's tone, less of the kind of muffled fear and controlled resolution found in the earlier ode. Images of light and darkness, or rather of skewed light, continue to dominate. Ketcham finds Wordsworth struggling in the "Evening" ode "to fix and domesticate a passing vision of his old, glorious world of spiritual insight," then "turning to a poignantly personal note, he views the evening's recovered moment of transcendence as almost bitter irony."[38] In the *Immortality Ode*, we remember, memories of a celestial light pervading everything give way to other memories of that light fading. The glory and dream of childhood and adolescence fade into the light of "common day." Yet no sooner have the sadness of loss, the remnants of time's relentless erosions been recognized than a counter-voice strikes a jubilant tone, celebrates the ability to recapture in age youthful rapture, cre-

new springs of thought and feeling, which the great events of our age have exposed to view, a similar tone of sentiment, imagery and expression" (*Correspondence*, ed. Roger Ingpen, in *Complete Works of Percy Bysshe Shelley*, ed. Roger Ingpen and Walter Peck, 10 vols. [New York: Gordian Press; London: Ernest Benn, Ltd., 1965], 10.95–96). See also Shelley's sonnet "To Wordsworth."

Note Keats's remark in his May 3, 1818 letter to John Hamilton Reynolds (*Letters*, 1:281) and Hazlitt's comment in *Complete Works of Hazlitt*, 5:156.

[37] Wordsworth, *Shorter Poems*, p. 16.
[38] Ibid.

ates a parade-like motif with the somber adult joining the jubilant ranks of the children. Closure seems forced as the speaker proclaims "O joy that is our embers / Is something that doth live" and ends with the apparent conviction that "To me the meanest flower that blows can give / Thoughts that do often lie too deep for tears."

The Fenwick note to the "Evening" ode describes it as "Felt and in a great measure composed upon the little mount in front of our abode at Rydal." We imagine the speaker at sunset, or rather at a particular point in sunset. He is struck by how the "effulgence," instead of disappearing "With flying haste" and triggering in him "a look / of blank astonishment," lingers, works itself out slowly, deliberately. The "effulgence" has "power to stay," indeed to "sanctify one closing day" in order that "frail Mortality may see / What is?—ah no, but what *can* be" (1–8). It has not simply the sense of an ending, or even of hope for the beginning of a bright new day, but rather, like Keats's autumn, a beauty and mystery of its own.

The speaker recalls, sharply echoing the *Immortality Ode*, "Time was when field and watery cove / With modulated echoes rang, / While choirs of fervent Angels sang / Their vespers in the grove." Yet such a "holy rite" is not something to be recaptured at the expense of the present realities of age, pain, time. Indeed, even if it could be repeated, and the clear implication is that it cannot, it "could not move / Sublimer transport, purer love, / Than doth this silent spectacle—the gleam— / The shadow—and the peace supreme!" (9–20).

The second stanza of the ode explores the nature of the peace that comes with maturing, ripening. Its greatest gift is silence as "a deep / And solemn harmony pervades / The hollow vale from steep to steep, / And penetrates the glades." Its beauties are not abstract, but "Far-distant images draw nigh, / Call'd forth by wond'rous potency / Of beamy radiance" (21–27). Yet it is a magnificence best captured by an interaction of mind and nature. The old confidence in the power of imagination still seems strong, although Wordsworth's language seems more deeply touched with solemn, even religious overtones. The beauty of the evening is undoubtedly a firm reality, yet its full range of meaning is lodged in the inner life, in "god-like wish, or hope divine" (34). A large part of this evening's gift comes "From worlds not quickened by the sun" (37).

This radiance of a summer evening will not be momentary. Rather, it will take on the qualities of one of the early "spots of time" in *The Prelude*, moments of intense absorption in nature which renovate and inspire for the future. Now, "rooted here" (50), firmly in touch with the real and all its demands and limitations, his mind's eye sees the ascending mountain-ridges as steps on Jacob's Ladder to heaven, and he summons Genii to arouse "some Traveller, weary of his road" "to meet the dow'r / Bestowed on this transcendent hour!" (55–60).

Stanza 4 follows hard upon the summons to the Genii as the speaker recalls how the hues from their urn "Were wont to stream before my eye, / Where'er it wandered in the morn / Of blissful infancy." Yet some of that "glimpse of glory" past is now renewed, if "only in my dreams." The somberness of an older Wordsworth emerges as he eschews any false or vain hopes, any sense of dream as panacea or escape. Addressing the "Dread Power" who presides over the present peace as well as the "threatening voice" of Nature, he prays in a manner reminiscent of Herbert or Vaughan. If ever he turns away from the Divine Power in any way, "Oh, let thy grace remind me of the light / Full early lost and fruitlessly deplored." It is a prayer, however, uniquely Wordsworthian, not for perpetual light, eternal peace on earth, never-ending childhood. Such ideals belie the reality of being human. Yet it is a prayer for glimpses such as those offered by this evening, a prayer for a Vaughan-like retreat, for the light "Which, at this moment, on my waking sight / Appears to shine, by miracle restored!" (61–76). This evening has given intimations of immortality, but only intimations.

There is a decisive pause before the closing couplet of the ode, creating the tone of the "Forlorn" of the last stanza of Keats's "Ode to a Nightingale." In the drama of Keats's poem, the "forlorn" of the fairylands his imagination has created for him becomes a bell that tolls him back to the reality of an aching heart and drowsy numbness relieved briefly by the song of the bird. In Wordsworth's poem, the light of youth, restored by miracle—" 'Tis past, the visionary splendour fades." And the speaker, caught up for a spell in the imagination's dalliance with splendor, returns to earth as "Night approaches with her shades" (79–80). This great ode of 1820 is evidence of what I have called "continuities with variations" in the later Wordsworth. The pressures of time, the demands of mortality, the undermining of ideals have not necessarily deadened the poetic impulse. They have taken it in new directions.

Published in May 1820, the River Duddon sonnets were more widely praised than any volume of his work to date.[39] Written over a number of years—probably as early as 1806 and as late as 1820—and dedicated to his brother, the Reverend Christopher Wordsworth, they continue to offer the image of a poet confident of his vocation as artist and teacher. The sonnets dramatize once again Wordsworth's imaginative encounter with history, his naturalism now more firmly penetrated by a classical-Christian dimension. Likening himself to Roman Horace praising the spring of Blandusia in his odes, he hails "ye mountains" (1.10) and "thou morning light" and seeks the "birthplace" (1.9) of "long-loved Duddon," "my theme" (1.14).[40] And he prays that the same creative force that moves the river will stir his poetic life, his shaping power of imagination. Mary Moorman reminds us that "Since infancy, flowing water had been for Wordsworth the most beloved of all 'natural objects' " and "the image and symbol of the dearest things."[41] And as he proceeds down the Duddon Valley, adds Melinda Ponder, "it is the eternality of the river that strikes the speaker, now more than ever convinced that enduring art is created by the imagination, the symbol-making power as Coleridge perceived it."[42]

Time passes, but not the river, impelled by some "awful Spirit" (14.9). The natural and the human are intertwined as the imagination, with the speaker at Seathwaite Chapel, calls up once again the memory of "Wonderful" Walker, a pastor in the tradition of Chaucer, Herbert, Goldsmith, and others, and one who ministered humbly

---

[39] The anonymous reviewer for *The British Review* (September 16, 1820) says that "Wordsworth brings intensity and originality of natural expression to the imbuing of external description with natural feeling." And the anonymous reviewer for *London Magazine; and Critical and Dramatic Review* (June 1, 1820) comments how "the sonnets beautifully adapt morality to description" and suggests that "Wordsworth's poems combine the meditative spirit of the metaphysical poets with the simplicity and love of nature of the Elizabethans." See Bauer, *William Wordsworth: A Reference Guide*, pp, 47–53.

[40] Citations to the sonnets are by sonnet number and line number.

[41] *William Wordsworth: A Biography*, 2:375.

[42] "Echoing Poetry with History: Wordsworth's Duddon Sonnets and Their Notes," *Genre*, 21 (1988), 164.

and tenderly for sixty-six of his ninety-three years, another Wordsworthian emblem of endurance honored at greater length in a later biographical note to the sonnet sequence.

Sonnet 32, certainly among the best in the sequence, evokes, perhaps for a moment, the earlier Westminster Bridge sonnet as we view the Duddon's movement on its course "in radiant progress toward the Deep" (32.4). In a picture of great serenity, the river expands and "Beneath an ampler sky a region wide / Is opened round him:—hamlets, towers, and towns, / And blue-topped hills, behold him from afar; / In stately mien to sovereign Thames allied" (32.9–12). "Sonnet 33—Conclusion" continues the image of movement as the speaker, the Duddon's patron, pleads for the freedom of the stream, for the energy in his own poetic life "to advance like Thee; / Prepared, in peace of heart, in calm of mind / And soul, to mingle with Eternity!" (12–14). There is more than a touch of the Romantic sublime here, the reaching for a state beyond sight and sound, the quest for a mingling with the transcendent.

The well-known "After-Thought" sonnet links the poet's life even more directly to the course of the stream, again supernaturalizing, as it were, the natural. On the one hand, he sees the river, *"my partner and my guide,"* *"As being past away"* (1-2). Yet he sees an eternality in the flowing stream as *"The Form remains, the Function never dies"* (6). His is a strong "be it so" (9); it is enough—and we hear the great "O joy that in our embers / Is something that doth live" of the *Immortality Ode* still alive and powerful but now more sharply, indeed, more religiously formulated—if as we move toward an ending, through the virtues of faith, hope, and love, *"We feel that we are greater than we know"* (14).

The more public poetic posture continues in the massive sequence of the *Ecclesiastical Sonnets* (called *Ecclesiastical Sketches* until 1837), first published in 1822 and added to later. In a long prefatory letter and in the later Fenwick note, we get a sense of the poet's mind at the time. Recalling a walk with Sir George Beaumont through his estate at Coleorton, "with a view to fix upon the site of a new Church which he intended to erect," they were led "to look back upon past events with wonder and gratitude, and on the future with hope." That sense of history and of thanks for a continuing tradition accompanied by the looming question of Catholic emancipation provided Wordsworth with the idea that "certain points in the Ecclesiastical History of our Country might advantageously be presented to view in verse." William Galperin cites Moorman as the source of his comment that "in reconstructing the development of the English Church, Wordsworth consistently relied on more than one source: Bede, Eusebius, Stillingfleet and Sharon Turner for the early period; Fuller, Daniel, Stowe, Drayton and Foxe for the Middle Ages through the reign of Elizabeth, and Walton, Heylin and Milton for the seventeenth century."[43]

The Fenwick note alerts the reader to Wordsworth's purpose in the collection: to trace "the introduction, progress, and operation of the Church in England, both previous and subsequent to the Reformation." There is a remarkable candor in Wordsworth's April 16, 1822 letter to Richard Sharp as he notes the disadvantages associated with his project, that the sonnets require readers pretty well acquainted with English history and that "as separate pieces, several of them suffer as poetry from the matter of fact," that there is something in all history "that enslaves the Fancy."[44] Wordsworth seems his own best critic on this matter, echoing Coleridge's complaint about the matter-of-factness of some of the *Lyrical Ballads* written years earlier. We continue to be reminded of the tension throughout the poetic life between the claims of the inner life and the larger demands of the world beyond.

Matter of fact notwithstanding, ecclesiastical history of Britain granted, the sonnets do, however, play a role in understanding Wordsworth's literary life, his continuing attempt to bring the force of his imagination to bear on the world and its institutions. Abbie Findlay Potts, an early editor of the *Sonnets*, regards them as "a memorial of the progress of religion as an element of poetry, a progress made by collective minds and traceable in ecclesiastical polity and history."[45] This attempt is especially evident in these post-1810 years as the pressures of the real compete strongly with the demands of the inner life and often find expression in a more stable, fixed

---

[43] *Revision and Authority*, p. 229.

[44] *LY* 4.1:119.

[45] *The Ecclesiastical Sonnets of William Wordsworth: A Critical Edition* (New Haven, Conn.: Yale University Press, 1922), p. 21. Citations give part number, sonnet number, and line numbers.

language and metaphor, just as his deepest yearnings for a point of reference, for something transcendent find a satisfaction in institutions like Tory politics and, in this case, the Church of England.

The *Ecclesiastical Sonnets*, says Mary Moorman, offers "a picture of the English Church felt as poetry"; "they were written as Wordsworth himself pointed out in later years, long before Ecclesiastical History and points of doctrine had excited the interest with which they have been recently inquired into and discussed by the scholars of the Oxford Movement." For Moorman the sonnets were not academic exercises, but expressions of "his own mature mind, nourished by his early sympathies and by his recent readings of history and biography."[46] I will have occasion, as we proceed in this section, to discuss the Wordsworth–Oxford Movement connections, but for now we turn to the poetry itself, to the literariness of the poet's continuing quest for meaning.

The sequence opens with the speaker linking himself to his fellow speaker "who accompanied with faithful pace / Cerulean Duddon from its cloud-fed spring," and "who essayed the nobler Stream to trace / Of Liberty" (1.1.1–5). His purpose here is less a celebration of nature, or of political ideals, and more the poetic task of seeking "upon the heights of Time the source / Of a HOLY RIVER" (1.1.9–10), knowing that for such a poet "Immortal amaranth and palms abound" (1.1.14).

It is a sweeping poetic quest that he undertakes, uneven, prosaic, even discontinuous at times, but at special moments catching, in Moorman's words, the Church "felt as poetry." We hear the speaker wondering whether Saints Paul and Peter wandered West and dwelt "a while in Britain" (1.2.6). We savor the legend of Catholic writers that Joseph of Arimathea, described in the Gospels as a secret disciple of Jesus who buried the Lord's body in his private tomb, first brought Christianity to Britain and built a church at Glastonbury. Rich and stark, almost mythic images mark the ominous fortunes of the Druids: "Screams round the Arch-druid's brow the sea-mew-white / As Menai's foam; and toward the mystic ring / Where Augurs stood, the Future questioning, / Slowly the cormorant aims her heavy flight" (1.3.1–4).

---

[46] *William Wordsworth: A Biography*, 2:394.

Out of the violence of the "Julian spear" come the "tidings" of
"Jesus crucified" (1.3.1–12) and the spread of those whose hope is
in their faith. Then followed Roman persecution, the death of Alban,
England's first martyr, and the final evacuation by the Romans as
they rush to defend their own nation against barbarian invasions. As
the sonnets continue, we view the Saxon conquest and the coming
of Augustine as first Archbishop of Canterbury. Wordsworth, paying
tribute to Bede's *Ecclesiastical History*, nevertheless again translates
history into poetry, most notably in his celebration of the ninth-
century reign of Alfred the Great, patron of learning and letters, as
King of the West Saxons, and renders Alfred's great and frequently
quoted speech in Bede in a special way. Addressing Alfred, he builds
on the central metaphor of the brevity of human life: "Man's life is
like a Sparrow, mighty King! / That—while at banquet with your
Chiefs you sit / Housed near a blazing fire—is seen to flit / Safe from
the wintry tempest." With short vowels predominating, we sense
the speed of the sparrow's coming, "Fluttering / Here did it enter."
And longer syllables catch the finality of its going: "there, on hasty
wing, / Flies out, and passes on from cold to cold; / But whence it
came we know not, nor behold / Whither it goes" (1.16.1–8).

More Danish invasions ravage the land after the abuses of Dun-
stan, the tenth-century Benedictine abbot and prelate, and King Ca-
nute II emerges as ruler of England and Denmark. A sober
Wordsworth berates "The Might of spiritual sway! his thought, his
dreams, / Do in the supernatural world abide," the evil of "virtues
pushed to extremes, / And sorceries of talent misapplied" (1.28.10–
14). Only "Gospel-truth," a simple, unadorned Christianity, can
calm rage and violence (1.29.5)

The Norman Conquest, the calling of the First Crusade by Pope
Urban II at the Council of Clermont to recover the Holy Places, the
violence of the Crusaders, the eventual emergence of the power of
"Peter's chair" (1.39.1)—these are the themes of the closing sonnets of Part 1. Ann Rylstone's summary comment is perceptive as
she views the substance and style of this section. Nature is close to
the divine, she argues, and "when the institution defies nature . . .
the poet realigns the work's imagery to isolate the foolish and offen-
sive behavior in a frightening dimension characterized by the absence of music and an unresponsive natural landscape." And, making

the case for the kind of continuity we have been tracing in Wordsworth's life, she contends that the poetic and philosophical power of the earlier poet of *The Prelude* "resonates in the *Ecclesiastical Sonnets* for those who recognize that he is devoting his attention to a different region of the vast cosmography of his works, epic in scope, but unified by a spiritual, synthetic vision."[47]

Part 2 of Wordsworth's ecclesiastical epic moves from the reign of Henry III to the turbulent years of Charles I, from medieval to Renaissance England, a period of calm to one of revolution and reformation. Ten sonnets at the outset moderate the critique of Papism immediately preceding and advance the contributions of Roman Catholicism. Sonnet 5 on "Monks and schoolmen" praises those devoted souls committed to solitude and the life of the mind and spirit, and Sonnet 6 bemoans the sad prospect if knights and retainers seeking the gifts of prayer and music were "forlorn of offices dispensing heavenly grace!" (2.6.14). The court of Edward II is a place "Of wisdom, magnanimity, and love" (2.7.10), a place where Church and State, lamb and lion, dove and eagle live in peace.

But the glories of Catholicism are undermined by the corruptions of the clergy and the persecutions of Protestant thinkers. Peter Waldo is harassed for opposing the doctrine of transubstantiation; John Wycliffe, for his satire of clerical vice. Yet the negative always seems tinged with some regret that the delicate balance of reforming and preserving has not been maintained, that change has brought the dissolution of the monasteries, the loss of devotion to the saints and especially the Virgin Mary, "Our tainted nature's solitary boast" (2.25.4), the decline of the artistic dimension of worship. Again we are reminded of the power of revolution in Wordsworth's imagination, the dangers posed by those turbulent spirits who, in Burke's phrase, would destroy in order to reform. The tension between individual and institution, between freedom and discipline, between change and tradition creates what Rylstone calls a "chaotic but rich ferment."[48]

A fundamental fairness emerges from Wordsworth's experience

---

[47] *Prophetic Memory in Wordsworth's "Ecclesiastical Sonnets"* (Carbondale and Edwardsville: Southern Illinois University Press, 1991), pp. 77–78.

[48] Ibid., p. 79.

of the tension between the claims of the heart and imagination and the need for an orderly body politic, a stable institutional church. The Church of England is, for him, human, made up of men and women. Some were responsible for the aberrations outlined in his overview; others, such as Thomas More and John Fisher, who held to their beliefs, refused the Oath of Supremacy and were executed in 1535. The revival of Popery under Queen Mary—ritual, the restoration of images, the martyrdom of Latimer and Ridley, the burning at the stake of Archbishop Cranmer—threatens genuine reformation and breeds chaos as reform gives way to reaction. As Wordsworth celebrates Elizabeth's coming to the throne—"Hail, Virgin Queen!" (2.38.1)—he wonders why the triumph yields to new violence, now against Mary and Roman Catholicism. Reformers like Hooker seek a middle course, only to be foiled by new sectarianism and the violence of the Gunpowder Plot. The Reign of Terror redivivus!

Two powerful sonnets, with the ring of Milton's political poetry, capture in powerful images disorder in nature matching the disarray of religious turmoil. There is something of Weiskel's romantic sublime in the epic simile that constitutes the entire sonnet, "The Jung-Frau and the Fall of the Rhine near Schaffhausen." The long vowels of the opening five lines capture the power of first sight: "The Virgin-Mountain, wearing like a Queen / A brilliant crown of everlasting snow, / Sheds ruin from her sides; and men below / Wonder that aught of aspect so serene / Can link with desolation" (2.43.1-5). The s-alliteration dominating a second scene suggests the peace of the Rhine—"Smooth," "seeming at a little distance slow" (2.43.5-6). Then in terrifyingly vague imagery the two forces meet. There is peace until a kind of madness takes possession of the river and turns it into "a fearful Thing whose nostrils breathe / Blasts of tempestuous smoke—wherewith he tries / To hide himself, but only magnifies; / And doth in more conspicuous torment writhe, / Deafening the region in his ireful mood" (2.43.10-14). And in Sonnet 44—"Troubles of Charles the First"—the writhing spasm of the Beast becomes a metaphor for destructive religious warfare. For Rylstone, however, out of this chaos will emerge the unique *via media* of the Anglican Church "whose stable but dynamic presence graces the

Church as an institution, the Anglican communion, and the British nation."[49]

Part 3 of the *Ecclesiastical Sonnets* moves from the Restoration to the present. And an impressive present it is, with Parliament having in 1818 voted £1,000,000 for the building of new churches in England. Again, however briefly, the themes of home and village and solitude and family return, in this case right at the beginning. The Fenwick note to the opening sonnet recalls Wordsworth's dream of his daughter Dora at the time of composition and how the poem reconstructs it. It was, he says, composed on the road from Grasmere to Ambleside, begun as he left the last house in the valley and completed exactly as it stands before he came in sight of Rydal village. Wordsworth's story evokes memories of his account of the composition of *Tintern Abbey*, spontaneous composition while walking and finally rendered verbatim in writing. The "lovely Maid" is "Seated alone beneath a darksome tree, / Whose fondly-overhanging canopy / Set off her brightness with a pleasing shade" (3.1.1–4). Yet the vision lasts just a while, as "form and face— / Remaining still distinct grew thin and rare, / Like sunny mist" (3.1.9–11). Sonnet 2, "Patriotic Sympathies," continues the motif of vision fading, here the vision not of a woman, but of a nation.

The Restoration of Charles II and the seeming recovery of tradition and order give way to "wantonness," to "misery, shame, / By poets loathed; from which Historians shrink!" (3.3.9–14). Yet all is not lost; witness the Church, the Cambridge Platonists, and, of course, Milton, "solitary," with "Darkness before and danger's voice behind," but with "the pure spirit of celestial light / . . . that he may see and tell / Of things invisible to mortal sight" (3.4.7–14). The shame of the Act of Conformity of 1662, of the persecution of the Scottish Covenanters, of the trial but final acquittal of the Bishop who opposed James II, "the vacillating Bondman of the Pope" (3.9.13), in 1688—these and other episodes fade with the return of William III.

Three sonnets—13, 14, and 15—range over history to deal with Christianity in America, and then in a sweeping review of things

---

[49] Ibid.

liturgical, he sums up the Church's sacramental care of the faithful from birth to death. William III emerges as hero, his legacy "A State—which balancing herself between / Licence and slavish order, dares be free" (3.37.13–14). New churches, chapels, cathedrals contend with time. The "Inside of King's College Chapel, Cambridge," is a place "Where light and shade repose, where music dwells / Lingering—and wandering on as loth to die" (3.43.11–12). The builders of Westminster, St. Paul's, King's College Chapel, Cambridge "dreamt not of a perishable home." In words that suggest the twentieth-century poet Philip Larkin, Wordsworth prays, "Be mine, in hours of fear / Or grovelling thought, to seek a refuge here" (3.45.1–3). Then, un-Larkin-like, he writes, "Glory to God" (3.46.1) in his "Ejaculation" and "let us seek the light" and "So, like the Mountain, may we grow more bright / From unimpeded commerce with the Sun / At the approach of all-involving night" (3.46.12–14). In the spirit of his late-career supernatural naturalism, he closes his ecclesiastical monument in the final sonnet with the image of water, urging his readers to behold the winding course of the stream they have traveled and to trust the vision. "Stained and polluted" though they be at times, the waters "brighten as they roll, / Till they have reached the eternal city—built / For the perfected Spirits of the just!" (3.47.12–14).

There is a notable tempering of the poetic spirit by the demands of history in the *Ecclesiastical Sonnets*. James Chandler looks back to Wordsworth's celebration of the power of Peele Castle as a vehicle of escape from the prison of the self and an image of a source of strength beyond. The poem, he says, "predicts in a very concrete way the themes of the later poetry: specifically, Wordsworth's postulate of the institution (Church, State) as the ultimate unassailable referent in a world terrorized by imagination."[50] The poet, now more overtly in search of monuments more lasting, beacons of hope and security, has found a magnificent one in the Christian Church of England. The price paid is candidly sketched in Wordsworth's Fenwick observation that "there is unavoidably in all History,—except as it is mere suggestion—something that enslaves the fancy." Yet

---

[50] *Wordsworth's Second Nature*, p. 102.

in those moments when the imagination is energized—the King's College Chapel visit is a classic example—there is the poet of the *Lyrical Ballads*, the 1807 *Poems*, *The Prelude* still at work, still pursuing the literary life in time.

8

Endings and Completions: The Full Poetic Life

Blessings be with them and enduring praise
. . . .
The Poets, who on earth have made us heirs
Of truth and pure delight by heavenly days;
Oh! might my name be numbered among theirs
Then gladly would I end my mortal days.

Wordsworth, "Written at the Request of Edward Moxon"

"If one points out that Wordsworth's poetry after 1807 is, if anything, more poetically engaged and more topical than what went before, the notorious conservatism of the later years remains a stumbling block. But merely to invoke this conservatism is not to understand how it functions in particular poems. . . . The late poems deliberately no longer offer the richly represented self of, say, *The Prelude*, but once understood within their historical situation, their contexts steadily widen and their procedures gain meaning."

Peter Manning, "Wordsworth at St. Bees"

"The most alluring clouds that mount the sky
Owe to a troubled element their forms,
Their hues to sunset. If with raptured eye
We watch their splendor, shall we covet storms,
And wish the Lord of day his slow decline
Would hasten, that such pomp may float on high?
. . . .
Peace let us seek,—to stedfast things attune
Calm expectations, leaving to the gay

And volatile their love of transient bowers,
The house that cannot pass away be ours.

Wordsworth, *Miscellaneous Sonnets* (1845)

THE PERIOD 1822–1830 brought little new and original work as Wordsworth increasingly assumes the role of guru, elder statesman, and
collector of his works, ensconced at the stately Rydal Mount, visited
by Scott, Canning, various Coleridges, the Wilberforces, Emerson—
indeed, a host of fans from Europe and America. He did deign to
write poems for a friend editing a volume called *The Keepsake*, but
among his major literary efforts was a translation of three books of
the *Aeneid*![1] The passing of old friends, notably Sir George Beaumont
in February 1827, also took its toll, although he remains a physical
marvel—climbing mountains, skating on Rydal Water, horsebacking
even after a bad accident, walking long distances with Dorothy until
she fell ill in 1829. John Keymer provides an interesting picture of
Wordsworth at this time in an account of his father's interview with
the poet. "I walked part of the way to Boxell's to whom he was going
to sit for his Portrait. . . . He was in fine health, full of talk but very
ready to listen, free from all affectation or dignity. He styled himself
a 'lively youth of sixty two.' "[2]

Travel, as always, was a major activity: July to November 1820, a
European tour with Dorothy, Mary, and others; May, June 1823, a
trip to Belgium and Holland with Mary; a trip to North Wales in
August and September 1824 with Mary, Dora, and old friend Robert
Jones that brought vivid memories of places first seen in 1791 and
1793; tours that took him to Belgium, Germany, and Holland with
Dora and Coleridge in 1828 and to Ireland with John Marshall of
Hallsteads and his son James in September 1829—these suggest the
energy and drive of the poet during these years. The Irish trip is
especially interesting, beginning in Dublin where he was the guest
of William Rowan Hamilton, the brilliant young Professor of Astronomy at Trinity College who had visited at Rydal Mount the previous

---

[1] See Bruce Graver,"Wordsworth's Georgic Beginnings," *Texas Studies in Language
and Literature*, 33, No. 2 (1991), 137–157.
[2] "Fragment of an account of an interview had by John Keymer with W. W."
(1832). Wordsworth Library (Grasmere) Manuscripts.

summer. Wordsworth regarded Coleridge and Hamilton as the two most extraordinary men he had ever met.[3] Also, although he was unimpressed by the Irish scenery, he, now more politically conservative, was anxious to see the people and to get a sense of their general welfare. He had feared the passage of the Catholic Relief Bill, and, before its passage in March 1829, had written to the Bishop of London in strong opposition.[4]

Still not particularly popular with the reviewers, Wordsworth was nevertheless gaining a certain fame in his role as elder statesman, poet, and adviser of poets.[5] Many political and religious causes are brought to his attention for his voice. W. P. Atkinson, a Boston abolitionist devoted to Wordsworth's poetry, writes to him asking for a contribution to a volume of poems in support of the cause, and Wordsworth, writing to his friend Henry Reed, offers a piece not "bearing directly on slavery," but "if you think this little piece would serve his cause indirectly pray be so kind as to forward it to him."[6]

---

[3] "Wordsworth's estimate of his contemporaries was not generally high. I remember his once saying to me, 'I have known many that might be called very *clever* men, and a good many of real and vigorous abilities, but few of genius; and only one whom I should call "wonderful." That one was Coleridge. . . . The only man like Coleridge whom I have known is Sir William Hamilton, Astronomer Royal of Dublin'" (Aubrey de Vere, Esq., "Recollections of Wordsworth," in *The Prose Works of William Wordsworth*, ed. Rev. Alexander B. Grosart, 3 vols. (London, 1876), 3:492.

[4] W. W. to Charles James Blomfield, March 3, 1829, LY 5.2:36–46.

[5] See Bauer, *William Wordsworth: A Reference Guide*, pp. 15–62. An anonymous 1814 review of *The Excursion* in the *New Monthly Magazine* had described the poem as "ponderous, overly metaphysical, and written in hobbling verse." Hazlitt, in his "Character of Mr. Wordsworth's New Poem, The Excursion" in *The Examiner* for 1814 proclaimed: "If Wordsworth's choice of materials had been equal to his genius and more readily communicable, *The Excursion* would seem less a half-finished structure." And in the *Edinburgh Review* in 1814, the ever-cruel Francis Jeffrey described Wordsworth's case in *The Excursion* as "now hopeless; habits of seclusion and ambition or originality can alone account for the combination in Wordsworth of bad taste and genius." *Peter Bell*, says the anonymus review in *The Monthly Review* in 1819, "is lisping drivel, suitable for the nursery or a Cheap Repository Tract." The anonymous reviewer for *The Literary Gazette* in 1822 comments in Bauer's account that in his *Ecclesiastical Sketches* "Wordsworth again sinks into weakness and doating, choosing a prosaic subject and an absurd plan." And an anonymous review in the *General Weekly Register* in 1822 saw Wordsworth in the *Sketches* abandoning the religious dimension of nature for that of "painted wood, gilt crosses, and priestcraft."

[6] W. P. Atkinson to W. W., May 25, 1845. Wordsworth Library (Grasmere) Manuscripts; and W. W. to Henry Reed, July 1, 1845. *LY* 7.4:688–689.

Dr. George Husband Baird, Principal of the University of Edinburgh, sought Wordsworth's assistance in providing new paraphrases of the Psalms for the Church of Scotland, although he ultimately refused with words that certainly take their place in the arguments for and against the compatibility of poetry and religious experience. "The sacred writings," he writes to Baird, "have a majesty, a beauty, a simplicity, an ardour, a sublimity, that awes and overpowers the spirit of poetry in uninspired men. Indeed, Sir, I dare not attempt it."[7] Both Dorothy and his friend Henry Crabb Robinson were concerned about his neglect of the great political movements for freedom after 1814—the opposition to the scandal of slavery, the plight of the Spaniards under Ferdinand, the Greek wars of independence in which Byron took such a strong interest. His attitude again is conservative as several of his *Miscellaneous Sonnets* reveal. In one we read, "Not Love, not War, nor the tumultuous swell / Of civil conflict, nor the wreck of change, / Nor Duty struggling with afflictions strange,— / Not these *alone* inspire the tuneful shell." The Muse is just as comfortable "where untroubled peace and concord dwell" (1–5).

It is, he argues cautiously in another sonnet, "To the solid ground / Of nature trusts the Mind that builds for aye; / Convinced that there, there only, she can lay Secure foundations" (5–8). Moorman sees the poet "in anxiety over a general election, while Catholic Emancipation and Parliamentary Reform, in the years immediately following, were a constant source of despondency and almost of despair." As Moorman describes it, the reason for his neglect of international issues stems from "the peculiar vividness with which Wordsworth's imagination had clothed the figures of revolutionary France and Napoleon," a depth of emotion that grew out of his own early involvement in and later indictment of the Revolution. With France in a state of collapse and Napoleon a fallen tragic figure, "the images which had inspired him to poetic achievement were removed and his muse fell silent."[8] And Stephen Gill sees Wordsworth, after the passing of the Reform Bill in 1832, as taking on "the mantle of Jeremiah. The Bill was bad, but its progeny, already to be descried,

---

[7] W. W. to George Husband Baird, June 15, 1827. *LY* 7.1:534.

[8] *William Wordsworth: A Biography*, 2:449–450.

would be terrifying. Filtering out much that he actually saw in France in the 1790s, the unity, the gaiety, the triumphal arches, Wordsworth now insisted that what he had witnessed were 'the calamities brought upon all classes, and especially the poor by a Revolution.' "[9]

Family matters concern him greatly in the 1820s. Greatly worried about the failure of his son John to achieve academic distinction, he supported him strongly and, thanks to the good offices of friends like Keble, Beaumont, and Lord Lonsdale, John took orders and secured a good curacy in Leicestershire in 1823. Son Willy was his greatest worry, a none-too-bright or -promising young man turned down for an Army commission and finally sent off to Germany to learn the language. Dorothy, for so long the center of his life, suffered not just physical weakness, but mental deterioration, and she eventually became John's housekeeper at his parish. Dora, his daughter, became the poet's new Dorothy after his sister's condition became hopeless. A more stunning blow met him on his September 20, 1831 visit to Sir Walter Scott. Once an overnight sensation, but now impoverished by bankruptcy and stricken with paralysis, he became for Wordsworth a kind of symbol of a fate he feared for himself as he grew older. Yet his own financial situation improved, and his own general health, except for his chronic trachoma, was very good for a man of his age.

Certainly, the pressures of the everyday reality in which he lived were never more strikingly evident. Yet once again the life of the imagination, the need for the mind to be its own place, became evident. His is still a literary life. For all its sadness, the visit to Scott triggered memories and images, past and present and future, as he completed the third in his trilogy of Yarrow poems, a range of writing that takes us from as early as October 1803 to the autumn of 1831. I pause here to talk about these poems as fertile episodes in a literary life, from work composed in his early thirties to that of his early sixties. While I make no claim for the paradigmatic character of the three poems, they do provide opportunities for dealing with those continuing questions of whether there is an "early" and "late" Wordsworth—that is, a notable shift from a trust in the reasons of

---

[9] *Wordsworth: A Life*, p. 378.

the heart to a moderating of that impulse in the face of the claims of the social, political, religious—or whether there is simply a significant decline in poetic power.

The earliest piece, "Yarrow Unvisited," proceeding from its epigraph from William Hamilton's *The Braes of Yarrow*, seems strangely titled, indeed seems to be an altogether unusual subject for a poem. Dorothy's September 18, 1803 note in her *Recollections of a Tour in Scotland* goes a way in explaining it: "At Clovenford, being so near to the Yarrow, we could not but think of the possibility of going thither, but came to the conclusion of reserving the pleasure for some future time, in consequence of which, after our return, William wrote the poem."[10] But perhaps the best approach is to move beyond journal-explanation and see it as an experiment in imagination.

There is a lively, engaging rhythm in the iambic tetrameter, eight-line stanzas and a notably fresh, concrete vernacular capturing the dialect of Scotland. The opening quickly sets a scene, introduces a cast of travelers/tourists, creates the image, the feeling of a tour. The only speakers are the narrator and his *"winsome marrow."* "From Stirling Castle we had seen / The mazy Forth unravell'd; / Had trod the banks of Clyde, and Tay, / And with the Tweed had travell'd." The *"winsome Marrow"* rather exuberantly proposes at this point: "Whate'er betide, we'll turn aside, / And see the Braes of Yarrow" (1–8). Abruptly the narrator dismisses the idea, calling attention to the immediate pleasures of the natural scene around them: "Dryborough, where with chiming Tweed / The Lintwhites sing in chorus," and "pleasant Triviot Dale, a land / Made blithe with plough and harrow." With such beauty "Why throw away a needful day / To go in search of Yarrow?" (19–24). His true love notwithstanding, it is "Enough if in our hearts we know / There's such a place as Yarrow" (47–48). With a sense of Simplon or of Coleridge's "Lime-Tree Bower," he imagines herons feeding, hares couching, rabbits burrowing. We must, he contends with the conviction of a true believer in the imagination, let it be "unseen, unknown," for "We have a vision of our own; / Ah! why should we undo it?" (51–52). Such a vision will prove a reservoir of strength greater than the reality of Yarrow. Yarrow imagined, the sense of something about to be, the power of

---

[10] *Journals*, 1:391.

the mind to make a reality, will in the future "soothe us in our sorrow" (62).

"Yarrow Visited," composed in early September 1814, translates imagination into reality. The Fenwick note to the poem recalls the first visit, made with James Hogg, the Ettrick shepherd, and expresses regret that Dorothy, who knew the occasion of the first poem, was not with him now. And Wordsworth's famous letter of November 23, 1814 to R. P. Gillies describes how, after a successful "Yarrow Unvisited," he was "anxious that there should be no falling off; but that was unavoidable, perhaps, from the subject, as imagination almost always transcends reality."[11]

Yet the reality is captured nicely in the poem, with its sense of the interaction of image and actual setting. There is the initial disappointment as the speaker exclaims, "And is this—Yarrow?" emphasizing the question with an intensified "*This* the Stream / Of which my fancy cherish'd, / So faithfully, a waking dream? / An image that hath perished!" (1–4). There is the familiar Wordsworthian tension, sadness in the midst of stunning natural beauty. Yarrow visited is a worthy rival of imagination, now called "fond": "Meek loveliness is round thee spread, / A softness still and holy" (42–46). Wild nature has given way to the things of cultivated nature, as the Yarrow winds its way past the ruins of "Newark's Towers" (55). The sense of time taking its toll, of youth passing into age, autumn passing into winter is captured strikingly in "The sober Hills thus deck their brows / To meet the wintry season" (71–72).

Although he is now physically present, aware of a Yarrow touched by time, there is a hint of the "O joy that in our embers / Is something that doth live" motif of the *Immortality Ode* in "I see—but not by sight alone, / Lov'd Yarrow, have I won thee; / A ray of Fancy still survives— / Her sunshine plays upon thee!" (73–76). Yarrow's waters still flow with a special music, and in the midst of fickle earthly things, the speaker knows "where'er I go, / Thy genuine image, Yarrow, / Will dwell with me—to heighten joy, / And cheer my mind in sorrow" (85–88).

"Yarrow Revisited" represents still a further removal from the direct experience of the river. Wordsworth's disciple Barron Field, in

---

[11] *MY* 3.2:170.

a December 17, 1836 letter, regarded the poem as the "climax of the triad—the sweetest strain of them all," and extends his comment saying that "all your new poems are dear to me. Your genius only mellows with your age. Not the smallest spark of decay is visible yet."[12] The river itself has become increasingly an emblem, a memory of something once "felt in the blood," but now experienced more empirically. The opening stanzas have a rollicking quality as the poet recalls "The gallant Youth, who may have gained, / Or seeks, a 'winsome Marrow,' / Was but an Infant in the lap / When first I looked on Yarrow." They are quickly matched and tempered by more somber lines; one hears long vowels, irregular meter, an unusual use of spondees—"Once more, by Newark's Castle–gate / Long left without a warder, / I stood, looked, listened, and with Thee, / Great Minstrel of the Border!" (1–7). Wordsworth, according to the Fenwick note, is recalling a happy visit he and Dora made to Sir Walter Scott before the latter's departure for Italy.

Wordsworth comments that there is "too much pressure of fact" in this last of the Yarrow poems. Whatever his emphasis in this comment, we note how language, rhythm, overall tone evoke a mood of time taking a toll, of age prevailing over youth. Uninspired meters, excessive lifeless personification, stock diction and imagery, a strong didacticism stand out. Scott's departure evokes a rather flat "May Heath return to mellow Age, / With Strength, her venturous Brother" (59–60). May Scott find in Italy the welcome that Yarrow gave to him.

There is melancholy in the poet's lament over the frailty and suffering of the world. Yet there is hope in the "poetic voice" (87), hope that "the visions of the past / Sustain the heart in feeling / Life as she is—our changeful Life, / With friends and kindred dealing" (3.93–96). It is a confidence in the power of mind to recall, to reshape joys of the past, to find secure resting-places. The poem closes with a plea to his friends to "Bear witness" (97), calling on "Yarrow Stream" to "Flow in for ever" (105). The river seems now almost ministerial, fulfilling a duty to be celebrated by future poets. But the poem ends in an awkwardly and cloyingly preachy manner that undermines the power of Yarrow. Now it is "To dream-light dear

---

[12] December 17, 1836. Wordsworth Library (Grasmere) Manuscripts.

while yet unseen, / Dear to the common sunshine, / And dearer still, as now I feel, / To memory's shadowy moonshine!" (109–112).

Death, always a reality even for the young Wordsworth, becomes more and more part of his literary life, with the deaths of writer-friends, Coleridge and Lamb in 1834, and James Hogg in 1835. Hogg's death stirs him to write one of the great pieces of the later years, the "Extempore Effusion" in which, in elegiac form, he mourns not only the death of Hogg, Scott, Coleridge, Lamb, George Crabbe, and Felicia Hemans, but the larger phenomenon of death itself. The poem, composed probably between November 21 and December 12, 1835, was probably first published on December 12, 1835 in the *Athenaeum*, and the Fenwick note records Wordsworth as saying, "These verses were written extempore, immediately after reading a notice of the Ettrick Shepherd's death in the Newcastle paper."

The poem, like so many of Wordsworth's, is a memory piece, eleven stanzas that both recall the symbolic centrality of the river Yarrow in his experience and the passing of brother and sister poets and friends. The eleven quatrains are perfectly crafted with the iambic rhythms capturing delicately the mournful tone. His imagination returns at the outset to a specific time, when, with Hogg as his guide, he walked the Yarrow valley. Quickly he violates chronology to call up the immediate past, a past caught in a richly suggestive autumnal image. Scott is the player in the later drama: "When last along its banks I wandered, / Through groves that had begun to shed / Their golden leaves upon the pathways, / My steps the Border-mistrel led" (5–8). But Hogg has perished, and Scott " 'Mid mouldering ruins low he lies" (10). One death suggests another, as the minstrel Scott is followed by Coleridge, "The rapt One, of the godlike forehead," and by Lamb, "the frolic and the gentle" (17–19).

The middle section of the poem gently interrupts the naming with the starkly mourning "How fast has brother followed brother, / From sunshine to the sunless land!" (23–24). The poet remains to bear witness, to affirm the reality of the darkness of death, onomatopoeically describing himself in the soft sounds of "A timid voice, that asks in whispers, / 'Who next will drop and disappear?' " (27–28).

Returning to his witness—this time beginning with the image of "Our haughty life is crowned with darkness," which he reinforced by a remarkable Blake-like simile, "Like London with its own black wreath"—he recalls a better time when he and the poet Crabbe gazed on the great city "from Hampstead's breezy heath" (29–30). But Crabbe is gone too, yet, sounding like Edgar, "why / O'er ripe fruit, seasonably gathered, / Should frail survivors heave a sigh?" (34–36). Mourn for Lycidas-like figures, dead too soon. Mourn for the gifted young poet Felicia Hemans befriended by Wordsworth, for a "holy Spirit," like Lucy, "For Her who, ere her summer faded, / Has sunk into a breathless sleep" (39–40).

The "Effusion" concludes the stoic eulogy with a farewell to "romantic sorrows" (41) for dead youth or lovelorn maidens. The grief of Yarrow is real, sharp, not to be sentimentalized or rationalized, "And Ettrick mourns with her their Poet dead" (44), the extra foot in the closing pentameter suggesting the finality of it all.

Wordsworth is busy as a poet in the 1830s, not always the inspired bard of the earlier years, though at times one hears exuberant tones. He continues to revise and publish collections of his poems and to edit *The Prelude*, always with the understanding that it would not be published until after his death.

And celebrity continues, as he is honored with doctorates at the University of Durham on July 21, 1838 and at Oxford on June 12, 1839. John Peace, City Librarian at Bristol, writes to Wordsworth shortly after the Oxford ceremony, including a note to Mary about the response of the audience:

> It was overpowering, and perhaps Mr. W. may recollect and coincide with what I said—that nowhere is applause bestowed with so much energy as in that theatre. That which he received, thundering as it was, had not to my ear an uproarious character, it had a beautiful tone about it; just such as one would expect to characterize a burst from the central heart of the best men of England at the best period of their lives.

And Peace, obviously an extravagant admirer, goes on to tell Mary how fortunate it was that the "congenial and heavenly minded John Keble" told the "fit audience not few, that the highest praise which

Christian life may utter belonged to the Christian Poet who stood before them."[13]

And there were more plaudits as he was honored, after originally refusing the title, with the Poet Laureateship on April 4, 1843, although he brought no great commitment to that post. He, like many a father in a similar situation, retired as Distributor of Stamps for Westmoreland, seeing to it that his feckless son Willy became his successor. Anxieties about money, always a concern for the poet, were eased, as the many collections of his works proved successful and brought him an annual income of £5,000. And Sir Robert Peel, the prime minister, saw to it that he received a civil service pension of £300 a year.

Browning's 1845 poem "The Lost Leader" bemoans the comfortable conservatism of the former radical turned Tory. Yet Wordsworth's fears about the drift of politics were not assuaged by what he saw as the leveling force of the great Reform Bill of 1832, the growing power of the Whigs, the widening of the electorate, the increasing dehumanization of science, the exclusion of religious tests from education and the increasing liberalism of its teaching, the generally poor state of poetry and the language.[14]

Dorothy's illness grew worse from 1829 to 1834, relieved only occasionally by periods of good health when she could assist her brother as in the past and when such assistance seemed a spur to his creative energies. Hunter Davies's words offer a poignant, if somewhat romanticized, picture of a failing Dorothy. Though she was housekeeper for her nephew John at his first ministerial assignment at Whitwick Church in Leicestershire, her health, especially her

---

[13] August 12, 1839 (note to Mrs. W. within). Wordsworth Library (Grasmere) Manuscripts.

[14] Eliza Fletcher offers an interesting firsthand description of the Wordsworth of these years in a Holiday Log Book for September 4–23, 1833. Wordsworth, she writes, "has two souls a practical Soul pure, elevated, Devotional,—conversant with nothing but images of moral and natural beauty." And she adds, "The prosaic soul is sordid and slavish.—cold, a good hater of Liberty and all who advocate its cause or sympathise in its aspirations after justice, humanity and truth.—a lover of the great after the fashion of *this* world." Fletcher later comments that Wordsworth "loved God and his Neighbor too.—but his aristocratic prejudices limit and darken his understanding on the love of his neighbor. . . . in short Nature which gifted him with Genius intended him for a great man but accident and circumstances have made him only a great poet." Wordsworth Library (Grasmere) Manuscripts.

mental condition, deteriorated. "From now," he says, "until the end of her life, she lived in her own twilight world, eventually confined to a wheel-chair, taken out round the garden on days of sunshine, though she often protested, determined to sit roasting by the fire, even on the hottest day."[15] The picture painted by George Douglas Campbell, 8th Duke of Argyll, is somewhat grimmer. Writing to the Reverend J. G. Hanson on September 8, 1848, he recalls walking to Rydal Mount with Chaplain Howard, only to find the family at church. "We saw," he writes, "a very old, shrivelled, and palsied woman, drawn in a Bath Chair by a servant where [whose?] paralytic countenance, and wandering eye struck us unpleasantly as she asked Howard with painful vacancy what His name was—and added that she had not the pleasure of his acquaintance."[16]

Wordsworth the poet emerges again in a notable series of poems called "Evening Voluntaries" of 1833, none more notable than the one called "On a High Part of the Coast of Cumberland." Mary Moorman sees these evening musings by Rydal Water or on the lawn at Rydal Mount as examples of change for the worse in the later poetry. The same sights and sounds of the earlier poetry that triggered "immediate contact with a visionary world of glory and joy" have now become " 'emblems' of moral or religious truths."[17] Moorman notwithstanding, however, "On a High Part" is an excellent example of the best Wordsworth poetry of the later years, as the poet, caught by a sublime moment of rapture close to nature, turns that moment into an occasion for reflective statement. The Fenwick note describes its composition—probably on Easter Sunday, April 7, 1833, his sixty-third birthday—as "on the road between Moresby and Whitehaven while I was on a visit to my Son, then Rector of the former place." The poem "originated in the concluding lines of the last paragraph," lines of deep and overt religious sentiment.

With childhood memories of Whitehaven "and the white waves breaking against the quays and piers, as the whole came into view from the top of the high ground down which the road . . . then descended abruptly," the poet in the first verse-paragraph sets a

---

[15] *William Wordsworth: A Biography*, p. 303.
[16] Wordsworth Library (Grasmere) Manuscripts.
[17] *William Wordsworth: A Biography*, 2.496.

scene of nature at peace. But as the poem proceeds with a splendid variety of iambic pentameter couplets, that peace is seen as the finale of a fierce battle of light and shade caught in a dazzling image: "The Sun, that seemed so mildly to retire, / Flung back from distant climes a streaming fire." The brilliant sun will not decline without a display of its power, yet the display is brief, "now subdued to tender gleams, / Prelude of night's approach with soothing dreams." With the darkness approaching, the speaker urges, "Look round," and catch the peace of a serene twilight. It is a splendid moment, and, almost as if to evoke with variation another moment—"the first mild day of March" in the early lyric "To My Sister"—he proclaims, " 'Tis the still hour of thinking, feeling, loving" (1–6).

From sunset above to the sea below, the mood is of silence, peace. Continuing the soft alliteration of the opening image, "Silent, and steadfast as the vaulted sky, / The boundless plain of waters seems to lie," the speaker questions whether the sound comes "from breezes rustling o'er / The grass-crowned headland that conceals the shore." But the answer is "No; 'tis the earth-voice of the mighty sea, / Whispering how meek and gentle he can be!" (7–12), an echo of the much earlier "mighty heart" or "mighty being" as power reveals itself in solitude and peace.

To this point we hear something of the Wordsworth of *The Prelude*, the *Immortality Ode*, the 1807 *Poems*. But the second verse-paragraph turns sharply prayerful, formulaically devout, as the speaker looks beyond nature and its nourishing power to something transcendent. The setting of the opening paragraph—sunset, a peaceful sky, silence and calm—becomes now more the visual aid, the allegorical representation of a God the speaker would image. "Thou Power supreme" (13), he prays; yet his prayer, unlike Donne's, is not for a manifestation of this power. He seeks another side of the Deity, "to rejoice / In Admonitions of thy softest voice!" (19–20). The poem closes in a more narrowly prayerful way, the posture of the speaker humble, the language abstract, the imagery conventional. Let me know "the blessing of Thy grace," and "rest absorbed in Thee!" (22–26). It is a prayer for peace uncomplicated by fear or doubt, a permanence unshaken by change.

A short trip to the Isle of Man in July 1833 with his son John and Crabb Robinson produced, along with those poems of the Scottish tour of 1831, thirty-six sonnets and other poems published in a new volume in 1835. His discouragement about the state of contemporary culture continues, but a notable visit to Italy with Crabb Robinson in 1837 brought him face-to-face with the Italian struggle for liberty, and some of his old political fervor and poetic genius re-emerged.

Heading for Italy, he makes his last visit to Caroline on March 26, 1837. His time in Italy was filled with all kinds of activity, as he took great pleasure in both the country and its people. He stayed in Rome at the Piazza di Spagna from April 25 until May 22, met Joseph Severn and talked to Keats, even posed for a now lost portrait. From Rome he moved about Florence, admiring the monasteries and on May 25 visiting Assisi and the famous church constructed over the house in which Saint Francis lived, Santa Maria degli Angeli called Portiuncula. A few days later, Wordsworth and Robinson climbed to the Franciscan convent by the summit of Laverna where he heard the song of the cuckoo that a month later, traveling through Austria on his return journey, occasioned a new poem, "The Cuckoo at Laverna." Homesick, suffering from a nervous disorder, he returned to England on August 7 with a packet of poems written on the trip.

Wordsworth's more firmly shaped conservative politics is matched by his religious orthodoxy, as the Church of England becomes still another source of stability in a fickle world, an institution standing, as E. Margaret Taylor puts it, "as a *via media* between the extremes of over-evangelical Methodism or the rigidity of Roman Catholic doctrines." For a good many years Wordsworth had not been anything like a regular churchgoer. We know that at Hawkshead he went dutifully to the local church or, in bad weather, to the nearby Quaker meeting house. At Cambridge he resented compulsory chapel rules. And the young radical of Cambridge and post-Cambridge days, the ardent supporter of the French Revolution, was not at all attracted to organized religion, finding meaning and transcendence in the nourishing powers of nature and imagination. Mary had, before their marriage, been a regular communicant at her own village church, and the marriage, the education of children, and the death of the poet's brother John brought before Wordsworth some sense of the importance of church attendance. But the notorious rector of St. Oswald's Church in Grasmere—a madman by all ac-

counts—and a bibulous curate/pastor kept them from even perfunc-
tory attendance. Taylor contends that it was not until 1806, "when
the Rev. Thomas Jackson was nominated as Rector by Lady Diana
de Fleming of Rydal Hall . . . that the Wordsworths took to regular
church attendance." And by 1813 Wordsworth was genuinely con-
nected to the Church of England.[18] Gill contends that "by 1822 [the
date of the publication of the *Ecclesiastical Sketches*] he had become
committed to the Church of England."[19]

Ironically, his devotion to the Anglican communion involved him
in a remarkable dalliance with a number of the younger generations
of the burgeoning Oxford Movement—Hugh James Rose, John
Keble, Roundell Palmer, Robert Aston Coffin, and F. W. Faber, who
served as a curate at the parish church of St. Mary the Virgin in
Ambleside from 1837 to 1842.[20] Faber, in a June 26, 1841 letter,
reminds Wordsworth of the poet's desire that he keep in touch after
his visit to Rydal Mount. Ill at Constantinople, he recalls drawing
upon the poet "for cheerfulness and thought" and speaks of reading
Laodamia "to a party of young Englishmen as we sailed up the Hellespont," finding great consolation "meditating on what I had just
read, when otherwise I should probably have been the victim of fret-
fulness and weary dissipation of mind."[21] Back in his rectory at Elton
on Halloween 1843, he is welcomed by his poor parishioners and
harassed by Methodist fanatics. A most important letter of Novem-

---

[18] "William Wordsworth and St. Oswald's Church, Grasmere" (Grasmere, 1979),
p. 14. I am greatly indebted to this pamphlet for information concerning the church
and the churchgoing habits of the Rydal Mount Wordsworths.

[19] *Wordsworth: A Life*, p. 344.

[20] See Moorman, *William Wordsworth: A Biography*, 2:397–398: "The morning
after the degree ceremony [at Oxford], Wordsworth was guest of honour at a breakfast party in Magdalen Cottage given by Francis Faber. Here he met, among others,
Faber's brother Frederick, John Keble, and John Henry Newman." In June 1839,
she writes: "they represented the intellectual core of the movement for spiritual
renewal within the Church of England, the Tractarian or Oxford Movement, and
when they gathered in Faber's rooms it was to meet the poet whose influence they
all acknowledged." Newman offered his tribute to Wordsworth. "When Newman
met Wordsworth in 1839" says Moorman, "he had just singled him out in an article
in *The British Critic* as a poet of 'philosophical meditation whose works addressed
themselves to . . . high principles and feelings,' and he was to return to this essay
as an important document in his intellectual development when he wrote *Apologia
Pro Vita Sua* (1864)."

[21] Wordsworth Library (Grasmere) Manuscripts.

ber 17, 184(5?) informs Wordsworth of Faber's reception into the Roman Church by the Catholic Bishop of Northampton.[22]

A pamphlet entitled "Ambleside Parish Church: Brief Guide" describes the interest Wordsworth took in the building of that church and the generosity of his contributions. Even though he died before the actual building began, English and American friends "subscribed toward the cost of a window in his memory—that at the east end of the north aisle. That part of the church was known as the Wordsworth Chapel from the church's earliest days." In 1952 it was furnished and officially designated to mark the centenary of the poet's death. Other windows in the chapel honored Mary, Dorothy, Dora, and Sara Hutchinson, and each window "bears the word VERI-TAS, motto of the Wordsworth family." George Fielding, a local resident, presented two chairs from Wordsworth's home; and Mary Wordsworth, attending the dedication of the church in 1854, presented a Bible for the lectern inscribed in her own handwriting, "in memory of William Wordsworth, poet, by Mary Wordsworth, his wife."

Faber had agreed to contribute to the *Lives of the English Saints* launched by the now retired Newman. He wrote nine of the lives and wrote to Wordsworth requesting permission to append his stanzas "Suggested in a Steamboat off Saint Bees' Heads, on the Coast of Cumberland" to his *Life of St. Bega*. The lines were printed at the end of the volume with a prefatory note by Faber drawing attention to the date of the poem—1833—as "a fresh instance of the remarkable way in which his poems anticipate the revival of catholic doctrines among us."[23] In 1833 Benjamin Bailey, once Keats's friend and now Colonial Chaplain in Ceylon, proposed that the *Ecclesiastical Sonnets* be printed as a book of devotion to accompany Keble's *Christian Year*.

In 1842 Samuel Wilkinson of Leeds, the Anglican editor of *The Christian Miscellany*, asked Wordsworth's permission to devote an entire issue to a series of passages from his poetry in *Contributions of William Wordsworth to a Revival of Catholic Truth* (1842). Newman him-

---

[22] Wordsworth Library (Grasmere) Manuscripts.

[23] See Gill, *Wordsworth: A Life*, p. 418; Moorman, *William Wordsworth: A Biography*, 2:480–481.

self, the inspiration for the Oxford Movement, had written that Wordsworth, Coleridge, and Scott, though very different poets and believers, "had all borne witness in their writings to a progress in religious thinking, 'to something deeper and truer than satisfied the last century.' "[24] Yet Wordsworth, flattered as always by attention to his work, was reluctant to take the next step: open support of the Tractarian Movement. "It would seem," he writes to Wilkinson, "to enroll me as a partisan; and the support which I might otherwise give to Catholic truth would, I fear, in numerous quarters, be impaired accordingly."[25]

There were many other voices of religion in Ambleside and Rydal during these years. Dr. Thomas Arnold came to Rydal Mount with his wife on a visit, fell in love with the natural beauty of the Lake District, and settled in a furnished house nearby. He preached at Rydal Chapel on Sundays, and walked regularly with Wordsworth. After Arnold's return to the headmaster duties at Rugby, Wordsworth negotiated for the Arnolds a small estate called Fox How.

Two women enter the Wordsworth circle around this time, and we pause briefly here to talk about them. The first, whose name is immediately recognized by Wordsworth students from the detailed notes to the poems he dictated to her in 1843, is Isabella Fenwick. A friend of Wordsworth's friend Henry Taylor of the Colonial Office, a woman of independent means, well read, sensible, engaging, and warm in temperament, she took a house in Ambleside, and Wordsworth, Mary, and Dora were as devoted to her as she to them. She was enthusiastic about his poetry—indeed, she was his companion when he traveled to Durham for his honorary degree—and she became, more or less, a member of the family, attending to Dorothy in her illness, and taking the side of Dora when the poet objected to her relationship and later marriage to Edward Quillinan. Wordsworth's visits to Fenwick's home in Ambleside, from all we know friendly visits by a man interested in the opposite sex all his life, triggered the predictable local gossip. Yet the great triumph of the relationship was her persuading Wordsworth, who was against a biography, to dictate to her his recollections of the poems and the cir-

---

[24] Moorman, *William Wordsworth: A Biography*, 2:480–481.
[25] September 21, 1842. *LY* 7.4:371.

cumstances of their writing. While far from definitive, the notes have become a key starting point for all kinds of biographical and literary studies of the poetry.

The other woman, the American writer Harriet Martineau—an eccentric of the first order—claiming miracles through her special gift of mesmerism, lecturing on a variety of topics from religion to economics, traveling across Europe, settled in the Lake District, eventually buying a parcel of land near Ambleside. Even though she was somewhat less than enthusiastic about the humble, rustic life of the neighborhood and the area, she nevertheless became a fan of Wordsworth's poetry, and her praise, unusual ideas, and disagreements with the poet made her a lively presence.

Not all fans came to England; at least one brought Rydal Mount to the United States. A brief note in Stephen Gill's biography drew me to a packet at the Wordsworth Library in Grasmere containing materials pertaining to a certain Mrs. Sarah P. Green of Charlestown, Massachusetts.[26] Among the materials is a letter of February 16, 1846, lavish in its praise of Wordsworth's poems and their impact on her personal and professional life. A lecture entitled "The Poetry of Nature" extends the praise and offers wide-ranging and effusively impressionistic commentary on the poems. But, wonder of wonders, she and her husband, the Reverend Henry K. Green, a progressive Baptist minister and pastor, following the principles set down in her lecture on the education of women called "Obsolete Idea," founded a school for young ladies, The Rydal Mount Ladies' Boarding School in Charlestown, committed to, among other things, Wordsworthian ideas about the place of the human affections in the education of the young. The lecture on education and a broadside with a lithograph of the school and an announcement of its curriculum and related matters are also part of the extraordinary packet at Grasmere.[27]

Wordsworth saw his return to England after Italy as being like Milton's return from exile. On a weekend visit to the Archbishop of Canterbury, he lamented the state of civil and public affairs as he had some thirty years before lamented the state of literary taste and

---

[26] *Wordsworth: A Life*, p. 412.

[27] See my "The Rydal Mount Ladies' Boarding School: A Wordsworthian Episode in America," *The Wordsworth Circle*, 23 (1992), 43–48.

the larger culture. The Italian poems, collected in *Memorials of a Tour in Italy*, were published in 1842. This was his last separate volume, although other, and rather impressive, poems appear until nearly the end of his life, and he would continue to prepare various collections of his complete poems.

These are busy years during which, despite failing eyesight, he is attentive to many things. He is interested in writing on "the deceased Poetesses of Great Britain," and bemoans in literary histories the lack of attention to such "female Writers" as "very ungallant."[28] His first published poem was "On Seeing Miss Helen Maria Williams Weep at a Tale of Distress." He had probably read the poems of Williams at Hawkshead and had met her later on his 1791 trip to revolutionary France. A poet from the previous century, Anne Finch, Lady Winchelsea (1661–1720), caught his attention early in his career, and Barron Field provides him with a biographical sketch of Finch in a letter of April 28, 1828.[29] In Wordsworth's sweeping review of British poetry in the "Essay Supplementary to the Preface to the *Lyrical Ballads* of 1815," he argues that "excepting the nocturnal Reverie of Lady Winchelsea, and a passage or two in the Windsor Forest of Pope, the Poetry of the period between the publication of the Paradise Lost and the Seasons does not contain a single new image of external nature" (3:73).

Wordsworth bought and read Charlotte Smith's *Elegiac Sonnets* while at Cambridge, "retaining for them a considerable admiration throughout his life."[30] Smith had, of course, provided him with letters of introduction to Helen Maria Williams when he went to France. And Wordsworth carried on a correspondence with the highly regarded Felicia Hemans, expressing concern for her good health and her work. In a long letter of April 30, 1834, he speaks of having read many of her poems, thanking her for the dedication copy of her *National Lyrics* and telling her of his special pleasure with her "The Pilgrim Song to the evening Star."[31] A February 12, 1829 letter

---

[28] W. W. to Dionysus Lardner, January 12, 182[9]. *LY* 5.2:4.

[29] Barron Field to W. W., April 28, 1828, in *Barron Field's Memoirs of Wordsworth*, ed. Geoffrey Little, Australian Academy of the Humanities Monograph 3 (Sydney: Sydney University Press, 1975), p. 141.

[30] Moorman, *William Wordsworth: A Biography*, 1:170.

[31] *LY* 5.2:705.

to Sir William Hamilton, Professor of Astronomy at Trinity College, Dublin and Astronomer Royal for Ireland, praises poetry Hamilton had sent, but goes out of his way to say that "I was also much gratified with your sister's [Eliza Mary Hamilton, 1807–1851] verses, which I have read several times over—they are well and vigorously expressed, and the feelings are such as one could wish should exist oftener than they appear to do in the bosoms of *male* astronomers."[32]

A most interesting episode involves Lydia Huntley Sigourney of Hartford, Connecticut, who had visited Wordsworth at Rydal Mount in 1842 and who wrote to him on April 8, 1842 to offer birthday greetings and to solicit a poem for the annual *Religion Souvenir*, which she edited. She also includes in her letter a poem by her daughter (a letter of September 25, 1843 reveals that she had written it) "On the Birthday of Wordsworth."[33] The September 25, 1843 letter also includes an oration on Wordsworth delivered by Francis Joseph Clerc ("now studying for the ministry of the Episcopal Church") at Christ Church, Hartford on August 3, 1843, Commencement Day for Washington College. The oration offers lavish praise for the poet, whose "principles" transcend "popularity" and "literary reputation." "Who that has studied his poems," says Clerc, "has failed to perceive his moral purpose, to discover a new charm in the beauties of nature and affections of home, to feel a warmer sympathy for the suffering and oppressed, a deeper reverence for wisdom, beauty, virtue and age, and a livelier enthusiasm for LIBERTY." For Clerc, Wordsworth is a "Christian poet," who goes beyond "the pride that advocates a senseless but intricate philosophy, that teaches of a cause and calls it Law; that points to a reason and calls it Nature."[34]

Although he lacked the Romantic flair of Scott and Byron, Wordsworth's literary reputation at home and abroad soared during these years, with, as we have already seen, offers for honorary degrees and honorary memberships in learned societies. Oxford undergraduates cheered his presence at his honorary degree award on June 12, 1839, and John Keble called him in his address "one who alone among poets has set the manners and religion of the poor not merely in a

---

[32] *LY* 5.2:30.
[33] Wordsworth Library (Grasmere) Manuscripts.
[34] Wordsworth Library (Grasmere) Manuscripts.

good but I might say even in a celestial light."[35] And his financial fortunes rose also. Crabb Robinson, visiting Rydal Mount at Christmas in 1835, talked at length about the sale of his poetry and estimated that his poems were bringing £200 a year. Another complete edition in 1836–1837 proved very lucrative.

Yet that other self remained also—the loner, the eccentric. Hunter Davies describes his

> shepherd's style of clothing—his rough plaid trousers, loose brown frock-coat and black handkerchief round his neck. He had allowed his hair to grow longer at the back, which gave him a very distinctive appearance, and he often wore a straw hat, with a veil to shade the sun. When his eyes were really bad, he wore green shades, though, in his last decade, his eyes don't seem to have bothered him as much as they did in earlier years.[36]

His health remained strong well into his eighth decade, as he walked, climbed, and helped with the hay gathering in Dora's field. John Kenyon, in a September 16, 1840 letter to Mary Wordsworth, speaks of Wordsworth as a "Happy Man to have the will and power to mount Helvellyn" at age seventy.[37] A great seventy-fourth birthday celebration brought together a large number of children and adults from the neighborhood, and Isabella Fenwick, who organized the celebration, paid for the expenses in the same spirit of generosity as she manifested when she gave the poet the celebrated cuckoo clock now at Dove Cottage.

Wordsworth fought hard for the beauty of the land and the bliss of solitude, and his efforts against the coming of the railroads are still evident in there being no train service beyond Windemere. The visitors to Rydal Mount continued and included celebrities like Queen Adelaide, the Royal Dowager and widow of William IV, in 1840. He met Tennyson, who was to be his successor as Poet Laurate, in London in 1842, and the great Victorian poet paid him high tribute for his influence on his own work and for the general cause of poetry. In 1845 Wordsworth was to meet Queen Victoria at the Fancy Dress Ball in London.[38] And Benjamin Haydon—one of his

---

[35] Quoted in Moorman, *William Wordsworth: A Biography*, 2:542–543.
[36] *William Wordsworth: A Biography*, p. 319.
[37] Wordsworth Library (Grasmere) Manuscripts.
[38] Moorman, *William Wordsworth: A Biography*, 2:574.

oldest London friends and a notable portrait painter of his day who had introduced him to Keats at the "immortal dinner party" of 1817 and included the poet, along with Voltaire and Newton, in his massive painting *Christ's Entry into Jerusalem*"—painted Wordsworth again, this time against the massive backdrop of Mount Helvellyn.

Although Wordsworth was never completely happy about the Dora–Edward Quillinan marriage, it was, as far as we can determine, a good one, and when they settled with Quillinan's two children at Loughrigg Holme, Wordsworth had his three children and grandchildren settled near him. Yet the blessing of family was shaken when Dora, the apple of his eye, caught cold while helping brother Willy set up house with his bride in Carlisle, and, after being taken to Rydal Mount by Mary and William, died July 9, 1847. This, along with the death of another favorite, Hartley Coleridge on January 6, 1849, nearly shattered him completely. Now only Mary remained as that ever-needed personal point of stability in his life. Still Wordsworth maintained a poetic life, uneven and less prolific, to be sure, but hardly the disastrous falling off that is often too glibly used to describe the later work. Indeed, certain of the poems of this period stand out as more than valedictories, but as having artistic lives of their own and as rich contributions to an understanding of Wordsworth's literary life.

The Fenwick note to his 1842 "A Poet! He hath put his heart to school" (*Miscellaneous Sonnets* 27) is an important example. Expressing his impatience with the word *artistical* borrowed from the German by contemporary writers, he would rather call the poetry and the theory behind it "artificial." Here, in the last ten years of his life, he mocks the poet who "must laugh / By precept only, and shed tears by rule" (3–4). To the poet he counsels, "Thy Art be nature" and "the live current quaff" (5). With a lovely "lilies-of-the-field" metaphor he closes the poem. The workings of nature are seen as vivid analogues of the creative process. The meadow-flower blooms because it is "free / Down to its root, and, in that freedom, bold." Likewise, "the grandeur of the Forest-tree / Comes not from casting in a formal mould / But from its *own* divine vitality" (10–14).

In the same collection is another sonnet that might well serve as a late model of the essential and one Wordsworth. The Fenwick note recalls how often he had seen clouds "hanging about and above the vale of Rydal, clouds that may gave given birth to this Sonnet, which was thrown off on the impulse of the moment one evening when I was returning home from the favourite walk of ours along the Rotha under Loughrigg." But the sonnet is far more than a journal entry or a geographical memoir. It makes metaphor out of the interaction of sun and cloud, of light and shadow, of calm and trouble. Clouds of rare beauty do not achieve their beauty in a static way. "The most alluring clouds that mount the sky / Owe to a troubled element their forms, / Their hues to sunset" (1–3). The powers lurking deep in a dynamic nature—wind, the revolution of the earth, storms—bring a special richness to the viewer. Joy tempered by sadness makes for the full life.

France continues to inform the Wordsworthian imagination, as in three somber, somewhat prosy poems—"In Allusion to Various Recent Histories and Notices of the French Revolution"—he warns against Carlylean romanticizing of the events of 1789 and thereafter that had touched his young life so deeply. There is a Burkean ring to his indictment, "Portentous change when History can appear / As the cool Advocate of foul device" (1–2), in his warning to "him / Who thus deceived shall lend an eager hand / To social havoc" (9–11), in his prayer "Long favoured England! be not thou misled / By monstrous theories of alien growth, / Lest frenzy seize thee" (1–3).

Among the poetic gems of the final years, the occasion for which is recorded in an R. P. Graves letter to Thomas Woodward, is "So fair, so sweet, withal so sensitive" in which a speaker notes the shadow of a daisy projected on a smooth stone in the light of a noonday sun.[39] In six rhyming triplets he proceeds, wishing that "the little Flowers were born to live, / Conscious of half the pleasure which they give" (1–3). The speaker's imagining takes him from flower to the larger universe. What if, he questions, the sun could reckon with "all that issues from his glorious fount" (9) or if the moon could know its power and "through the clouds break through on human sight!" (15)? Yet these are "fond fancies" (16), like Coleridge's "vain babblings of the unregenerate mind." Better to be in tune with hard realities, to temper the ventures of imagination, to quell "All vain desires" and be impelled to "love and praise" (19–20).

---

[39] Wordsworth Library (Grasmere) Manuscripts.

One of Wordsworth's last poems, "How Beautiful the Queen of Night," written in 1846 and published in the 1849–1850 *Miscellaneous Poems*, might serve as an epitaph. It is a genuinely rich short poem on the flight of the moon through the clouds of night, light moving through the darkness and beyond. Though the moon's head is shrouded "in dense obscurity," the speaker nevertheless urges "But look," for to those with eyes to see, "A frightening edge will indicate that soon / We shall behold the struggling Moon / Break forth,—again to walk the clear blue sky" (1–8). Skewed light as always, but now the promise of a brightness beyond.

There is an even stronger confidence in the very short "On the Banks of a Rocky Stream." In the "eddying balls of foam" he sees an emblem of the human mind "Crowded with thoughts that need a settled home." Sounding like Coleridge and his "Epitaph," he turns to the listening stranger and offers a final reassurance of comfort, of stability: "if such disquietude be thine, / Fall on thy knees and sue for help divine" (1–8).

Ever the travel-planner, Wordsworth envisioned another European tour in 1849, but it was not to be. His last Lakeland tour had been in 1844 when he journeyed with Mary, his son-in-law Edward Quillinan, and others up the serene and beauteous Duddon Valley. He is increasingly not just a figure of solitude, but a lonely man saddened by Dorothy's wretched physical and mental condition, by the deaths of Mary's sister Joanna in 1843, of Christopher in his Sussex rectory in Buxstead in 1846, of John's wife in Italy in 1848.

Interesting at this point is a letter of September 8, 1848 from George Douglas Campbell, 8th Duke of Argyll, to the Reverend G. Howson, later to become Dean of Chester. The letter provides a vivid glimpse of the poet on the Duke's and his wife's visit to Rydal Mount in 1848. Reaching the poet's home on a Saturday, he finds Wordsworth "a little languid in manner" at first, then talking "incessantly—but not generally interestingly." The next day the picture of the poet was quite different as he visits to say goodbye. Wordsworth was "unwilling that we should go away soon," and walked with the group to the mound in front of the house. The Duchess "asked Him if he w^d repeat some of his own lines to us," and Wordsworth agreed to read *Tintern Abbey* in preference to any part of *The Excursion*."

After recounting how he composed the poem in four days—"the last 20 lines or so being composed as he walked down the hill from Clifton to Bristol"—he read "the introductory lines descriptive of the scenery in a low clear voice. But when he came to the thoughtful and reflective lines his tone deepened, and he poured them forth with a fervour and almost passion of delivery which was very striking and beautiful." The emphasis on the lines to Dorothy—"My *dear, dear* friend," "In thy wild eyes"—seemed "almost unnatural at the time," but became clearer after the reading when "we found out that the old Paralytic and *doited* woman we had seen in the morning" was Dorothy.[40]

During March of his final year he could be seen walking around his beloved Grasmere, seeking out the company of friends. He was clearly weak physically, and yet he moved about with his familiar walking-stick. He made his last visit to Rydal Chapel on Sunday, March 10, and then, remarkably enough, proceeded to Grasmere in the late afternoon. On March 12, according to Christopher's *Memoir*, he "went towards Grasmere, to meet his two nieces, who were coming from Town–End." He called at a house near the White Moss quarry, and—how powerfully the image continues to the end—when no one was home, "he sat down on the stone seat of the porch to watch the setting sun."[41]

He was taken ill with pleurisy the following week, and his condition continued to worsen although he seemed to enjoy his eightieth birthday on April 7 amid the sights and sounds of a Lakeland spring. On April 20 he took Holy Communion from his son John, according to "a young lady, a near connection of Mr. Wordsworth," telling his son, "That is just what I want." With the end near, Mary Wordsworth "said gently to him, 'William, you are going to Dora,'" words echoed by the poet the next day as he, in a conscious response to the presence of a niece, echoes Mary's poetic farewell with the question, "Is that Dora?" On April 23, the date of Shakespeare's birth and death, he died, his son John recalling for Robert Percival Graves

---

[40] Wordsworth Library (Grasmere) Manuscripts.

[41] Unless otherwise noted, details of Wordsworth's final days are from Christopher Wordworth's *Memoirs of William Wordsworth*, 2:15–18.

that he died "peacefully and without a struggle,"[42] and his son-in-law Edward Quillinan noting in his journal that he "breathed his last calmly, passing away almost insensibly, exactly at twelve o'clock, while the cuckoo clock at the bedroom door was striking the hour."[43]

Wordsworth was buried in St. Oswald's churchyard in Grasmere on Saturday, April 27. A letter written by Mary Howitt, along with her husband friends and admirers of Wordsworth and according to Carl Woodring a poet whose "American reputation in 1845 was higher than any other living foreign poet," provides a valuable picture of the funeral. Writing to a Professor John Seely Hart in Philadelphia in May 1850, she quotes from "a letter before me."

> Dear Mrs. Wordsworth bears this heaviest of all her trials with truly Christian resignation. It was touching and beautiful to see the manner in which she went through the mournful duties on Saturday when we saw him laid to rest beside the daughter he so deeply mourned. The whole country rich and poor seemed to have assembled in Grasmere Church yard to pay the last mark of respect to him who was so deservedly loved and venerated.
>
> The Americans loved and honoured him; they will miss him in their visit to the old Mother Country and they who have seen him will feel themselves privileged.[44]

Tributes of all kinds honor the poet, especially those that remember Wordsworth as poet and that convey the sense of continuity in his life. Elizabeth Fletcher, widow of an Edinburgh lawyer and a contemporary of Wordsworth's, composed in his honor "Lines written on leaving Grasmere Churchyard after Mr. Wordsworth's funeral." Catching the image of the poetic teacher—"The beautiful realities he taught"; "his teaching simple yet sublime"—she remembers the spirit of the man. "His was no narrow creed; he loved mankind / Because God's law is love and many hearts / In loneliness and grief have felt his power."[45]

---

[42] Most helpful are James A. Butler, "Wordsworth's Funeral: A Contemporary Report," *English Language Notes*, 13 (1975), 27–29; and Carl Woodring, *Victorian Samplers* (Lawrence: University of Kansas Press, 1952), pp. 69–75, 112–113.

[43] Quoted in Gill, *William Wordsworth: A Life*, p. 494*n*129.

[44] Quoted in Butler, "Wordsworth's Funeral," 29.

[45] Wordsworth Library (Grasmere) Manuscripts.

Writing to Wordsworth's son John on April 27, 1850, John Kenyon had just heard the news of the poet's death. He recalls "the happy hours I had passed" at Rydal Mount and counts knowing Wordsworth as "among the good fortunes of my life." And, he continues, "like all those who knew your father's writings well—my mind has been indebted to them for mere pleasure but for, I would fain believe, no small moral gain."[46] And Wordsworth's friend John Peace offers his sympathy to Mary in a letter of May 1, 1850. "What a difference," he says, "between the world with that great and good man on it and the same world without him. . . . That he should have quitted earth the very day upon which the other great William was called is very noticeable indeed."[47]

Among the most memorable condolences are those of a Mrs. Hughes, sister of Robert Jones, Wordsworth's dear friend and the traveling companion of his youth. Although they saw little of each other in later years, they maintained a lively correspondence. Jones, now rector of Souldern, Oxen, wrote to the poet on October 11, 1815: "I can assure you that a Day seldom passes that I do not think of you with feelings of inexpressible affection not unmingled with regret that we see and have seen for a long series of years so little of each other."[48] In a February 23, 1821 letter he speaks of fond memories of their earlier, revolutionary years, and wonders whether Wordsworth is seeing things differently in Switzerland twenty years later. "We were," he says, "early risers in 1790 and generally walked 12 or 15 miles before breakfast and after feasting on our Dejeuner of whatever the house might afford!"[49]

Wordsworth had written to Mrs. Hughes when he heard the news of Jones's death on April 3, 1835. Speaking of the "consolation of religion" at a time of loss, he remembers Jones as "a man, I doubt not, esteemed wherever he was known, by me he will always be remembered with hearty interest." Out of touch they may have been of late, but, says Wordsworth, "we loved each other with a faithful affection, and that mutual respect which gives a strength to friendships formed in early life, which none of more recent origin can

---

[46] Wordsworth Library (Grasmere) Manuscripts.
[47] Wordsworth Library (Grasmere) Manuscripts.
[48] Wordsworth Library (Grasmere) Manuscripts.
[49] Wordsworth Library (Grasmere) Manuscripts.

have."[50] Mary Wordsworth acknowledged Jones's sister's letter on the occasion of Wordsworth's death. Writing to Mrs. Hughes on August 10, 1850, Mary says that "it will be pleasing to you to hear that the friendship of former days, was to the last a cherished remembrance in the heart of him whom it has been the will of our heavenly Father to remove."[51]

---

[50] W. W. to Mrs. Hughes, April 3, 1835. *LY* 6.3:86, 87.
[51] Wordsworth Library (Grasmere) Manuscripts.

EPILOGUE

"And now my heart with pleasure fills
And dances with the daffodils."

William Wordsworth

"Now that we're middle aged, we're reciting Wordsworth on the front porch on a Sunday afternoon finally savoring the words like the strawberries in the colander between us, letting the words bypass our minds and slip into our hearts so that even the most innocent phrase catches at our feelings like a thorn and makes us weep. It's odd when a friend or worse a stranger arrives and we're on the verge of tears over a line that once bored us.

"There is no explaining the impact of words. The kids are half grown, some of our parents have died, we have lived half our lives and in that time, enough has happened to strip daffodils down to their truth. Perhaps we should hide poems from the children until words take on the power of memory or hope, until they darken like storm clouds or glitter like the face of the sea under the moon. Then the poems are spoken with the import of weather, of celebration and defeat, then words swell like silk banners far above the page and simple conversation is as tender as a hand stroking your hair."

Judith Steinbergh, *Past Time*

Recently the above poem by a fine American poet came to my attention. What engaged me at first was the epigraph, especially a small but notable shift in the adverb from "then" in the original to "now" in Steinbergh's adaptation. Indeed, in that shift we sense a kind of continuity—from pleasure in the daffodils not just "then" but "now"—and that continuity has been a key motif in the preceding pages.

Steinbergh's Wordsworth is seen from the vantage point of someone "middle aged," when youthful exuberance, which once seemed
never-ending, has given way to a mellow sense of acceptance or resignation. There is, I think, a remarkably Wordsworthian feeling in
her speaker's self-portrayal, "reciting" with a spouse the poems "on
the front porch on a Sunday afternoon." And the intensity of youthful joy which "once bored us" has given way to a pleasure in "finally
savoring / the words like the strawberries in the colander between /
us" as the words "bypass our minds and slip into our / hearts," as
"even the most innocent phrase catches at / our feelings like a thorn
and makes us weep."

The second stanza might very well serve as a coda for Wordsworth's poetry and for his poetic life as we have been following it. In
a categorical line the speaker confesses, "There is no explaining the
impact of words." Children becoming adults, some parents gone,
half a life lived, "enough has happened to strip daffodils down to
their truth." Perhaps, as Wordsworth himself might have said, it is
not so bad that the young do not respond as the poet might like.
"There was a time," "There was a boy," but now no more. Sunlight
dims, light gives way to shadow, joy to sorrow, budding to ripening.
The young may not be ready for the time when "words take on the /
power of memory or hope," when poems "darken like storm / clouds
or glitter like the face of the sea under the moon." Peele Castle in a
storm, or "It is a beauteous evening, calm and free"? Only then are
poems fully known and felt "with the import of weather, / of celebration and defeat."

These pages have followed a poetic life, to the extent that
Wordsworth can be revealed through the poems. And, as I have often
noted, it is a long poetic life—from the early loco-descriptive pieces,
to the poems of humble and rustic life, to explorations of the inner
life, to the poetry of age. In the process of such a biography I have
tried to minimize categories and to search for continuities. And
while there is certainly early and late, youthful radical and mature
oracle, there is the continuing poet with a deep faith in the mind's
power and a developing awareness of the encounter of mind and a
larger reality. Wordsworth's is an unfolding poetry, with the vigor of
youth nuanced by sadness, with the wisdom of age touched by hope.

Perhaps, like Steinbergh's speaker, we can see all of Wordsworth's life in the poems as "words swell[ing] like silk / banners far above the page and simple conversation is / as tender as a hand stroking your hair."

Hawkshead Grammar School, Wordsworth's school, 1779–1787.

Rydal Mount, Wordsworth's home, 1813–1850.

St. Oswald's Churchyard, burial place of Mary, Dorothy, and William
Wordsworth and of Sarah Hutchinson.

BIBLIOGRAPHY

Abrams, M. H. *Natural Supernaturalism: Tradition and Revolution in Romantic Literature.* New York: W. W. Norton, 1971.

————. "Structure and Style in the Greater Romantic Lyric." In *The English Romantics: Major Poetry and Critical Theory.* Ed. John L. Mahoney. Lexington, Mass.: D. C. Heath, 1978. Pp. 655–659.

Alger, John Goldworth. *Paris in 1789–1794: Farewell Letters of Victims of the Guillotine.* New York: AMS Press, 1970.

Allenback, Steven, and Alexander Medlicott, Jr. "A Visit with Wordsworth: From the Unpublished Journals of Anne Eliot Ticknor." *The Wordsworth Circle,* 9, No. 1 (1978), 88–91.

Arnold, Matthew. "Wordsworth." *Essays in Criticism, Second Series: Contributions to the "Pall Mall Gazette" and Discourses in America.* The Works of Matthew Arnold in Fifteen Volumes. New York: AMS Press, 1903–1904.

Averill, James. *Wordsworth and the Poetry of Human Suffering.* Ithaca, N.Y.: Cornell University Press, 1980.

Bakhtin, Mikhail. *The Dialogic Imagination.* Ed. Michael Holquist. Trans. Caryl Emerson and Michael Holquist. Austin: University of Texas Press, 1981.

Barfield, Owen. *Saving the Appearances: A Study in Idolatry.* New York: Harcourt, Brace, Jovanovich, 1965.

Bate, W. Jackson. *The Burden of the Past and the English Poet.* Cambridge, Mass.: Harvard University Press, 1970.

————. *Coleridge.* Cambridge, Mass., and London: Harvard University Press, 1987.

————. *From Classic to Romantic: Premises of Taste in Eighteenth-Century England.* Cambridge, Mass.: Harvard University Press, 1946.

————. *Samuel Johnson.* New York and London: Harcourt, Brace, Jovanovich, 1975. Repr. 1977.

Bateson, F. W. *Wordsworth: A Re-Interpretation.* London: Longmans, 1954.

Batho, Edith. *The Later Wordsworth.* Cambridge: Cambridge University Press, 1933.

Bauer, N. S. *William Wordsworth: A Reference Guide to British Criticism, 1793–1899.* Boston: G. K. Hall and Co., 1978.

Beer, John. *Wordsworth and the Human Heart.* New York: Columbia University Press, 1978.

Bialostosky, Don. *Wordsworth, Dialogics, and the Practice of Criticism*. New York and Cambridge: Cambridge University Press, 1992.

Bloom, Harold. *The Anxiety of Influence: A Theory of Poetry*. New York: Oxford University Press, 1973.

————. *The Visionary Company: A Reading of Romantic Poetry*. Ithaca, N.Y.: Cornell University Press, 1971.

Bober, Natalie. *William Wordsworth: The Wandering Poet*. Nashville and New York: Thomas Nelson, Inc., 1975.

Broch, Herman. Introduction to *On the Iliad.*, by Rachel Bespallof. Trans. Mary McCarthy. New York: Pantheon, ca. 1947.

Bush, Douglas. "Wordsworth: A Minority Report." In *The English Romantics: Major Poetry and Critical Theory*. Ed. John L. Mahoney. Lexington, Mass.: D. C. Heath, 1978. Pp. 691–692.

Butler, James. "Wordsworth's Funeral: A Contemporary Account." *English Language Notes*, 13 (1975), 37–39.

Byatt, A. S. *Wordsworth and Coleridge in Their Time*. London: Thomas Nelson, Inc., 1970.

Chandler, James. *Wordsworth's Second Nature: A Study of the Poetry and Politics*. Chicago and London: The University of Chicago Press, 1984.

Clancey, Richard. "Wordsworth's Classical Undersong: Rhetorical Learning and the 'Blended Might' of a New Creation." Unpubl., 1993.

Coleridge, Hartley. *Letters of Hartley Coleridge*. Ed. Grace Evelyn Griggs and Earl Leslie Griggs. London: Oxford University Press, 1936.

Coleridge, Samuel Taylor. *Biographia Literaria*. Ed. James Engell and W. Jackson Bate. 2 vols. Princeton, N.J.: Princeton University Press, 1983.

————. *Coleridge's Poems and Prose*. Selected by Kathleen Raine. London: Penguin, 1957.

————. *Collected Letters of Samuel Taylor Coleridge*. Ed. Earl Leslie Griggs. 6 vols. Oxford: Oxford University Press, 1912.

Curtis, Jared. *The Fenwick Notes of William Wordsworth*. London: Bristol Classical Press, 1993.

Damrosch, Leopold. *The Imaginative World of Alexander Pope*. Berkeley and Los Angeles: University of California Press, 1987.

Darlington, Beth, ed. *The Love Letters of William and Mary Wordsworth*. Ithaca, N.Y.: Cornell University Press, 1981.

Davies, Hunter. *William Wordsworth: A Biography*. New York: Atheneum, 1980.

De Selincourt, Ernest. *The Early Wordsworth*. The English Association Presidential Address, November, 1936. Oxford: Oxford University Press, 1936.

De Vere, Aubrey, Esq. "Recollections of Wordsworth." In *The Prose Works of William Wordsworth.* Ed. Rev. Alexander B. Grosart. 3 vols. London: Norton, 1876. Pp. 386–399.

Douglas, Wallace W. *Wordsworth: The Construction of a Personality.* Kent, Ohio: Kent State University Press, 1968.

Faber, Frederick William. *Faber: Poet and Priest—Selected Letters by Frederick William Faber, 1833–1863.* Ed. Raleigh Addington. Cowbridge, Wales: D. Brown and Sons, Ltd., 1974.

Ferry, David. *The Limits of Mortality: An Essay on Wordsworth's Major Poems.* Westport, Conn.: Greenwood Press, 1978.

Field, Barron. *Barron Field's Memoirs of Wordsworth.* Ed. Geoffrey Little. Australian Academy of the Humanities Monograph 3. Sydney: Sydney University Press, 1975.

Fielding, Gabriel. *William Wordsworth Centenary, 1850–1950.* The Wordsworth Memorial Chapel in St. Mary's Church, Ambleside.

Fletcher, Eliza. *Holiday Log Book, 1833.* Wordsworth Library (Grasmere) Manuscripts.

Friedman, Michael H. *The Making of a Tory Humanist: William Wordsworth and the Idea of Community.* New York: Columbia University Press, 1979.

Galperin, William. *Revision and Authority in Wordsworth: The Interpretation of a Career.* Philadelphia: University of Pennsylvania Press, 1989.

Gates, Barbara T. "Wordsworth's Mirror of Mortality: Distortions of Church History." *The Wordsworth Circle,* 12, No. 2 (1981), 129–132.

Gill, Stephen. *Wordsworth: A Life.* Oxford: Clarendon, 1989.

Gilley, Sheridan. *Newman and His Age.* London: Darton, Longman and Todd, 1990.

Gilligan, Carol. *In a Different Voice: Psychological Theory and Women's Development.* Cambridge, Mass.: Harvard University Press, 1982.

Gittings, Robert, and Jo Manton. *Dorothy Wordsworth.* Oxford: Clarendon, 1985.

Graver, Bruce. "Wordsworth and the Language of Epic." *Studies in Philosophy.* 83, No. 3 (1986), 261–285.

———. "Wordsworth's Georgic Beginnings." *Texas Studies in Language and Literature,* 33, No. 2 (1991), 137–157.

———. "Wordsworth's Georgic Pastoral." *European Romantic Review.* 1, No. 2 (1991), 119–134.

Grosart, Rev. Alexander B., ed. *The Prose Works of William Wordsworth.* 3 vols. London: Norton, 1876.

Harper, George Maclean. *William Wordsworth: His Life, Work, and Influence.* 2 vols. New York: Charles Scribner's Sons, 1916.

———. *Wordsworth's French Daughter.* Princeton, N.J.: Princeton University Press, 1921.

Hartman, Geoffrey. *The Unremarkable Wordsworth*. Theory and History of Literature 34. Minneapolis: University of Minnesota Press, 1987.

———. *Wordsworth's Poetry, 1787–1814*. Cambridge, Mass. and London: Harvard University Press, 1987.

Hazlitt, William. *The Complete Works of William Hazlitt*. Ed. P. P. Howe. 21 vols. London: J. W. Dent, 1930–1934.

Heath, William. *Wordsworth and Coleridge: A Study of Their Literary Relations in 1801–1802*. Oxford: Oxford University Press, 1970.

Heffernan, James. "History and Autobiography: The French Revolution in Wordsworth's *Prelude*." *Representing the French Revolution: Literature, Historiography, and Art*. Hanover, N.H.: University Press of New England, 1992.

Holmes, Richard. *Footsteps: Adventures of a Romantic Biographer*. New York: Viking, 1985.

Jordan, Frank, ed. *The English Romantic Poets: A Review of Research and Criticism*. New York: Modern Language Association, 1972.

Jordan, John. *Why the "Lyrical Ballads"? The Background, Writing, and Character of Wordsworth's 1798 "Lyrical Ballads."* Berkeley: University of California Press, 1976.

Johnston, Kenneth R. *Wordsworth and the Recluse*. New Haven, Conn.: Yale University Press, 1984.

Keats, John. *The Letters of John Keats, 1814–1821*. Ed Hyder Edward Rollins. 2 vols. Cambridge, Mass.: Harvard University Press, 1958.

———. *The Poems of John Keats*. Ed. Jack Stillinger. Cambridge, Mass.: Harvard University Press, 1978.

Kelley, Theresa M. *Wordsworth's Revolutionary Aesthetics*. Cambridge: Cambridge University Press, 1988.

Ker, Ian. *John Henry Newman: A Biography*. Oxford: Clarendon, 1988.

Ketcham, Carl, ed. *The Letters of John Wordsworth*. Ithaca, N.Y.: Cornell University Press, 1969.

Keymer, John. "Fragment of an account of an interview had by John Keymer with W. W. (1832)." Wordsworth Library (Grasmere) Manuscripts.

Langbaum, Robert. *The Poetry of Experience: The Dramatic Monologue in Modern Literary Tradition*. New York: W. W. Norton, 1963.

Latham, Edward Connery, ed. *The Poetry of Robert Frost: The Collected Poems, Complete and Unabridged*. New York: Holt, Rinehart and Winston, 1975.

Legouis, Émile. *The Early Life of Wordsworth*. Trans. J. W. Matthews. London: J. W. Dent, 1921.

———. *Wordsworth and Annette Vallon*. New York: E. P. Dutton, 1922.

———. *Wordsworth in a New Light*. Cambridge, Mass.: Harvard University Press, 1923.

Levin, Susan. *Dorothy Wordsworth and Romanticism*. New Brunswick, N.J.: Rutgers University Press, 1987.

Levinson, Marjorie. *Wordsworth's Great Period Poems: Four Essays*. Cambridge: Cambridge University Press, 1986.

Lindenberger, Herbert. *On Wordsworth's "Prelude."* Princeton, N.J.: Princeton University Press, 1963.

Lipking, Lawrence. *The Life of the Poet: Beginning and Ending Poetic Careers*. Chicago and London: The University of Chicago Press, 1981.

Liu, Alan. *Wordsworth: The Sense of History*. Stanford, Calif.: Stanford University Press, 1989.

Lyon, Judson. *The Excursion: A Study*. New Haven, Conn.: Yale University Press, 1950.

McGann, Jerome. *The Romantic Ideology: A Critical Investigation*. Chicago and London: The University of Chicago Press, 1983.

McGhee, Richard. " 'And Earth and Stars Composed a Universal Heaven': A View of Wordsworth's Later Poetry." *Studies in English Literature*, 11 (1971), 641–657.

MacGillivray, James Robertson. "Wordsworth and His Revolutionary Acquaintances." Ph.D. Diss., Harvard University, 1930.

Maclean, Catherine Macdonald. *Dorothy and William Wordsworth*. New York: Octagon Books, 1972.

Maclean, Kenneth. *Agrarian Reform: A Background for Wordsworth*. New Haven, Conn.: Yale University Press, 1950.

Magnuson, Paul. *Coleridge and Wordsworth: A Lyrical Dialogue*. Princeton, N.J.: Princeton University Press, 1988.

Mahoney, John L. "Reynolds and Wordsworth: The Development of a Post-Romantic Aesthetic." *European Romantic Review*, 3, No. 2 (1992), 147–158.

———. "The Rydal Mount Ladies' Boarding School: A Wordsworthian Episode in America." *The Wordsworth Circle*, 23 (1992), 43–48.

———. *The Whole Internal Universe: Imitation and the New Defense of Poetry in British Criticism, 1660–1830*. New York: Fordham University Press, 1985.

———. Review of *Wordsworth, Dialogics, and the Practice of Criticism*, by Don Bialostosky. *European Romantic Review*, 17, No. 2 (1993), 269–275.

Mahoney, John, ed. *The English Romantics: Major Poetry and Critical Theory*. Lexington, Mass.: D. C. Heath, 1978.

Manning, Peter. "Wordsworth at St. Bees: Scandals, Sisterhoods, and Wordsworth's Later Poetry." *Reading Romantics: Texts and Contexts*. New York and Oxford: Oxford University Press, 1990. Pp. 273–299.

Mason, Michael. *Lyrical Ballads*. London and New York: Longman, 1992.

Meisenhelder, Susan Edwards. *Wordsworth's Informed Reader: Structures of*

Experience in His Poetry. Nashville, Tenn.: Vanderbilt University Press, 1988.

Mellor, Anne. *Romanticism and Gender*. New York and London: Routledge, 1993.

Miller, Arthur. "Tragedy and the Common Man." In *Tragedy: Vision and Form*. Ed. Robert W. Corrigan. San Francisco: Chandler Publishing Co., 1965. Pp. 148–151.

Miller, J. Hillis. *The Linguistic Moment: From Wordsworth to Stevens*. Princeton, N.J.: Princeton University Press, 1985.

Moorman, Mary. *William Wordsworth: A Biography*. I. *The Early Years: 1770–1803*. Oxford: Clarendon, 1957; II. *The Later Years: 1803–1850*. Oxford: Clarendon, 1965.

Newton, Annabel. *Wordsworth in Early American Criticism*. Chicago: The University of Chicago Press, 1928.

Noyes, Russell. *William Wordsworth*. Rev. John Hayden. Boston: Twayne, 1991.

Owen, W. J. B. *Wordsworth as Critic*. Toronto: University of Toronto Press, 1980.

Parrish, Stephen. *The Art of the Lyrical Ballads*. Cambridge, Mass.: Harvard University Press, 1973.

Peacock, Markham. *The Critical Opinions of William Wordsworth*. Baltimore: The Johns Hopkins University Press, 1950.

Perkins, David. *The Quest for Permanence: The Symbolism of Wordsworth, Shelley, and Keats*. Cambridge, Mass.: Harvard University Press, 1959.

———. *Wordsworth and the Poetry of Sincerity*. Cambridge, Mass.: Harvard University Press, 1964.

Ponder, Melinda. "Echoing Poetry with History: Wordsworth's Duddon Sonnets and Their Notes." *Genre*, 21 (1988), 157–178.

Potts, Abbie Findlay. *The Ecclesiastical Sonnets of William Wordsworth: A Critical Edition*. New Haven, Conn.: Yale University Press, 1922.

Prickett, Stephen. *Coleridge and Wordsworth: The Poetry of Growth*. Cambridge: Cambridge University Press, 1970.

Pritchard, William. *Robert Frost: A Literary Life Reconsidered*. New York: Oxford University Press, 1984.

Rader, Melvin. *Presiding Ideas in Wordsworth's Poetry*. New York: Gordian Press, 1968.

Rawnsley, Hardwick Drummond. *Reminiscences of Wordsworth Among the Peasantry of Westmoreland*. London: Dillon's, 1968.

Read, Herbert. *Wordsworth*. London: Faber & Faber, 1930. Repr. 1948.

Reed, Mark. "Wordsworth on Wordsworth and Much Else: New Conversational Memoranda." *Papers of the Bibliographical Society of America*, 81 (1987), 451–458.

Critical Theory. Ed. John L. Mahoney. Lexington, Mass.: D. C. Heath, 1978. Pp. 698–706.

phen, Leslie. "Wordsworth's Ethics." *Hours in a Library*. 4 vols. New York and London: Putnam's, The Knickerbocker Press, 1904. 3:125–178.

ingle, L. J. *The Obstinate Questionings of English Romanticism*. Baton Rouge: Louisiana State University Press, 1987.

lor, E. Margaret. *William Wordsworth and St. Oswald's Church, Grasmere*. Grasmere, 1979.

ompson, Lawrence. *Robert Frost: The Early Years, 1874–1915*. New York: Holt, Rinehart and Winston, 1966.

———. *Robert Frost: The Years of Triumph, 1915–1938*. New York: Holt, Rinehart and Winston, 1970.

ompson, Lawrence, with R. H. Winnick. *Robert Frost: The Later Years, 1938–1963*. New York: Holt, Rinehart and Winston, 1976.

ompson. T. W. *Wordsworth's Hawkshead*. Ed. Robert Woof. London: Oxford University Press, 1970.

lotson, Geoffrey. Introduction. In Hardwick Drummond Rawnseley. *Reminiscences of Wordsworth Among the Peasantry of Westmoreland*. London: Dillon's, 1968.

aiting for the Palfreys: The Great Prelude Debate." *The Wordsworth Circle*, 17, No. 1 (1986).

tson, J. R. *Wordsworth's Vital Soul: The Sacred and Profane in Wordsworth's Poetry*. Atlantic Highlands, N.J.: Humanities Press, 1982.

iskel, Thomas. *The Romantic Sublime: Studies in the Structure and Psychology of Transcendence*. Baltimore and London: The Johns Hopkins University Press, 1986.

son, J. Dover. *Leslie Stephen and Matthew Arnold as Critics of Shakespeare*. Cambridge: Cambridge University Press, 1939.

dring, Carl. *Politics and English Romantic Poetry*. Cambridge, Mass.: Harvard University Press, 1970.

———. *Victorian Samplers: William and Mary Howitt*. Lawrence: University of Kansas Press, 1952.

dsworth, Christopher. *Memoirs of William Wordsworth*. 2 vols. London, 1851.

dsworth, Dorothy. *Journals of Dorothy Wordsworth*. Ed. Ernest De Selincourt. 2 vols. Hamden, Conn.: Archon Books, 1970.

dsworth, John. *The Letters of John Wordsworth*. Ed. Carl Ketcham. Ithaca, N.Y.: Cornell University Press, 1969.

dsworth, Mary. *The Letters of Mary Wordsworth, 1800–1855*. Ed. Mary E. Burton. Oxford: Clarendon, 1958.

———. *Wordsworth: The Chronology of the Early Years, 1770–*
Mass.: Harvard University Press, 1967.

———. *Wordsworth: The Chronology of the Middle Years,*
bridge, Mass.: Harvard University Press, 1975.

Richardson, Alan. "Archaism and Modernity: Poetic Dicti
and the Romantic Canon." *Southern Humanities Review,*
228.

———. *Literature, Education, and Romanticism: Reading as So*
York: Cambridge University Press, 1994.

Robinson, Jeffrey. *Radical Literary Education: A Classroom*
Wordsworth's "Ode." Madison: University of Wisconsin

Ruoff, Gene. "Romantic Lyric and the Problem of Belief.'
Recent Revisionary Criticism. Ed. Karl Kroeber and G
Brunswick, N.J.: Rutgers University Press, 1993. Pp. 2⁴

Russell, John. "Art Born in the Fullness of Age." *The New Y*
23, 1987. Section 1. Pp. 1, 11.

Rylstone, Ann. *Prophetic Memory in Wordsworth's "Ecclesiasti*
bondale and Edwardsville: Southern Illinois University

Rzepka, Charles J. " 'A Gift That Complicates Employ': Po
in 'Resolution and Independence.' " *Studies in Romant*
226–246.

Salvesen, Christopher. *The Landscape of Memory: A Study*
Poetry. Lincoln: University of Nebraska Press, 1965.

Schneider, Ben Ross. *Wordsworth's Cambridge Education.* C
bridge University Press, 1957.

Shelley, Percy Bysshe. *Correspondence.* Vols. 8–10. Ed. Rog
plete Works of Percy Bysshe Shelley. 10 vols. Ed. Roger In
E. Peck. New York: Gordian Press; London: Ernest Ber

Simpson, David. *Wordsworth and the Figurings of the Real.* Atla
N.J.: Humanities Press, 1982.

———. *Wordsworth's Historical Imagination: The Poetry of D*
York and London: Methuen, 1987.

Siskin, Clifford. *The Historicity of Romantic Discourse.* New Yo
versity Press, 1988.

Smith, Elsie. *An Estimate of William Wordsworth by His Conte*
1822, Oxford: Basil Blackwell, 1932.

Smyser, Jane Worthington. "Wordsworth's Dream of Poetr
The Prelude." *PMLA,* 71 (1956), 269–275.

Sperry, Willard. *Wordsworth's Anti-Climax.* New York: Russ
1955. Repr. 1966.

———. "Wordsworth's Decline." In *The English Romantics: M*

Wordsworth, Jonathan. *William Wordsworth: The Borders of Vision.* Oxford: Clarendon, 1982.

Wordsworth, William. *The Borderers.* Ed. Robert Osborn. Ithaca, N.Y.: Cornell University Press, 1982.

———. *Descriptive Sketches.* Ed. Eric Birdsall. Ithaca, N.Y.: Cornell University Press, 1984.

———. *The Ecclesiastical Sonnets of William Wordsworth: A Critical Edition.* Ed. Abbie Findlay Potts. New Haven, Conn.: Yale University Press, 1922.

———. *An Evening Walk.* Ed James Averill. Ithaca, N.Y.: Cornell University Press, 1984.

———. *Lyrical Ballads and Other Poems.* Ed. James Butler and Karen Green. Ithaca, N.Y.: Cornell University Press, 1992.

———. *Poems, in Two Volumes, and Other Poems, 1800–1807.* Ed. Jared Curtis. Ithaca, N.Y.: Cornell University Press, 1983.

———. *Poetical Works.* Ed. Ernest De Selincourt and Helen Darbishire. 5 vols. Oxford: Oxford University Press, 1940–1949.

———. *The Prelude, 1799, 1805, 1850.* Ed. Jonathan Wordsworth, M. H. Abrams, and Stephen Gill. New York: W. W. Norton, 1979.

———. *The Prose Works of William Wordsworth.* Ed. W. J. B. Owen and Jane Worthington Smyser. 3 vols. New York: Oxford University Press, 1974.

———. *Salisbury Plain Poems.* Ed. Stephen Gill. Ithaca, N.Y.: Cornell University Press, 1975.

———. *Shorter Poems, 1807–1820.* Ed. Carl Ketcham. Ithaca, N.Y.: Cornell University Press, 1989.

———. *The White Doe of Rylstone; or, The Fate of the Nortons.* Ed. Kristine Dugas. Ithaca, N.Y.: Cornell University Press, 1988.

Wordsworth, William, and Dorothy Wordsworth. *The Letters of William and Dorothy Wordsworth.* Ed. Ernest De Selincourt. 7 vols.: *The Early Years, 1787–1805.* Rev. Chester L. Shaver. Oxford: Clarendon, 1967. *The Middle Years, Part I. 1806–1811.* Rev. Mary Moorman. Oxford: Clarendon, 1969. *The Middle Years. Part II. 1812–1820.* Rev. Mary Moorman and Alan G. Hill. Oxford: Clarendon, 1970; *The Later Years, 1821–1853.* Rev. Alan G. Hill. 4 vols. Oxford: Clarendon, 1978–1988.

Wordsworth at Cambridge: A Record of the Commemoration Held at St. John's College, Cambridge, April 1850. Cambridge: Cambridge University Press, 1950.

Wu, Duncan. "The Wordsworth Family Library at Cockermouth: Towards a Reconstruction." *The Library*, 14, No. 2 (1992), 127–135.

———. *Wordsworth's Reading, 1770–1799.* Cambridge: Cambridge University Press, 1993.

INDEX